AWS Certified Security –
Specialty Exam Guide

Build your cloud security knowledge and expertise as an
AWS Certified Security Specialist (SCS-C01)

Stuart Scott

BIRMINGHAM - MUMBAI

Packt.com

Subscribe to our online digital library for full access to over 7,000 books and videos, as well as industry leading tools to help you plan your personal development and advance your career. For more information, please visit our website.

Why subscribe?

- Spend less time learning and more time coding with practical eBooks and Videos from over 4,000 industry professionals

- Improve your learning with Skill Plans built especially for you

- Get a free eBook or video every month

- Fully searchable for easy access to vital information

- Copy and paste, print, and bookmark content

Did you know that Packt offers eBook versions of every book published, with PDF and ePub files available? You can upgrade to the eBook version at www.packt.com and as a print book customer, you are entitled to a discount on the eBook copy. Get in touch with us at customercare@packtpub.com for more details.

At www.packt.com, you can also read a collection of free technical articles, sign up for a range of free newsletters, and receive exclusive discounts and offers on Packt books and eBooks.

AWS Certified Security – Specialty Exam Guide

Commissioning Editor: Vijin Boricha
Acquisition Editor: Meeta Rajani
Content Development Editor: Carlton Borges
Senior Editor: Rahul Dsouza
Technical Editor: Sarvesh Jaywant
Copy Editor: Safis Editing
Project Coordinator: Neil Dmello
Proofreader: Safis Editing
Indexer: Rekha Nair
Production Designer: Joshua Misquitta

First published: August 2020

Production reference: 1040820

Published by Packt Publishing Ltd.
Livery Place
35 Livery Street
Birmingham
B3 2PB, UK.

ISBN 978-1-78953-447-4

www.packt.com

Contributors

About the author

With over two decades in the IT industry, **Stuart Scott** has an extensive background covering a range of technologies, but his passion is centered around **Amazon Web Services (AWS)**.

Stuart is the AWS content and security lead at Cloud Academy where he has created over 80 courses teaching over 100,000 students. His content focuses on cloud security and compliance, and how to implement and configure AWS services to protect, monitor, and secure customer data in AWS.

Stuart has written many cloud security blogs and regularly hosts webinars with AWS and leading AWS partners.

He is a certified expert within the Experts-Exchange community. In January 2016 he was awarded 'Expert of the Year' for his sharing of knowledge on cloud services with the community.

> *A huge thank you to my family for their continued support throughout this book, in particular, my loving wife Lisa!*
>
> *Also, to my mum and dad, who have always encouraged me to do my best to achieve my goals – thank you for everything!*

About the reviewer

Sriya Potham is an experienced security professional and cloud evangelist and is currently a cloud security architect managing e-commerce, AWS, and SaaS security. She has obtained both the AWS Solutions Architect – Associate and AWS Security – Specialty certifications and has been involved in the development of cloud programs at major Fortune 500 companies in the travel, financial, and consumer goods sectors. Outside of work, she enjoys practicing and teaching yoga.

> *I'd like to thank my family and friends for their part in helping me grow and learn every day.*

Packt is searching for authors like you

If you're interested in becoming an author for Packt, please visit `authors.packtpub.com` and apply today. We have worked with thousands of developers and tech professionals, just like you, to help them share their insight with the global tech community. You can make a general application, apply for a specific hot topic that we are recruiting an author for, or submit your own idea.

Table of Contents

Section 3: Security - a Layered Approach

Preface

This book will provide you with a deep understanding of the different security mechanisms that can be applied when architecting within the cloud, specifically within AWS. Security should always be the number one factor when deploying solutions, and understanding the impact of security at every layer is a requirement for any security practitioner.

You will be guided through every layer of AWS security from the following perspectives:

- Access management and the different techniques that can be applied to enforce it

- Policy management to understand how to define permissions that should be applied
- Host security, defining best practices on protecting instances
- Network and application security, ensuring neither are left vulnerable to exposures, vulnerabilities, or attacks
- Incident response, and how to manage security incidents to minimize the blast radius
- Log management, allowing full tracking and tracing of your solutions to automatically detect and remediate any issues found
- How to accurately record and audit your infrastructure to maintain compliance with governance standards
- Data protection, covering different encryption mechanisms to ensure your data is protected at rest and in transit

Who this book is for

The AWS Certified Security – Specialty certification is recommended for those who have at least 2 years of practical AWS production deployment experience, due to the level of depth and technical ability that is expected from the candidate.

You should also have some basic knowledge of security principles and concepts and, ideally, come from a background in IT security and governance. Also, if you are responsible for maintaining and implementing AWS security across production environments and are in a position similar to the following roles, then you are ideally suited to certify in this area:

- Cloud security consultant
- Cloud security architect
- Cloud security engineers
- DevSecOps engineer
- Cloud security specialist

If you are looking to validate your knowledge of being able to architect, implement, maintain, and operate security features, techniques, and services within AWS, then this certification is the one for you!

What this book covers

Chapter 1, *AWS Certified Security Specialty Exam Coverage*, provides you with an understanding of the different assessment topics that will be covered throughout the exam across the five different domains, including incident response, logging and monitoring, infrastructure security, identity and access management, and data protection.

Chapter 2, *AWS Shared Responsibility Model*, looks at the different security models (infrastructure, container, and abstract) that define where your responsibility as a customer implementing, controlling, and managing security in AWS starts and ends, in addition to the responsibilities of AWS, which controls the security of the cloud.

Chapter 3, *Access Management*, outlines the core concepts of identity and access management through the use of users, groups, and roles, and the differences between them. It also dives into the different types of roles available and EC2 instance profiles, before finishing with an understanding of how to implement multi-factor authentication.

Chapter 4, *Working with Access Policies*, takes a deep look at the multitude of different access policies that exist across the AWS environment, and which policy type should be used in different circumstances.

You will also learn how to read JSON policies to evaluate their permissions and the steps involved to implement cross-account access.

Chapter 5, *Federated and Mobile Access*, provides you with a comprehensive understanding of different federated access methods, including enterprise identity and social identity federation to provide a single sign-on approach to your AWS environment. In addition, you will also be introduced to the Amazon Cognito service to understand access control through mobile applications and devices.

Chapter 6, *Securing EC2 Instances*, tackles the best approach to secure your instance infrastructure using a variety of techniques. These include performing vulnerability scans using Amazon Inspector, how to manage your EC2 key pairs, using AWS Systems Manager to effectively administer your fleet of EC2 instances, and also, should a security breach occur, how to isolate your EC2 instances for forensic investigation.

Chapter 7, *Configuring Infrastructure Security*, enables you to gain a full understanding and awareness of the range of **Virtual Private Cloud** (**VPC**) security features that AWS offers to effectively secure your VPC environments. By the end of the chapter, you will be able to confidently build a secure multi-subnet VPC using internet gateways, route tables, network access control lists, security groups, bastion hosts, NAT gateways, subnets, and virtual private gateways.

Chapter 8, *Implementing Application Security*, looks at how to minimize and mitigate threats against your application architecture using different AWS services to prevent them from being compromised. You will also be introduced to the configuration of securing your elastic load balancers using certificates and how to secure your APIs using AWS API Gateway.

Chapter 9, *DDoS Protection*, highlights how to utilize different AWS features and services to minimize threats against this very common attack to ensure that your infrastructure is not hindered or halted by the threat. You will gain an understanding of the different DDoS attack patterns and how AWS Shield can be used to provide added protection.

Chapter 10, *Incident Response*, explains the process and steps to manage a security incident and the best practices to help you reduce the blast radius of the attack. You will understand how to prepare for such incidents and the necessary response actions to isolate the issue using a forensic account.

Chapter 11, *Securing Connections to Your AWS Environment*, provides you with an understanding of the different methods of securely connecting your on-premise data centers to your AWS cloud environment using both a **Virtual Private Network** (**VPN**) and the AWS Direct Connect service.

Chapter 12, *Implementing Logging Mechanisms*, focuses on Amazon S3 server access logs, VPC flow logs, AWS CloudTrail logs, and the Amazon CloudWatch logging agent to enable you to track and record what is happening across your resources to allow you to monitor your environment for potential weaknesses or signs of attack indicating a security threat.

Chapter 13, *Auditing and Governance*, looks at the different methods and AWS services that can play key parts in helping you to maintain a level of governance and how to provide evidence during an audit. You will be introduced to AWS Artifact, the integrity controls of AWS CloudTrail, AWS Config, and how to maintain compliance with Amazon Macie.

Chapter 14, *Automating Security Threat Detection and Remediation*, provides you with an understanding of how to implement automation to quickly identify, record, and remediate security threats as and when they occur. It looks at Amazon CloudWatch, Amazon GuardDuty, and AWS Security Hub to help you detect and automatically resolve and block potential security incidents.

Chapter 15, *Discovering Security Best Practices*, covers a wide range of different methods of implementing security best practices when working with AWS in an effort to enhance your security posture. It highlights and reviews a number of common best practices that are easy to implement and could play a huge role in protecting your solutions and data.

Chapter 16, *Managing Key Infrastructure*, takes a deep dive look into the world of two data encryption services, the AWS **Key Management Service** (**KMS**) and CloudHSM. You will learn how to implement, manage, and secure your data through AWS encryption services and the best service to use to meet your business requirements.

Chapter 17, *Managing Data Security*, introduces you to a variety of different encryption features related to a range of different services covering both storage and database services, including Amazon **Elastic Block Store** (**EBS**), Amazon **Elastic File System** (**EFS**), Amazon **Simple Storage Service** (**S3**), Amazon **Relational Database Service** (**RDS**), and Amazon DynamoDB.

Chapter 18, *Mock Tests*, provides you with two mock exams. Each of them is 65 questions in length to review your understanding of the content covered throughout this book to help you assess your level of exam readiness.

To get the most out of this book

Throughout this book, there are a number of demonstrations that you can follow to help with your learning. As a result, I suggest you have your own AWS account created that is *not* used for any production environments. You can follow along on either a Linux-based or windows-based operating system, however, I suggest you also have the AWS CLI installed.

Software/Hardware covered in the book	OS Requirements
Amazon Web Services Management Console	Any device with a modern browser
AWS Command Line Interface	Linux/Windows

To create a new AWS account, please follow the guide found at: `https://aws.amazon.com/premiumsupport/knowledge-center/create-and-activate-aws-account/`.

To install the AWS CLI, please follow the guide found at: `https://docs.aws.amazon.com/cli/latest/userguide/cli-chap-install.html`.

On completion of this book, I suggest you get as much hands-on experience with AWS as possible to use the different AWS services that are discussed to help reinforce the material from each of the chapters.

Code in Action

Code in Action videos for this book can be viewed at (`https://bit.ly/33jnvMT`).

Download the color images

We also provide a PDF file that has color images of the screenshots/diagrams used in this book. You can download it here: `http://www.packtpub.com/sites/default/files/downloads/9781789534474_ColorImages.pdf`.

Conventions used

There are a number of text conventions used throughout this book.

`CodeInText`: Indicates code words in text, database table names, folder names, filenames, file extensions, pathnames, dummy URLs, user input, and Twitter handles. Here is an example: "The `Principal` parameter is used within resource-based policies to identify the user, role, account, or federated user."

A block of code is set as follows:

```
{
  "Version": "2012-10-17",
  "Statement": {
    "Effect": "Allow",
    "Principal": {"AWS": "arn:aws:iam::356903128354:user/Stuart"},
    "Action": "sts:AssumeRole",
    "Condition": {"Bool": {"aws:MultiFactorAuthPresent": "true"}}
  }
}
```

When we wish to draw your attention to a particular part of a code block, the relevant lines or items are set in bold:

```
[default]
exten => s,1,Dial(Zap/1|30)
exten => s,2,Voicemail(u100)
exten => s,102,Voicemail(b100)
exten => i,1,Voicemail(s0)
```

Any command-line input or output is written as follows:

```
$ mkdir css
$ cd css
```

Bold: Indicates a new term, an important word, or words that you see onscreen. For example, words in menus or dialog boxes appear in the text like this. Here is an example: "Select **Route Tables** from the menu on the left and click the blue **Create Route Table** button."

 Warnings or important notes appear like this.

 Tips and tricks appear like this.

Get in touch

Feedback from our readers is always welcome.

General feedback: If you have questions about any aspect of this book, mention the book title in the subject of your message and email us at customercare@packtpub.com.

Errata: Although we have taken every care to ensure the accuracy of our content, mistakes do happen. If you have found a mistake in this book, we would be grateful if you would report this to us. Please visit www.packtpub.com/support/errata, selecting your book, clicking on the Errata Submission Form link, and entering the details.

Piracy: If you come across any illegal copies of our works in any form on the Internet, we would be grateful if you would provide us with the location address or website name. Please contact us at copyright@packt.com with a link to the material.

If you are interested in becoming an author: If there is a topic that you have expertise in and you are interested in either writing or contributing to a book, please visit authors.packtpub.com.

Reviews

Please leave a review. Once you have read and used this book, why not leave a review on the site that you purchased it from? Potential readers can then see and use your unbiased opinion to make purchase decisions, we at Packt can understand what you think about our products, and our authors can see your feedback on their book. Thank you!

For more information about Packt, please visit packt.com.

Section 1: The Exam and Preparation

The primary objective of this section is to summarize the exam topics you will come across, along with their weighted percentages, so that you are aware of the critical points of focus.

This section comprises the following chapter:

- Chapter 1, *AWS Certified Security Specialty Exam Coverage*

1
AWS Certified Security Specialty Exam Coverage

The AWS Certified Security Specialty Exam has been designed to assess and validate the ability of the candidate across a number of AWS security domains to demonstrate their knowledge, awareness, understanding, and capability in securing AWS architecture, services, resources, and data.

This initial chapter will explain in detail the requirements that you need in order to pass the exam, and highlight the domains and topics that will be assessed. It is important to understand these requirements before progressing through the rest of this book to ensure that you are aware of what you will be tested on. This will allow you to determine where your strengths and weaknesses lie, thereby allowing you to spend more time on those areas.

This chapter will take you through the following topics:

- Aim of the certification
- Intended audience
- Domains accessed
- Exam details

Aim of the certification

The aim of the certification is to validate the candidate's knowledge across the following areas, as defined by AWS (source: *AWS Certified Security Specialty (SCS-C01) Exam Guide*):

- An understanding of specialized data classifications and AWS data protection mechanisms
- An understanding of data encryption methods and AWS mechanisms to implement them

- An understanding of secure internet protocols and AWS mechanisms to implement them
- A working knowledge of AWS security services and the features of services used to provide a secure production environment
- Competency gained from two or more years of production deployment experience using AWS security services and features
- The ability to make trade-off decisions with regard to cost, security, and deployment complexity given a set of application requirements
- An understanding of security operations and risks

Upon completion of this book, you will feel ready to take and sit this exam with confidence, and achieve the much sought-after AWS Certified Security – Specialty certification.

Intended audience

This exam is intended for candidates like you who are responsible for maintaining and implementing AWS security across a range of environments. Those of you in the following roles or similar would be ideally suited to attempt this certification:

- Cloud security consultant
- Cloud security architect
- Cloud security engineer
- DevSecOps engineer
- Cloud security specialist

Although these roles are typically the target audience of this certification, the certification itself is available to anyone; there are no prerequisites in terms of other certifications for taking this exam.

Domains assessed

In the exam, there are five domains that have been defined by AWS that you will be assessed against, each with a different percentage weighting level, as shown in the following table:

Domain	Weighting level
Incident response	12%
Logging and monitoring	20%

Infrastructure security	26%
Identity and access management	20%
Data protection	22%

Attention must be paid to each domain to ensure you feel confident and comfortable with the topics, services, and features that may crop up in your exam. Let me break down these domains further to allow you to gain a deeper understanding of exactly what is tested within each domain.

Domain 1 – Incident response

This domain tests your understanding of how best to identify, respond to, and resolve AWS incidents across a range of services, and has been broken down into the following three elements:

- **1.1: Given an AWS abuse notice, evaluate the suspected compromised instance or exposed access keys**: Here, you will be expected to know how to respond to such an incident and the steps required to remediate the issue and take the appropriate action, depending on the affected resource in question.
- **1.2: Verify that the incident response plan includes the relevant AWS services**: When an incident occurs within an AWS environment, you must be able to utilize the appropriate AWS resources to identify, isolate, and resolve the issue as quickly as possible, without affecting or hindering other AWS infrastructure and resources.
- **1.3: Evaluate the configuration of automated alerting, and execute possible remediation of security-related incidents and emerging issues**: Proactive monitoring and speed are two key elements when analyzing your infrastructure for potential issues, in addition to utilizing automated services. You must have a solid understanding of these features, and how they can assist you to spot a potential problem and help you to resolve the issue.

Being able to identity, verify, and remediate incidents as they occur within your environment allows you to effectively isolate your resources before the blast radius of the security incident travels deeper within your infrastructure.

Domain 2 – Logging and monitoring

This domain determines your ability to implement and troubleshoot solutions relating to logging, monitoring, and alerting. You will need to be able to deploy, operate, and troubleshoot solutions relating to these four components within your AWS infrastructure:

- **2.1: Design and implement security monitoring and alerting**: You must have full comprehension of the available monitoring and alerting services within AWS. In addition, you must also be aware of how these can be utilized and integrated to implement an effective solution for monitoring your infrastructure for security threats and vulnerabilities.
- **2.2: Troubleshoot security monitoring and alerting**: Implementing a monitoring and alerting system is one thing, but being able to resolve issues with the solution and design is another. You must be aware of how the architecture is coupled together and the prerequisites for specific AWS features.
- **2.3: Design and implement a logging solution**: Data held in logs generated from services and applications can provide a wealth of information to help you identify a potential security breach. Therefore, it's imperative that you have a sound awareness of how to implement a solution to capture and record log data.
- **2.4: Troubleshoot logging solutions**: Similar to 2.2, your knowledge of logging solutions has to go deeper than implementation; you have to understand the key components, concepts, and how components depend on one another to enable you to resolve any incidents.

You must understand the complexities and importance of monitoring and logging and how they can be used together as an effective security tool.

Domain 3 – Infrastructure security

The infrastructure security domain assesses your ability to architect security best practices across your AWS architecture, from an individual host, to your VPC, and then to the outer reaches of your edge infrastructure. This domain carries the highest percentage mark across your certification, so it's key that you understand all the concepts and components:

- **3.1: Design edge security on AWS**: A thorough understanding of Amazon CloudFront and its security capabilities and controls is a must, in addition to other edge services offered by AWS.

- **3.2: Design and implement a secure network infrastructure**: Here, you will be tested on your knowledge of **Virtual Private Cloud** (**VPC**) infrastructure, and how to architect an environment to meet different security needs using route tables, NACLs, bastion hosts, NAT gateways, IGWs, and security groups.
- **3.3: Troubleshoot a secure network infrastructure**: This follows on from point 3.2, which ensures that you have a deep level of security architecture, enabling you to quickly pinpoint the most likely cause of misconfiguration from a security perspective.
- **3.4: Design and implement host-based security**: This will focus on security controls that can be enabled and configured on individual hosts, such as your EC2 instances.

Implementing a VPC is one of the first elements you are likely to build within your AWS account. Understanding how to protect your VPC is key in maintaining a level of protection to the rest of your resources running within it.

Domain 4 – Identity and access management (IAM)

This domain will focus solely on everything access control-related regarding the IAM service and how to control access to your AWS resources. IAM must be understood inside out and it is essential that you have the knowledge and confidence to spot errors in IAM JSON policies:

- **4.1: Design and implement a scalable authorization and authentication system to access AWS resources**: I can't emphasize enough the importance of understanding IAM at a deep level. This point will test your knowledge of authentication and authorization mechanisms, from multi-factor authorization to implementing conditional-based IAM policies used for cross-account access.
- **4.2: Troubleshoot an authorization and authentication system to access the AWS resources domain**: Here, you will be required to demonstrate your ability to resolve complex permission-based issues with your AWS resources.

Access control is covered in detail within the exam, so you must be familiar with all things relating to access management, and specifically the IAM service. You need to be able to read access policies to determine the resulting access of that policy.

Domain 5 – Data protection

The last domain requires you to have a solid understanding and awareness of how data within AWS can be protected through an encryption mechanism, both at rest and in transit. You will be assessed on services relating to encryption, specifically the **Key Management Service** (**KMS**):

- **5.1: Design and implement key management and use**: This point requires you to demonstrate your knowledge when it comes to encryption using KMS. You must be aware of when, how, and why this service is used, and which services can benefit from the features it offers.
- **5.2: Troubleshoot key management**: Data encryption keys are a powerful tool to help protect your data, but you must understand how you can configure the permissions surrounding these keys and what to look for when troubleshooting issues relating to data encryption and customer master keys.
- **5.3: Design and implement a data encryption solution for data at rest and data in transit**: Here, you will be assessed on your understanding of encryption as a whole. You must demonstrate that you have the knowledge to encrypt data in any state using the correct configuration, depending on a set of requirements.

It is of no surprise that the security specialty will assess your understanding of encryption, which will be centered around two key services, AWS **Key Management Service** (**KMS**) and AWS CloudHSM. The KMS service integrates with many different AWS services to offer a level of encryption, so make sure that you are familiar with all the components of KMS.

Exam details

Much like all other AWS certifications, the format consists of multiple choice questions. You will have 170 minutes to answer 65 questions, which is just over 2.5 minutes per question. You should have plenty of time, provided you have studied well and are confident in the domain areas I just discussed.

Some questions can be scenario-based and do take a little longer to process and answer, but don't panic; focus on what's being asked and eliminate the obviously wrong answers. It is likely there are two that you can rule out. Take your time and re-read the question before deciding on your final answer.

The passing score for this certification is 750 out of 1000 (75%). The exam itself is USD 300 and it must be taken at an AWS authorized testing center, which can all be booked online through the AWS website, at: https://aws.amazon.com/certification/.

Summary

In this chapter, I primarily focused on the different domains that you will be assessed against when taking your exam. I wanted to provide a deeper understanding of what each of the domain points might assess you against in order to allow you to understand where your strengths and weaknesses might lie. As you progress through the chapters, you will gain an understanding sufficient to cover all elements that have been discussed within this chapter to ensure that you are prepared for your certification.

In the next chapter, we begin by looking at the foundation of security on AWS, the AWS shared responsibility model, and how an understanding of this plays an important part in understanding AWS security as a whole.

Questions

As we conclude, here is a list of questions for you to test your knowledge regarding this chapter's material. You will find the answers in the *Assessments* section of the *Appendix*:

1. True or false: You need to complete a few other certifications as a prerequisite for the AWS Certified Security – Specialty certification.
2. How many domains have been defined by AWS that you will be assessed against in the exam?
3. The AWS Certified Security – Specialty certification consists of how many questions? (choose any one)
   - 55 questions
   - 60 questions
   - 65 questions
   - 75 questions

Further reading

For more information on this certification, please visit the AWS site, where you can download the exam guide and sample questions, at: https://aws.amazon.com/certification/certified-security-specialty/.

2
Section 2: Security Responsibility and Access Management

Throughout this section, you will be introduced to one of the most fundamental principals of working with AWS Security: the AWS shared responsibility model. This will help you understand where your security responsibility, both as a customer and as part of AWS, starts and ends. You will then be introduced to a number of different AWS services that allow you to effectively manage and implement solid access control policies so that you can control who has access to which resources within your AWS account. You will also learn about the best practices regarding **identity and access management (IAM)**, in addition to how to create and configure many of the available components.

To implement stringent access control, you will need a solid understanding of how access policies work. To ensure you have this in your tool belt, we'll dive into how to create them and the parameters that are used to define and control access. Finally, we'll look at how to manage access control at scale using federated access to create a single sign-on approach, in addition to how to manage access to AWS resources when using mobile applications.

By the end of this section, you will have a strong understanding of AWS access management and the different techniques and mechanisms that can be used to implement access security.

This section comprises the following chapters:

- Chapter 2, *AWS Shared Responsibility Model*
- Chapter 3, *Access Management*
- Chapter 4, *Working with Access Policies*
- Chapter 5, *Federated and Mobile Access*

2

AWS Shared Responsibility Model

Before I delve into the deeper technical aspects of AWS security in this book, it is essential that you gain an understanding of the AWS shared responsibility model. All security-related principles and concepts are derived from having a full comprehension of this model, and so you must be aware of why it is used.

From its very name—**shared responsibility model**—it's clear from the outset that there is more than just one party involved. The concept of this model defines where your responsibility as a customer for implementing, controlling, and managing security within AWS starts and ends, compared to that of the cloud service provider—in this case, AWS.

The roles and responsibilities of managing security require a shared awareness between the two parties. The model itself doesn't actually form a legal agreement in any way; it's simply down to you to be aware of the model and understand the importance surrounding it in order to allow you to architect and protect your resources effectively.

AWS has three different shared responsibility models—**infrastructure**, **container**, and **abstract**—all of which have varied levels of responsibility between the cloud customers and AWS. In this chapter, I will explore each model to help you understand their differences and how this affects security *in* and *of* the cloud.

The following topics will be covered in this chapter:

- Shared responsibility model for infrastructure services
- Shared responsibility model for container services
- Shared responsibility model for abstract services

Technical requirements

There are no hardware or software requirements for this chapter.

Shared responsibility model for infrastructure services

The infrastructure shared responsibility model is probably the most common model that AWS engineers are aware of today. It looks as in the following diagram and covers **Infrastructure as a Service (IaaS)** services, such as Amazon **Elastic Compute Cloud (EC2)**:

Customer Responsibility (Security 'in' the Cloud)	Customer Data		
	Platforms, Applications, Identity and Access Management		
	Operating System, Network and Firewall Configuration		
	Data-Side Data Encryption and Data Integrity Authentication	Server-Side Encryption (Filesystem and/or Data)	Network Traffic Protection (Encryption/Integrity/Identity)
AWS Responsibility (Security 'of' the Cloud)	AWS Foundation Services Compute Storage Database Network		
	AWS Global Infrastructure Regions Availibility Zones Edge Locations		

Let me break this down a bit further to help explain what this diagram represents. The diagram is split into two very distinct sections—a green area and a yellow area. This color-split defines the division of responsibility between the customer (green) and AWS (yellow).

We can also see that the customer is responsible for maintaining security *in* the cloud and AWS maintains the security *of* the cloud. But what does that mean?

Let's take a look at what AWS is responsible for:

- **AWS global infrastructure**: You can see that AWS provides security for the global infrastructure, including regions, Availability Zones, edge locations, and regional edge caches. This global infrastructure forms the physical data centers and point-of-presence locations that AWS uses globally to physically store your AWS resources. We as customers do not have physical access to AWS data centers; we are not allowed to turn up at the door of an AWS data center and ask to see our cloud resources. As a result, it is down to AWS to ensure that the physical security of their data centers meets stringent security controls and global security standards.

 For more information on AWS' global infrastructure, you can read my blog post on the subject, which describes each element in further detail:

    https://cloudacademy.com/blog/aws-global-infrastructure/

- **AWS foundation services**: AWS also provides foundation services, as defined in the model, covering compute, storage, database, and network components. This means they are physically providing the hardware and underlying infrastructure to allow us as customers to create resources from the pooled hardware that AWS provisions. Again, as customers, we do not have access to these hosts, the physical infrastructure, or the underlying hypervisor software on each host. All access and security to ensure the separation of resources on a single host are controlled and managed by AWS. This helps to prevent their customers' EC2 instances from being aware of other EC2 instances running on the same underlying host, but being used by another customer. This segregation and separation of resources at the hypervisor level is managed by AWS.

So, within this infrastructure shared responsibility model, AWS provides global reach via various data centers, as well as provisioning the underlying hardware and infrastructure required to allow their customers to create cloud resources from the AWS provisioned and pooled hardware resources. These two components effectively make up the AWS cloud; as such, within this model, we can summarize AWS' responsibility as providing the security *of* the cloud.

Now, let's compare this to the customer's responsibility for providing security *in* the cloud.

Essentially, anything that we as customers provision by using AWS foundation services across the global infrastructure, we have ultimate security responsibility for:

Customer Responsibility (Security 'in' the Cloud)	Customer Data		
	Platforms, Applications, Identity and Access Management		
	Operating System, Network and Firewall Configuration		
	Data-Side Data Encryption and Data Integrity Authentication	Server-Side Encryption (Filesystem and/or Data)	Network Traffic Protection (Encryption/Integrity/Identity)

Using the EC2 service as an example, let's look at each point relating to the customer's responsibilities from the preceding diagram:

- **Customer data**: The customer has to maintain the security of the data that they import into or create within their AWS environment—for example, any data stored on EC2 volumes, ephemeral or persistent.
- **Platform, application, and Identity and Access Management (IAM)**: Any platform or application installed on top of your EC2 instance has to be secured and protected by controls configured and implemented by you as the customer. In addition to this, you are solely responsible for maintaining any access control to your EC2 instance and applications. AWS provides the IAM service to implement these controls, but it's down to you as the customer to implement effective security measures using the features offered by IAM.
- **Operating system and network and firewall configuration**: As we saw, the responsibility of AWS ends at the hypervisor level. EC2 instances fall within the infrastructure model, and so maintaining the security of the operating system itself is the customer's responsibility. As a result, the customer must maintain and implement patching for the relevant operating system. EC2 instances are deployed within a VPC, and therefore, network configuration, including firewall restrictions, such as security groups (which are effectively virtual firewalls operating at the instance level), have to be configured and associated appropriately to protect your EC2 fleet.
- **Client-side data encryption and data integrity authentication**: This relates to the protection of data generated by or stored on your EC2 instances via an encryption mechanism. If you plan to encrypt your data, you as the customer are responsible for doing so.

- **Server-side encryption (filesystem and/or data)**: Again, if you plan to use any form of encryption to protect your data using server-side mechanisms—perhaps through the use of the **Key Management Service (KMS)**, which will be discussed in-depth in a later chapter—it is down to the customer to use the service effectively for data protection.
- **Network traffic protection (encryption/identity/integrity)**: When network traffic is being sent to and from your EC2 instance, you can configure, where applicable, to encrypt the communications with a protocol such as SSL or HTTPS.

So, in summary, when working with services that fall within the infrastructure shared responsibility model, AWS is responsible for the security *of* the cloud, which includes everything from the hypervisor stack and below. The customer is then responsible for security *in* the cloud, which starts from the operating system stack and up.

Understanding each of these models will help you define a more robust security strategy and strengthen your security posture across your AWS account. Fully understanding what you are responsible for and what AWS is responsible for will help to ensure that you are not left open to any unexpected vulnerabilities.

Shared responsibility model for container services

The second model we will cover is the container model. The word container is frequently used to describe software packages that contain code, and all associated dependencies that can be run across a range of different compute environments. Examples of common container technologies include Docker and Kubernetes. However, the word *container* when used here refers to a slightly different concept.

This model focuses on services that essentially reside on top of infrastructure services, meaning the customer does not have access to some of the infrastructure-level components—for example, the operating system. Examples of services in the container model include the following:

- AWS **Elastic MapReduce (EMR)**
- AWS **Relational Database Service (RDS)**
- AWS Elastic Beanstalk

This diagram shows the responsibility model for container services:

Customer Responsibility (Security 'in' the Cloud)	Customer Data				Customer IAM
	Data-Side Data Encryption and Data Integrity Authentication	Network Traffic Protection (Encryption/Integrity/Identity)		Firewall Configuration	
AWS Responsibility (Security 'of' the Cloud)	Platforms, Applications, Identity and Access Management				AWS IAM
	Operating System, Network and Firewall Configuration				
	AWS Endpoints	AWS Foundation Services			
		Compute Storage Database Network			
		AWS Global Infrastructure			
		Regions Availibility Zones Edge Locations			

As you can see, AWS still maintains the same level of security responsibility as retained from the infrastructure model, plus more additional responsibilities. Platform and application management and operating system and network configuration are now the responsibility of AWS.

Let's take the example of RDS. In this case, we as customers do not have access to the underlying operating system that the RDS databases are running on; as such, customers are not able to patch the operating system. This security element has been abstracted away from the customer and transferred over to AWS. In addition, platform and application management has also been passed to AWS. This is because RDS is a managed service, and as a result, all the maintenance of the application itself is undertaken by AWS. This takes a huge administrative burden off the customer, but also introduces a level of restriction at the same time, as we are only presented with the platform and everything above that stack.

As this is a managed service, AWS will have to maintain access control over the underlying operating system to perform any maintenance at the operating system level. Again, as customers, we do not have access to these elements.

You may also notice that from the customer's point of view, we have a level of IAM permissions to maintain; this is for users who require access to use the service in question, such as RDS.

Shared responsibility model for abstract services

The final model we will look at is the abstract shared responsibility model, shown here:

Customer Responsibility (Security 'in' the Cloud)	Customer Data		Customer IAM
	Client-Side Data Encryption and Integrity Authentication		
AWS Responsibility (Security 'of' the Cloud)	Data-Side Data Encryption provided by the platform (Protection of data at rest)	Network Traffic Protection provided by the platform (Protection of data in transit)	AWS IAM
	Platforms and Application Management		
	Operating System and Network Configuration		
	AWS Endpoints	AWS Foundation Services — Compute Storage Database Network	
		AWS Global Infrastructure — Regions Availibility Zones Edge Locations	

Right away, from a visual perspective, we can see that the shift in responsibility leans even greater toward AWS.

This model retains the level of security AWS has to manage from both the previous two models (infrastructure and container), with the addition of server-side encryption and network traffic protection. Example AWS services that fall within this model are the Amazon **Simple Queue Service** (**SQS**), Amazon DynamoDB, and Amazon S3.

These are defined as abstract services as almost all the control and management of the service has been abstracted away from the end customer; we simply access these services through endpoints. Customers do not have access to the underlying operating system (infrastructure) or to the actual platform that is running these services (container); instead, the customer is presented with the service frontend or endpoint to configure as required.

As a result, the customer has been totally abstracted away from having to maintain security updates for the operating system or any platform patches and security management. This also means that AWS now has the responsibility to implement and control any server-side encryption options, such as Amazon **S3 Server-Side Encryption** (**S3-SSE**), where the customer has no control over the access keys used for this encryption method; it's all managed by AWS.

Also, AWS will manage the secure transfer of data between the service components—for example, when S3 automatically copies customer data to multiple endpoints across different Availability Zones. As a customer, we have no control over how this data is transferred, and so the traffic has to be secured by AWS.

Summary

To review, the three different models discussed in this chapter were the shared responsibility model for infrastructure services, the shared responsibility model for container services, and the shared responsibility model for abstract services. It is clear to see that across these models, from infrastructure to abstract, the level of security responsibility shifted more toward AWS and away from the customer. This is down to the fact that AWS has more control over the level of management of services falling within the container and abstract models.

It is certainly worth understanding these models and being able to differentiate between them; this will serve you in good stead when you come to implement your security strategies across different solutions. You will have a clear understanding of where your responsibility ends and where AWS' starts. This will help to ensure that you do not leave any vulnerabilities across your AWS infrastructure within your accounts.

In the next chapter, we will be looking at access control within AWS and one of the key security services—AWS IAM. I will explain the core components of this service and show you how to create and configure IAM users, groups, roles, and multi-factor authentication.

Questions

As we conclude, here is a list of questions for you to test your knowledge regarding this chapter's material. You will find the answers in the *Assessments* section of the *Appendix*:

1. Which shared responsibility model offers the most customization and control for the customer?

2. Which shared responsibility model offers the least customization and control for the customer?

3. In which model would you expect to find the EC2 service?

4. Which model focuses on services that essentially reside on top of infrastructure services, such as Amazon EMR and Amazon RDS?

5. True or false: the customer's responsibility is defined as security *in* the cloud.

Further reading

For additional information on the AWS shared responsibility model and an underlying foundation to AWS security, please take a look at the following resources.

- Introduction to AWS security: `https://d1.awsstatic.com/whitepapers/Security/Intro_to_AWS_Security.pdf`
- The shared responsibility model: `https://aws.amazon.com/compliance/shared-responsibility-model/`

3
Access Management

Access management is one of the biggest elements of AWS security. It governs how, when, who, and what can access your resources at any given time. In this chapter, we will dive deep into each element of access management security that you will need to be aware of and master for the AWS security specialty certification.

You must be able to confidently implement and manage access controls across a range of different authentication mechanisms and understand all principles of permissions-based access policies. You also need to be aware of some of the specific services and features in place that are specifically designed to enrich and enhance the access control method selected.

Within this chapter, we shall be focusing on the following topics:

- Understanding **Identity and Access Management (IAM)**
- Provisioning users, groups, and roles in IAM
- Configuring **Multi-Factor Authentication (MFA)**

Technical requirements

To perform the tasks mentioned within this chapter, you will need to have the correct permissions to allow you to perform a number of different actions within the IAM service, including the creation and management of users, groups, and roles, in addition to configuring MFA. The permissions given in the IAMFullAccess policy will be sufficient to carry out all the actions in this chapter.

Understanding Identity and Access Management (IAM)

IAM is probably going to be one of the very first security services that you will use when setting up an AWS account. It contains the details and credentials of your root user account, which was set up during the creation of your account and also has full admin privileges to your entire AWS account by default. The power and privilege of this root user make it vulnerable as a credential compromise would put your entire AWS account and all of its resources at risk.

Due to this risk, it's best practice to *not* use this account for daily administration and operations. Instead, you should create another user account with relevant privileges, enabling you to control your resources within your account. It's also against best practice to configure access keys for the root account; limiting access methods for this user is essential due to the unlimited permissions that it has. To understand the use cases for access keys, we will explore them in detail in this chapter. You should definitely configure **MFA** for the root user, as it provides an additional step for authenticating to your AWS account in addition to the password. Again, we will be looking into MFA in great detail later in the chapter.

Now we have highlighted the security privileges of a root account, and why it is important for us to keep it secure, let's look at users, groups, and roles to help us configure and implement accounts that we can use for daily operational tasks.

Provisioning users, groups, and roles in IAM

You need to understand the differences between users, groups, and roles and their overall purpose within access control. This will help you architect and implement the most appropriate and effective access control for users and identities.

Creating users

Users within IAM are objects defined as identities that have the ability to log in and authenticate using defined credentials in the form of an associated password. Additional authentication may also be used in the form of **MFA**. Once authenticated, the user can then access resources as defined by their associated set of permissions.

With this basic understanding of what a user is, let's create our first one:

1. From within the AWS Management Console, select **IAM**.
2. Select **Users** from the menu and select **Add user**:

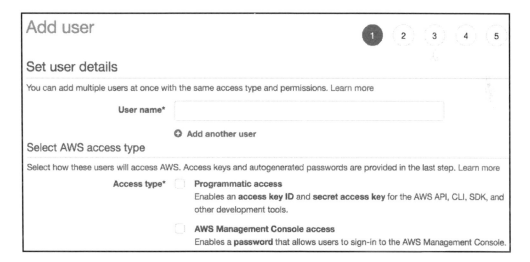

3. Enter a username, which will be the login name of the user. It can only contain alphanumeric characters, or any of the following: _+=,.@-.
4. If required, you can add more than one user at a time by selecting the **Add another user** option.

5. At the bottom of the **Add user** window, you can see that you have options for an AWS **Access type**. You can select either of the following:

- **Programmatic access**: This will issue access keys for the user, enabling that identity to authenticate to access AWS resources programmatically using the AWS CLI, SDK, or other development tools.

- **AWS Management Console access**: This will issue a password for that identity to authenticate to access AWS resources using the Management Console. If you select this option, the following will be displayed:

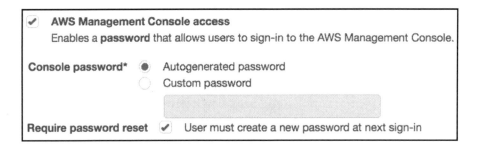

Here, you must choose an IAM autogenerated password or enter a custom password defined by you. You can also select whether the user should be forced to create a new password the next time this new user logs in. I would recommend this option for additional security.

6. Once you have selected the required option for **Access type – Programmatic access**, **AWS Management Console access**, or both if required, click on the **Next: Permissions** button, which will display the following permissions screen:

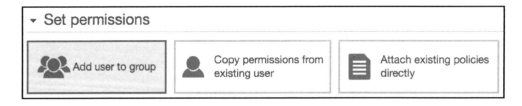

You then have three options, as shown in the preceding screenshot:

- **Add user to group**: This is a best practice, adding a new user to a group that already has a defined set of permissions attached to it. Adding users to a group reduces the amount of administration required when access control changes are needed. For example, assume you have a team of 30 people all performing the same job who require the same access. If you configured permissions associated with the individual user accounts, that's 30 permission policies. Now, if a change of access was required for the whole team, to perhaps support a new resource in a solution, you would have to update 30 different policies, one for each user. However, if you created a group for the team and added all 30 users to that group, you would simply need one set permission policy associated with the group. Any changes required would then mean just updating the single policy attached to the group.

- **Copy permissions from existing user**: If you did have a requirement of associating permissions directly with a user account and you needed to repeat the same set of permissions for a new user, then this option would be used. It allows you to select an existing user to copy permissions from. However, do be sure you understand exactly what permission that existing user has to ensure you do not grant overly permissive access for this new user.

- **Attach existing policies directly**: This option again allows you to attach permission policies to a user directly, and if required to do so, this will present a list of both managed and custom policies for you to select. We will discuss more on policies (both managed and custom) in the next chapter, Chapter 4, *Working with Access Policies*.

7. Once you have selected the appropriate option, click on the **Next: Tags** button.
8. Here, you can enter any key/value pair tags that you want to associate with the user, for example, a **Key** of **Department** and a **Value** of **Development**, or a **Key** of **Cost Center** and a **Value** of **41123**:

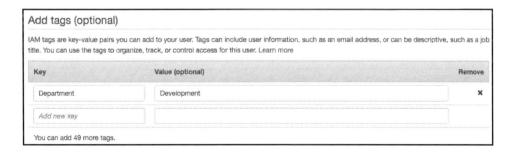

9. When you have completed your tags configuration, select the **Next: Review** button:

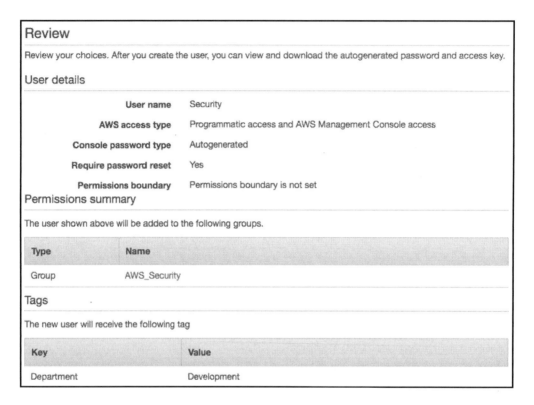

10. This **Review** screen will allow you to verify the options you have selected up to this point during the creation of the user. When you have confirmed all details are correct, select the **Create user** button. This will then create the user and display a screen as shown here, with credential details:

11. Using the **Send email** option, we can send the details of how to log in to your account, including a link to the management console for your account.

12. **Download.csv** will download the programmatic access key details, including both the **Access key ID** and **Secret access key**.

With that, we have successfully created our first user. Users allow us to plan permissions for individuals in our organization. However, we can also associate permissions with a set of accounts, which we will explore next with groups.

Creating groups

Groups within IAM are objects that are associated with a set of permissions allowing any users that are members of that group to inherit the permissions of the group. The group itself does not have any credentials associated with it and so you are unable to authenticate to AWS using group details; it is simply an object within IAM containing users.

In order to create a group, follow these steps:

1. From within the AWS Management Console, select **IAM**.
2. Select **Groups** from the menu.
3. Now select **Create Group**. You will arrive at the following screen:

4. Enter a **Group Name**, which can have a maximum of 128 characters and can contain only alphanumeric characters and/or the following: +=,.@-_. In this example, we have entered AWS_Security as the name. Once your name is entered, select **Next Step**.

5. As shown in the following screenshot, you can attach a policy and these policies contain permissions to access resources. We have selected the **AmazonS3FullAccess** policy in this screenshot:

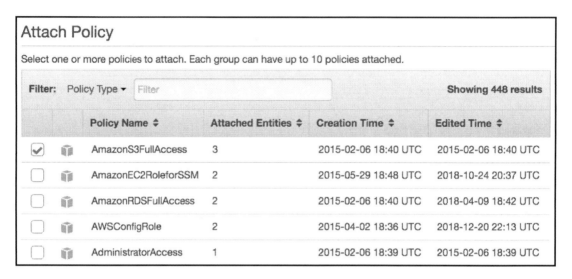

6. Once you have added your policies, select **Next Step**. The final review screen is then shown to confirm your configuration based on the previous steps.

7. When you are happy with the configuration, select **Create group**:

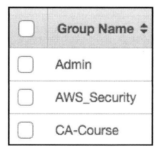

You will now be able to see the new group in the list of groups within the IAM dashboard.

Creating roles

Similar to users, roles are also identities. They have an associated set of permissions that allows them to access AWS resources. However, they are not associated with users or groups. Instead, a role can be assumed by other identities and resources such as users in your AWS account, by a user in a different AWS account, by a federated user, or another AWS service such as EC2. When the role is assumed by one of these methods, the identity will inherit the associated permissions of the role. It's important to understand that the roles themselves do not have static credentials; instead, they are dynamically created when the role is assumed.

There are a number of different types of roles available, which are as follows:

- Service roles
- User roles
- Web identity federated roles
- SAML 2.0 federated roles

We will discuss each of these roles and learn how to create them in the following subsections.

Service roles

These service roles allow other AWS services to perform actions on our behalf. As you work within AWS and begin to utilize and configure various services, there will be requirements whereby the service will create service roles in order to perform specific steps and functions. For example, during the configuration of AWS Elastic Beanstalk, a service role will be created allowing Elastic Beanstalk to use other AWS services on your behalf. This role will have all of the required permissions to allow the service to carry out the necessary tasks that it needs to. It's important to understand that service roles exist *only* in the account in which they were created and can't be used for cross-account access.

These service roles are often created during the configuration of the service itself, but it's also possible to create service roles within IAM. Let's see how to do it:

1. From within the AWS Management Console, select **IAM**.
2. Select **Roles** on the menu and select **Create Role**.

3. Select the **AWS service** option as the trusted entity.

4. As you can see from the screenshot, there are a number of supported AWS services that can use service roles. Select the service you would like to configure the role for, for example, AWS **Lambda**:

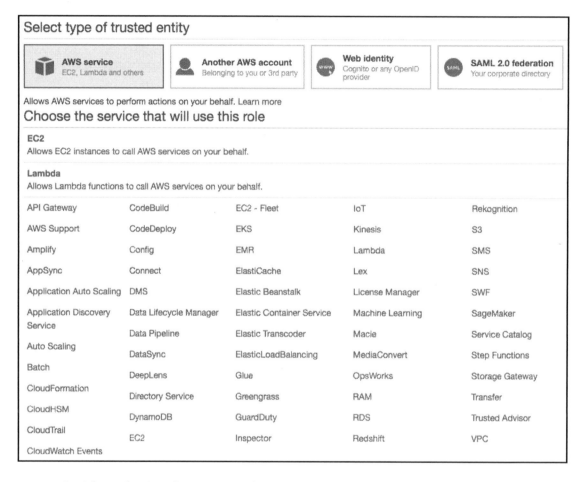

5. After selecting the service, select **Next: Permissions**. You can add permissions to the role by filtering on the policies that exist. Alternatively, you can also create a new policy at this point by selecting **Create policy**. For this example, I have filtered on S3 and selected the **AmazonS3FullAccess** policy:

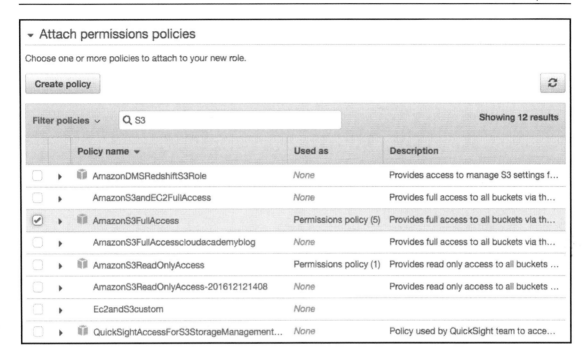

6. On this same screen, you also have an option to set a permission boundary, which allows you to restrict the maximum permissions granted to the role:

▾ Set permissions boundary

Set a permissions boundary to control the maximum permissions this role can have. This is an advanced feature used to delegate permission management to others. Learn more

◉ Create role without a permissions boundary
◯ Use a permissions boundary to control the maximum role permissions

7. Once you have configured and selected your permissions for the role, click **Next: Tags**.

8. Add any tags required for the role and click **Next: Review**:

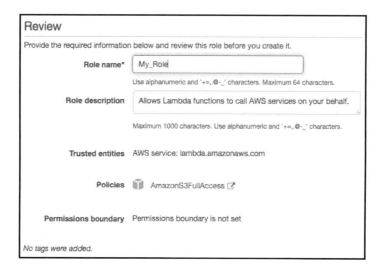

9. The **Review** page will then be displayed allowing you to confirm the configuration you have specified throughout the previous screens. You must also specify a name for the role. When you are happy with the configuration and you have added your role name, select **Create role**:

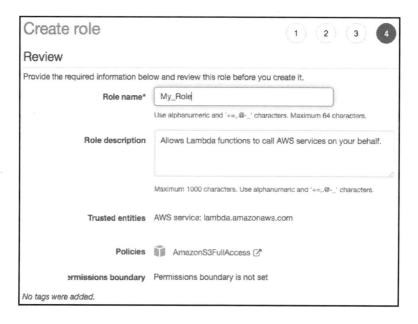

10. The role is now created. If you select the role from within the role list you can find metadata information for that role, such as the ARN, in addition to trusted relationships. As we created this role as a service role for Lambda, we can see that, under **Trusted entities**, we have the Lambda service listed. This restricts this role to only be used by Lambda when configured to do so:

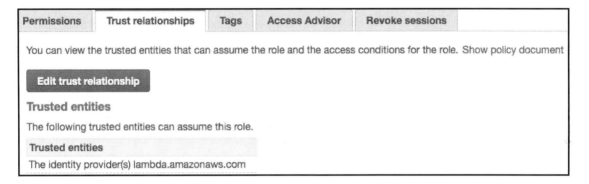

As we can see, a role contains two different policies. One contains the permissions of the role itself, which allows the identity using the role to access resources. The second policy contains the trust relationship and this is used to govern who or what can assume the policy. In the next chapter, `Chapter 4`, *Working with Access Policies*, I will discuss how you can change parameters within this trust relationship policy to specify specific principals.

You may have noticed when selecting a trusted entity during the role creation that EC2 was listed first. Using EC2 roles are key when deploying and running applications on your EC2 instances that may need access to other AWS resources. One way of managing this access would be to hardcode user credentials, such as access keys, into the application, which would then allow access. However, this would be a security risk if a malicious user was able to gain unauthorized access to the instance as they could gain access to those credentials. Instead, it is a best practice to associate the EC2 instance with a role. This enables a dynamic set of credentials to be used for the instance and then applications running on that instance can inherit the permissions of the associated role. This removes the need to store credentials on any instance, which again is a security risk.

When you create a service role for EC2 via the console, two components are created: the role itself and also an instance profile, both with the same name. The instance profile is essentially a container for your role and it's used to pass data to the EC2 instance from the role itself. If you use the EC2 console to create your instance and use the drop-down list of roles to associate with the instance, the list actually displays a list of instance profiles and not the role (however, they are of the same name).

If you were to configure the roles for EC2 via the command line, then you would have to create the role and the instance profile as two separate actions, and by doing so, you can have it create a different name for the instance profile than that of the role.

 For more information on the commands used to perform this process, please visit https://docs.aws.amazon.com/IAM/latest/UserGuide/id_roles_use_switch-role-ec2_instance-profiles.html.

User roles

Next, we have roles that can be assumed by a user in either the same or a different AWS account. When a user assumes a role, their current set of permissions associated with their user identity is temporarily replaced with the permissions associated with the role. To assume a role, the identity needs to have the relevant permissions to do so; without these configured permissions, accessing the role is not possible. These permissions can be associated with a group or with the user identity themselves.

The role can be assumed either through the Management Console or programmatically via the AWS **Command-Line Interface (CLI)**. If the user switches to the role from within the Management Console, then the identity can only do so for 1 hour. If the role was assumed programmatically using the `assume-role` command on the CLI or the `AssumeRole` API operation, then the role can be assumed for a minimum of 15 minutes or up to 1 hour by using the `duration-seconds` parameter on the CLI or the `DurationSeconds` API.

In order to create a role to be assumed by the user, follow these steps:

1. From within the AWS Management Console, select **IAM**.
2. Select **Roles** from the menu and select **Create role**.
3. Select **Another AWS account** as the trusted entity.
4. You must then enter the AWS account that can use this role. If you want a user within the same account, then enter your AWS account number. Alternatively, if it should be used by another user in another account to perform cross-account access, then you must enter the AWS account number of that account (cross-account access will be explained in the next chapter, Chapter 4, *Working with Access Policies*). For this demonstration, we will add the AWS account number of the same account:

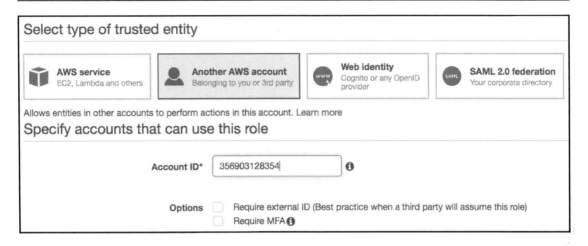

5. Next, you have a couple of options to choose from. If you are going to allow a third party access to your resources via this role, then you should check the relevant checkbox, which allows you to enter an optional external identifier. This means, when assuming this role, the exact identifier will also have to be entered, adding an additional layer of security. Besides this, you also have an option to include MFA to be used when assuming the role. Again, this is an additional layer of authentication for the role.

6. When you have selected the relevant configuration and added your trusted account, click on **Next: Permissions**.

7. Much like in the previous example, when creating our service role, you will then be asked to add the relevant permissions. In this example, I have selected the **AmazonS3FullAccess** policy. When you have added your policies to the role, select **Next: Tags**.

8. Add your tags and then click **Next: Review**.

9. Add a role name and then click **Create Role**.

Your role has now been created and can be found within the list of roles.

So, we have now covered service roles, which allow other AWS services to perform actions on our behalf, and user roles that can be assumed by a user to temporarily replace their permissions with those associated with the role. Next, let's look at web identity federated roles.

Web identity federated roles

This option allows users who have been granted federated access to your AWS resources through a web identity provider to assume these roles instead of via a user that has been created within IAM.

Federated access simply means that the user has been authenticated by an external source, and in the case of web identity federation, this could be via well-known **identity providers** (**IdPs**) such as Amazon, Google, Facebook, or even Amazon Cognito (which will be discussed later in this chapter). Federation allows a **Single Sign-On** (**SSO**) approach.

Before creating a role for a web identity, there are a number of prerequisites that need to be completed:

1. You will need to either gain an **Application ID** or **Audience** from the IdP, depending on which option you select, by signing up as a developer with the IdP.
2. Once you have received the information (application ID or audience), you will then need to set up an OpenID Connect IdP within IAM.
3. Finally, you will need to ensure you have both the permission policy and the trusted identity policy configured.

Once you have this information, you can complete your role setup by following a similar process to the previous examples, including the assigning of permissions (using the policy created in *step 3*, tagging, review, and role creation).

SAML 2.0 federated roles

The final option when creating a new role is the SAML 2.0 federation option, which allows you to create roles that have been federated through your own internal corporate directory.

This differs from web identity in the fact that the external authentication system is your own corporate directory of users, for example, your own **Microsoft Active Directory** (**MSAD**). Using the **Lightweight Directory Access Protocol** (**LDAP**), you can query MSAD as your authentication into your AWS account, again providing an SSO approach to your AWS environment.

Users authenticated in this way can then assume SAML 2.0 federation roles, allowing them to adopt permissions required to perform the required actions and tasks within your AWS account.

Again, there are a couple of prerequisites for using this option:

- Create a SAML provider within IAM.
- Ensure you have your policies configured, again both a permission policy and a trusted identity policy.

Once you have fulfilled the prerequisites, you can complete your role setup by referring to the following screenshot and executing the steps that follow:

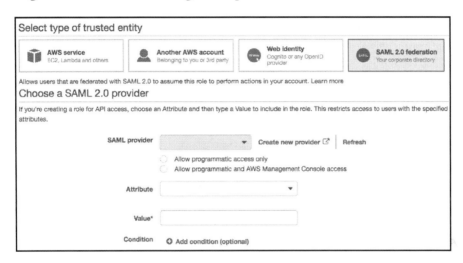

1. Select your newly created SAML provider.
2. Decide whether you need to allow only programmatic access or both programmatic and AWS Management Console access.
3. The **Attribute** and **Value** fields are only used if you selected the **Allow programmatic access only** option from the previous step. They can be used to restrict the role's access to users from the IdP whose SAML response includes the attribute/value that is defined by the IdP selected.
4. Optionally, you can also include conditions that will exist in the trust policy relating to SAML attributes. More information on conditional values will be discussed in Chapter 4, *Working with Access Policies*.

You should now have an understanding of users, groups, and roles within IAM. The knowledge that you've acquired here will not only help you in access management but will also be used to configure various other AWS security services discussed in this book. I now want to dive into an access control mechanism that can help you to enforce stronger authentication methods for your users.

Configuring Multi-Factor Authentication (MFA)

In addition to a password that is required for users to authenticate to AWS, it is recommended to implement MFA to add a second layer of authentication. This is best practice for your AWS root account and any other user accounts that have elevated privileges.

By using MFA, you are required to enter a randomly generated 6-digit number once you have entered your password when using the Management Console. This 6-digit number changes very frequently, making it difficult to compromise. It is very easy to set up MFA for a user so let me run through it:

1. From within the IAM dashboard of the AWS Management Console, select **Users** and then the user requiring MFA.

2. Click on the **Security Credential** tab and you will notice under **Sign-in Credentials** that it states **Not assigned** for your MFA device:

> **Assigned MFA device** Not assigned | Manage

3. Click on **Manage.** Here, you can then select your chosen device for using MFA. I will use Google Authenticator, which is a simple app I have on my phone. So, in this example, we have selected **Virtual MFA device**. Once done, click **Continue**:

4. Using the Google Authenticator app, we scan the QR code and enter the first 6 digits that appear within the app for our user and add those digits into the entry of **MFA code 1**. We must then wait for the numbers to change and add those consecutive digits into the **MFA code 2** field:

5. At this point, we will get a message stating that we have successfully assigned a virtual MFA device for that user:

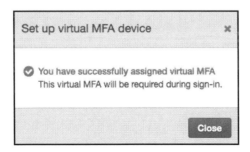

6. The following screenshot shows how the screen appears when logging in as the user once the username and password have been entered:

MFA can also be used in other areas of AWS, for example, policies. You can configure your policies to only allow a user to perform an action if they have done so via MFA within the conditional parameters. The following example policy shows a trust policy relating to a role that checks to make sure that the user Stuart has authenticated via MFA. If Stuart did not use MFA, then access is not permitted:

```
{
  "Version": "2012-10-17",
  "Statement": {
    "Effect": "Allow",
    "Principal": {"AWS": "arn:aws:iam::356903128354:user/Stuart"},
    "Action": "sts:AssumeRole",
    "Condition": {"Bool": {"aws:MultiFactorAuthPresent": "true"}}
  }
}
```

As you can see, MFA is very easy to configure and set up and provides a great way of strengthening authentication to your AWS account and resources. MFA provides a great way of enhancing the security posture within your access control policies.

Summary

This chapter covered some of the key, essential components when managing access to your resources, including users, groups, roles, and MFA. With an understanding of these components within IAM, you are now able to successfully and securely control access and boost your security. The policies that underpin the permissions that are assigned to the identity objects help tie together the authentication and authorization functions of your access control mechanisms.

In the next chapter, we will be focusing on these policies, and how to implement and change them to suit your security needs.

Questions

As we conclude, here is a list of questions for you to test your knowledge regarding this chapter's material. You will find the answers in the *Assessments* section of the Appendix:

1. Which type of role allows other AWS services to perform actions on our behalf?
2. True or false: Adding users to an IAM group is considered best practice.
3. True or false: Rules can only be assumed by other services within AWS.
4. What does MFA stand for (which acts as an authentication control mechanism)?

Further reading

The AWS Identity and Access Management Documentation can be found at: `https://docs.aws.amazon.com/iam/index.html#lang/en_us`.

4

Working with Access Policies

Access control is a crucial step in implementing a secure foundation for your environment. You need to define who can access your AWS resources, as well as when, why, and how. Much of this access is governed by different access policies associated with your identities. This chapter dives deep into how to create and manage your access policies to effectively and securely govern permissions across your infrastructure.

The following topics will be covered in this chapter:

- Understanding the difference between policy types
- Identifying policy structure and syntax
- Configuring cross-account access
- IAM policy management
- Policy evaluation
- Using bucket policies to control access to S3

Technical requirements

To complete all the steps detailed in this chapter, you will need to have access to two AWS accounts and be able to administer the IAM service.

Understanding the difference between policy types

We looked into different policies when discussing users, groups, and roles in the previous chapter. So now, we will dive deeper into these policies and discuss the various different types of policies and what they look like.

Policies are associated with users, groups, roles, or resources and define who or what can or can't access AWS resources. You may already be familiar with some policy types, but AWS supports a number of different types of policies, including the following:

- Identity-based policies
- Resource-based policies
- Permissions boundaries
- **Access Control Lists (ACLs)**
- Organization **Service Control Policies (SCPs)**

We will discuss these policies one by one in the following subsections.

Identity-based policies

If you have been using AWS for any length of time, then this type of policy is probably the most familiar to you. You can attach these policies to identities that have been created within the IAM service and they essentially associate specific permissions associated with the identity. For example, if a group had a policy allowing full Amazon **Simple Storage Service (S3)** access, then that is an identity-based policy as users of the group would be granted permissions based on the policies bound to that group.

Identity-based policies can either be AWS-managed, customer-managed, or in-line policies, which we will discuss now:

- **AWS-managed policies**: These are predefined policies that can be found within IAM and are available to use without having to create your own. The following screenshot shows a sample of the EC2-managed policies that are available:

○ ▶ 📦	AmazonEC2FullAccess	
○ ▶ 📦	AmazonEC2ReadOnlyAccess	
○ ▶ 📦	AmazonEC2ReportsAccess	
○ ▶ 📦	AmazonEC2RoleforAWSCodeDeploy	
○ ▶ 📦	AmazonEC2RoleforDataPipelineRole	
○ ▶ 📦	AmazonEC2RoleforSSM	
○ ▶ 📦	AmazonEC2SpotFleetAutoscaleRole	
○ ▶ 📦	AmazonEC2SpotFleetRole	
○ ▶ 📦	AmazonEC2SpotFleetTaggingRole	

As you can see, there is a wide range of policies for each service with varying levels of access. At the time of writing this book, there are over 480 AWS-managed policies to choose from. They can all be accessed by selecting **Policies** from within the IAM management console.

- **Customer-managed policies**: These are policies that have been customized by us as customers. There might not be an AWS-managed policy that is correct; as a result, you may need to either copy and customize an existing managed policy or create your own from scratch by using the visual editor or writing it using **JavaScript Object Notation (JSON)** format. Customer-managed identity-based policies give you far more granular control over how you want to manage access for identities than AWS-managed policies.

- **In-line policies**: These are different from both AWS- and customer-managed policies in the sense that in-line policies are embedded directly into the identity object; for example, customer-managed policies are stored in IAM as separate objects and can then be assigned to multiple identities, such as groups, roles, and users. In-line policies are *not* stored as separate objects; they only exist within the identity that they are created—users or roles.

As a general rule, it's a best practice to use managed policies over in-line policies where possible as you have a clear view of managed policies within IAM, whereas in-line policies are embedded into identities and are not as visible.

Resource-based policies

These are essentially in-line policies, but instead of being attached to an identity object, they are attached to resources themselves. For example, one of the most frequently used resource-based policies is Amazon S3 bucket policies.

As these policies are not attached to an identity, there needs to be a parameter within the policy that defines a principal so that AWS knows who or what these permissions apply to. This principal relates to an identity and can either reside in the same AWS account or in a different account. We will discuss principals later in this chapter when we look at the structure of policies.

Permissions boundaries

These are policies that govern the maximum permissions that an identity-based policy can associate with any user or role; however, the permissions boundary policy itself does not apply permissions to users or roles. It simply restricts those given by the identity-based policy.

To create a permissions boundary, you can perform the following steps:

1. From within the IAM management console, select your user or role. In this example, we have selected a user who has been assigned permissions from a group, **AmazonS3FullAccess** (as per the best practices), giving full access to S3. However, if you wanted to restrict this level of access to S3 either temporarily or permanently for this particular user, you could set a permissions boundary:

2. Select the arrow next to **Permissions boundary** (not set). This will open a drop-down menu:

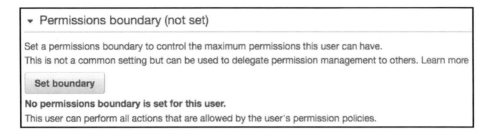

3. Select **Set Boundary**. This will then take you to a screen showing all the managed policies (both AWS- and customer-managed). From here, you can select a new policy to act as the maximum boundary—for example, **AmazonS3ReadOnlyAccess**. Once you have selected your policy, click **Set boundary**:

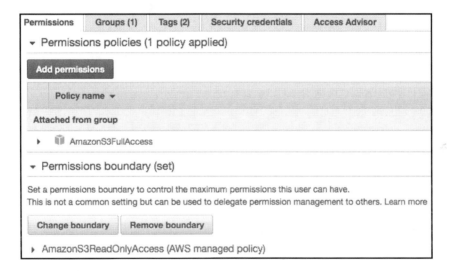

4. This new boundary will restrict that user's permissions to S3 as read-only based on the associated managed policy of that boundary. This is despite the user being a member of a group that has access to **AmazonS3FullAccess**.

If you want to explore permissions boundaries in greater depth and understand how they are evaluated against all other permissions, please refer to `https://docs.aws.amazon.com/ IAM/latest/UserGuide/access_policies_boundaries.html`.

Access control lists

Firstly, do not confuse ACLs with **network access control lists** (**NACLs**), which are used to control network traffic (discussed later in this chapter). ACLs are used in Amazon S3 and act much like resource-based policies, as these ACLs can be attached to buckets. They can also be attached to S3 objects, whereas bucket policies (discussed later in this chapter) can't. However, ACLs are used *only* to control cross-account access from a different AWS account or public access.

When configuring your ACLs, you have a number of options as to who can access the object or bucket via an ACL:

- **Access for other AWS Accounts**: Using this option, you can enter the email address of the account owner or the canonical ID of the AWS account.
- **Public Access**: This is a pre-configured S3 group created by AWS and allows anyone with internet access to have access to your object. This should be used with extreme caution and should only be used if necessary. Ensure that no sensitive or confidential data is stored within an object or bucket that has public access.
- **S3 Log Delivery Group**: Again, this is another pre-configured S3 group created by AWS. This option allows write permission to the bucket for S3 server access logging. If this logging is configured, these logs can be useful from a security and audit point of view.

To view these options and the permission level, do the following:

1. From the AWS management console, select **S3**:

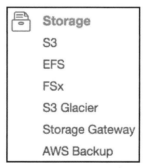

2. Select the bucket that you would like to configure permissions for.
3. Select the **Permissions** tab:

4. Select the **Access Control List** option:

5. You will then see that there are minimal permissions that can be assigned for each of the three options, in addition to the bucket owner, as shown:

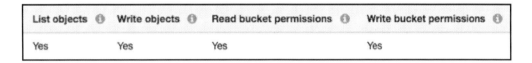

In fact, these are the only policies that are not written in JSON format. The permissions are as follows:

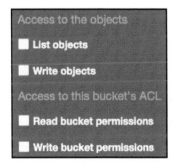

In this section, we looked at how we can use ACLs to control cross-account access from a different AWS account, as well as public access or access for server-access logging on a per bucket basis.

Organization SCPs

These are policies that are used by AWS organizations, which are used to manage multiple AWS accounts. Organizations can be used to allow you to centrally manage your AWS accounts in a hierarchical structure, and grouping can be done through **Organization Units (OUs)**. **SCPs** act in a similar manner to permissions boundaries within identity objects. They set the maximum permission level that can be given to members of an associated AWS account or OU. They restrict what level both identity-based and resource-based policies can grant permission for both users and roles, but the SCPs do not themselves grant any permissions.

For example, the following SCP would deny anyone within the AWS account associated with the SCP from deleting VPC Flow Logs, even if they had access via an identity-based policy:

```
{
  "Version": "2012-10-17",
  "Statement": [
    {
      "Effect": "Deny",
      "Action": [
        "ec2:DeleteFlowLogs",
        "logs:DeleteLogGroup",
        "logs:DeleteLogStream"
      ],
      "Resource": "*"
    }
  ]
}
```

With this, we come to the end of the section covering the various access policies. Remember that since these policies determine who or what can or can't access AWS resources, they are very important to understand in order to ensure the security of your environment is maintained. The syntax of this policy, as well as other JSON policies used (for example, those within IAM) are covered in the next section. So, let's take a look at that next.

 For more information on AWS organizations, please see my blog post on the topic at https://cloudacademy.com/blog/multiple-aws-account-management-using-aws-organizations/.

Identifying policy structure and syntax

All of the policies discussed in the previous section, other than ACLs, are written in JSON format and follow a specific policy structure. Understanding this structure will enable you to quickly and easily identify what permissions are being granted or denied within a policy and for who and what service. You must be able to confidently review and interpret these policies.

An example of policy structure

The following screenshot shows an example policy. Take a note of the various parameters:

```
 1 {
 2     "Version": "2012-10-17",
 3     "Statement": [
 4         {
 5             "Sid": "SamplePolicy",
 6             "Effect": "Allow",
 7             "Action": [
 8                 "s3:PutObject",
 9                 "s3:GetObject"
10             ],
11             "Resource": "arn:aws:s3:::awssecuritycert/*",
12             "Condition": {
13                 "IpAddress": {
14                     "aws:SourceIp": "10.0.0.0/16"
15                 }
16             }
17         }
18     ]
19 }
```

Let's understand these parameters one by one:

- Version: The 2012-10-17 version number shows the version of the policy language being used by AWS. The latest version at the time of writing this book is 2012-10-17.
- Statement: This acts as a group for the parameters that follow, and each policy can have a number of statements within them.
- Sid: This is simply a statement identification, the value of which can be anything to make logical sense of the statement itself. In this example, we have simply added a value of SamplePolicy, allowing us to easily identify what we are using the policy for.

- `Effect`: This can either be a value of `Allow` or `Deny`. This simply allows or denies access to the resources within the statement using the actions listed.
- `Action`: Here you can list a number of different actions that you want to either allow or deny access to, depending on the value of the previous parameter (`Effect`). In this example, we have listed two actions: `s3:PutObject` and `s3:GetObject`. The action is first defined by its service, such as S3, and is then followed by a colon (`:`), which precedes the action itself within the service.
- `Resource`: This provides the **Amazon Resource Name (ARN)** that tells us which resource these permissions apply to. In our example, we have an ARN: `aws:s3:::awssecuritycert/*`. `*` is a wildcard that stipulates any object within the `awssecuritycert` bucket.
- `Condition`: The `Condition` element is an optional parameter and allows you to dictate under what conditions or circumstances that the policy comes into effect. In my example policy, I have a single condition, which contains condition operators that specify the values of the condition. This condition is based on the IP address of the identity. For this condition to be met, the source IP address of the identity trying to access the `aws:s3:::awssecuritycert/*` resource, using either `s3:PutObject` or `s3:GetObject`, *must* be in the network range of `10.0.0.0/16`.

  It's also possible to have multiple conditions, which are known as condition blocks (more than one condition). In a condition block, the conditions are evaluated together using a logical `AND` statement, meaning all conditions in the block must be met before the permissions are put into effect.

The parameters discussed in this example are similar to what you would expect to see in a resource-based policy. In the next section, we will focus on the core difference between the two.

The structure of a resource-based policy

The policy structure for resource-based policies is essentially the same; however, there is one significant difference. As mentioned previously, when working with resource-based policies, the policy itself is attached to a resource and not an identity. As a result, another parameter is needed within the policy to identify who or what the policy should be associated with. This parameter is known as `Principal`:

```
1   {
2       "Id": "Policy1548357720488",
3       "Version": "2012-10-17",
4       "Statement": [
5           {
6               "Sid": "SamplePolicy",
7               "Action": [
8                   "s3:GetObject",
9                   "s3:PutObject"
10              ],
11              "Effect": "Allow",
12              "Resource": "arn:aws:s3:::awssecuritycert/*",
13              "Condition": {
14                  "IpAddress": {
15                      "aws:SourceIp": "10.0.0.0/16"
16                  }
17              },
18              "Principal": {
19                  "AWS": [
20                      "arn:aws:iam::730739171055:user/Stuart"
21                  ]
22              }
23          }
24      ]
25  }
```

Principal is used within resource-based-policies to identify the user, role, account, or federated user that the permissions should be applied to in order to either allow or deny access. The preceding screenshot shows the same policy as the previous one but applied to an S3 bucket policy. The Principal parameter shows the ARN of the identity that these permissions should be applied to.

 For more information about ARN structure, please refer to https://docs. aws.amazon.com/general/latest/gr/aws-arns-and-namespaces.html.

Understanding the difference between identity-based and resource-based policies will help you resolve access control and permission issues. If you can easily read a policy and understand what it allows or denies, and if that policy is associated with an identity or a resource, that will be of great benefit. Next, we'll learn to configure cross-account access.

Configuring cross-account access

To allow another identity from another AWS account to access your resources with your account, you need to configure a role to grant the access required.

Imagine we have two AWS accounts—account A (the trusting account) and account B (the trusted account). User **Stuart** using account B needs to have access to your **Relational Database Service (RDS)** database in account A:

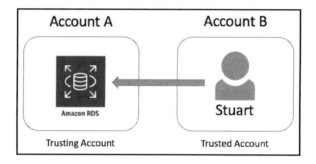

To configure this access, we need a new cross-account access role, which will need to be configured as follows.

Creating a cross-account access role

Execute the following steps to create a cross-account access role:

1. From the trusting account (in our example, this is account A), open IAM from the AWS management console.
2. Select **Roles** from the menu, and then select **Create Role**.
3. Select **Another AWS account** as the trusted identity.
4. You must then enter the trusted AWS account ID; in this case, this is the ID for account B:

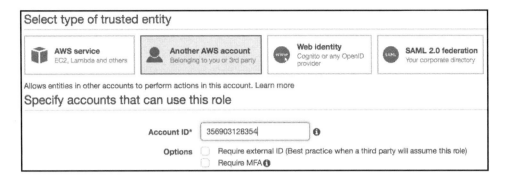

5. Click on **Next: Permissions**.

6. We can now add the permissions we want the role to have. I have selected **AmazonRDSFullAccess**, as shown:

7. Once the permissions have been selected, select **Next: Tags**.

8. For this demonstration, we don't need to add any tags, so click on **Next: Review**.

9. Add a role name—we will call it `CrossAccountRDS`—and then click **Create Role**:

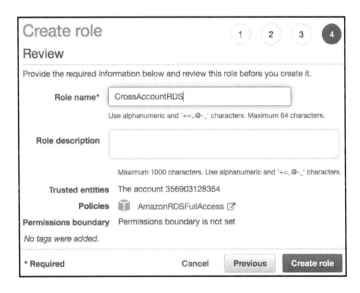

10. Select the **CrossAccountRDS** role in the list of roles that displays additional information about the role. From here, select the **Trust relationships** tab:

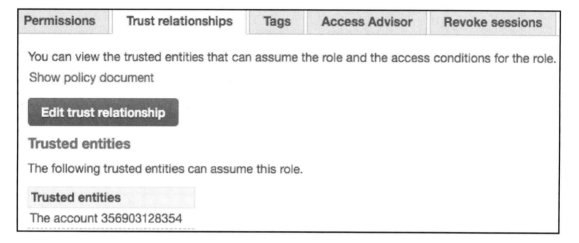

11. You can see that the account that we listed is under **Trusted entities**. However, we need to narrow this access down to a specific user (**Stuart**) within that account, ensuring that only **Stuart** can assume the role. To do this, select **Edit Trust Relationship.**

12. This will open up a policy editor that will allow us to directly edit the JSON policy. We now need to change the Principal line from "AWS": "arn:aws:iam::356903128354:root" to "AWS": "arn:aws:iam::356903128354:user/Stuart".

13. This ensures that the only principal that can assume the role is user Stuart within the 356903128354 AWS account:

> **Trusted entities**
> arn:aws:iam::356903128354:user/Stuart

Now that we have configured a cross-account role and associated the trust relationship between two different accounts, we need to create a policy to allow an identity to assume this role.

Creating a policy to assume the cross-account role

For Stuart to assume this role via the AWS management console, he also needs the required permissions to allow him to assume the role. Again, a policy is required to enable the user to do that, and it looks as follows:

```
{
  "Version": "2012-10-17",
  "Statement": {
    "Effect": "Allow",
    "Action": "sts:AssumeRole",
    "Resource": "arn:aws:iam::730739171055:role/CrossAccountRDS"
  }
}
```

This role uses an `Action` parameter, which uses the **Secure Token Service (STS)** permission of `AssumeRole` against the resource in the trusting account. You can also use, for example, wildcards in the ARN of `Resource`. If you wanted Stuart to assume any role in the trusting account, you could use * as a wildcard, which would then look as follows:

```
"Resource": "arn:aws:iam::730739171055:role/*"
```

Now, the cross-account role has been created, and a policy that allows user `Stuart` to assume that role. So, the last step in this process is to assume that role to gain the temporary permissions that are granted in the new role.

Assuming the cross-account role

Now that I have assigned this policy allowing Stuart to assume the specific role, he can perform the following steps to assume the `CrossAccountRDS` role:

1. From within the trusted account, Stuart can select the drop-down list in the top-right corner that shows the AWS account.
2. Select **Switch Role**, as in the following screenshot:

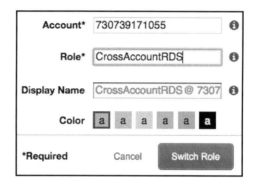

3. Enter the AWS account number of the trusting account (account A), which is where the role exists.
4. Enter the name of the role, `CrossAccountRDS`, and click **Switch Role**.
5. To show you that the role has been assumed, the drop-down list from which you selected **Switch Role** initially will have changed to something similar to what is shown in the following screenshot, displaying the role name and which account it exists in:

In this section, we looked at how to create, configure, and assume a temporary set of credentials in the form of a cross-account access role. By assuming roles, it allows us to access resources in a different account without having to have an additional IAM user created within that account.

IAM policy management

Over time, you are likely to accumulate and use a long list of policies, especially as you dive into the realms of creating your own custom identity-based policies that enable you to be very precise and specific in your permission set for a user, group, or role. As a result, it's important to understand some of the features available to you from within IAM to help you manage these roles.

When you access a policy within the AWS management console—for example, a custom policy that you have created—you will be presented with a page that looks as follows:

It will provide you with the policy ARN and the description of the policy that you added when you created the policy. Underneath this, you have the following tabs:

- **Permissions**
- **Policy usage**
- **Policy versions**
- **Access advisor**

Each of these tabs will help you to gain a better understanding of how the policy is configured. I now want to dive into each of these tabs to help you understand what each of them provides.

Permissions

The **Permissions** tab allows you to view a policy summary, which gives you a high-level breakdown of the permissions, which are broken down into the **Service**, **Access level** (such as read/write), **Resource**, and **Request condition** sections. From this tab, you can also view the policy in JSON format by clicking on the {}JSON tab. Finally, you can edit the policy by selecting **Edit Policy**:

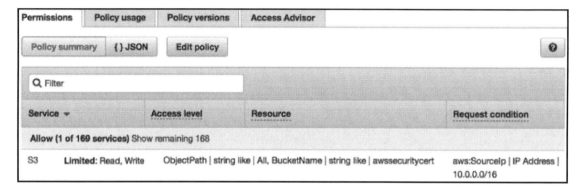

This is a great way to gain a quick view of the permissions associated with the policy.

Policy usage

From this tab, you can attach the policy to identities, such as users, groups, and roles. In the following screenshot, you can see that this policy is attached to three users. You can also remove policies from any of these identities by selecting the user and selecting **Detach**:

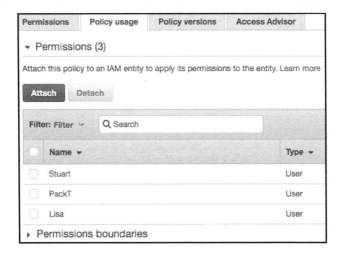

This provides a very quick method of adding and removing users to and from your policies.

Policy versions

Each time a change is made to a policy, the AWS version controls that change and date-stamps it, allowing you to revert to a previous version of the policy. Using the **Set as default** and **Delete** options, you can easily switch between the versions of your policy and remove any unwanted and old policies to ensure they do not get used again as an additional security measure:

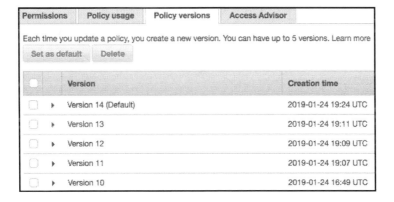

This version control is very useful when testing out new policy controls as it allows you to quickly roll back should an issue occur with your new policy.

Access Advisor

The **Access Advisor** tab allows you to determine when your identities associated with the permissions accessed the different services relating to the policy. In the following screenshot, we can see that user Stuart has not accessed S3 using these permissions for 917 days. With that in mind, it would be a good idea to remove this level of permission for the user as we can safely assume that he is not using it. Leaving these excessive permissions causes a security risk, should his credentials be compromised:

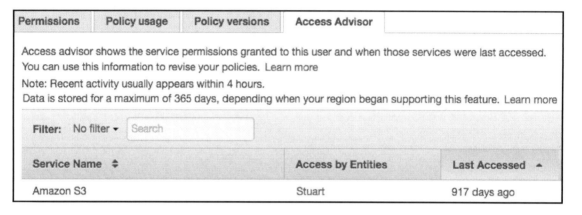

This tab can help you easily identify any policies that are granting more permission than is actually being used, which can lead to a security risk. Removing unnecessary permissions is essential in helping to ensure you have a robust security posture.

With this, we have come to the end of our section on managing policies. Remember that since you are likely to accumulate and use a long list of policies over time, managing these policies efficiently becomes of paramount importance. Next, we will move on to the topic of policy evaluation.

Policy evaluation

As your environment grows, so will your users, groups, roles, and resources. As a result, there will be times when an identity will have multiple policies that affects it, so how does AWS manage the logic of these policies?

When a request is received to gain access to a resource within AWS, the following four steps are performed to determine the permissions allowed:

1. **Authentication**: AWS determines who the principal of the request is by way of authentication.
2. **Determine the context of the request**: The access request is processed to define which policies should be used for permission verification. In this step the actions, resources, principals, environment data, and resource data are examined.
3. **Policy evaluation**: AWS evaluates the policy types being used as a specific order is applied when processing the policies to determine the evaluation of permissions within a single account. Policies will be evaluated in the order of identity-based, resource-based, IAM permissions boundaries, and SCPs.
4. **Permission result**: After the evaluation of policies has been carried out, access is either granted or denied.

As long as `Allow` exists in any one of the policies associated with the request, then access will be allowed for the relevant action. However if `Deny` exists in *any* of the policies that apply to the same resource and action as `Allow`, then access will be denied.

Let's look at an example to help explain this policy logic.

User `Lisa` has got an identity-based policy attached that allows a subset of S3 permissions, including `s3:putobject` and `s3:getobject`, against a bucket of `MyBucket`. However, in addition to this, a bucket policy attached to `MyBucket` allows additional permissions to the principal `Lisa` user with permissions of `s3:deletebucket` and `s3:deleteobject`. What permissions does `Lisa` ultimately have?

In this instance, all the permissions are set to `Allow`, and so the permissions are accumulated, and the end result will be that `Lisa` has the following:

```
S3:putobject
S3:getobject
S3:deletebucket
S3:deleteobject
```

If at this point an IAM permission boundary was associated to `Lisa` that had a `Deny` effect for the action of `S3:deletebucket` against the resource of `MyBucket`, then the permissions for `Lisa` would be reduced to the following:

```
S3:putobject
S3:getobject
S3:deleteobject
```

Again, if at this point an SCP was added to the account where the Lisa identity was created that had a Deny effect for the action of S3:putobject against the resource of MyBucket, then Lisa's permissions would be reduced to the following:

```
S3:getobject
S3:deleteobject
```

Remember, *any* deny action will overrule *any* allow action.

Ensure you have a good understanding of policy evaluation as you will need to understand how AWS manages this to resolve permission and access control-related issues. To do this, you will also need to be able to read policies effectively to understand the exact permissions they are enforcing.

Using bucket policies to control access to S3

As we covered previously, Amazon S3 bucket policies are a resource-based policy as the policy is directly attached the resource itself—in this case, the bucket. If you remember, resource-based policies have to have the additional parameter of Principal within the policy, so it knows which identity the permissions apply to.

We will see how to create a policy for an S3 bucket and how to apply this policy to a bucket. For this example, we have a bucket called awsbucketpolicy and we will add a bucket policy to this allowing user Lisa in a different AWS account to access the bucket. Now, previously, we looked at using roles to create cross-account access; however, for S3 resources it's also possible to emulate this cross-account access by using resource-based policies (bucket policies) and an identity-based policy attached to Lisa in the second account.

So, first, let's create the bucket policy:

1. Once you have navigated to your bucket in S3, select it, and then click on the **Permissions** tab and select **Bucket Policy**, as in the following screenshot:

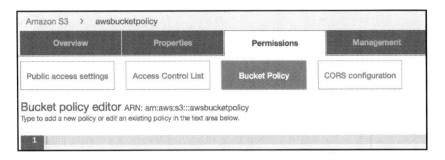

2. From here, we can either directly use the JSON editor provided to write the policy or, at the bottom of the screen, there is an option to use a policy generator. Now, this is a great tool if you are not confident with JSON or familiar enough with how to create policies from scratch. For those of you who are unfamiliar with the policy generator, refer to `https://awspolicygen.s3.amazonaws.com/policygen.html`.

   It doesn't just cater to S3 bucket policies; it can also be used to manage IAM policies, which we have already discussed (in addition to **Simple Queue Service (SQS)** Queue, SNS topics, and VPC endpoint policies, too).

3. Once you have created the policy using either the policy generator or by adding it directly into the JSON editor from the bucket, it will look as follows:

```
1  {
2      "Id": "MyBucket",
3      "Version": "2012-10-17",
4      "Statement": [
5          {
6              "Sid": "MyBucket",
7              "Action": "s3:*",
8              "Effect": "Allow",
9              "Resource": "arn:aws:s3:::awsbucketpolicy",
10             "Principal": {
11                 "AWS": [
12                     "arn:aws:iam::356903128354:user/Lisa"
13                 ]
14             }
15         }
16     ]
17  }
```

   As you can see, this policy allows user `Lisa` from account `356903128354` to access all S3 API calls to the `awsbucketpolicy` bucket.

4. Now, we need to apply an identity-based policy to allow `Lisa` in account `356903128354` to access that bucket. The following policy is applied as follows:

```
{
  "Version": "2012-10-17",
  "Statement": [
    {
      "Sid": "S3BucketAccess",
      "Action": "s3:*",
      "Effect": "Allow",
      "Resource": "arn:aws:s3:::awsbucketpolicy"
    }
  ]
}
```

As you can see, the S3 bucket doesn't actually detail the account that created it. This is because each S3 bucket is globally unique, and the namespace is shared by all AWS accounts.

5. Now, both policies have been applied, and `Lisa` in account `356903128354` has full access to the `awsbucketpolicy` bucket, which is managed and administered by a different account.

As this is a JSON policy, you can, of course, add conditional elements, such as the ones we discussed earlier in this chapter when discussing the policy structure, to add a greater level of control if required.

Bucket policies can be used to control access not only for other AWS accounts, as we saw in this example, but also within your own account as well. You simply need to enter the ARN of the user for your own account.

Summary

This chapter took you through the various types of access policies, their structure, and how to effectively and securely manage access to your AWS resources. You need to be fully aware of the different policies that exist within AWS and how they work together to either grant or deny access to resources based on different actions.

Regardless of which policy you are using, one key point is to always implement security based on the Principle of **Least Privilege (PoLP)**. This essentially means that you should only ever grant permissions for an identity that they actually need, and no more. For example, let's say a user needed access to be able to stop and terminate instances using `ec2:stopinstances` and `ec2:terminateinstances`. Then, you wouldn't issue a policy that allowed access to all `ec2` APIs—for example, `ec2:*`. If this happens, you are increasing the potential of security threats, especially from an internal perspective. For the certification exam, ensure you can read access policies with ease to determine what the policy allows or denies access to.

In the next chapter, we are going to look at access control through federation, allowing a single sign-on approach, covering both enterprise and social identity federation. We will also look at Amazon Cognito and see how it is used for access control across the mobile environment.

Questions

As we conclude, here is a list of questions for you to test your knowledge of this chapter's material. You will find the answers in the *Assessments* section of the *Appendix*:

1. Which format are AWS policies written in?
2. What type of policy are Amazon S3 bucket policies?
   - Identity-based policies
   - Resource-based policies
   - Organization SCPs
3. What parameter is needed within a resource-based policy to identify who or what the policy should be associated with?
4. After configuring cross-account access, from which account do you assume the cross-account role from – the trusted account or the trusting account?
5. True or false: the **Access Advisor** tab allows you to determine when identities accessed different services.

Further reading

- The IAM user guide can be found at: `https://docs.aws.amazon.com/IAM/latest/UserGuide/introduction.html`.

Federated and Mobile Access

5

This is the final chapter focusing on access security. So far, we have discussed access control from within your own AWS account, and even from a cross-account perspective. But what if you have hundreds or even thousands of users who need to access your resources? Configuring and setting up IAM users for so many people is not feasible, or even possible (due to user limitations within IAM). So what options do you have to simplify user management for your employees within a large organization? Also, how can you grant access to tens of thousands or even millions of users who are all competing for that high score on your latest viral mobile gaming app to store their accomplishments in one of your AWS databases? This chapter will help you answer all these questions.

The following topics will be covered in this chapter:

- What is AWS federated access?
- Using SAML federation
- Using social federation

Technical requirements

To follow the exercises within this chapter, you must have access to an AWS account and have permissions to configure federation options within the IAM service. For more information on granting access to services, please refer to the topics discussed in Chapter 4, *Working with Access Policies*.

What is AWS federated access?

Federated access within AWS allows access to your AWS resources without having the need to create an associated IAM user account. Instead, credentials are federated by an **identity provider** (**IdP**), for example, your corporate accounts, such as your Microsoft Active Directory accounts (enterprise federation), or even by a social IdP, for example, using the credentials from your Google, Facebook, or even Amazon account (social identity federation).

Federation allows you to manage your account centrally and reduces the administration required in creating multiple accounts to access your AWS resources.

There are a number of different options that organizations use to implement federation. We will be looking at two of the most common ones:

- SAML federation
- Social federation

We will then look at how Amazon Cognito uses federation to manage access to web and mobile applications with ease.

We'll start by explaining how you can allow users to authenticate and access your AWS resources using their corporate identities, such as their MS-AD account.

Using SAML federation

Before we go any further, let's just explain in a sentence what SAML actually is. **Security Assertion Markup Language** (**SAML**) is a standard that allows you to securely exchange authentication data between different domains by using security tokens between an **identity provider** (**IdP**) and a SAML consumer. In this case, the IdP will be **Microsoft Active Directory** (**MS-AD**) and the SAML consumer will be AWS, specifically IAM roles.

In this section, we will see how you can use SAML to enable **single sign-on** (**SSO**) to gain federated access to your AWS Management Console.

Gaining federated access to the AWS Management Console

For this example, let's say we are using MS-AD. We may have tens or even hundreds of users who may need access to our AWS resources via the Management Console, but instead of creating AWS user accounts for each and every user, we can set up IAM federation using IAM roles and SAML. MS-AD is a SAML 2.0 compliant IdP, and using IAM roles you can allow the IdP to grant MS-AD identities access and permissions to access the AWS Management Console to perform tasks and actions.

To begin with, you need to configure your enterprise network as a SAML provider to AWS. As a part of this configuration, you will need to do the following:

1. Configure MS-AD to work with a SAML IdP, for example, Windows Active Directory Services.

2. You must then create a `metadata.xml` document via your IdP, which is a key document in the configuration. This `metadata.xml` document also includes authentication keys.

3. Using your organization's portal, you must ensure that any requests to access the AWS Management Console are routed to the correct AWS SAML endpoint, allowing that user to authenticate via SAML assertions.

> To help you with this part of the configuration, please visit the following URL, which will help you integrate third-party SAML solution providers with AWS: `https://docs.aws.amazon.com/IAM/latest/UserGuide/id_roles_providers_saml_3rd-party.html`.

Once you have created your `metdata.xml` document, you need to create a SAML provider via the IAM service. To do this, you can follow these steps:

1. Open the IAM dashboard from within the IAM Management Console and select **Identity providers**:

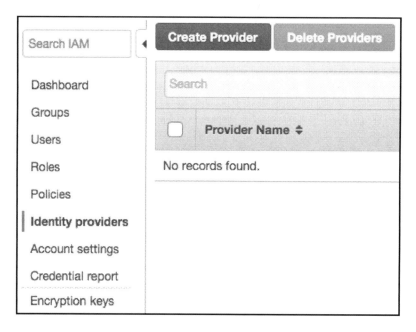

2. Select the **Create Provider** button in blue, as shown in the preceding screenshot.
3. Select **SAML** as the provider type:

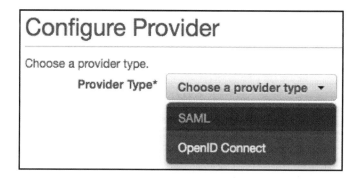

4. Enter a provider name and select your `metadata.xml` document:

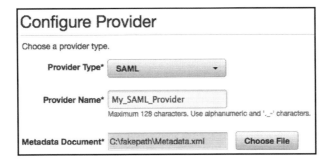

5. Select **Next** and verify your provider information, and if it's correct, select **Create**:

6. Once your SAML provider has been created within IAM, you then need to create a role from within IAM that your federated users will assume to gain permissions within your AWS environment. When creating your role, select the **SAML 2.0 federation** option:

7. Once you have selected your SAML provider, which was created in the previous section, continue to add permissions to the role. The permissions policy of the role will dictate the permissions that federated users will gain when authenticated and follows the same configuration as any other role. The trust policy of the role creates a trust relationship between the IdP and IAM organizations. In this trust, the IdP we just created in IAM is used as a principal for the federation.

The following shows an example of what the trust policy might look like, where I have the AWS account ID as `123456789012` and the IAM IdP as `My_SAML_Provider`:

```
{
    "Version": "2012-10-17",
    "Statement": {
      "Effect": "Allow",
      "Action": "sts:AssumeRoleWithSAML",
      "Principal": {"Federated": "arn:aws:iam::123456789012:saml-
provider/My_SAML_Provider"},
      "Condition": {"StringEquals": {"SAML:aud":
"https://signin.aws.amazon.com/saml"}}
    }
  }
```

Within this trust policy, you can also include additional conditions that relate to SAML attributes that must match the user for them to assume the role.

8. The final part of the configuration requires you to notify your organization's SAML IdP about AWS, which is now a service provider. This is completed by installing the following `saml-metadata.xml` file, which can be found at `https://signin.aws.amazon.com/static/saml-metadata.xml`.

Once the configuration is complete, users from your organization's Active Directory can be federated through to the AWS Management Console using the permissions set out in the role, as follows:

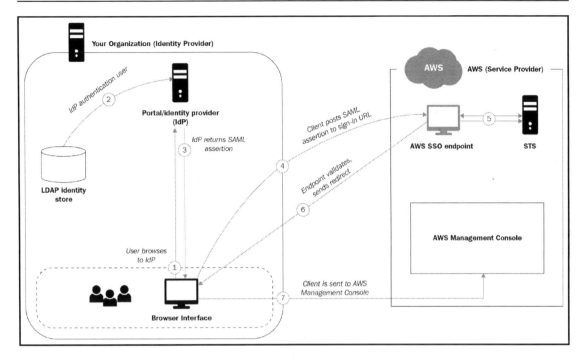

As illustrated in the preceding diagram, this federated access can be granted in seven steps:

1. Using a portal, which is a part of an organization's IdP, the user within the enterprise uses their organization's portal to direct them to the AWS Management Console. This portal manages the exchange of information between AWS and **Active Directory Federation Services (ADFS)**.

2. When the portal receives the request, verification of the user is performed via the **Lightweight Directory Access Protocol (LDAP)** identity store.

3. If the user is verified, then the portal creates a SAML authentication response. This response can also include assertions that identify the user.

4. These assertions are then received by the client and are sent to the AWS Management Console sign-in URL.

5. At this point, the **security token service (STS)** is contacted to gain temporary credentials and to create a console sign-in URL using the credentials generated by the STS. The STS allows you to request temporary credentials for IAM users or for authenticated federated users. For more information on STS, please see the documentation at: `https://docs.aws.amazon.com/STS/latest/APIReference/Welcome.html`

6. This new URL is sent back to the user.
7. The user is then redirected to this new URL, gaining access to the Management Console using the role associated with the user's attributes.

 If you have users who don't need to access the AWS Management Console, but need federated access to your AWS resources, then you can follow the process at: `https://docs.aws.amazon.com/IAM/latest/ UserGuide/id_roles_providers_saml.html`. Much of the configuration and steps are the same as we just discussed.

Now we have discussed SAML federation using your own organization as an IdP to help simplify access management for hundreds or even thousands of corporate users.

We now know how federation works and the key benefit of using federation. However, sometimes you may need to federate users to your AWS resources, without ever knowing who those people are. An example of this would be if you had a mobile app where users who download the app may need to store high scores, or details in the app that are stored on a DynamoDB database within your AWS environment. How do you manage the access to these resources by users who you have no record of or control over? You could store credentials within the app that would authenticate access, however, this is a bad practice and should be avoided at all costs. Instead, you should use social federation.

Using social federation

Social federation allows you to build your applications to request temporary credentials. Much like in the previous discussion relating to enterprise federation where we used SAML, these temporary credentials with social federation map to an AWS IAM role that has the relevant permission to access your DynamoDB database.

Instead of using your internal ADFS servers to authenticate users, the users of your app can use widely known social IdPs, for example, Facebook, Amazon, and Google. In fact, as long as the IdP is **OpenID Connect (OIDC)** compatible, then you can use them for authentication. Using these social IdPs, the user can get an authentication token, which in turn is exchanged for temporary credentials, and these credentials are associated with your specific IAM role with the required permissions.

When creating applications that require social IdPs for authentication, you need to write specific code to interact with the IdP to allow you to call the `AssumeRoleWithWebIdentity` API, which allows you to replace the token with temporary credentials. However, if you want to remove the need to have to write this specific code for the IdP, then there is another method, and it's actually recommended by AWS. This preferred and best practice method is to use Amazon Cognito.

Amazon Cognito

Amazon Cognito was built purely for the simplification of enabling secure authentication and access control for new and existing users accessing your web or mobile applications. It not only ingrates well with enterprise federation but also social federation. One of the biggest features of Amazon Cognito is that it has the capability to scale to millions of new users, which is great when working with mobile applications, which will be the focus of this discussion.

There are two main components of Amazon Cognito that you should be aware of, these being *user pools* and *identity pools,* and they perform different actions that we will see in the following topics.

User pools

User pools are essentially scalable user directories that allow new and existing users to log in to your mobile application using the user pool or they can alternatively federate their access via a social or enterprise IdP. Either way, a profile within the user pool is created for each and every user. These profiles contain no permissions for access to your AWS infrastructure; they allow them to log in to your mobile app as a user and use it.

Once a user is authenticated via the user pool, either from the user pool itself or via a third-party IdP, Amazon Cognito will generate tokens that manage the access to your mobile app.

It is also possible to enable additional features using user pools, such as the ability to enable **multi-factor authentication (MFA)**, providing additional security to your user base. You can also create user pool groups and assign different permissions to different groups. This provides greater access control and prevents all users from having the same access, which might cause a security risk.

Identity pools

Identity pools are different from user pools. Identity pools actually provide you with the ability to assign permissions to users to access your AWS resources used within the mobile app by using temporary credentials. This access can be granted to both federated users and anonymous guest users. Identity pools support federated access for users that have been authenticated by user pools, OpenID Connect IdPs, SAML IdPs, social IdPs, and developer-authenticated identities. These permissions are assigned through IAM roles and can be mapped to different users to provide different permissions sets.

Once a user has authenticated either via a user pool or a social IdP, the token received and managed by Amazon Cognito can then be exchanged for temporary credentials using the identity pools. These credentials can then be used to access the AWS services required when using your mobile app.

Gaining access using user and identity pools

These two types of pool, both user and identity, can be used together or separately, depending on the functional requirements of your mobile app. The following diagram shows gaining access to AWS resources via the user pool for token generation:

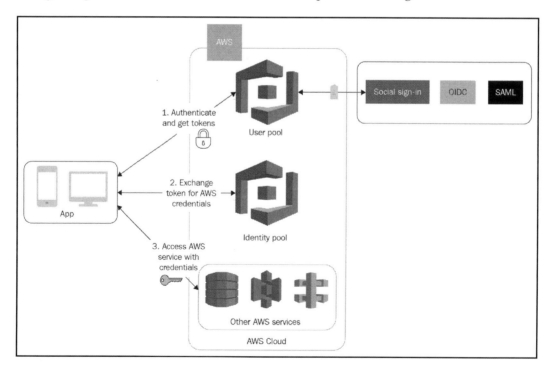

This diagram is explained in the following steps:

1. Tokens are received from a third-party IdP, such as Facebook. The user pool then manages these tokens and authenticates the user to the app.
2. The tokens are then exchanged for temporary credentials, based upon an associated IAM role with set permissions through the identity pool.
3. When these permissions have been assumed, the user of the mobile app is then authenticated and authorized to access the appropriate AWS services.

The diagram that follows shows users gaining access to AWS resources via the identity pool without the user pool:

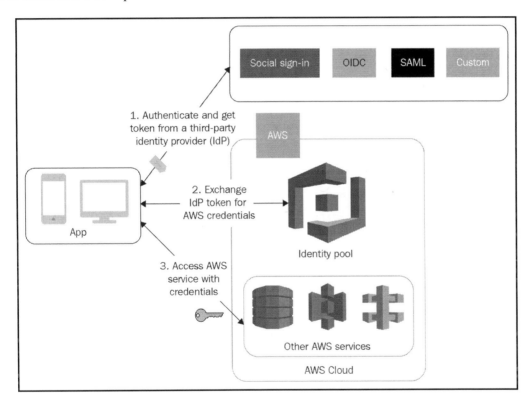

This diagram is explained in the following steps:

1. A user authenticates with a third-party IdP, such as Facebook. The social IdP generates tokens, which are sent back to the mobile app.
2. The tokens are then sent to the Amazon Cognito identity pool to be exchanged for temporary credentials, based upon an associated IAM role.
3. When these permissions have been assumed, the user of the mobile app is then authenticated and authorized to access the appropriate AWS services.

If you are building applications to run on a mobile client, then using Amazon Cognito is a great way to implement access management with simplicity and ease using social federation.

Summary

This chapter highlighted some of the alternative methods for providing access to your AWS resources for identities that sit outside of the IAM service. Introducing federated access allows you to quickly and easily scale your user base, who might require access to your AWS Management Console, or simply require the ability to run APIs to perform actions against your resources.

Enterprise federation allows you to use your existing corporate identities, such as your Active Directory using SAML 2.0. Social federation allows you to scale to millions of users with the introduction of Amazon Cognito managing this elasticity and control of your token and authentication mechanism.

In the next chapter, we'll be looking at how to secure your EC2 instances through the use of Amazon Inspector, key pairs, and EC2 Systems Manager. We'll also look at how to isolate your instance should it become compromised.

Questions

As we conclude this chapter, here is a list of questions for you to test your knowledge regarding its material. You will find the answers in the *Assessments* section of the *Appendix*:

1. True or false: Federated access within AWS allows access to your AWS resources without needing to create any permissions.
2. Which AWS service uses federation to manage access to web and mobile applications with ease?

3. What are the two common types of federated access with AWS?
4. What is IdP short for in relation to federated access?
5. True or false: Identity pools actually provide you with the ability to assign permissions to users to access AWS resources used within a mobile app by using temporary credentials.

Further reading

- Amazon Cognito Documentation: https://docs.aws.amazon.com/cognito/index.html#lang/en_us
- AWS identity federation: https://aws.amazon.com/identity/federation/

Section 3: Security - a Layered Approach

3

In this section, you will learn how to design and implement a level of security that surrounds your EC2 instances via different techniques. You'll do this by applying vulnerability scans, using key pairs, and isolating your instance for forensic analysis. You'll also learn how to use AWS Systems Manager to administer your EC2 instances.

You will then master how to secure a multi-subnet virtual private cloud through a variety of infrastructure security controls, including route tables, network access control lists, NAT gateways, security groups, and more!

Using a variety of different AWS services specifically designed to secure your applications, we'll look at how to both implement and manage the security configuration of many of them to ensure your applications remain protected.

Unfortunately, there will always be malicious attackers who have a sole aim to harm and hinder your infrastructure. As a result, we'll learn how to implement a number of different features so that you can protect your environment from a distributed denial-of-service attack, as well as some of the best practices that you can implement to reduce the negative effects of such an attack.

Recovering from a security incident takes a lot more than restoring a service, so we will be dedicating a chapter to learning how to respond to an incident and the different steps and recommendations on what to do and when. This will help you identify, isolate, and remediate security incidents across your infrastructure.

Finally, we'll look at how to implement secure connectivity options from your on-premise data center to your AWS infrastructure through the use of a virtual private network and a Direct Connect connection, as well as the components involved to implement such a solution.

By the end of this section, you will have a solid understanding of how security can be implemented across a variety of different layers within your AWS architecture, as well as how each layer plays its own important and effective role.

This section comprises the following chapters:

- Chapter 6, *Securing EC2 Instances*
- Chapter 7, *Configuring Infrastructure Security*
- Chapter 8, *Implementing Application Security*
- Chapter 9, *DDoS Protection*
- Chapter 10, *Incident Response*
- Chapter 11, *Securing Connections to Your AWS Environment*

6
Securing EC2 Instances

EC2 is the most common of the compute services that AWS offers within its library. This is largely due to its vast variety of instance family types offering different performance and cost options. With this wide acceptance of EC2 by millions of customers, there is an inherent need to ensure that we are able to secure the resource when in operation to prevent it from being compromised by those with malicious intent.

In this chapter, we will be looking into a number of security points relating to EC2 and how they can be configured and implemented. We will be studying the following topics:

- Performing a vulnerability scan using Amazon Inspector
- Creating and securing EC2 key pairs
- Isolating instances for forensic investigation
- Using AWS Systems Manager to administer EC2 instances

Technical requirements

To complete some of the examples within this chapter, you will need to have an AWS account with an EC2 Linux instance running and permissions to access the instance. You will also need permissions to run and configure Amazon Inspector and AWS Systems Manager. For more information on permissions and access control, please refer to Chapter 4, *Working with Access Policies*.

Performing a vulnerability scan using Amazon Inspector

Amazon Inspector is a fully managed service that allows you to secure your instances and the applications that run on top of them by performing vulnerability assessments via an agent.

The assessments that are run are based upon rules packages that contain hundreds of different known security weaknesses, threats, and vulnerabilities that could exist within your EC2 instance. These rules packages are pulled from five different sources:

- The **Center for Internet Security** (**CIS**) Benchmarks, which is a list of global standards and best practices
- A publicly known reference of well documented security threats and flaws found within the common vulnerabilities and exposures list, also known as the CVE
- General security best practices known across the industry, which helps you find deviations within your infrastructure
- Runtime behaviour analysis, which is used to assess and monitor security weaknesses as your EC2 instance is running during an assessment made by Amazon Inspector
- Network reachability, which looks at the configuration of your network settings to discover security vulnerabilities

At the end of the assessment, a report is generated showing your findings that were discovered based upon the packages selected for the assessment.

As I mentioned previously, the service uses an agent to help perform the assessments. This agent allows Amazon Inspector to monitor the behavior of the instance during a scheduled assessment. It will look at activity across the entire EC2 instance, from network activity to processes that are being run at the time of the assessment. When the assessment ends, the data is collected, and this telemetry data that has been captured is then sent back to Amazon Inspector for review and assessment. By utilizing an agent, you can easily implement Amazon Inspector across your existing fleet of instances.

There are a number of different ways you can install this agent, which are as follows:

- You can install the agent on each EC2 instance by logging into the resource and running one of the appropriate scripts.
- You can install the agent on a group of EC2 instances or a single instance by using the `Run` command from within Systems Manager. We shall be discussing Systems Manager in more depth later in this chapter, and we will see how to use the service to administer our EC2 instances.
- When defining your targets that you want Amazon Inspector to assess, you have the option to install the agent as a part of that initial assessment.

- Alternatively, you could use an Amazon AMI that already has the agent installed, meaning you do not have to perform any manual installation. This AMI is called the Amazon Linux AMI with Amazon Inspector Agent, as shown in the following screenshot, and can be found in the AMI Marketplace (`https://aws.amazon.com/marketplace/search/results?x=0y=0searchTerms=Amazon+Linux+AMI+with+Amazon+Inspector+Agent`):

As we will be discussing Systems Manager later in the chapter, let's see instead how to install the agent on a Linux-based EC2 instance using the script method mentioned previously.

Installing the Amazon Inspector agent

To begin with, you will need to have an EC2 Linux instance that has access to the internet running within your AWS account. Then follow these steps:

1. Connect to your EC2 Linux instance.
2. Run either of the following commands to download the script required to install the agent:

```
wget https://inspector-agent.amazonaws.com/linux/latest/install
```

```
curl -O https://inspector-agent.amazonaws.com/linux/latest/install
```

We get the following output when we execute the `wget` command:

```
[ec2-user@ip-10-0-1-222 ~]$ wget https://inspector-agent.amazonaws.com/linux/latest/install
--2019-02-21 17:16:09--  https://inspector-agent.amazonaws.com/linux/latest/install
Resolving inspector-agent.amazonaws.com (inspector-agent.amazonaws.com)... 54.192.28.7, 2600:9000:200a:f600:
Connecting to inspector-agent.amazonaws.com (inspector-agent.amazonaws.com)|54.192.28.7|:443... connected.
HTTP request sent, awaiting response... 200 OK
Length: 35963 (35K)
Saving to: 'install'

100%[===================================================================================================>]

2019-02-21 17:16:09 (13.4 MB/s) - 'install' saved [35963/35963]
```

3. Once it is downloaded, you then need to run the script by entering the `sudo bash install` command, and you will get the following output:

```
Total size: 37 M
Installed size: 37 M
Downloading packages:
Running transaction check
Running transaction test
Transaction test succeeded
Running transaction
  Installing : AwsAgent-1.1.1150.0-102150.x86_64
Redirecting to /bin/systemctl reload crond.service
  Verifying  : AwsAgent-1.1.1150.0-102150.x86_64

Installed:
  AwsAgent.x86_64 0:1.1.1150.0-102150

Complete!
HTTP/1.1 200 OK
x-amz-id-2: qTo6kHsf8N7Y1PrRalevT8tNnbNaMq2cC5A238DW1Ua10/NYQCABi5wzkwSq30HrEdfGiX3c2vQ=
x-amz-request-id: 153D6133B49E76D2
Date: Thu, 21 Feb 2019 17:18:34 GMT
Last-Modified: Mon, 11 Feb 2019 14:08:08 GMT
ETag: "c7244490f462f8f88b3d8f59a0d387f6"
Accept-Ranges: bytes
Content-Type:
Content-Length: 872
Server: AmazonS3

Installation script completed successfully.

Notice:
By installing the Amazon Inspector Agent, you agree that your use is subject to the terms of your existing
AWS Customer Agreement or other agreement with Amazon Web Services, Inc. or its affiliates governing your
use of AWS services. You may not install and use the Amazon Inspector Agent unless you have an account in
good standing with AWS.
* * *
Current running agent reports to arsenal endpoint:
Current running agent reports version as: 1.1.1150.0
This install script was created to install agent version:1.1.1150.0
In most cases, these version numbers should be the same.

[ec2-user@ip-10-0-1-222 ~]$
```

Now the agent is installed, let's now go ahead and configure Amazon Inspector to perform a vulnerability scan on the EC2 instance.

Configuring assessment targets

To configure Amazon Inspector, we need to create a number of components within the Amazon Inspector service, starting with the assessment target. An assessment target is a grouping of AWS EC2 instances that you want to run an assessment against. This grouping is defined and managed by the tags associated with your EC2 instances within your environment:

1. From within the AWS Management Console, select the **Amazon Inspector** service found in the **Security, Identity & Compliance** category.
2. Select **Assessment targets** in the left menu:

Dashboard

Assessment targets

Assessment templates

Assessment runs

Findings

3. Select the blue **Create** button, and this will display the following options:

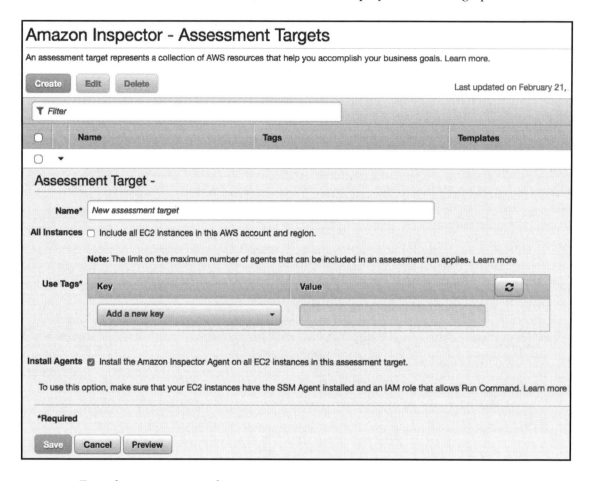

From here, you create the assessment targets:

- Enter a name for your assessment target.
- If you want to include all of your EC2 instances in your AWS account and your current region, then you can tick the appropriate box to do so.

- Using the drop-down lists for the **Key** and **Value** options, select the tags that you have configured for your EC2 instances. You can select more than one tag to refine your EC2 groupings. For example, you might have tags associated with your EC2 fleets such as the following:

Key	Value
Department	Finance
Department	Operations
Environment	Production
Environment	Dev

  Here, you might want to only select EC2 instances that are in the Production environment and the Operations team, and so you could select a **Key** of Department with **Value** set to Operations, and then another **Key** set to Environment with a **Value** of Production.

- Finally, you can choose to install the Inspector Agent on the targets if they do not already have it running using the checkbox.

4. Once you have configured your assessment target, click the blue **Save** button.
5. Click on the **OK** button to accept the creation of a service-linked role by Amazon Inspector:

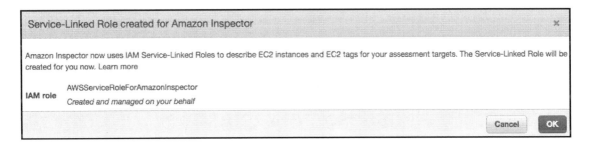

6. Your assessment target is now completed and will appear in the console. In this example, my configuration looked as follows:

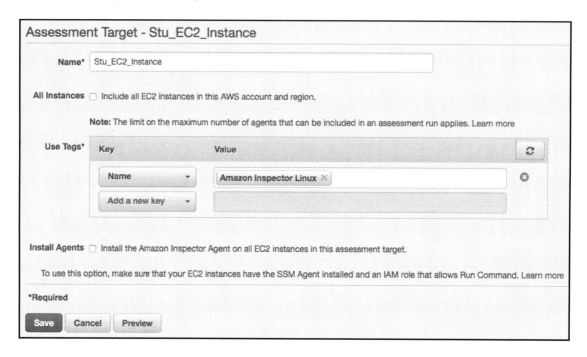

I selected a single instance that I had named `Amazon Inspector Linux`, which was the instance that I installed the agent on earlier in this chapter. You can now, of course, configure additional assessment targets with a different EC2 instance grouping as required.

Once you have configured your assessment targets, you then need to configure an assessment template.

Configuring an assessment template

The assessment template consists of a number of configurable options that defines how an assessment will be run against your EC2 instances that you just defined as targets. To configure it, follow these steps:

1. Remain within the Amazon Inspector console and select **Assessment Template** on the left-hand side.
2. Click the blue **Create** button and the following configurable page will appear:

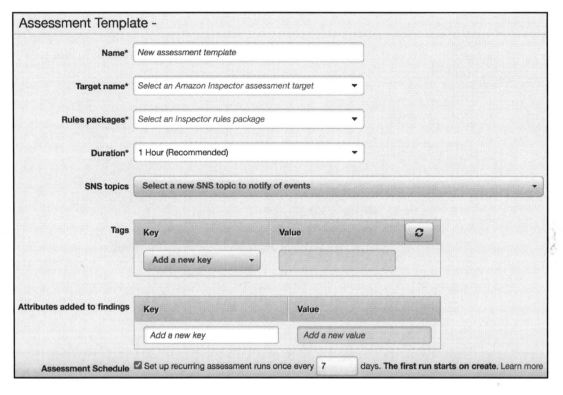

3. Similar to the assessment targets, you now have a number of configurable parameters to define your assessment starting with a name for the assessment template. Ensure it is something meaningful that will identify its use.

4. You must then select a **Target name** using the drop-down list. Now this will list all of your assessment targets that you have created in Amazon Inspector. Select the appropriate assessment target. In this example, I have a single assessment target that I created in the previous demo called **Stu_EC2_Instance**:

5. Next, you need to select a **Rules package**. Rules packages are used to define what the telemetry data will be assessed against during an assessment run and each of these rules packages contains a number of individual rules that the telemetry data is checked against. These rules packages are as follows:

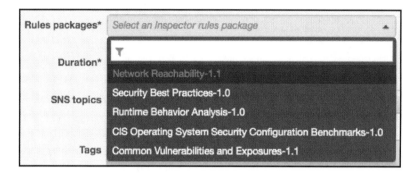

6. You can select one or more of these rules packages, but do be aware that not all of the packages are available on all operating systems. The following constraints exist:

- **Network Reachability**: Does not support EC2 classic networks. Besides, you do not need an agent on the EC2 instance for this rules package.
- **Security Best Practices**: The rules in this package will only discover findings for Linux-based OSes and not for Windows-based OSes.
- **Runtime Behaviour Analysis**: This package can be run against both Linux-based and Windows-based OSes; however, not all rules in the package will be applied to Windows-based OSes.
- **CIS Operating System Security Configuration Benchmarks**: This package contains set rules for both Linux-based and Windows-based OSes.
- **Common Vulnerabilities and Exposures**: This package contains set rules for both Linux-based and Windows-based OSes.

For a full analysis of which packages support which OSes, please see: https://docs.aws.amazon.com/inspector/latest/userguide/ inspector_rule-packages_across_os.html.

7. Once you have chosen your rules packages, you must then decide how long you want to run the assessment for. The longer the assessment is running, the greater the chance that additional security weaknesses will be found. However, AWS recommends at least running the assessment for one hour. You should also perform these assessments when the EC2 instances are in heavy use as this will yield the greatest amount of findings. The options for setting a time frame are as follows:

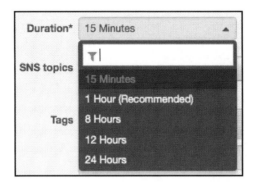

8. Next, you are able to define an SNS topic to send your findings to once they are available following the assessment. Use the drop-down list to select an SNS topic that you may already have created within your AWS account.

9. You can then add an optional tag to the assessment template as you would do for another AWS resource if you need to use the appropriate drop-down lists:

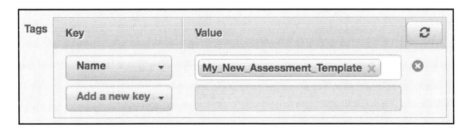

10. At the bottom of the configuration page you are able to set up a recurring schedule of when you want this assessment to run by selecting the checkbox and choosing how often you want the assessment to run, in days:

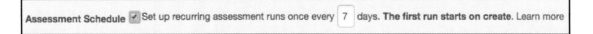

11. We're almost done. My configuration of the assessment template looks as follows:

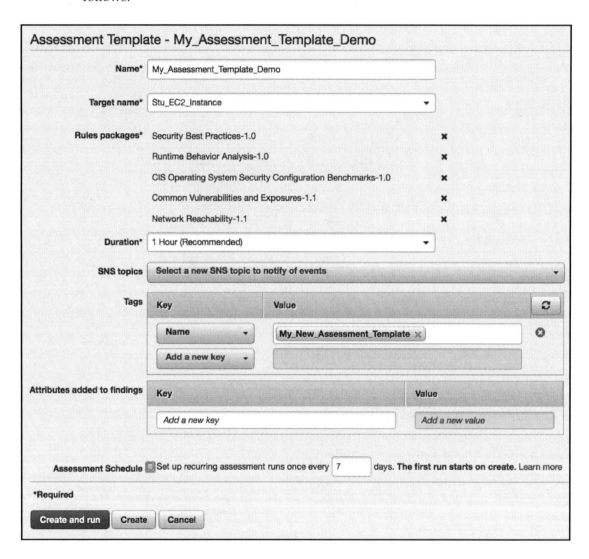

12. At this stage, you can either select **Create and run**, **Create**, or **Cancel**. For this demonstration, select **Create**.

At this point, your assessment template is now created and ready to run against the assessment targets defined within your assessment template. Do bear in mind that once your template is created, it is not possible to update it. The template will also be listed within the assessment template dashboard, as shown here:

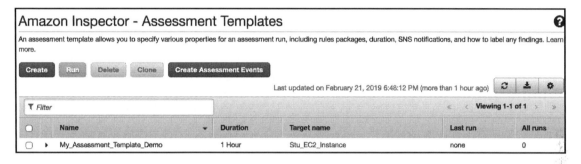

You are now in a position to run the assessment against your targets.

Running an assessment

Execute the following steps to run an assessment:

1. From the **Assessment Templates** dashboard in Amazon Inspector, select the assessment template you would like to run.
2. Select the blue **Run** button. A message will then appear stating that the assessment has started.
3. At this point, the **Last run** column status will update to **Preparing to run**:

4. While the assessment is taking place, you can view more information by selecting **Assessment Runs** in the left menu. Here, you will find the status of the assessment as it runs, for example, **Collecting data**:

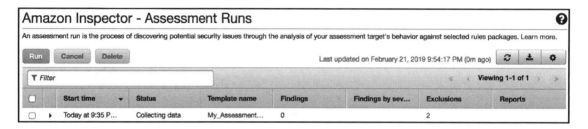

5. Once the assessment duration has completed, the status will change to **Analyzing**.
6. Once the analysis is complete, the assessment run will show the number of findings. In my example, we can see that Amazon Inspector has **20** findings for my Linux instance:

Getting these findings after you have run the assessment, isn't the end. Let me now explain how you can dive into these findings to gather more information.

Viewing findings

Let's execute the following steps to view the findings:

1. From within the **Amazon Inspector** dashboard, select the **Findings** option from the left menu:

Dashboard

Assessment targets

Assessment templates

Assessment runs

| **Findings**

2. This will display all of the findings that were recorded in your assessment. The findings that I have looked for are as follows:

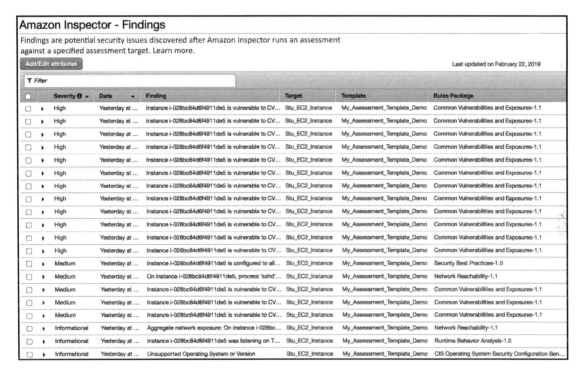

Amazon Inspector - Findings

Findings are potential security issues discovered after Amazon Inspector runs an assessment against a specified assessment target. Learn more.

Add/Edit attributes   Last updated on February 22, 2019

		Severity	Date	Finding	Target	Template	Rules Package
☐	▶	High	Yesterday at ...	Instance i-028bc84d6f4911de5 is vulnerable to CV...	Stu_EC2_Instance	My_Assessment_Template_Demo	Common Vulnerabilities and Exposures-1.1
☐	▶	High	Yesterday at ...	Instance i-028bc84d6f4911de5 is vulnerable to CV...	Stu_EC2_Instance	My_Assessment_Template_Demo	Common Vulnerabilities and Exposures-1.1
☐	▶	High	Yesterday at ...	Instance i-028bc84d6f4911de5 is vulnerable to CV...	Stu_EC2_Instance	My_Assessment_Template_Demo	Common Vulnerabilities and Exposures-1.1
☐	▶	High	Yesterday at ...	Instance i-028bc84d6f4911de5 is vulnerable to CV...	Stu_EC2_Instance	My_Assessment_Template_Demo	Common Vulnerabilities and Exposures-1.1
☐	▶	High	Yesterday at ...	Instance i-028bc84d6f4911de5 is vulnerable to CV...	Stu_EC2_Instance	My_Assessment_Template_Demo	Common Vulnerabilities and Exposures-1.1
☐	▶	High	Yesterday at ...	Instance i-028bc84d6f4911de5 is vulnerable to CV...	Stu_EC2_Instance	My_Assessment_Template_Demo	Common Vulnerabilities and Exposures-1.1
☐	▶	High	Yesterday at ...	Instance i-028bc84d6f4911de5 is vulnerable to CV...	Stu_EC2_Instance	My_Assessment_Template_Demo	Common Vulnerabilities and Exposures-1.1
☐	▶	High	Yesterday at ...	Instance i-028bc84d6f4911de5 is vulnerable to CV...	Stu_EC2_Instance	My_Assessment_Template_Demo	Common Vulnerabilities and Exposures-1.1
☐	▶	High	Yesterday at ...	Instance i-028bc84d6f4911de5 is vulnerable to CV...	Stu_EC2_Instance	My_Assessment_Template_Demo	Common Vulnerabilities and Exposures-1.1
☐	▶	High	Yesterday at ...	Instance i-028bc84d6f4911de5 is vulnerable to CV...	Stu_EC2_Instance	My_Assessment_Template_Demo	Common Vulnerabilities and Exposures-1.1
☐	▶	High	Yesterday at ...	Instance i-028bc84d6f4911de5 is vulnerable to CV...	Stu_EC2_Instance	My_Assessment_Template_Demo	Common Vulnerabilities and Exposures-1.1
☐	▶	Medium	Yesterday at ...	Instance i-028bc84d6f4911de5 is configured to all...	Stu_EC2_Instance	My_Assessment_Template_Demo	Security Best Practices-1.0
☐	▶	Medium	Yesterday at ...	On instance i-028bc84d6f4911de5, process 'sshd'...	Stu_EC2_Instance	My_Assessment_Template_Demo	Network Reachability-1.1
☐	▶	Medium	Yesterday at ...	Instance i-028bc84d6f4911de5 is vulnerable to CV...	Stu_EC2_Instance	My_Assessment_Template_Demo	Common Vulnerabilities and Exposures-1.1
☐	▶	Medium	Yesterday at ...	Instance i-028bc84d6f4911de5 is vulnerable to CV...	Stu_EC2_Instance	My_Assessment_Template_Demo	Common Vulnerabilities and Exposures-1.1
☐	▶	Medium	Yesterday at ...	Instance i-028bc84d6f4911de5 is vulnerable to CV...	Stu_EC2_Instance	My_Assessment_Template_Demo	Common Vulnerabilities and Exposures-1.1
☐	▶	Informational	Yesterday at ...	Aggregate network exposure: On instance i-028bc...	Stu_EC2_Instance	My_Assessment_Template_Demo	Network Reachability-1.1
☐	▶	Informational	Yesterday at ...	Instance i-028bc84d6f4911de5 was listening on T...	Stu_EC2_Instance	My_Assessment_Template_Demo	Runtime Behavior Analysis-1.0
☐	▶	Informational	Yesterday at ...	Unsupported Operating System or Version	Stu_EC2_Instance	My_Assessment_Template_Demo	CIS Operating System Security Configuration Ben...

We can see that the **Findings** page provides information for each finding based on the following:

- The severity of the finding
- The date it was found
- The finding itself, which relates to a rule in one of the rules packages
- The target the finding was found on

- The template assessment used to find the finding
- The rules package that the finding relates to

It is worth noting that the severity range is **High**, **Medium**, **Low**, and **Informational**. In my example, we can see that we have a lot of **High** severity findings that need investigation, and these should always be investigated first as there is a chance that my instance can be or already has been compromised.

3. To drill down into a finding, you can select it from the list. The following screenshot shows one of my **High** severity findings detected using the CVE package:

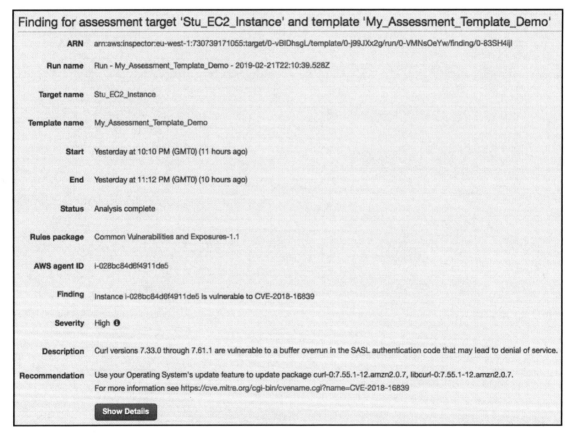

Finding for assessment target 'Stu_EC2_Instance' and template 'My_Assessment_Template_Demo'	
ARN	arn:aws:inspector:eu-west-1:730739171055:target/0-vBIDhsgL/template/0-j99JXx2g/run/0-VMNsOeYw/finding/0-83SH4ijl
Run name	Run - My_Assessment_Template_Demo - 2019-02-21T22:10:39.528Z
Target name	Stu_EC2_Instance
Template name	My_Assessment_Template_Demo
Start	Yesterday at 10:10 PM (GMT0) (11 hours ago)
End	Yesterday at 11:12 PM (GMT0) (10 hours ago)
Status	Analysis complete
Rules package	Common Vulnerabilities and Exposures-1.1
AWS agent ID	i-028bc84d6f4911de5
Finding	Instance i-028bc84d6f4911de5 is vulnerable to CVE-2018-16839
Severity	High ❶
Description	Curl versions 7.33.0 through 7.61.1 are vulnerable to a buffer overrun in the SASL authentication code that may lead to denial of service.
Recommendation	Use your Operating System's update feature to update package curl-0:7.55.1-12.amzn2.0.7, libcurl-0:7.55.1-12.amzn2.0.7. For more information see https://cve.mitre.org/cgi-bin/cvename.cgi?name=CVE-2018-16839

Show Details

This provides additional data on the finding and provides all the information you need to help mitigate the issue. Amazon Inspector does a great job of identifying remediation steps to help you secure your infrastructure.

4. The remediation information is provided at the bottom of this page, and the parts that I am most interested in are the following:

Finding	Instance i-028bc84d6f4911de5 is vulnerable to CVE-2018-16839
Severity	High ❶
Description	Curl versions 7.33.0 through 7.61.1 are vulnerable to a buffer overrun in the SASL authentication code that may lead to denial of service.
Recommendation	Use your Operating System's update feature to update package curl-0:7.55.1-12.amzn2.0.7, libcurl-0:7.55.1-12.amzn2.0.7. For more information see https://cve.mitre.org/cgi-bin/cvename.cgi?name=CVE-2018-16839

Here, you can see that it provides additional information on the finding. In this example, we can see that the instance is vulnerable to **CVE-2018-16839**. It also shows a description of the security weakness and finally a remediation option to resolve the issue and to help protect the instance. Within this remediation, it also provides a URL link to the CVE in question in case you wanted to gather further information on this finding.

For further examples of findings that I received, see the following screenshots to see some of the variations found by different deployment packages:

Network Reachability package finding:

Finding	On instance i-028bc84d6f4911de5, process 'sshd' is listening on tcp port 22 which is associated with 'SSH' and is reachable from the internet
Severity	Medium ❶
Description	On this instance, tcp port 22, which is associated with SSH, is reachable from the internet with a process listening on the port. The process has name 'sshd', process id 3287, and uses binary /usr/sbin/sshd. The instance i-028bc84d6f4911de5 is located in VPC vpc-f495a290 and has an attached ENI eni-030e95b4e23a679f8 which uses network ACL acl-9ab640fd. The port is reachable from the internet through Security Group sg-01610096c08781bba and IGW igw-21268a45
Recommendation	You can edit the Security Group sg-01610096c08781bba to remove access from the internet on port 22

Security Best Practices package finding:

Finding	Instance i-028bc84d6f4911de5 is configured to allow users to log in with root credentials over SSH, without having to use a command authenticated by a public key. This increases the likelihood of a successful brute-force attack.
Severity	Medium ⓘ
Description	This rule helps determine whether the SSH daemon is configured to permit logging in to your EC2 instance as root.
Recommendation	To reduce the likelihood of a successful brute-force attack, we recommend that you configure your EC2 instance to prevent root account logins over SSH. To disable SSH root account logins, set PermitRootLogin to 'no' in /etc/ssh/sshd_config and restart sshd. When logged in as a non-root user, you can use sudo to escalate privileges when necessary. If you want to allow public key authentication with a command associated with the key, you can set **PermitRootLogin** to 'forced-commands-only'.

Runtime Behaviour Analysis finding:

Finding	Instance i-028bc84d6f4911de5 was listening on TCP port(s) 111, but no connections to these port(s) were seen during the assessment run.
Severity	Informational ⓘ
Description	This rule detects listening TCP ports that may not be required by the assessment target.
Recommendation	To reduce the attack surface area of your deployments, we recommend that you disable network services that you do not use. Where network services are required, we recommend that you employ network control mechanisms such as VPC ACLs, EC2 security groups, and firewalls to limit exposure of that service.

In this example, we were able to review any findings that had been identified and captured by Amazon Inspector. Analyzing these findings allows you to implement the necessary steps to remediate any security issues, threats, or vulnerabilities detected, and hence Amazon Inspector is a very useful tool.

Creating and securing EC2 key pairs

As a part of the process for creating an EC2 instance you are asked to create or select an existing key pair. In this section, we will be looking into the importance of these key pairs and how to manage them.

Key pairs are used to allow you to connect to your instance, whether it is Linux-based or Windows-based. The method for connecting to each of these OSes with key pairs differs, and we shall look into these methods shortly.

Each key pair uses public key cryptography using 2,048-bit SSH-2 RSA keys and are used to encrypt and decrypt administrative logs on credentials to the instance. Public key cryptography uses two separate keys to encrypt and decrypt data; these are known as the public key and the private key. The public key is maintained by the EC2 instance, and the private key is kept by us as the customers. We must download and store this private key securely, as it is unrecoverable if we lose it. The public key encrypts the credentials, and our private key will decrypt them, allowing us to gain access to the instance.

Creating key pairs

Without the creation of these key pairs, it is not possible to connect to your EC2 instance when it has been deployed. You can still create your EC2 instance without a key pair, but you would not be able to connect to it locally to perform any kind of maintenance or local administration.

The two methods for creating key pairs that we will be looking into are as follows:

- Creating key pairs during EC2 deployment
- Creating key pairs within the EC2 console

Creating key pairs during EC2 deployment

You can create a key pair for your instance during its creation. To do so, follow these steps:

1. At the end of the configuration option, and just as you click on **Launch Instances**, the following window will appear:

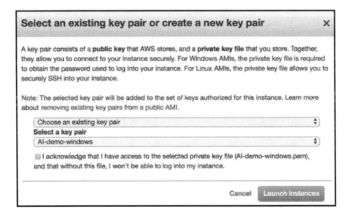

2. EC2 asks you to either select an existing key pair or create a new one. However, in fact you have three choices. Select the drop-down list and then click on **Choose an existing key pair**:

> ✓ Choose an existing key pair
> Create a new key pair
> Proceed without a key pair

You don't have to create a new key pair for each and every instance that you would like to connect to. By selecting the first option here, you can use the same key pair that you have already used for a previous instance from the second drop-down box. This means that EC2 will use the same public key associated with that saved key pair, and you have to ensure that you still have the matching private key.

3. If you want to create a new key pair, you can do so by selecting the second option, and this will prompt you to give the key pair a name and explains that you need to download the key pair as you will not get another opportunity to do so:

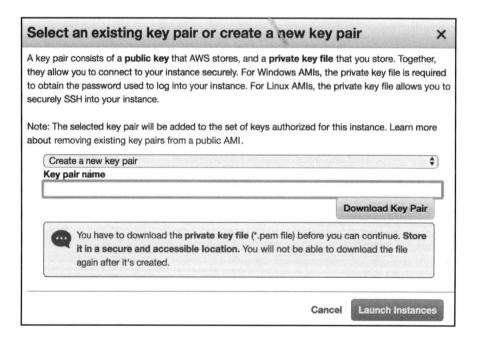

4. Select the option of proceeding without a key pair will still allow you to launch the instance. It simply means that you will not be able to connect to it locally to administer it, which isn't always required. In fact, this option effectively adds another layer of security by removing the potential threat of a key pair breach. The only option of connecting to the instance would be if you know the password built into the AMI:

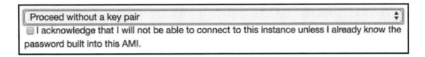

You can also create your key pairs from within the EC2 dashboard of the Management Console, which we will be looking into next. You can then select these key pairs during the creation of an EC2 instance.

Creating key pairs within the EC2 console

To create a new key pair from the EC2 dashboard, follow these steps:

1. From the EC2 console, select **Key Pairs** from the left menu in the **NETWORK & SECURITY** category:

2. Select **Create Key Pair**.
3. Add a name for your new key pair:

Your key pair will now appear in the list of active key pairs and can be used as a key pair when you create new EC2 instances.

With this, you have learned how to create a key pair. But what if you ever need to delete it? The next subsection will deal with this.

Deleting a key

Over time, you may want to delete a key pair for any number of reasons. When you delete a key pair from the EC2 Management Console, you are no longer able to use that key pair for any new EC2 instances. However, this deletion simply only deletes the copy of the public key that AWS holds; it does not delete the public keys that are attached and associated to any EC2 instances that are already created with it. Therefore, as long as you have the private key to the same pair, you can still connect to that same EC2 instance.

Deleting a key using the EC2 console

To delete a key using the EC2 Management Console, follow these steps:

1. From the EC2 console, select **Key Pairs** from the left menu in the **NETWORK & SECURITY** category.
2. Select the key pair that you need to delete and select **Delete**:

3. Confirm the deletion by selecting **Yes**.

Next, we will see how we can recover a lost private key.

Recovering a lost private key

If you lose your private key, then you could be in a situation of never being able to access you EC2 instance again; however, this is dependant on what storage was selected for the root device of your EC2 instance. If your EC2 instance was EBS-backed and you lost your private key, then you can recover it. However, if it was an instance store-backed instance, then this is not possible.

To view the process of recovering this key, follow the steps detailed at: `https://docs.aws.amazon.com/AWSEC2/latest/UserGuide/ec2-key-pairs.html#replacing-lost-key-pair`.

To determine if your EC2 instance is EBS-backed or instance store-backed, follow these steps:

1. Open the EC2 dashboard within the AWS Management Console.
2. Select **Instances** and then select the instance you want to check.
3. In the **Details** pane at the bottom of the screen, look for the **Root device type:**

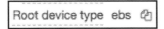

If the instance is EBS-backed, then the value will be **ebs**, as shown in the preceding screenshot; alternatively, it will be **instance store** for an instance store-backed device.

Connecting to a Linux-based instance with your key pair

Once you have downloaded your private key to your Linux instance, you can connect to the resource:

1. Open the EC2 dashboard from within the AWS Management Console.
2. Select **Instances** and then select the instance that you would like to connect to.
3. Select **Actions | Connect:**

4. This will then provide further information and instructions on how to connect to your instance using a four-step process, as shown here:

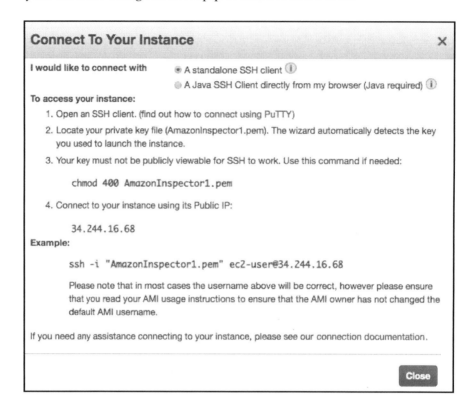

5. Once you have followed *steps 1 to 4*, you can then use the command shown in the **Example** section in the preceding screenshot to connect. So, to connect to this instance we simply need to copy and paste the following command into the client:

```
ssh -i "AmazonInspector1.pem" ec2-user@34.244.16.68
```

AmazonInspector1.pem is the name of the private key and ec2-user is the name of the user configured on the instance using the AMI. Finally, the IP address 34.244.16.68 is the address of the instance connected.

Connecting to a Windows-based instance with your key pair

Connecting to a Windows instance is slightly different and uses the key differently:

1. Open the EC2 dashboard from within the AWS Management Console.
2. Select **Instances** and then select the instance that you would like to connect to.
3. Select **Actions** | **Connect**.
4. This will then provide further information and instructions on how to connect to your instance:

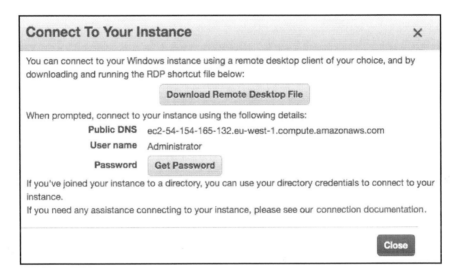

The **Download Remote Desktop File** button uses your RDP client to directly connect to your Windows instance, much the same as the **Example** link when connecting from a Linux box. Once you are presented with the Windows logon screen, you will then be asked for a username and password. The username is displayed. In this example, it is Administrator; however, you will need to get the password using the private key.

5. To get the password, click on **Get Password** and you will see the following screenshot:

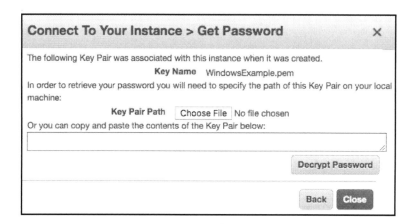

This screen allows you to navigate to your private key to decrypt the administrator password.

6. Select **Choose File** next to **Key Pair Path** and locate the same key as shown under **Key Name**. Once you have done this, the contents of the private key will be displayed in the box:

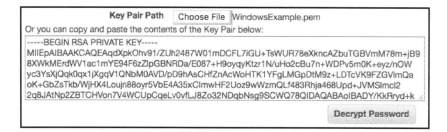

7. Select **Decrypt Password**. This will use the date from the private key to provide you with the password for the administrator:

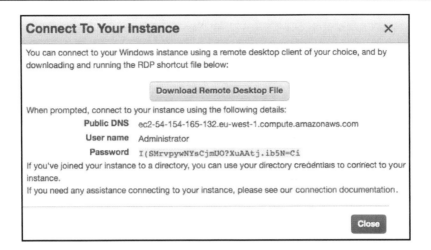

You can now connect to the instance using the RDP shortcut with the username and password provided.

In this section, we focused on the importance of creating, deleting, recovering, and using your key pairs with both Windows and Linux-based instances. Remember, if you want to connect to your EC2 instance to perform any kind of administration then you will need to ensure you create a key pair for that instance.

In the next section of this chapter, I want to explain how to isolate your instance should it become compromised to minimize the blast radius affecting your other infrastructure.

Isolating instances for forensic investigation

When you encounter a security threat within your AWS environment and have identified that an EC2 instance may have been compromised, what actions should you take to help prevent the threat from extending further into your network and affecting and compromising even more resources?

AWS monitoring and logging services

Thankfully, AWS provides a number of monitoring and logging services and features that you should implement and architect into your environment to help you in such a situation. The more information you have, the quicker you can detect and block the attack or threat. This will ultimately reduce the blast radius within your infrastructure and the effect it has both on your customers and on your business from a financial perspective.

Some of these logging and monitoring services and features are detailed in the following sections.

AWS CloudTrail

This is a service that tracks and records just about all API calls made within your AWS account. This is a fantastic service to have at your side. For every API call made, AWS will track the following:

- The API that was called
- The service to which the API call was made against
- The timestamp when it was called
- The source IP address of the requester

This is all great information when trying to identify when and how an incident occurred within your environment.

More on AWS CloudTrail will be discussed in `Chapter 12`, *Implementing Logging Mechanisms*.

AWS Config

AWS Config can provide a whole realm of resource management activities, including the following:

- Acting as a resource inventory for your infrastructure.
- Ability to capture and log any changes to your resources.
- You can take a snapshot of your configurations.
- Storing and reviewing the configuration history of resources.
- It integrates with AWS CloudTrail and will show you which API call made specific changes.
- Identify relationships held between different resources, for example, which EBS volumes are associated to which instances, and which instances are within which subnet.
- Through the use of compliance checks underpinned by AWS Lambda you can implement automatic checking for compliance rules, for example, to check all EBS volumes provisioned are encrypted.

All of this helps you to perform security analysis across your environment. More on AWS Config will be discussed in `Chapter 13`, *Auditing and Governance*.

Amazon CloudWatch

CloudWatch is probably the most common monitoring service provided by AWS. It collates and collects metrics across a variety of your resources running in your AWS account. This allows you to monitor your resources' performance over time and configure and respond to alerts that meet customized and defined thresholds.

On top of this metric monitoring, you can use CloudWatch along with a unified Cloud Agent to collect logs of your applications running on EC2 instances and a number of different AWS services. This log's data can be read from within CloudWatch, providing you with a real-time logstream of data. Using CloudWatch Logs in this way essentially allows you access to central repository of real-time log data.

More on Amazon CloudWatch will be discussed in `Chapter 12`, *Implementing Logging Mechanisms*.

VPC Flow Logs

VPC Flow Logs can capture all IP traffic from network interfaces on your instances, a subnet for the **Virtual Private Cloud** (**VPC**), or the VPC itself. This data is then sent to CloudWatch logs, allowing you to view the data as a stream showing all the entries. This data and information can help you resolve incidents and help with security remediation by identifying traffic that shouldn't be destined for a specific resource.

These are just a few of the logging capabilities offered by AWS. The point is, there are services and features, but you need to architect them into your solution in order to get the maximum benefit. As a general rule, you should ensure you have some form of logging enabled within your account.

So, going back to our first point at the start of this section, when you encounter a security threat and have identified that an EC2 instance may have been compromised, what action should you take? The key point is isolation.

VPC Flow Logs will be discussed in more depth in `Chapter 12`, *Implementing Logging Mechanisms*.

Isolation

Once you have identified a compromised instance, you must isolate it from everything else and remove it from your production network, thus preventing anything else from gaining access to it. There are a number of different steps you could take to do this:

- You should build in a forensic security group within your production environments. This allows you to quickly change the EC2 instance security group to one that prevents it from communicating with any other resource on your network. This effectively removes it from the network as no other connection can be made to or from it. If and when you need to connect to the resource, configure the security group using very specific ports and protocols (such as SSH and RDP) and configure the inbound source as a single IP address of the engineer that will be connecting.
- Create a snapshot of the EC2 instance, allowing you to restore it somewhere else in a secure environment for further analysis.
- If possible, take a memory dump of the instance.
- Store any log data to a dedicated S3 bucket. You could also use S3, again with dedicated buckets, to store information from the memory dump and disk information.
- Implement bucket-level permission on any S3 buckets used to a single identity.
- Create a separate forensic VPC purely for compromised resources.
- This forensic VPC should not be connected to any other VPCs.
- Enable logging, such as VPC Flow Logs.
- Create specific IAM roles that only allow read-only access to resources. This prevents you from inadvertently changing any data on the instance, preserving the condition for thorough forensic analysis.

Your main goals are to remove the compromised instance from the production network as quickly as possible (usually achieved by changing the security group of the instance). You will also want to preserve the instance in its exact state as much as possible to ensure you are not responsible for making any changes to it that could show up in logs during the investigation of the cause and impact and that would slow the investigation down. By taking a snapshot of the instance you can restore it within a different environment, allowing you to analyze it in safer and more restrictive circumstances.

In this section, I introduced you to some of the logging services that can be used to capture important data, including AWS CloudTrail, AWS Config, Amazon CloudWatch, and VPC Flow Logs. These services will be covered in greater detail in Chapter 12, *Implementing Logging Mechanisms* and Chapter 13, *Auditing and Governance*. I also explained some of the methods that can be used to help you isolate an instance should it become compromised, which will help you to reduce the chances of the malicious user gaining access to other resources.

In the next section, we will see how we can use the AWS Systems Manager to administer EC2 instances.

Using Systems Manager to administer EC2 instances

AWS Systems Manager is a powerful tool that allows you to easily and quickly administer and perform operational actions against your instances (both Windows- and Linux-based) at scale for both on-premise resources and within AWS without having to SSH or RDP to those instances. From a security standpoint, being able to remove these protocols from security groups reduces the attack surface of your instances even further. Having a single dashboard providing this administration also allows you to gain insights into your EC2 fleet and as a result provides you with greater visibility of your infrastructure. You will, for example, be able to see systems configurations and the patching levels of your instances, as well other software installations on the instance. Systems Manager can also aid with your compliance requirements by scanning instances against set patch baselines and anti-virus definitions.

System Manager works on the basis of resource groups. These groups are simply a customized collection of regional resources based on resource types and tags. These groups are then saved and used by Systems Manager to both simplify the management of your resources and to provide an overview and visibility of the groupings operational data. When you have resources grouped together, it makes performing actions such as deploying patches and security updates far easier.

Creating resource groups in Systems Manager

In this example, we will create a resource group of your EC2 instances tagged with the following information, but feel free to use your own tags:

Key	Value
Project	AWS
Domain	Security

Create a resource group with the following steps:

1. Log into your AWS Management Console.

2. Navigate to the **Systems Manager** service found within the **Management & Governance** category:

3. In the left-hand menu, select **Find Resources**:

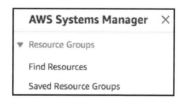

The following screen will then appear, which allows us to create our resource group:

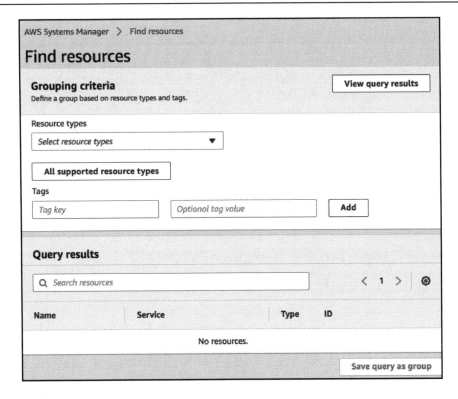

4. To define your resources for your group, select the **Resource types** drop-down box and select **AWS::EC2::Instance**:

5. Next, you need to add your tag keys and values into the appropriate box and click **Add**:

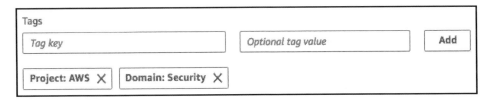

6. At this point, you have defined the resource type that you want to be a part of this group (EC2 instances) and filtered them using tag keys and values. To identify the resources that meet this criterion you must then click the **View query results** button. This will then display any resources that match your query of the resource type and matching tags. As you can see in the following screenshot, we have two EC2 instances that match. To save these results as your group, click the orange **Save query as group** button:

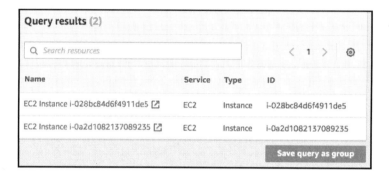

7. You are then prompted to enter a name for your group. In our example, we have named the group `My-EC2-Instances`. You also have the option of adding a description for the group, in addition to applying tags. When you have entered the details, click the orange **Create group** button to save this group:

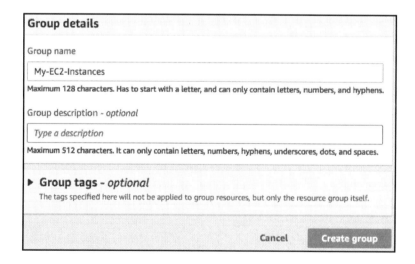

8. Lastly, you will be notified that the group has been created successfully within your region:

⊘ **The resource group "My-EC2-Instances" has been successfully created in the current region (eu-west-1).**

We have now created a resource group with specific tags relating to our environment, which will enable us to manage them easier within Systems Manager. The feature that we will be exploring next is the built-in insights.

Built-in insights

AWS Systems Manager uses built-in insights (integrations with other AWS services and features) to provide you with an overview of how your resources are operating within your resource groups. Currently, these built-in insights can review your resources groups against the following:

- Configuration compliance and history (integration with AWS Config)
- CloudTrail
- Personal Health Dashboard
- Trusted Advisor

We will discuss these one by one. But first, let's access these insights using the left menu by selecting **Built-in Insights**:

This will present the following simple dashboard, where you can then select each of the following insights:

- **Config:** This shows the config details, where you can filter to see how your resources are responding to compliance checks configured within AWS Config, in addition to the resource history:

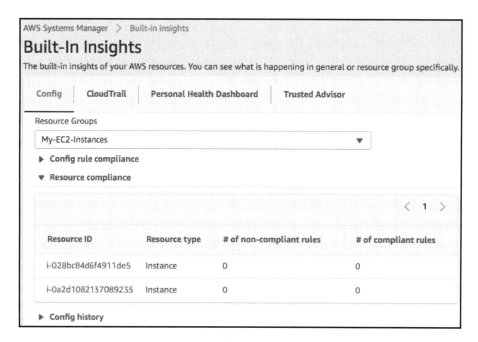

- **CloudTrail**: This shows the latest AWS calls made to the instances within the group:

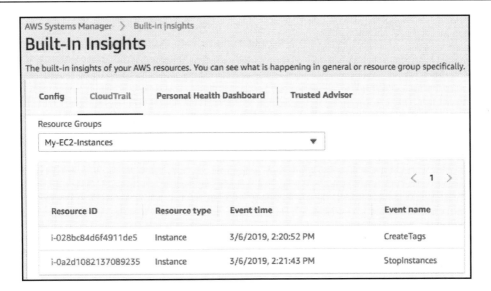

- **Personal Health Dashboard**: If there were any outages or incidents within AWS that affected your resources, then they will be shown here:

- **Trusted Advisor**: This will display any issues that are detected using the Trusted Advisor checks. As we can see in the following screenshot, it has detected one issue where investigation is recommended, and another issue where action is recommended. If we select the **View all check details** link at the bottom, it takes us to Trusted Advisor to identify the issue, and we can then resolve the problem:

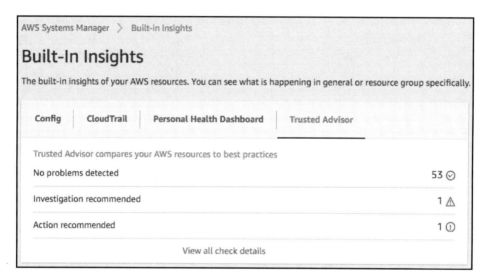

These built-in insights allow you to gain great visibility into the state of your EC2 instances, such as any non-compliance or best practices that are not being followed, thanks to resource groups and its integration with other AWS services and features.

AWS Systems Manager has a wide range of administration features, but we will just run through a few of the key components of the service to highlight what they are used for.

Actions

In this section, we will focus on the actions of AWS Systems Manager. These actions allow you to perform a number of different tasks and operations against your resources, from implementing a level of automation to creating packages to distribute to your fleet of instances. Let's take a look at each of them.

The **Actions** list can be found in the menu on the left of the dashboard:

We will go through each of these actions in the following sections.

Automation

Here, you can automate processes against groups of resources through a series of steps via *SSM documents*. This helps to simplify the management of your resources and your EC2 fleet, as it enables you to implement common tasks using both custom and pre-defined documents, which are written in JSON. These SSM documents enable you to perform recurring and common operational tasks automatically, for example, patching your EC2 instances or creating AMIs. Another common use is to implement operational changes at scale, with the inclusion of approval steps and controls to prevent unexpected behavior.

In order to access the automation documents, you can navigate to the **Shared Resources** menu on the left and select **Documents**:

Automation should be used where ever possible to ensure tasks and operations are carried out predictably and accurately without human intervention, so the automation action is a great feature of SSM.

Run Command

The Run Command allows you to manage your fleet of EC2 instances remotely and securely, allowing you to perform maintenance and management without ever having to log into the instances. Much like with the Automation section, the Run Command also uses SSM documents to help you perform administrative tasks and configuration changes.

As an example, we will see how to update the SSM agent on a EC2 instance. The SSM agent is preinstalled with most versions of Linux and Windows, and its main purpose is to process requests from AWS Systems Manager. To update the SSM agent using the Run Command, execute the following steps:

1. From within the Systems Manager console, select **Run Command** from the **Actions** section:

2. In the **Command document** list, search for AWS-UpdateSSMAgent:

3. The **Command parameters** section is optional; you can specify a specific version of the agent you want to install, or if you want to downgrade to a previous agent:

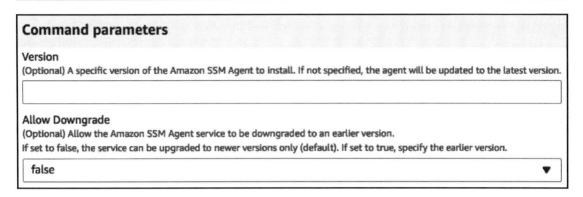

4. Next, you can select your target EC2 instances that you want to update the agent on, you can do this by tag selection or by manually selecting the instances. Do bear in mind that for your EC2 instances to be visible here you must have configured the EC2 instances with permission to communicate with SSM. This is done by associating the EC2 instances with a role with the permissions set out in the AWS managed policy of AmazonEC2RoleforSSM:

For more information on how to set this up, please visit `https://docs.aws.amazon.com/systems-manager/latest/userguide/sysman-configuring-access-role.html`.

5. Next, you configure the **Other parameters** section. Here, you can add any additional comments (optional) regarding the command and set a timeout in seconds for how long the command should wait before failing should an issue arise:

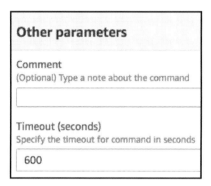

6. Next is the **Rate Control**, which allows you to customize how many resources should be updated at once, either as a number of targets or the percentage of targets. In addition, you can also set the command to fail once it has reached a set number of errors or percentage of failures:

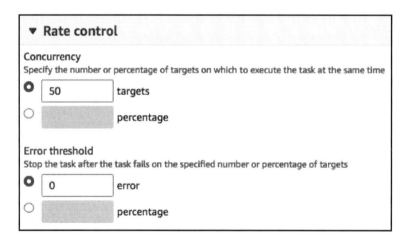

7. The next section to complete is the **Output options**. This section allows you to send output generated by the results of the Run Command to either **S3** or **Amazon CloudWatch Logs**, or both:

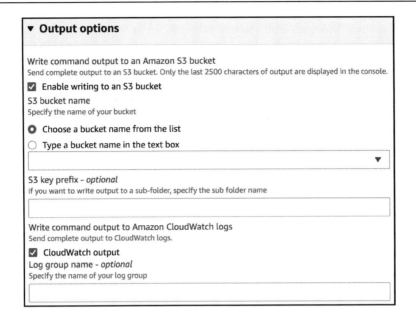

8. If you would also like notifications generated by SNS of the status of your Run Command, then this can be configured in the **SNS Notifications** section by simply selecting **Enable SNS notifications**:

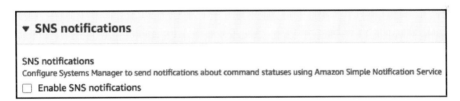

9. Finally, you are given the option of using the AWS CLI to perform the same actions as defined during the configuration, and it provides you with the complete command, as shown here:

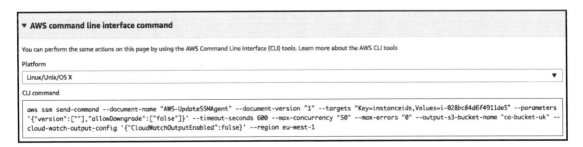

10. Once you have configured all of your options, you then click **Run**, and this will then execute the Run Command and provide a status screen showing you the progress:

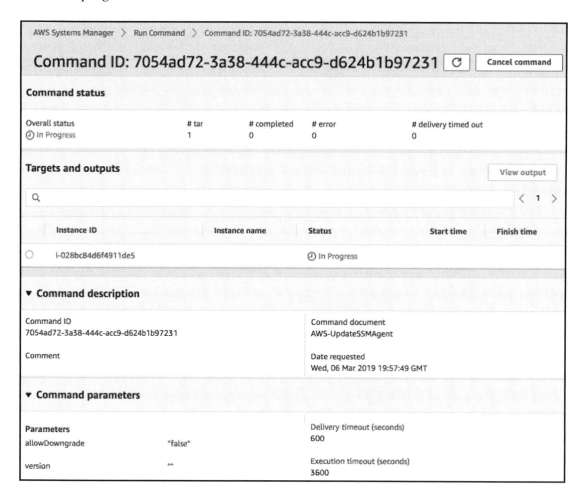

11. Once the command has finished, the status will change to **Completed**. For reference, the following output is what was sent to S3 by SSM on completion:

```
Updating amazon-ssm-agent from 2.3.372.0 to latest

Successfully downloaded
https://s3.eu-west-1.amazonaws.com/amazon-ssm-eu-west-1/ssm-agent-m
anifest.json
Successfully downloaded
https://s3.eu-west-1.amazonaws.com/amazon-ssm-eu-west-1/amazon-ssm-
```

```
agent-updater/2.3.479.0/amazon-ssm-agent-updater-linux-amd64.tar.gz
Successfully downloaded
https://s3.eu-west-1.amazonaws.com/amazon-ssm-eu-west-1/amazon-ssm-
agent/2.3.372.0/amazon-ssm-agent-linux-amd64.tar.gz
Successfully downloaded
https://s3.eu-west-1.amazonaws.com/amazon-ssm-eu-west-1/amazon-ssm-
agent/2.3.479.0/amazon-ssm-agent-linux-amd64.tar.gz

Initiating amazon-ssm-agent update to 2.3.479.0
amazon-ssm-agent updated successfully to 2.3.479.0
```

In this example, we looked at how you can use the Run Command to update the SSM agent on an EC2 instance, both remotely and securely, showing you that it's possible to perform administrative tasks and configuration changes.

Session Manager

The Session Manager helps to maintain security and audit compliance across your fleet. It helps to reduce the level of access control required on your instances, in addition to optimizing your security groups by closing inbound ports for your resources too, for example, by removing SSH. Session Manager allows you to connect securely to your instances via a browser-based shell or the CLI without having to maintain and configure bastion hosts or manage SSH keys. Any access gained to the instances is fully audited via session logs for additional compliance requirements. This allows an instance access activity to be monitored and tracked and enables an overview of user access. The session logs also allow you to track any actions or changes that were performed.

To connect to an instance using Session Manager from within the console, follow these steps:

1. Select **Session Manager** from the **Actions** menu on the left side of the console.
2. Select the orange **Start session** button.
3. Select your instance you want to connect to:

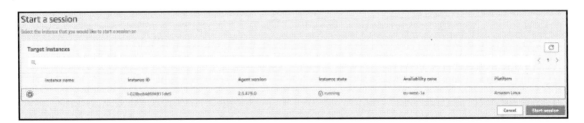

4. Select **Start session**.

5. You will then be securely connected to the instance via your browser, as shown in the following screenshot:

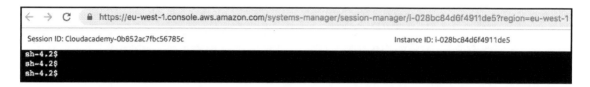

In this example, I showed you how you can access your instances through a browser-based shell using Session Manager.

Distributor

The Distributor allows you to create packages to distribute your own software across your instances. Alternatively, there are also a range of AWS managed and compiled packages that you can also take advantage of, such as AWSKinesisTap, which would install the Windows Kinesis agent on an instance. If you create your own package, it is published to AWS Systems Manager, where it can then be deployed by using the Run Command as explained earlier, or by using State Manager.

State Manager

This is used to help you maintain a consistent and measurable state of your EC2 instances. Some of the key uses of State Manager include the following:

- Configuring network settings
- Bootstrapping your instances, allowing you to install specific software on boot
- Ensuring the installation of specific agents are updated on a regular schedule
- Joining Windows-based instances to a domain
- Running scripts on instances

By using State Manager, you can help to reduce the configuration drift that can be experienced by instances over time through various different updates and configuration changes. This helps to maintain your compliance requirements across your fleet of instances.

I now want to pay additional attention to the Patch Manager feature, as it's important to understand how patching is managed through Systems Manager.

Patch Manager

Quite simply, this provides a method of automating the management of patch updates across your fleet of EC2 instances. This is great way to push out a newly released patch that protects you from new vulnerabilities across your whole fleet with a few clicks. It also has the ability to scan your instances to see which patches are missing, and if configured to do so it will update any missing patches for you.

Before you use Patch Manager, ensure that you meet all the prerequisites of using System Manager found at: `https://docs.aws.amazon.com/ systems-manager/latest/userguide/systems-manager-prereqs.html`.

There are four key points to Patch Manager, as highlighted by the AWS Systems Manager Patch Console:

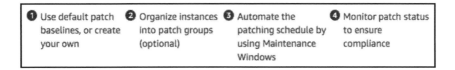

So, let's take a look at each of these in turn.

Use default patch baselines, or create your own

A key element of Patch Manager is patch baselines. They simply provide a patch baseline for each supported OS. There are a number of predefined patch baselines that AWS provides. To view them from within the Systems Manager console, follow these steps:

1. Select **Patch Manager** from the menu on the left.
2. Select **View predefined patch baselines**:

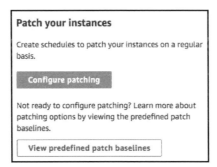

3. This will then present a list of predefined patch baselines that have been created by AWS for each OS:

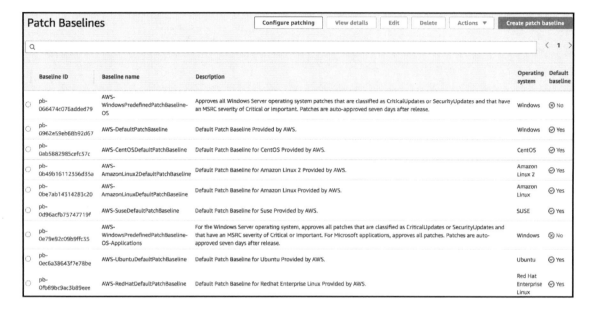

4. To view the settings of a baseline, select the Baseline ID:

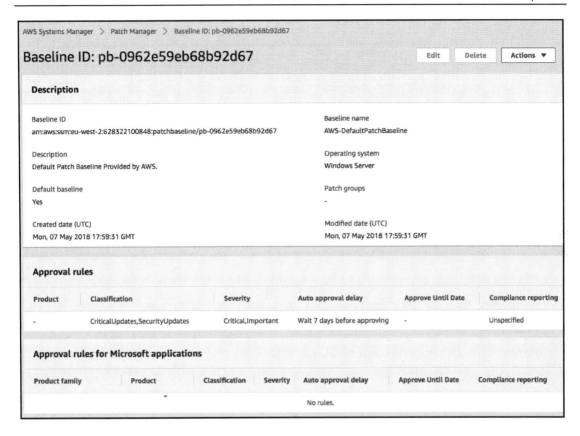

5. Here, you can see the description and, importantly, the approval rules of the baseline, which determine the classification of patches included, the severity of patches, and any auto-approval delay.

Depending on the settings within these predefined patch baselines you can determine if you would like to use one of these baselines or create your own.

I now want to show you how to create your own patch baseline:

1. From the list of predefined AWS patch baselines, select **Create patch baseline**:

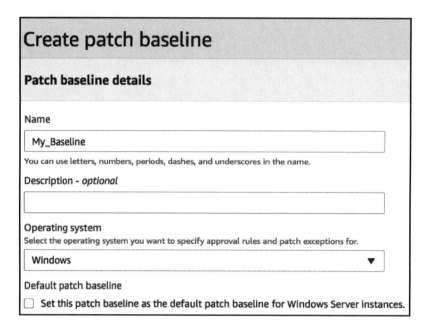

Here, there are a few selections to be made:

- The first elements you will need to configure are the name and optional description of your baseline.
- You must also select which OS this baseline will be associated with.
- If required, you can select a checkbox to make this baseline a new default for instances with the same OS.
- Following this section, you will then need to configure the approval rules for the OS. You must have a minimum of 1 rule and a maximum of 10:

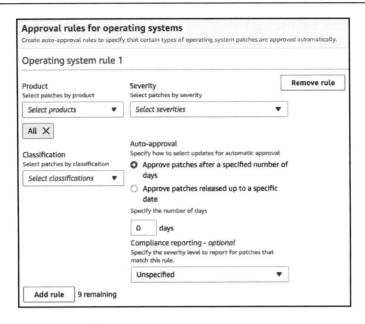

2. The **Product** dropdown allows you to select from the list the version of the OS; for example, if Windows was selected, you could select the version of Windows you wanted:

3. The **Classification** dropdown allows you to select patches as per their classification, the options here are as follows:

So, going back to our predefined default baseline for the Windows OS we saw earlier, the classification contained **CriticalUpdates** and **SecurityUpdates**. If we wanted our patch baseline to include **ServicePacks** as well, for example, then we would need to create our own baseline as we are doing here, and add the required classifications.

4. Next, we have **Severity**, which allows you to select your patches by the defined severity:

5. Next is the **Auto-approval** component. This allows you to configure when the patches defined by the severity, classification, and product settings already made will be approved by your baseline. You can either approve the patches after a specified number of days once they are released, or all patches up to a specific release date:

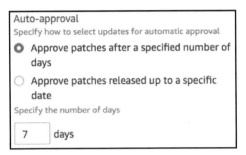

6. The last part in this section allows you to select a level of severity for patches that match this rule for optional compliance reporting:

7. If you would like to add an additional rule, select **Add rule**:

8. Further down the configuration screen, you will see **Patch exceptions**:

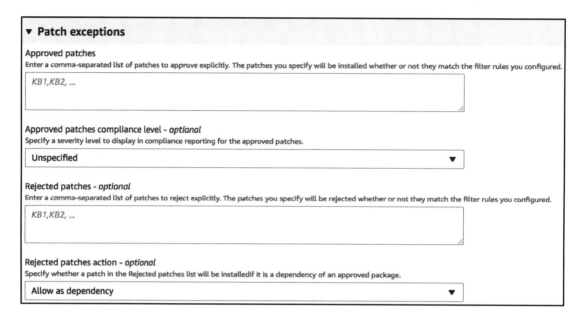

This section allows you to provide a list of approved patches regardless of whether the rules specified within the patch baseline match it or not. You just need to add them to the **Approved patches** box. You can also explicitly reject any patches that you do not want installed as a part of your patch baseline, even if the rules in your baseline allow it. For these rejected patches, you can specify whether you would like to have them installed if they are a dependency on another patch, or block it completely regardless of any dependencies:

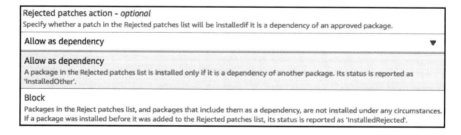

9. Finally, select **Create Patch Baseline**. Your baseline will now appear in the list of predefined patch baselines.

Next, I want to talk about how to organize instances into patch groups, which is an optional step.

Organizing instances into patch groups (optional)

Once you have your baselines defined and configured, even if that means using the default predefined baselines created by AWS, you can then choose to create patch groups if required.

Patch groups are exactly what you would expect them to be: they allow you to associate a number of instances with a group, which is then associated with a single patch baseline. This helps you to organize your instances and patches more easily by grouping similar instances together, perhaps within the same environment. For example, you could group together all Windows instances within your test environment.

Also, any instance that is not associated with a patch group will automatically receive the default patch baseline for that OS.

So, when a task is run to apply patches to your instances, SSM will know if the instance belongs to a patch group. If it does, the associated patch baseline of that group will be used to apply any patches. If an instance does not belong to a patch group, then the instance will use the default patch baseline available, which, as we know, could be a patch baseline that you have configured yourself instead of the predefined ones created by AWS.

 As this is an optional step, please take a look at the following documentation to see how to create a patch group, available at: `https://docs.aws.amazon.com/systems-manager/latest/userguide/sysman-patch-group-tagging.html`.

Automate the patching schedule by using maintenance windows

You can use maintenance windows to schedule specific times when maintenance activities should occur to reduce the performance impact for your end users. Actions to be run within these configured windows could include patch updates or software installations.

There are three options to select from a patching schedule perspective:

1. **Select an existing maintenance window**: This allows you to use an existing maintenance window that you have already configured.
2. **Schedule in a new maintenance window**: You can create a new maintenance window when configuring patching.
3. **Skip scheduling and patch instances now**: Lastly, you can simply decide to carry out your patch update immediately outside of any preconfigured maintenance windows.

The final element of using Patch Manager is monitoring your patch status to ensure compliance.

Monitoring your patch status to ensure compliance

Once you have completed your patch installations on your instances, compliance data is available immediately to you. AWS Systems Manager provides three different methods of viewing your patch compliance data:

- AWS Systems Manager Explorer (`https://docs.aws.amazon.com/systems-manager/latest/userguide/Explorer.html`)
- AWS Systems Manager Configuration compliance (`https://docs.aws.amazon.com/systems-manager/latest/userguide/systems-manager-compliance.html`)
- AWS Systems Manager Managed Instances (`https://docs.aws.amazon.com/systems-manager/latest/userguide/managed_instances.html`)

Each of these capabilities will provide you with a method of obtaining and viewing your EC2 patch compliance.

Now we have looked at patch baselines, patch groups, automating the patching schedule, and the different capabilities of monitoring your patch compliance. I now want to quickly walk you through setting up your patch configuration:

1. From the Patch Manager dashboard within Systems Manager, select **Configure Patching**.
2. You will then be taken a configuration page, where you will need to define the following:
   - Which instances to patch
   - A patching schedule
   - The patching operation:

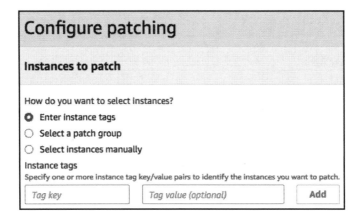

3. Firstly, you must select which instances you would like to patch, either via instance tags, a patch group, or by manually selecting them.

4. Next, you must select a patching schedule. As I explained earlier, there are three options. The following screenshot shows the configuration options for creating a new maintenance schedule for your patching:

5. Finally, you must select which patching operation you would like to use:

Patching operation

◉ **Scan and install**
Scans each target instance and compares its installed patches with the list of approved patches in the patch baseline. Downloads and installs all approved patches that are missing from the instance.

○ **Scan only**
Scans each target instance and generates a list of missing patches for you to review.

As we can see, **Scan and install** will scan each target instance and download any patches that are approved and missing from the instance that fall within the patch baseline settings. **Scan only** will simply identify the missing patches for you to review without installing them.

6. Once you have select the options required for your patching, select **Configure Patching**.

Your patching will then be configured and will be run as per your patching schedule, instance selection, and patching operation.

In this section, we looked at how you can use Patch Manager within Systems Manager to create, define, and run patch updates across your EC2 fleet for all different OSes using patch baselines to determine the patches of interest using classifications and severity levels.

Summary

This chapter covered a range of methods and services that can be used to help you protect and manage your EC2 instances. Compute resources, which of course includes EC2 instances, are likely to be widely used within your environment, and as a result you should be familiar with an array of techniques and methods to protect and secure them at all levels. This includes being able to detect potential threats and vulnerabilities, access management, compliance, and operational maintenance. All of these points are essential when looking at how best to secure you EC2 instances. Some of the topics and services that are mentioned here will be covered in more detail in later chapters of the book.

In the following chapter, my focus will be moving onto securing your infrastructure within AWS.This will include your VPC and its core components, including **Network Access Control Lists (NACLs)**, security groups, network segmentation, NAT gateways, and internet gateways.

Questions

As we conclude, here is a list of questions for you to test your knowledge regarding this chapter's material. You will find the answers in the *Assessments* section of the *Appendix*:

1. True or False: AWS Systems Manager is a fully managed service that allows you to help secure your instances and the applications that run on top of them by performing vulnerability assessments via an agent.
2. True or False: Amazon Inspector requires an agent to be installed to remotely run assessments.
3. Is the public key of an EC2 instance key pair held by AWS or you as the customer?
4. Which service is used to track and record API calls made within your AWS account?
5. Which service allows you to easily and quickly administer and perform operational actions against your instances (both Windows- and Linux-based) at scale for both on-premise resources and within AWS without having to SSH or RDP into those instances?

Further reading

For more information on some of the best practices when securing EC2 instances, please review the following info from AWS, at: `https://aws.amazon.com/answers/security/aws-securing-ec2-instances/`.

7
Configuring Infrastructure Security

As you saw in the previous chapter, it's very easy using the Wizard to create your VPC, but you might want more control and management over how your VPC is configured. To do this, it's best to create your VPC from scratch and configure the components as you go, such as your route tables and **network access control lists** (**NACLs**).

When looking at your cloud architecture and infrastructure from an IaaS perspective, you as the customer are responsible for implementing, maintaining, and managing the security of that infrastructure. This includes your **virtual private cloud** (**VPC**) and all of the components that make up that VPC.

This chapter will focus on these points to show you the different areas of interest that you need to pay particular attention to in order to ensure the security of your network and resources running across it.

In this chapter, we will cover the following topics:

- Understanding a VPC
- Creating a VPC using the Wizard
- Understanding the VPC components
- Building a multi-subnet VPC manually

Technical requirements

In order to perform the activities in this chapter, you will need to have access to an AWS account and have the necessary permissions to create and manage a Virtual Private Cloud and Launch EC2 instances. Access control and permissions were covered in Chapter 4, *Working with Access Policies*.

Knowledge of how to create an EC2 instance within a VPC is essential. You must have a basic understanding of the TCP/IP protocol and subnetting, and lastly, an understanding of the AWS global infrastructure is important.

 More on this can be found at: `https://cloudacademy.com/blog/aws-global-infrastructure/`.

Understanding a VPC

A **VPC** is a **Virtual Private Cloud**, and you can think of this as your own private section of the AWS network. It allows you to create a virtual network infrastructure that you can segment into different networks. These networks can be made both public-facing and private and they use TCP/IP for addressing. They can essentially emulate a local area network that you would be running on-premises within your own data center:

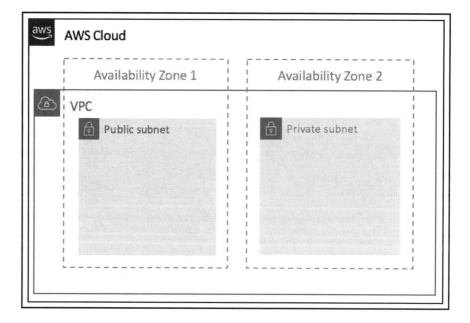

During the creation of your VPC, you can configure multiple subnets to reside in different Availability Zones, helping you to architect for resilience from the get-go. When you have your VPC configured and up and running, you can then deploy other AWS resources within these subnets. For example, you could have a public-facing subnet hosting EC2 web servers accessible by the public, which can then pass traffic to your application servers within a private subnet. This in turn could talk to your database infrastructure, within another private subnet. This setup can be seen in the following diagram:

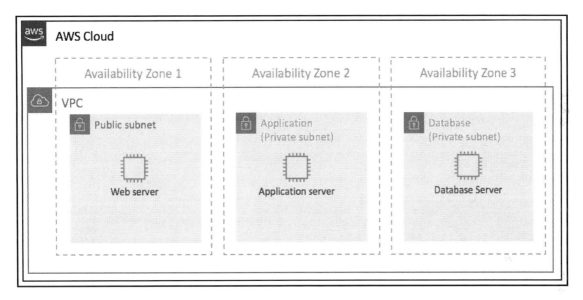

As these VPCs are all virtual, they are very easy to create, and there are two different ways to do this within the AWS Management Console – by using the VPC Wizard or manually from scratch. In the upcoming section, we will use the Wizard and see the different options available within it before looking at how to create the VPC manually from scratch.

Creating a VPC using the Wizard

Execute the following steps to create a VPC using the Wizard:

1. Open the VPC dashboard from with the AWS Management Console.
2. Select the blue **Launch VPC Wizard** button:

3. You will then be asked to select a configuration type for your VPC. There are four different options to select, and each is configured differently, offering you different solutions:

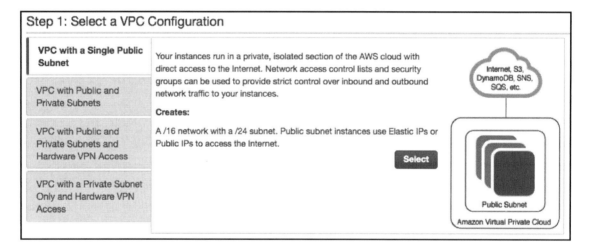

4. For this demonstration, select **VPC with a Single Public Subnet** and click **Select**.

To clarify at this point, a public subnet is a subnet that is reachable by the internet. So any resources within that subnet can reach out to internet traffic and also receive internet traffic. How this is configured and the components used will be discussed when we manually configure a VPC. For now, let's complete the Wizard.

5. You are now presented with the following page, where you are asked to provide additional configurable parameters that will dictate how your VPC and public subnet are configured from a CIDR block perspective. **CIDR** stands for **Classless Inter-Domain Routing** and defines the IP address ranges of your VPC and potential subnets:

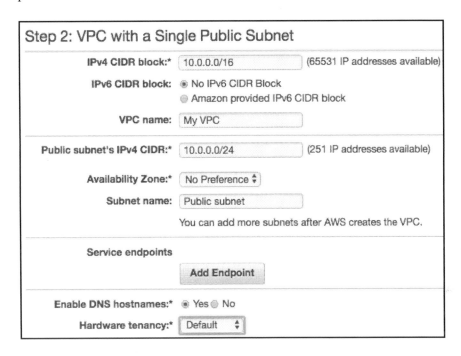

6. In the first section at the top, enter the size of your CIDR block, which must be between **/16** and **/28**. If you want to use an IPv6 CIDR block range, then this will be allocated by AWS. Also, add a name for your VPC.

7. Next, configure the CIDR block for your public subnet (remember, this Wizard will configure a single public subnet). Select the availability zone of your public subnet. Be aware that subnets are *not* able to span more than one availability zone. Add a name for your subnet.

8. Now add a service endpoint if required. A service endpoint allows you to connect to services that sit outside of your VPC, such as S3 or DynamoDB, without traversing the internet. Instead, an interface would be created within your VPC to directly connect to the service using only the internal AWS network.

9. Select whether you would like to enable DNS hostnames or not.
10. Select the tenancy required. The available tenancy options include **Default** or **Dedicated**. Default tenancy means that the underlying host hardware of your instances run within your VPC will be shared by other customers. Dedicated tenancy ensures that only your account will be using the underlying host hardware of your instances and not sharing it with anyone else. You might need this option for specific compliance reasons.
11. Finally, select **Create VPC**.

AWS will now create the VPC and the associated public subnet, which will also include components such as an IGW, route tables, NACLs, and many more automatically. So let's first take a look at these components and what they are. This will give you a much deeper insight into how to implement security across your environment.

Understanding the VPC components

In this section, we will be looking at the different VPC components that can be used to help you implement a level of protection in helping you to secure your resources. We will be looking at subnets, IGWs, route tables, NACLs, security groups, bastion hosts, NAT instances, and NAT gateways and virtual private gateways.

Subnets

A subnet is a network segment that falls within the CIDR block of the VPC. For example, if your VPC CIDR block is `10.0.0.0/16`, you could have subnets configured as follows:

- `10.0.1.0/24`
- `10.0.2.0/24`
- `10.0.3.0/24`

From a TCP/IP perspective, this would give you 256 addresses in each subnet. However, the first address is the network address, and the last address is the broadcast address and so they are not available as host addresses. In addition to this, AWS reserves the first three host addresses in any subnet. The first available host address is reserved for internal AWS VPC routing, the second address is then reserved for AWS DNS, and the third address is reserved for future use.

This means that a /16 subnet would produce 251 available host addresses to use for your resources within that subnet. In our example, this would be as follows:

- 10.0.1.0 - Network address
- 10.0.1.1 - Reserved for AWS routing
- 10.0.1.2 - Reserved for AWS DNS
- 10.0.1.3 - Reserved for AWS future use
- 10.0.1.255 - Broadcast address

There is a good analogy to help understand the relationship between VPCs and subnets. You could think of your house as your VPC. Within your house, you have a number of different rooms, the kitchen, the lounge, bedrooms, study, and washrooms. Each of these rooms could be thought of as your subnets. Each room in your house performs a different function. The same can apply to your subnets. Each subnet should be configured to perform a specific use. Perhaps a subnet contains all of your application servers, and another your database servers.

This segmentation helps to maintain security. By having multiple subnets with similar grouped resources, it helps to enforce security management through the use of NACLs filtering traffic through specific ports. Within your database subnet, you might only allow ports applicable to MySQL, both inbound and outbound, which would then drop all other traffic.

By selecting a subnet from within the VPC dashboard within the AWS Management Console, under **Subnets** on the left-hand menu, you will see that each subnet has a number of attributes and associations.

The Description tab

The **Description** tab provides an overall summary description of how the subnet is configured:

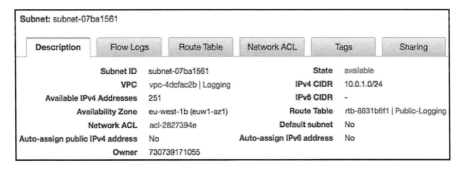

The main points to highlight at this stage are **VPC**, **Availability Zone**, **Network ACL**, **IPv4 CIDR**, and **Route Table:**

- **VPC**: When a subnet is created, it will exist within a single VPC. In this example, we can see the associated VPC ID and its name, **Logging**.
- **Availability Zone**: As mentioned previously, a subnet can only reside in a single availability zone; in this instance, it is located in the `eu-west-1b` AZ.
- **Network ACL**: A network ACL will always be associated with a subnet. If you don't specify a particular NACL on creation, then it will use the VPC default NACL. As shown, the NACL will also have a corresponding ID, **acl-2827394e**.
- **IPv4 CIDR**: The IPv4 CIDR value shows the current CIDR block for this subnet.
- **Route Table**: Finally, **Route Table** shows the associated route table that this subnet will use to route traffic. Again, during the creation of your subnet, if no route table is defined, it will use the default VPC route table. So, in essence, both the NACL and route table can be changed for each subnet.

To reiterate, network segmentation through subnets helps with security to maintain network borders, whereby protective measures are in place to filter network traffic, both inbound and outbound.

The flow logs tab

The **Flow Logs** tab allows you to set up and configure flow logs. These allow you to capture IP traffic sent between the network interfaces of your subnet. Flow logs can also be configured at the VPC level and for each of your network interfaces on your instances. However, this tab will only configure flow logs for this particular subnet. The data captured in these logs can help you resolve incidents relating to network communication issues and traffic flow. They are also useful to help identify traffic that shouldn't be traversing the network, so from a security stance, they are also very useful at IP traffic analysis. All flow log data is captured within CloudWatch Logs.

Flow logs will be covered in greater detail in `Chapter 12`, *Implementing Logging Mechanisms*.

The Route Table and Network ACL tabs

Both the **Route Table** and **Network ACL** tabs allow you to view the associated route table and NACL with the subnet and make changes as necessary.

The following screenshot shows a default route (local) with another route pointing to an **Internet Gateway** (**IGW**). Routing will be covered in more detail in the *Rout tables* section of this chapter:

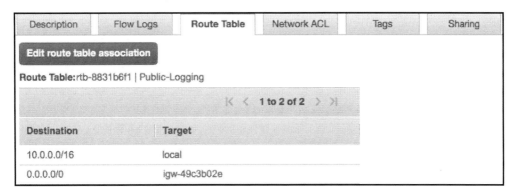

In the following network ACL, we can see two rules, including a default rule denying **ALL** traffic to the subnet that doesn't meet any other rules in the access control list. NACLs are covered in more detail in a later section of this chapter titled *Network Access Control Lists*:

Description	Flow Logs	Route Table	Network ACL	Tags	Sharing

Edit network ACL association

Network ACL: acl-2827394e

Inbound rules

Rule #	Type	Protocol	Port Range / ICMP Type	Source	Allow / Deny
100	ALL Traffic	ALL	ALL	0.0.0.0/0	ALLOW
*	ALL Traffic	ALL	ALL	0.0.0.0/0	DENY

Outbound rules

Rule #	Type	Protocol	Port Range / ICMP Type	Source	Allow / Deny
100	ALL Traffic	ALL	ALL	0.0.0.0/0	ALLOW
*	ALL Traffic	ALL	ALL	0.0.0.0/0	DENY

It's worth pointing out at this stage that a subnet can *only* be associated with a single NACL and a single route table, but multiple subnets can share the same NACL and route table. I will cover more on both of these components in the upcoming sections in this chapter.

The Tags tab

The **Tags** tab allows you to tag this resource with key-value pairs that you would like to configure:

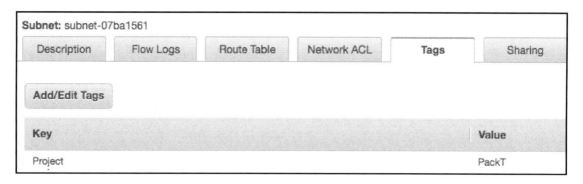

Tags can be used to help you organize and group your resources.

Internet gateways

An **internet gateway**, commonly referred to as an **IGW**, is used to help create a public subnet. It is a logical component that you must create and attach to your VPC to allow traffic to traverse from your subnet in your VPC out to the internet and vice versa. Without an IGW, there is no link or connection between your VPC and the outside world.

Later in this chapter, I will show you how to build a multi-subnet VPC with an IGW. This will look at how to create and attach it to your VPC.

Route tables

Route tables simply provide a way of directing network traffic where to go. When a network packet leaves a subnet, it needs to know how to get to its destination, and it uses a route table to find that route.

Whenever a new VPC is created, by default, a main route table will also be created and will typically look as shown in the following screenshot if the VPC has been created from scratch rather than from a Wizard template:

Destination	Target	Status	Propagated
10.0.0.0/16	local	active	No

It is very basic and will contain a single route, and this **local** route simply allows every subnet created within the VPC to route to each other. This main route table can't be deleted, however, you can modify it and add additional routes as and when you need to.

You aren't just limited to this single route table for your VPC, however; you can create additional route tables and associate different route tables to different subnets. Every route table you create will *always* have this default "local" route within it though.

The route table itself is comprised of a number of different tabs, just like the subnets.

The Summary tab

The **Summary** tab provides a high-level overview of data surrounding the route table, detailing which VPC it resides in, the account owner, the route table ID, and any explicit associations, as can be seen here:

These explicit associations relate to any subnets that have been configured to use this route table using the **Route Table** tab within the subnet configuration. Whenever you create a new subnet, it will automatically, by default, use the main route table created by your VPC. However, as I mentioned earlier, you can create different route tables. If you then configured your VPC to use one of these new route tables, then it would be implicitly associated.

The Routes tab

This tab shows the actual routes that are in place to direct traffic and contains a number of different fields, as seen here:

Let's understand these fields one by one:

- **Destination**: This shows a CIDR block range for a network that your traffic needs to route to.
- **Target**: This is essentially a gateway that allows you to reach the destination. In this example, we have a route with a destination of 0.0.0.0/0. This destination is used to imply any destinations that are not known by the route table (for example, an internet address). The **Target** for this route is **igw-1220de77**, which is an ID for an IGW. This route means that for any destination that isn't listed within the route table that resides outside of your subnet, then use the IGW to get to that address.
- **Status**: This shows the status of your routes within the table, for example **active**.
- **Propagated**: Route propagation is used when working with a virtual private gateway, which can automatically propagate routes if configured to do so, meaning that you don't need to manually enter VPN routes to your route tables.

When routes are added to the route table, we need to ensure that the correct subnets are using the right route table. This is achieved by configuring the subnet associations. Let's look at this next.

The Subnet Associations tab

This tab shows any explicit subnet associations with this route table that have taken place, along with any subnets within the VPC that are using the main route table:

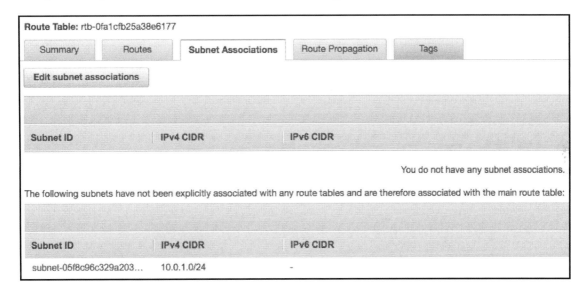

You can have multiple subnets associated with a single route table, but only a single route table can be associated with a subnet.

The Route Propagation tab

If you have a virtual private gateway configured, you can configure the route propagation setting here:

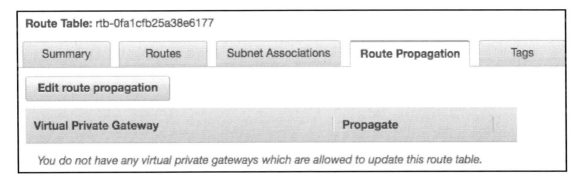

Route propagation allows the automatic population of detected routes across your VPN connection. This helps to ensure that the correct routing is in place between your gateways.

 As with all AWS resources, you can also set up key-value pairs that can be associated with your route table using the **Tags** tab.

Now we have covered route tables, I now want to look at NACLs, commonly referred to as NACLs, which help restrict traffic at a subnet level.

Network Access Control Lists

Network Access Control Lists (**NACLs**) are virtual network level firewalls that are associated with each and every subnet within your VPC and control ingress and egress traffic moving in and out of your subnet. Much like route tables, a default VPC NACL will be created when your VPC is also created. As a result, for any subnet that does not have an explicit NACL associated with it, this default NACL will be used.

For each NACL, there are two fundamental components: inbound rules and outbound rules. These rules control what traffic flows in and out of your subnet at a network level. NACLs are stateless, meaning that any response traffic generated from a request will have to be explicitly allowed and configured in either the inbound or outbound ruleset depending on where the response is coming from.

Let's look at the configuration of an NACL to explain how they work.

The Details tab

This provides an overview of the NACL itself, showing the VPC association and any associations with subnets within your VPC. It also details the NACL ID as well, as shown in the following screenshot:

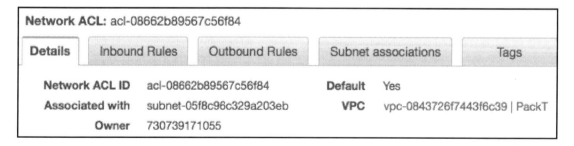

To understand the configuration of the NACL itself, we need to look at the rules, both inbound and outbound.

The Inbound Rules and Outbound Rules tabs

These are used to control what traffic flows into and out of your subnet. The inbound and outbound rules table is comprised of six fields:

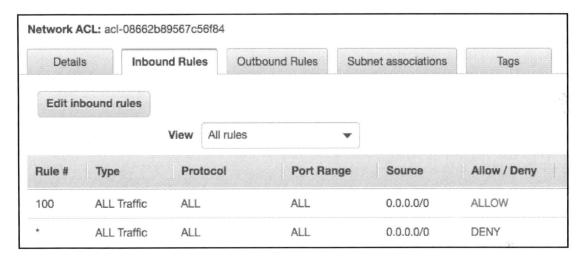

Let's go over these fields one by one:

- **Rule #**: The rule numbers are used to ascertain the order in which the rules are read. When your NACL processes traffic, the rules will be read in ascending order until a rule match is found. With this in mind, it's a best practice to leave number gaps within your rules to allow you to add more in over time without having to move everything around.
- **Type**: Here, you can select a number of common protocol types, such as LDAP, HTTP, DNS, and so on. You can alternatively specify custom TCP/UDP/ICMP protocols as well.
- **Protocol**: Depending on your selection in the previous **Type** field, you might be able to select a specific protocol (number).
- **Port Range**: Here, you can enter the port range for any custom protocol entries that you selected.

- **Source**: Much like the **Source** entry with your route tables, this can be a network subnet CIDR range, a single IP address using a /32 mask, or exposed to traffic from anywhere (using 0.0.0.0/0).
- **Allow / Deny**: With every NACL rule, you must specify whether the traffic that matches this rule should **ALLOW** or **DENY** the traffic coming into the subnet.

You will notice in this default NACL that all traffic is allowed by default, which makes using the default NACL very insecure. It doesn't actually provide any protection at all, so you should always look to update the default or, even better, create your own NACL and associate it with the relevant subnet.

The final rule in an NACL will always have an explicit *Deny* rule, which will drop all traffic that does not match any rule within the NACL. This is a safeguard mechanism to prevent any traffic from getting through to your subnet that you haven't specified.

 The **Outbound Rules** tab shows exactly the same fields as mentioned for the **Inbound Rules** tab, however, the rules affect traffic going out of the subnet rather than coming into the subnet.

The Subnet associations tab

This section shows which subnet is associated with this NACL, and as I mentioned when discussing subnets, you can have multiple subnets associated with a single NACL, but only a single NACL can be associated with a subnet:

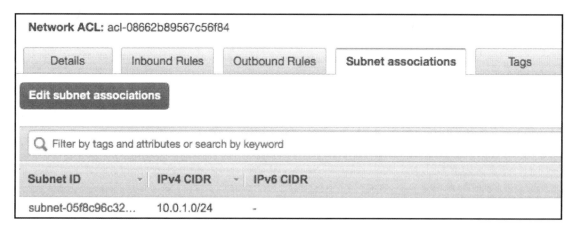

If you fail to associate your NACLs with the correct subnets, then your subnet might not have the correct security safeguards in place and could allow unwanted network traffic to be processed. Otherwise, your NACLs would be created and configured, but not associated with any subnet, and therefore would provide no security measures.

 The **Tags** tab, just as we discussed previously, helps you create key-value pairs that can be associated with your NACL.

Now we have looked at controlling security at the subnet/network level, let's now move on to a layer of security that operates at the instance level, security groups.

Security groups

Security groups are much like NACLs in that they provide a virtual firewall level of protection, but this time at the instance level, rather than the network. Security groups are associated with instances rather than subnets and control the traffic to and from your instances within your VPC. Again, only a single security group can be applied to an instance, but the same security group can be associated with multiple instances.

Unlike NACLs, which are stateless by design, security groups are stateful, which means you do not have to configure specific rules to allow returning traffic from requests. There are also other subtle differences within the rule base, so let's take a closer look at security group tabs.

The Description tab

Again, an overview is provided showing the security group ID, its name, VPC association, and rule counts:

Security Group: sg-0a8629e30947f2b8e			
Description	Inbound Rules	Outbound Rules	Tags

Group ID	sg-0a8629e30947f2b8e	**Group Name**	Allow_SSH
VPC ID	vpc-0843726f7443f6c39	**Description**	Allow SSH Traffic from custom IP Address
Owner	730739171055	**Inbound rule count**	1
Outbound rule count	1		

To look at the security configuration of the security group, we need to look at the inbound and outbound rulesets.

The Inbound Rules and Outbound Rules tab

This shows the inbound traffic rules that are associated with this security group, which contains five fields of information:

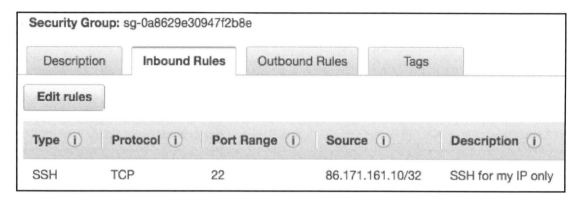

Let's take a closer look:

- **Type**: This represents the type of protocol that you would like to open up to network traffic (for example, SSH).
- **Protocol**: This shows the protocol associated with the **Type**.
- **Port Range**: This shows the port range of the protocol. If using a customer **Type** and **Protocol**, you can manually enter a custom port range.
- **Source**: Much like the **Source** entry with your route tables/NACL, this can be a network subnet CIDR range, a single IP address using a /32 mask, or exposed to traffic from anywhere (using 0.0.0.0/0).
- **Description**: An optional field allowing you to describe what this rule is used for.

Notice that there is not a field for **Allow** or **Deny** as we have with NACLs. This is because security groups only provide **Allow** rules by default, therefore, if a rule is in a security group, it is considered to be allowed. If a match for traffic is not found within the security group, the traffic is simply dropped. Also, there is no **Rule#** field, because all rules are evaluated by a security group before a decision is made about whether access should or should not be allowed.

The following table shows a quick comparison of how NACLs and security groups operate:

Security Method	Operates at	Rule Types	State	Rule processing
Network Access Control Lists	Subnet Level	Allow/Deny	Stateless	Rules read in ascending order until a match is found
Security Groups	Instance Level	Allow	Stateful	All rules are evaluated before a decision is made

 The **Outbound Rules** tab shows exactly the same fields as on the **Inbound Rules** tab, however, the rules affect traffic going out of the subnet rather than coming into the subnet.

The Tags tab

Here, you can create key-value pairs that can be associated with your security group. So, through the use of both NACLs and security groups, you can create layered security. For example, imagine you had an inbound NACL that looked as follows associated with a subnet:

Rule #	Type	Protocol	Port Range	Source	Allow / Deny
100	ALL TCP	TCP (6)	0 - 65535	0.0.0.0/0	ALLOW
*	ALL Traffic	ALL	ALL	0.0.0.0/0	DENY

Within that same subnet, you had an EC2 instance associated with the following security group:

Type ⓘ	Protocol ⓘ	Port Range ⓘ	Source ⓘ	Source ⓘ
HTTP	TCP	80	0.0.0.0/0	0.0.0.0/0
RDP	TCP	3389	86.171.161.10/32	86.171.161.10/32

Now if a host was trying to SSH to your EC2 instance, from a security standpoint it would have no problem traversing your NACL as SSH is a TCP protocol and you are allowing all TCP connections through to the subnet. However, it would not reach the instance as the security group for that instance would drop SSH as it's not listed as an allowed protocol.

Similarly, if an engineer was trying to RDP to the EC2 instance, then again access would be allowed through the NACL. If that engineer's IP address did not match `86.171.161.10/32`, then again RDP would be dropped as the source is not a match in the security group. If it was a match, then RDP would be allowed.

Finally, if anyone, anywhere was trying to use HTTP to the EC2 instance then it would be allowed both through the NACL and the security group. As you can see, using NACLs and security groups allows you to layer your security at both the network and instance level.

Next, we'll discuss the bastion host, which also offers a level of protection for your instances.

Bastion hosts

Bastion hosts are used to gain access to your instances that reside within your private subnets from the internet and the bastion itself resides within the public subnet. The difference between a public subnet and a private subnet is this: subnets only become classed as public when an IGW is attached to a VPC and a route exists within the route table associated with the subnet with a **Destination** of `0.0.0.0/0` via the **Target** of an IGW, for example:

Destination	Target
10.0.0.0/16	local
0.0.0.0/0	igw-49c3b02e

Any subnet associated with a route table pointing to an IGW with a destination address of 0.0.0.0/0 is considered a public subnet as it has direct access to the internet. Any subnet without this route is considered private, as there is no route to get out to the internet or vice versa.

So, to clarify, for a subnet to be public:

- The VPC must have an IGW attached.
- The subnet must have a route pointing to the internet (`0.0.0.0/0`) with a target of the IGW.

When a subnet is public, instances within this subnet will have a publicly accessible IP address and can communicate with the outside world. This allows your engineers to have the ability to SSH into your public-facing instances for support and maintenance if needed (providing NACLs and security groups have been configured to allow this access).

However, should you experience issues with your instances within your private instances, how can those same engineers SSH into them from the internet, perhaps as a remote fix? The answer is they can't, as they are private and there is no route to the outside world. To get around this, a bastion host needs to be installed within the public subnet.

The bastion host is a hardened EC2 instance with restrictive controls that acts as an ingress gateway between the internet and your private subnets without directly exchanging packets between the two environments. Hardening the host ensures that the chances of the systems being compromised are significantly reduced, and as this is a gateway to your internal private instances, you need to ensure you follow best practices to harden your instance.

As a part of the security group configuration associated with the bastion host, the source must be restricted as much as possible to restrict access from a small CIDR block or a single IP address. The security group for the private instances should allow SSH from the bastion host IP address *only*.

When connecting to instances, you use a key pair for authentication, which for Linux instances is stored as a *.pem file and is downloaded when the instance is created. However, once you connect to your bastion host (using a *.pem file), you will need to use the *.pem file associated within the private instance to connect, however, this will not be stored on the bastion host and should not be stored on the bastion host for security purposes, so how can you then connect to the private instance once you are connected to the bastion host? The answer is to use SSH forwarding, which provides a method of connection from your bastion host to your EC2 instance in your private subnet, without running the risk of storing your private key on your bastion host.

 For detailed information on how to configure SSH-forwarding, see:
https://aws.amazon.com/blogs/security/securely-connect-to-linux-instances-running-in-a-private-amazon-vpc/.

NAT instances and NAT gateways

A NAT instance/gateway can be thought of as performing the opposite role of a bastion host, in that it allows instances in the private subnets to initiate a connection out to the internet via the NAT resource, while blocking all inbound public-initiated traffic. NAT instances/gateways are much like bastion hosts provisioned within a public subnet and are typically used to allow your private instances access to the internet for maintenance-related tasks, such as obtaining OS updates and patch fixes, which is essential for maintaining a healthy and secure operating system.

One of the differences between a NAT instance and a NAT gateway is that the gateway is an AWS managed resource that offers enhanced bandwidth and availability when compared to that of a NAT instance. It always requires far less administrative configuration than that of a NAT instance. The following link shows a definitive difference between a NAT gateway and a NAT instance:

`https://docs.aws.amazon.com/vpc/latest/userguide/vpc-nat-comparison.html`

When deploying a NAT gateway, you will need to ensure you update the route tables of your private subnets that need to communicate with the gateway by adding a route **Destination** that points to the outside world of '`0.0.0.0/0`' with a **Target** of `Your_NAT_Gateway`. It's also important to remember that the route table of your public subnet where your NAT gateway is provisioned must also have a configured route to the internet via your IGW.

One final point on NAT is that, by design, any connections initiated from the internet will not reach your private subnets or instances.

Virtual private gateways

In addition to using the internet to gain access to your VPC via an IGW, you can also connect to it via a VPN connection from your own data center. This enables you to create a link between your own on-premises network and your VPC without using the public internet.

To do this, a "customer gateway" is configured at your own data center, which can either be a physical or software appliance. The other end of this customer gateway then connects a virtual private gateway, which is configured within your VPC in AWS. The VPN connection is then established between these two gateways.

A VPN connection is comprised of a dual connection, meaning there are two connections in place between the customer gateway and the virtual private gateway. This helps to establish a level of resiliency, should a connection problem occur affecting one of the lines.

It's very easy using the Wizard to create your VPC as all of these components that we just discussed will be created automatically, but you might want more control and management over how your VPC is configured. To do this, it is best to create your VPC from scratch and configure these components as you go, such as your route tables and NACLs. So let's try this out.

Building a multi-subnet VPC manually

Now you have a greater understanding of some of the key VPC components, let's build our very own VPC. This allows you to have full control and customization of how the VPC is configured, allowing you to optimize its design from an architectural and security standpoint.

This will encompass the following tasks:

- The creation of a new VPC
- The creation of two subnets, one public and one private across different Availability Zones
- The creation and configuration of an IGW and a NAT gateway
- The creation and configuration of new route tables, security groups, and NACLs
- The launch of instances in both subnets

By the end of this section, you will have built the following network infrastructure:

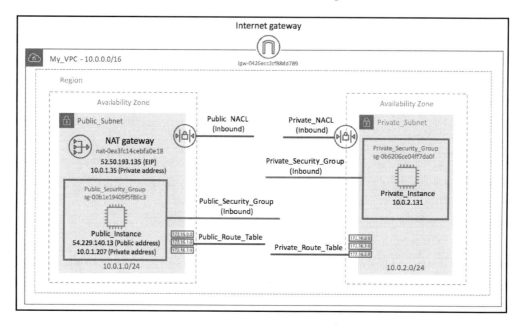

The corresponding rout tables can be seen in the image below:

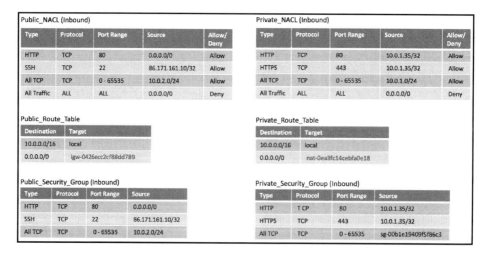

Although this diagram might look complicated, when it's broken down into the individual parts it's very easy to digest and understand as long as you have an understanding of the VPC components, which we have already discussed.

Creating a VPC

In this section, we are going to create a VPC from scratch without using a Wizard. This will allow us to customize every step of the creation process. The creation of the VPC is dependant on all other VPC components.

Execute the following steps to create a VPC:

1. From within the AWS Management Console, select the **VPC** service form within the **Networking and Content Delivery** category.
2. Select **Your VPCs** from the menu on the left and then select the blue **Create VPC** button:

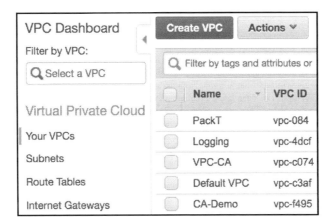

3. When prompted, enter the following VPC configuration details and then click the blue **Create** button:

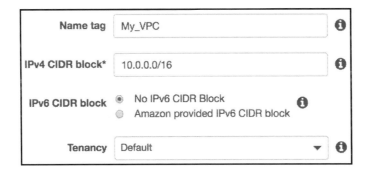

4. Acknowledge the confirmation of the VPC creation by selecting **Close**. Your VPC has now been created.

You may notice that under both the **Route Tables** and **Network ACLs** menus a new entry exists. This is the default main route table for your new VPC and the default NACL.

Now we have our VPC in place, we can now create our VPC subnets – both public and private.

Creating public and private VPCs

Execute the following steps to create public and private VPCs:

1. Select **Subnets** from the **VPC Dashboard** menu and then select the blue **Create subnet** button:

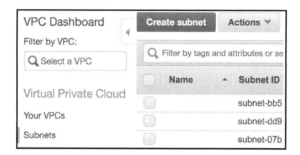

2. Configure the first subnet, which will become our public subnet, as shown in the following screenshot. Depending on your region, select the first availability zone within the region:

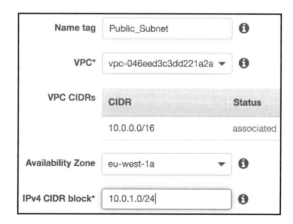

3. Select **Create**. Your subnet named `Public_Subnet` has now been created. Now you need to repeat that process for a second subnet, which will become our private subnet. Configure the second subnet as shown in the following figure. This time, select the second availability zone within the region:

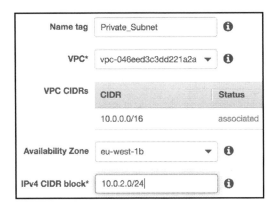

4. Once done, select **Create**. Your subnet named `Private_Subnet` has now been created.

Your infrastructure will now look as shown here:

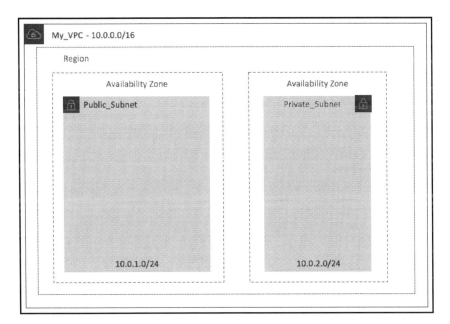

Now we have our VPC and subnets, and in particular, our `Public_Subnet` created, we can create and attach an IGW.

Creating an internet gateway

The IGW will provide a means of connecting our VPC to the internet. Execute the following steps to create an IGW:

1. Select **Internet Gateways** from the menu on the left of the console and then select the blue **Create Internet Gateway** button:

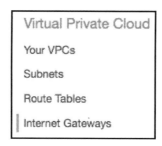

2. Enter a name for your IGW and select **Create**:

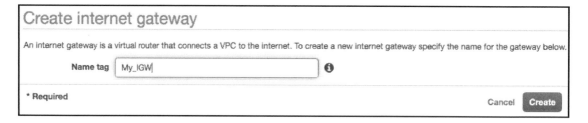

3. Your IGW will now be created. At this point, the status of the IGW is **detached** and that is because we have not attached it to our VPC as yet:

4. Select the IGW that you just created, select the **Actions** menu, and select **Attach to VPC**:

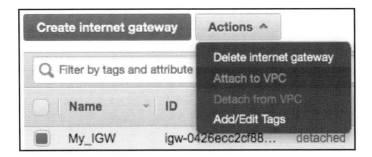

5. Select your newly created VPC from the drop-down list and click **Attach**:

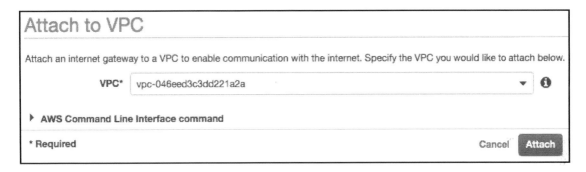

6. Your VPC now has an IGW attached:

However, no subnets currently have a route pointing to this IGW to access the internet. We are now going to create a new route table with a route pointing to the internet, which will go via the target of the IGW. This route table will then be associated with our `Public_Subnet`.

Creating a route table

We must create a route table to ensure that our subnets know how and where to route specific traffic. Execute the following steps to create a route table:

1. Select **Route Tables** from the menu on the left and click the blue **Create Route Table** button:

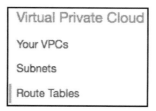

2. Configure the route table name as shown, select your VPC, and click **Create**:

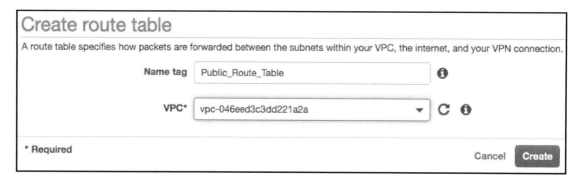

3. Select your new route table from the list of route tables shown. This will present you with the configuration options of the route table at the bottom of the screen (see the following screenshot).

4. Select the **Routes** tab, and you will see that it only has one route – the default local route that all route tables have, enabling all subnets to talk to each other:

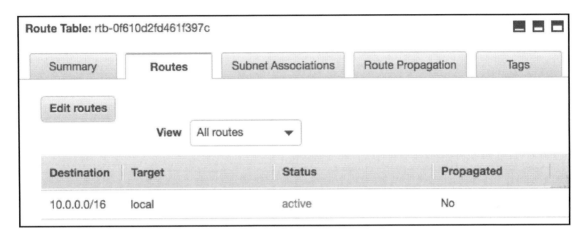

5. Select **Edit routes** in order to Add routes.
6. Add the configuration as shown in the **Destination** field of the second route and select your own IGW as the **Target**. This route sends all traffic without a known route to the IGW, which will then send it out to the internet. Once done, select **Save routes**:

7. Now select the **Subnet Associations** tab. You will notice that this route table does not have any subnet associations listed as we have just created this route table as a new route table. Select **Edit subnet associations**:

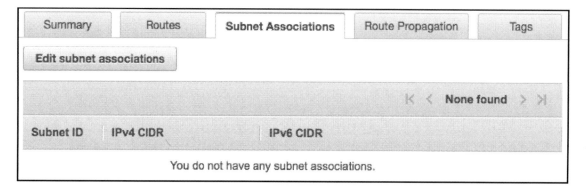

8. Select **Public_Subnet** and select **Save**:

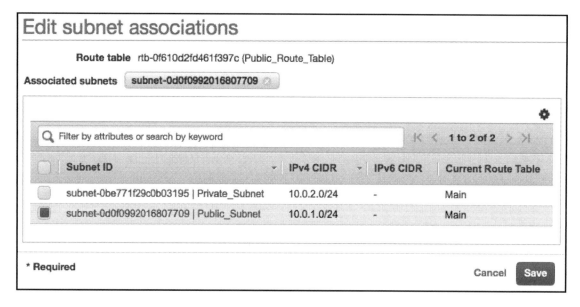

9. **Public_Subnet** is now associated with **Public_Route_Table**. This association now means that the **Public_Subnet** knows how to route internet traffic to the internet, which is via the IGW, as identified in **Public_Route_Table**:

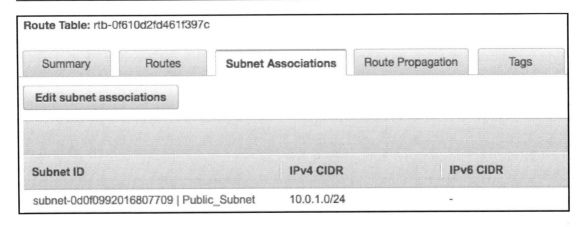

As a recap, your infrastructure will now look as shown here:

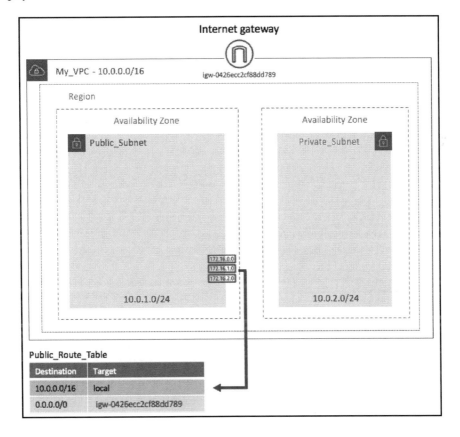

We now have an IGW attached to the VPC and a new route table associated with our public subnet with a route to the IGW for internet traffic. Now this configuration is in place, our **Public_Subnet** now has a direct link to the internet, with a route of how to get there.

Creating a NAT gateway

A NAT gateway allows instances in a private subnet to initiate a connection to the internet, for example, for essential operating system updates, but it prevents any inbound access to the private subnet being initiated from the internet.

Now it's time to create our NAT gateway:

1. Select **NAT Gateways** from the **VPC Dashboard** menu on the left and select the blue **Create NAT Gateway** button:

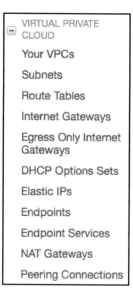

2. Configure the NAT gateway by selecting '**Public_Subnet**' for the subnet and then select the **Create New EIP** button to populate **Elastic IP Allocation** ID. A NAT gateway uses **Elastic IP (EIP)** addresses for its addressing:

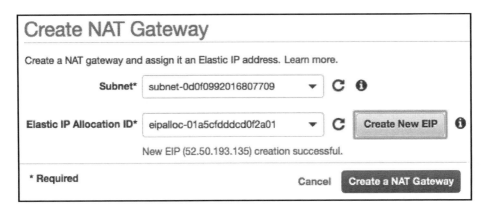

3. Select **Create a NAT Gateway** and then select **Close** to go to the confirmation message.

Your NAT gateway will now be deployed within your **Public_Subnet** using an EIP.

Creating security groups in our subnets

To recap from earlier, security groups provide a virtual firewall level of protection at the instance level. Security groups are associated with instances rather than subnets and control the traffic to and from your instances within your VPC. So let's create security groups for our instances.

For instances in your 'Public_Subnet'

To create a security group for instances in your public subnet, follow these steps:

1. From within the EC2 console, select **Security Group** on the menu on the left and select the blue **Create Security Group** button.
2. Configure the security group as shown here:

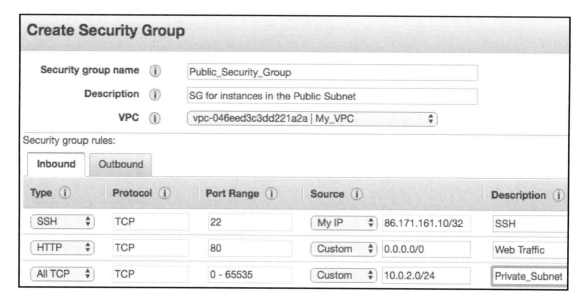

3. We will leave the outbound rules as the default and select **Create**.

This security group allows my own IP address inbound SSH connectivity as well as allowing inbound HTTP traffic from the internet and all TCP communications from **Private_Subnet**.

For Instances in your Private_Subnet

To create a security group for instances in your private subnet, follow these steps:

1. From within the EC2 console, select **Security Group** on the menu on the left and select the blue **Create Security Group** button.
2. Configure the security group as shown here:

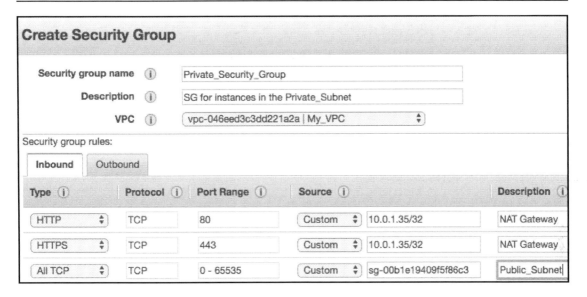

3. For the first and second rule, use the private IP address of your NAT gateway. For the third rule, use the security group ID of the **Public_Security_Group** you created in the previous step.

4. Leave the outbound rules as the default and select **Create**.

This security group allows HTTP and HTTPS inbound from the NAT gateway. This will allow any instances in the private subnet to be able to update their OS (once a route has been provisioned). This security group also allows all TCP traffic from **Public_Security_Group**.

Now our security groups are configured, we can create our EC2 instances and associate these security groups to our instances.

Creating EC2 instances in our subnets

We can now create an EC2 instance in each of our subnets – both the public and private subnets – and associate the security groups that we just created.

Creating E2C instances in the Private_Subnet

To create E2C instances in the private subnet, follow these steps:

1. Select an Amazon Linux AMI.
2. Create a `t2.micro` instance within your **My_VPC** and **Private_Subnet**.
3. Add a **Tag** of `Name` with a **Value** of `Private_Instance`.
4. Select the **Private_Security_Group** security group when prompted to select a security group in *step 6*.
5. Accept all other defaults.
6. Download a new key pair.

We'll now follow the same process for our public subnet.

Creating E2C instances in the Public_Subnet

To create E2C instances in the public subnet, follow these steps:

1. Select an Amazon Linux AMI.
2. Create a `t2.micro` instance within your **My_VPC** and **Public_Subnet**.
3. Select the **Auto-assign Public IP** option as **Enable**.
4. Add a **Tag** of `Name` with a **Value** of `Public_Instance`.
5. Select the **Public_Security_Group** security group when prompted to select a security group at *step 6*.
6. Accept all other defaults.
7. Download a new key pair.

With our EC2 instances created, our next step is to create a route table for our private subnet.

Creating a route table for Private_Subnet

We must now create our route table for the private subnet to ensure the private instance knows how to get to the internet via the NAT gateway:

1. Navigate to the **VPC** service under the **Networking & Content Delivery** category:

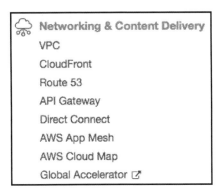

2. Select **Route Tables** from the menu on the left and click the blue **Create Route Table** button.
3. Configure the route table name as shown, select your VPC, and click **Create**:

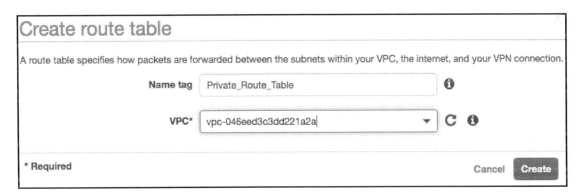

4. Now select your new route table from the list of route tables that will be shown. This will present you with the configuration options of the route table at the bottom of the screen.
5. Select the **Routes** tab | **Edit routes** | **Add routes**.

6. Add the configuration as shown in the **Destination** field of the second route and select your newly created NAT gateway as the target. This route sends all traffic without a known route to the NAT gateway, which will then send it out to the internet. Once done, click on **Save routes**:

7. Now select **Edit subnet associations**.
8. Select **Private_Subnet** and select **Save**:

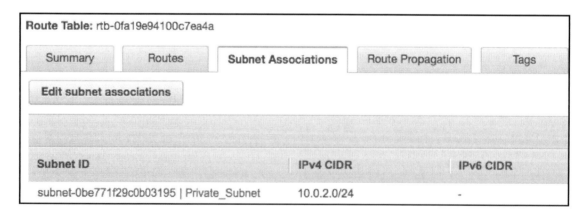

Our infrastructure is now configured as shown:

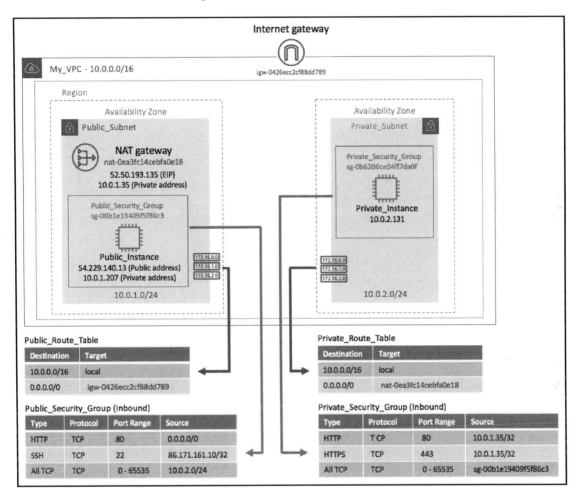

As you can see, we have created our VPC, and the two subnets (public and private). We have attached our IGW and created route tables for each subnet and added the appropriate routes to get to the IGW and the NAT gateway. We have also configured our security groups and associated them with our EC2 instances.

Finally, I want to create a new NACL for each subnet as they are currently using the default NACL when the VPC was created, which allows all traffic through – this is not best practice.

Creating an NACL for our subnets

Using the default NACL of your VPC provides no security protection whatsoever. It allows *all* network traffic, both inbound and outbound. As a result, we need to create new NACLs and configure them to restrict only the network traffic we want to allow.

Creating an NACL for the public subnet

To create an NACL for the public subnet, follow these steps:

1. Navigate to the **VPC** service within the Management Console.
2. Select **Network ACLs** from the menu on the left and select the blue **Create network ACL** button.
3. Configure the NACL as shown in the following screenshot by selecting your VPC:

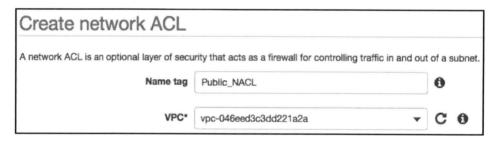

4. Now select the newly created NACL in the list that appears and it will display its configuration at the bottom of the screen.
5. Select the **Inbound Rules** tab. By default, a newly created NACL will **DENY** all traffic:

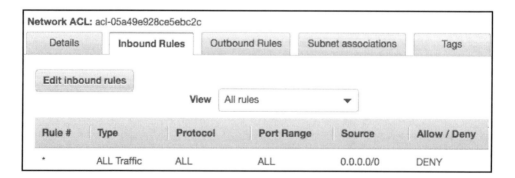

6. Select **Edit inbound rules** and configure the NACL as shown here:

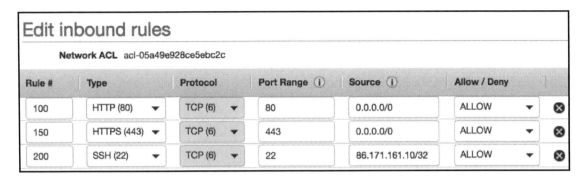

7. Click **Create**. By default, an explicit **DENY** will be added at the bottom of the NACL when you click **Create**, as shown here:

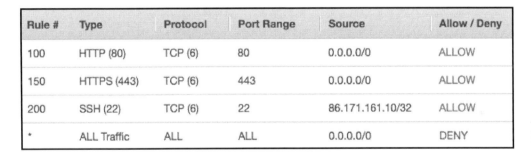

Rule #	Type	Protocol	Port Range	Source	Allow / Deny
100	HTTP (80)	TCP (6)	80	0.0.0.0/0	ALLOW
150	HTTPS (443)	TCP (6)	443	0.0.0.0/0	ALLOW
200	SSH (22)	TCP (6)	22	86.171.161.10/32	ALLOW
*	ALL Traffic	ALL	ALL	0.0.0.0/0	DENY

8. Select the **Outbound Rules** tab and configure the outbound rules as shown here. Once done, select **Create**:

9. Much like the route tables, we now need to associate this NACL with a subnet. Select the **Subnet Associations** tab | **Edit subnet associations**. Select **Public_Subnet** and click on **Edit**:

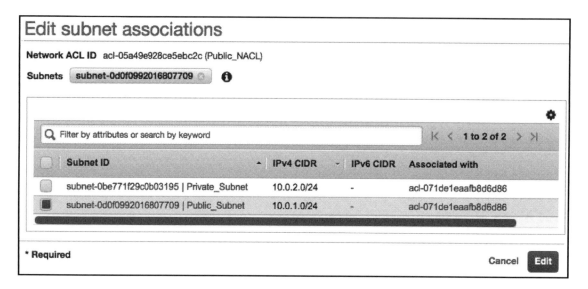

This NACL is now associated with your **Public_Subnet** rather than the default NACL that was created when the VPC was first created. This prevents any traffic from entering the public subnet that isn't using either HTTP or HTTPS.

Create an NACL for the private Subnet

To create an NACL for the private subnet, follow these steps:

1. Navigate to the **VPC** service within the Management Console.
2. Select **Network ACLs** from the menu on the left and select the blue **Create network ACL** button.

3. Configure the NACL as shown in the following screenshot by selecting your VPC:

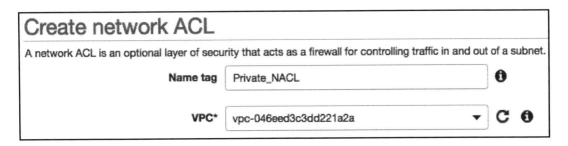

4. Select the newly created NACL from the list and it will display its configuration at the bottom of the screen.
5. Select the **Inbound Rules** tab | **Edit inbound rules** and configure the NACL as shown in the following screenshot. Once done, click on **Create**:

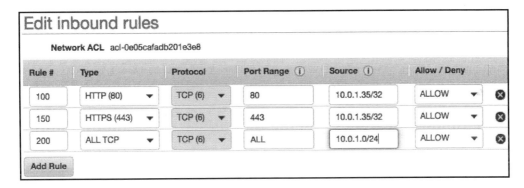

6. Now go to the **Outbound Rules** tab and configure the outbound rules as shown in the following screenshot. Once done, select **Create**:

7. Now, just like we did for the public subnet, select the **Subnet Associations** tab | **Edit subnet associations**. Select **Private_Subnet** and click on **Edit**.

This NACL is now associated with your **Private_Subnet**. That is now all of the configuration required for this scenario, and as a result, your infrastructure will now look as follows:

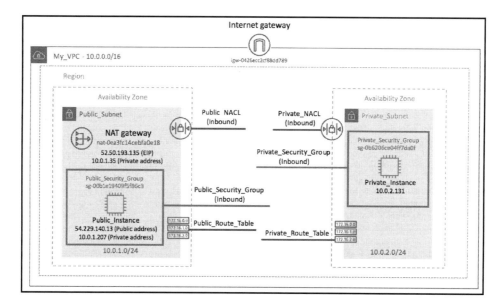

The corresponding rout tables can be seen in the image below:

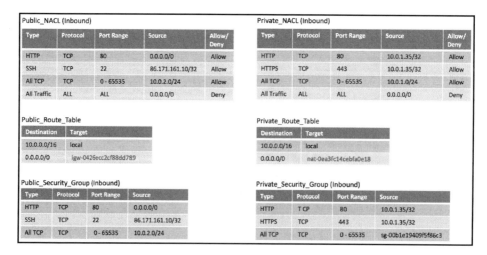

Public_NACL (Inbound)

Type	Protocol	Port Range	Source	Allow/Deny
HTTP	TCP	80	0.0.0.0/0	Allow
SSH	TCP	22	86.171.161.10/32	Allow
All TCP	TCP	0 - 65535	10.0.2.0/24	Allow
All Traffic	ALL	ALL	0.0.0.0/0	Deny

Private_NACL (Inbound)

Type	Protocol	Port Range	Source	Allow/Deny
HTTP	TCP	80	10.0.1.35/32	Allow
HTTPS	TCP	443	10.0.1.35/32	Allow
All TCP	TCP	0 - 65535	10.0.1.0/24	Allow
All Traffic	ALL	ALL	0.0.0.0/0	Deny

Public_Route_Table

Destination	Target
10.0.0.0/16	local
0.0.0.0/0	igw-0426ecc2cf88dd789

Private_Route_Table

Destination	Target
10.0.0.0/16	local
0.0.0.0/0	nat-0ea3fc14cebfa0e18

Public_Security_Group (Inbound)

Type	Protocol	Port Range	Source
HTTP	TCP	80	0.0.0.0/0
SSH	TCP	22	86.171.161.10/32
All TCP	TCP	0 - 65535	10.0.2.0/24

Private_Security_Group (Inbound)

Type	Protocol	Port Range	Source
HTTP	TCP	80	10.0.1.35/32
HTTPS	TCP	443	10.0.1.35/32
All TCP	TCP	0 - 65535	sg-00b1e19409f5f86c3

This infrastructure allows the following:

- SSH connectivity from your own client to Public_Instance, through the use of Public_NACL and Public_Security_Group, allowing SSH from your IP address only, as well as the IGW and Public_Route_Table to allow outside connectivity to your VPC.
- Public_Instance can communicate with the internet, receiving HTTP traffic only as specified in Public_Security_Group, despite HTTPS being open on Public_NACL.
- Public_Instance can communicate with any instance within Private_Subnet using TCP, as detailed in the NACLs and security groups.
- Private_Instance can perform OS updates using the NAT gateway with its associated Private_Route_Table and Private_Security_Group.

Now we have completed our VPC build with our networking components, we can be confident that we have applied a certain level of security to help protect our infrastructure. Our EC2 instances are protected by security groups with set protocols and ports. These instances are also isolated within their own subnets, which are protected by NACLs and their own route table, directing network traffic to where we want it to go, via the IGW or the NAT gateway. So, we have put effective measures in place to allow only certain traffic to be allowed to and from specific resources.

Summary

This chapter focused heavily on the VPC and how the different components of this infrastructure can come together to restrict and control access both at a network- and instance-level through the use of **Network Access Control Lists** (**NACLs**) and security groups. It also covered how segmenting a network can also prevent unauthorized access through layered network protection by keeping some subnets private and some public.

A VPN acts as a base for your resources that can be deployed across different regions and Availability Zones, and so understanding where you can control access and how is fundamental in ensuring its protection. All rules added to NACLs and security groups, as well as rules added to route tables should be refined and as detailed as possible in line with the **principle of least privilege** (**PoLP**).

In the next chapter, we are going to look at how we can protect our web applications through the use of AWS Web Application Firewall, Elastic Load Balancers, and AWS API Gateway.

Questions

As we conclude this chapter, here is a list of questions for you to test your knowledge regarding its material. You will find the answers in the *Assessments* section of the *Appendix*:

1. What does VPC stand for?
2. Which VPC component provides a connection between your VPC and the outside world?
3. Which VPC component allows instances in a private subnet to initiate a connection to the internet, for example, for essential operating system updates, but prevents any inbound access to the private subnet being initiated from the internet?
4. True or false: Security groups provide a virtual firewall level of protection at the instance level.
5. True or false: Using the default NACL of your VPC provides enhanced security protection blocking *all* network traffic, both inbound and outbound.

Further reading

Consult the following AWS whitepapers for more information:

- Building a Scalable and Secure Multi-VPC AWS Network Infrastructure: https://d1.awsstatic.com/whitepapers/building-a-scalable-and-secure-multi-vpc-aws-network-infrastructure.pdf
- Extend your IT Infrastructure with Amazon Virtual Private Cloud: https://d1.awsstatic.com/whitepapers/extend-your-it-infrastructure-with-amazon-vpc.pdf

8
Implementing Application Security

A huge amount of effort goes into developing your web applications and services on AWS and they are often a target of intrusion attacks looking for weaknesses and vulnerabilities. To minimize and mitigate these threats, you must be able to implement solutions using different AWS services to help protect your application from being compromised. This is exactly what we will be doing in this chapter.

In this chapter, we will look at how to create a web **access control list (ACL)** using the AWS Web Application Firewall service, in addition to how you can set up, configure, and create firewall access policies using Firewall Manager.

This chapter will focus on the following:

- Exploring AWS **Web Application Firewall (WAF)**
- Managing the security configuration of your **Elastic Load Balancers (ELBs)**
- Securing APIs with AWS API Gateway

Technical requirements

To complete the exercises in this chapter, you will require the following:

- Access to an AWS account
- Permissions to configure services within AWS WAF
- A CloudFront distribution configured to be used only for testing
- Access to create and manage ELBs
- Access to AWS Certificate Manager

More information on how to assign and grant permissions can be found in Chapter 4, *Working with Access Policies*.

Exploring AWS Web WAF

The main function of the AWS WAF service is to provide protection for your web applications from malicious attacks from a wide variety of attack patterns, many of which correspond to the OWASP top 10. AWS WAF is used in conjunction with Amazon CloudFront and its distributions, the Application Load Balancer, or API Gateway to analyze requests over HTTP or HTTPS to help distinguish between harmful and legitimate requests to your applications and site. AWS WAF will then block and restrict access that is detected as forbidden.

I just mentioned OWASP in the previous paragraph, and for those who are unfamiliar with what or who that is, let me briefly explain.

As we know, there are a huge amount of security vulnerabilities embedded in applications of all sorts, and it's important that we identify and assess the risks of potential exposure to allow us to resolve these weak points as soon as they are identified. The **Open Web Applications Security Project (OWASP)**, https://www.owasp.org/, is a not-for-profit organization that helps the industry to improve security in software for all to benefit from.

The OWASP also provides a top-10 list, which is often updated, of the most critical security risks around application architecture facing enterprises worldwide. At the time of publication, this list includes the following:

- Injections
- Broken authentication and session management
- **Cross-site scripting (XSS)**
- Insecure direct object references
- Security misconfiguration
- Sensitive data exposure
- Missing function-level access control
- **Cross-site request forgery (CSRF)**
- Using known vulnerable components
- Unvalidated redirects and forwards

 For an up-to-date list, please visit `https://www.owasp.org/index.php/Category:OWASP_Top_Ten_Project`.

Going back to AWS WAF, to understand how it offers protection against these security risks, we need to look at the components involved in its design. There are three primary elements:

- **Web ACL**: Also known as a web ACL, this is used to provide protection for your AWS resources, as we shall see going forward in this chapter. They contain rules and rule groups, which are used to define what should be inspected within your requests.
- **Rules**: The rules themselves are essentially comprised of if/then statements and help to define specific criteria for what the web ACL should be inspecting, and what action (allow/block/count) to take upon the result of that inspection.
- **Rule groups**: Rule groups simply allow you to group a set of rules together.

In order to make this more clear, let me show you how to create a web ACL. During this process, we shall cover rules and rule groups to explain how each of these combine together to provide the protection given.

Creating a web ACL

To start with, we need to create a web ACL, which, during its configuration, comprises five steps. Follow along:

1. From within your AWS Management Console, select **WAF & Shield** from the **Security, Identity, & Compliance** category:

2. Select the **Create web ACL** button:

This will then take you to the first page of the creation of the web ACL. The configuration itself comprises five steps:

1. Describe the web ACL and associate it with AWS resources.
2. Add rules and rule groups.
3. Set rule priority.
4. Configure metrics.
5. Review and create the web ACL.

Let's complete these steps in an orderly fashion.

Step 1 – Describing the web ACL and associating it with AWS resources

In this step, we need to provide some basic information when we create the web ACL. Let's take a look:

1. On the **Describe Web ACL and associate it to AWS resources** page, you will be asked to enter the first part of your configuration information, as well as to select the resources you'd like the web ACL to protect. Fill out the details as shown in the following screenshot. For this walk-through, I have selected CloudFront by selecting the **Global (CloudFront)** option in the **Region** list. The CloudWatch metric name is automatically created when you create a new web ACL:

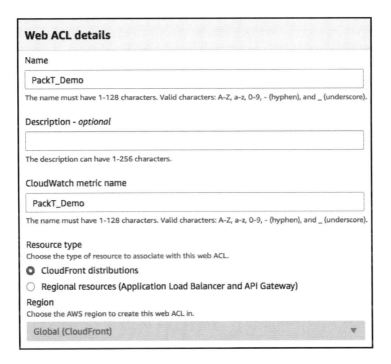

If you needed to select either an Application Load Balancer or API Gateway as a resource, you could select a specific region from the **Region** list and then select your resource from the **Associated AWS resource** section further down the page.

2. Next, you will need to associate your resources with this web ACL:

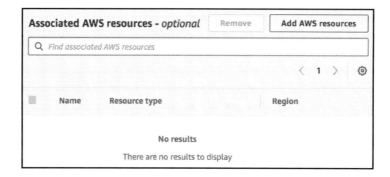

3. Select the **Add AWS resources** button. This will present you with the following screen. Select a CloudFront distribution that you would like to associate and click **Add**:

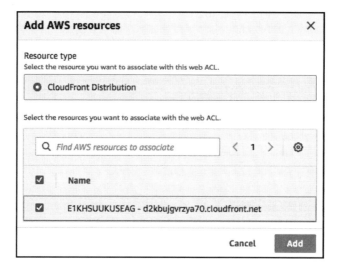

 You will need to select your own CloudFront distribution from the list. For this demonstration, I have created a test distribution that is not used for production services.

4. Your resource will now be shown as associated. Click the **Next** button at the bottom of the page:

You will now be on the next step, where you can add rules and rule groups.

Step 2 – Adding rules and rule groups

In this section, we are going to focus on rules and rule groups for the web ACL:

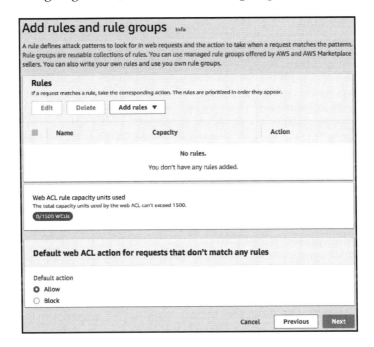

As you can see, there are three different sections here. Firstly, the rules themselves. To add a rule, do the following:

1. Select **Add rules**:

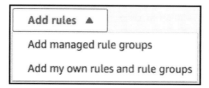

This will give you two options:

- **Add managed rule groups**: Selecting this option allows you to select pre-built rule groups with preconfigured rules.
- **Add my own rules and rule groups**: This option allows you to build your own rules and rule groups.

2. For the sake of this demonstration, select **Add managed rule groups**. This will provide you with a list of managed rule groups. The AWS managed rule groups are free to use; all other options are available through AWS Marketplace at a cost:

3. Select the AWS managed groups. This will provide you with a list of managed rule groups – far more than you see here in this screenshot:

▼ **AWS managed rule groups**		
Name	**Capacity**	**Action**
Admin protection Contains rules that allow you to block external access to exposed admin pages. This may be useful if you are running third-party software or would like to reduce the risk of a malicious actor gaining administrative access to your application.	100	⬤ Add to web ACL
Amazon IP reputation list This group contains rules that are based on Amazon threat intelligence. This is useful if you would like to block sources associated with bots or other threats.	25	⬤ Add to web ACL
Anonymous IP list This group contains rules that allow you to block requests from services that allow obfuscation of viewer identity. This can include request originating from VPN, proxies, Tor nodes, and hosting providers. This is useful if you want to filter out viewers that may be trying to hide their identity from your application.	50	⬤ Add to web ACL
Core rule set Contains rules that are generally applicable to web applications. This provides protection against exploitation of a wide range of vulnerabilities, including those described in OWASP publications.	700	⬤ Add to web ACL

4. Scroll down the list and select the **Add to web ACL** button for the following rule groups:
   - **Amazon IP reputation list**
   - **Core rule set**

An explanation of what these rule groups protect against can be seen in their description. The **Capacity** column that you see here relates to the number of web ACL rule capacity units used for that rule. I'll focus more on this metric shortly.

5. Select the **Add rules** button. You will now see these managed rule groups within your configuration:

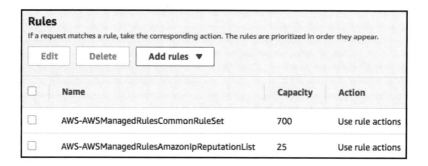

 Note that it is not possible to edit the rules of managed rule groups.

6. Under your newly added rule groups, you will see your **web ACL rule capacity units (WCUs)**:

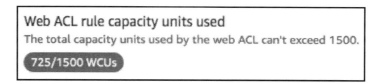

As you can see, this is the sum of our managed rules that we added (725). Web ACLs use rule capacity units to determine the maximum amount of rule configurations used on a single web ACL. Currently, this is defined as 1,500 WCUs. The complexity of each rule and rule group will affect the number of WCUs.

7. Finally, you need to determine the actions against any requests that do not match any defined rules. **Allow** will simply allow the traffic to pass through as a trusted request. **Block** will block the request and prevent it from reaching its destination. As I have selected rule groups that are looking to block bad traffic, I will **Allow** any traffic that doesn't match these rules to pass through as trusted traffic:

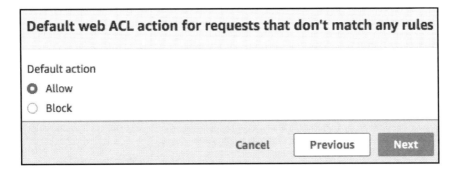

8. Finally, click **Next**.

We have now created our rule groups, which give the web ACL instructions on what to inspect and what action to take. Let's now take a look at setting rule priority.

Step 3 – Setting rule priority

This step allows you to adjust the order of your rules as they are executed by your web ACL. It is important to note that WAF rules are executed in the order that they appear within a web ACL, and as soon as a match is found, no other rules are checked for that request. So, ensure you set these rules in the correct order to filter your requests appropriately. A common method of high-level management is to list them in order of the following:

1. WhiteListed IPs – **Allow**
2. BlackListed IPs – **Block**
3. Bad Signatures – **Block**

WhiteListed IP addresses are IP addresses that are trusted and allowed to communicate with your associated resource. BlackListed IP addresses are addresses that have been defined as malicious or bad and are therefore explicitly blocked. Finally, bad signatures relate to any rules that meet other conditions, such as other attack patterns.

To adjust the order of your rules, follow these two simple steps:

1. Select the rule and then select either the **Move up** or **Move down** button:

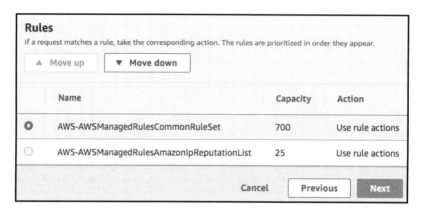

2. Click **Next**.

Great! The rules are now ordered as per your preference. Let's move on to our next step.

Step 4 – Configuring metrics

In this step, you can create and configure Amazon CloudWatch metrics against your rules and rule groups that you selected in *step 2*. By default, it will add in the metric names, but you can change them as necessary. The default names in our case can be seen in the following screenshot:

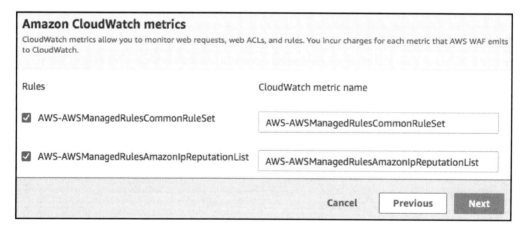

These metrics can be used to help you monitor the number of web requests, web ACLs, and rules that you have within your environment. Understanding how your web ACLs are managing traffic and to what extent can be useful in understanding how much traffic you are receiving and from where.

Make any name changes to new metrics as necessary. Alternatively, if you do not want to create CloudWatch metrics for your rules/rule groups, you can deselect the checkbox. Once done, click **Next**.

Step 5 – Reviewing and creating the web ACL

This section allows you to review your choices from the previous four steps before creating your web ACL. Once you click on the **Next** button (seen in step 4), you will arrive at the following screen, presented in four different steps (I have broken down the screenshot here to focus on each step separately).

This screenshot provides us with a summary of the selections we made in step 1:

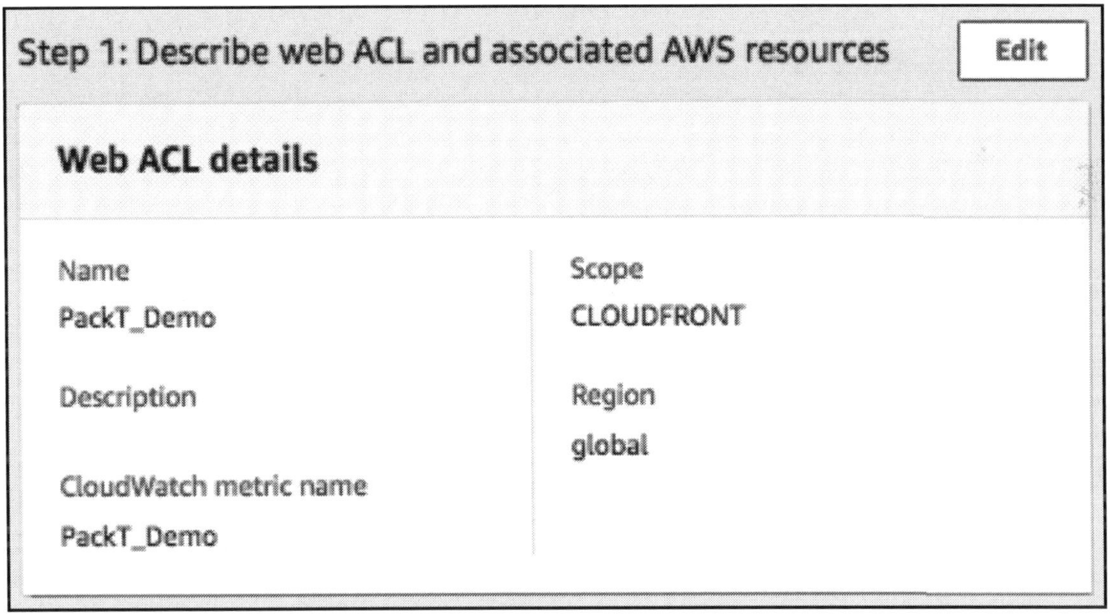

This screenshot provides us with a summary of the selections we made in steps 2 and 3:

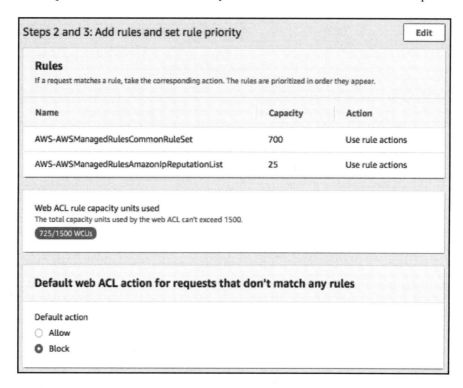

Finally, here is a summary of the choices we made for step 4:

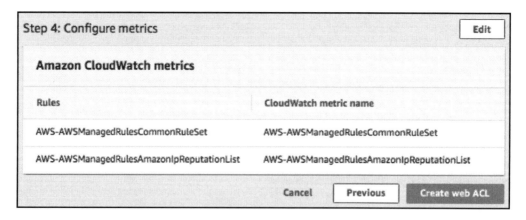

When you are happy with your configuration, click **Create web ACL** and your web ACL will then appear on the dashboard of your WAF console:

Your web ACL is now associated with your CloudFront distribution and is providing additional protection to your infrastructure. Now, every time a request is received by your CloudFront distribution, that web request will be processed by your newly configured AWS WAF web ACL, with the rules and rule groups that you configured, which will provide an enhanced level of protection for your web apps by only allowing traffic that has been deemed trustworthy.

Using AWS Firewall Manager

AWS Firewall Manager is closely linked with AWS WAF and is accessed from within the same dashboard within the AWS Management Console. AWS Firewall Manager allows you to manage WAF rules across a multi-account environment when using AWS Organizations.

 For more information on AWS Organizations, see the following link:
`https://aws.amazon.com/organizations/`.

If, for example, you had a number of CloudFront distributions across multiple accounts, it would be administratively heavy if you had to create your rules within each AWS account where you wanted to utilize the benefits of AWS WAF. Instead, with AWS Firewall Manager, you can centrally organize and manage your AWS WAF rulesets from a single console. One key benefit of the service is that it will protect your resources automatically as and when they are provisioned.

To enable you to utilize AWS Firewall Manager, you need to carry out a number of steps first. These include the following:

1. Adding your AWS account to an AWS organization
2. Selecting an AWS account to act as a primary account
3. Enabling AWS Config on all accounts you want to administer

Let's complete these steps one by one.

Adding your AWS account to an AWS organization

You must first add your AWS account to an AWS organization that has *all* features enabled (not just consolidated billing). The AWS organization account owner will need to invite you to join the organization, at which point, you can choose to accept the invitation from the AWS organization dashboard within the AWS Management Console. Alternatively, you could set up the AWS organization yourself on your own account.

For more information on how to add your account to an AWS organization, please see the following link: https://docs.aws.amazon.com/organizations/latest/userguide/orgs_tutorials_basic.html.

Selecting your primary account to act as the Firewall Manager administrative account

The organization's master account must delegate which AWS account within the organization will become the administrator account for Firewall Manager. To do this, you can follow these steps:

1. From within the AWS Management Console of the organization master, select **AWS Firewall Manager** under the **Security, Identity, & Compliance** category:

Security, Identity, & Compliance

IAM

Resource Access Manager

Cognito

Secrets Manager

GuardDuty

Inspector

Amazon Macie ↗

AWS Single Sign-On

Certificate Manager

Key Management Service

CloudHSM

Directory Service

WAF & Shield

AWS Firewall Manager

Artifact

Security Hub

Detective

2. Select **Getting started** under the **AWS Firewall Manager** option in the menu on the left:

 AWS Firewall Manager

Getting started

Security policies

Settings

You will see a list of the prerequisites I mentioned previously:

Prerequisites for using AWS Firewall Manager

⊘ **This account must be part of AWS Organization**
Your AWS account must be in an organization in AWS Organization, and the organization must have all features enable (not just consolidated billing).

⚠ **This account must be set as AWS Firewall Manager administrator**
Only the AWS account set as AWS Firewall Manager administrator account can configure security policies. The master account in your AWS Organization can designate this account as Firewall Manager administrator account.

AWS Config must be enabled in every account you want to protect resources using AWS Firewall Manager
You must enable WAF Config for each member account in your organization in AWS Organizations and for each AWS Region that contains the resources that you want to protect using AWS Firewall Manager security policies.

3. Select **Get started**:

Get started with AWS Firewall Manager

To get started designate an account in your organization as AWS Firewall Manager Administrator account.

Get started

4. Enter the AWS account ID (a 12-digit number) that you want to designate as the AWS Firewall Manager administrative account, and then click **Set administrator account**:

Set Firewall Manager administrator account

AWS Firewall Manager administrator account

To use AWS Firewall Manager, you need to set an account in your AWS Organization as the AWS Firewall Manager administrator account. The administrator account will be able to create and manage AWS WAF rules, security group, Shield Advanced across all accounts within the organization. This administrator can be either the AWS Organization master account, or a member account in the organization.

Administrator account ID
Enter the AWS account that you want to set as Firewall Manager administrator

730739171055

Cancel   **Set administrator account**

5. You will then see a message stating that is has been successfully set:

⊘ **Successfully set the AWS Firewall Manager administrator account.**
It may take some time to propagate the changes to in your organization. Please check Settings page after a few minutes.

It is worth noting that to set a different administrator, the current administrator must go to AWS Firewall Manager settings and remove their account as the administrator before the AWS organization owner can designate a new account.

Next, we need to enable AWS Config.

Enabling AWS Config

For instructions on how to enable and configure AWS Config within your account, please refer to Chapter 13, *Auditing and Governance*. AWS Config allows you to review, assess, and audit the configurations of your resources across your AWS account, including relationships between resources, configuration history, and compliance.

Once you have completed all the prerequisites of enabling the AWS Firewall Manager service, you can then create and apply an AWS Firewall Manager AWS WAF policy.

Creating and applying an AWS WAF policy to AWS Firewall Manager

These policies contain rule groups much as we discussed earlier when configuring our web ACL. In our example earlier, we used third-party rule groups, which provide a number of benefits over creating your own, such as the following:

- A reduction in the time it takes to configure and deploy. The rule groups are already built by both AWS-approved partners and AWS themselves.
- Depending on the rule group, they could help you to meet compliance controls that might be required for HIPAA or PCI.
- Some of them have been carefully curated to help mitigate against known vulnerabilities, such as those listed by the OWASP top 10. This is a great help to many organizations that might not have the skills in-house to put together rule groups that can achieve this level of security.

Now let's see how to create and apply a WAF policy to AWS Firewall Manager. Follow these steps:

1. From within the AWS Firewall Manager console, select **Security policies** from the menu on the left:

2. Select **Create policy**:

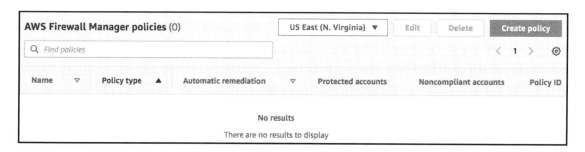

3. You will now have a five-step process to follow. These steps include the following:

    1. Choose the policy type and region.

    2. Describe the policy.

    3. Define the policy type.

    4. Configure policy tags.

    5. Review and create the policy:

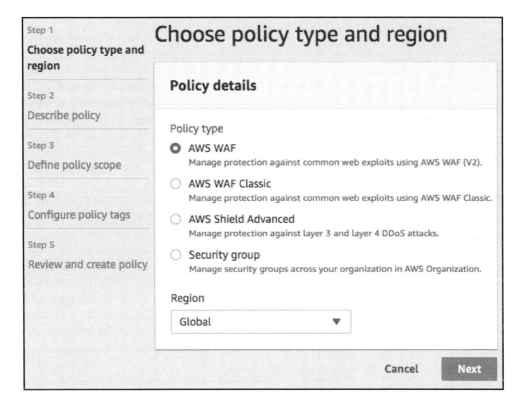

4. The first step is **Choose policy type and region**. In the preceding example, I have already selected **AWS WAF** and the **Global** region. Select **Next** to move on to **Step 2 -Describe policy**.

5. Add a name for the policy:

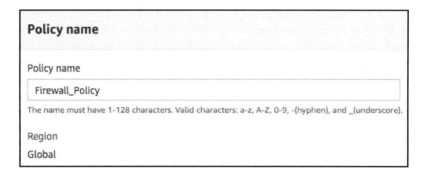

6. Next, you need to add the rule groups that you would like Firewall Manager to enforce across the different accounts in the AWS organization. You can select your own rule groups that you might have created within AWS WAF, or select from a list of predefined rule groups:

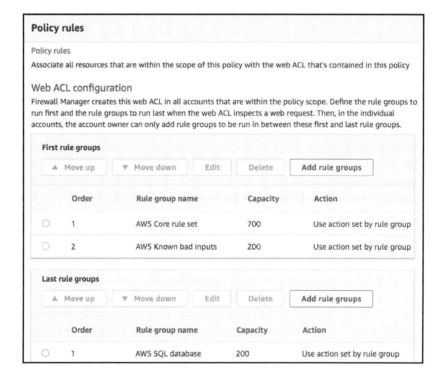

As you can see, there are two sections, **First rule groups** and **Last rule groups**. Any rule groups that are selected within **First rule groups** are run across all accounts associated with the web ACL that is being created *before* any account-specific rule groups are run. Additionally, any rule groups that are selected within **Last rule groups** will be run *after* any account-specific rule groups. In this example, I have selected **2** to be run first and **1** to be run last.

You can add your rule groups in the same way as we did when we configured them for AWS WAF.

7. We then need to determine a default action to be taken for any requests that do not match any of the rules selected. In this example, I have selected **Allow** for trusted traffic to pass through:

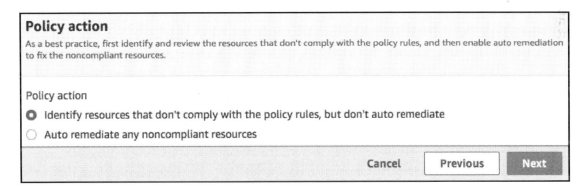

8. Finally, you must select a policy action. For this demonstration, I have selected the default option:

Policy action

As a best practice, first identify and review the resources that don't comply with the policy rules, and then enable auto remediation to fix the noncompliant resources.

Policy action

⦿ Identify resources that don't comply with the policy rules, but don't auto remediate

◯ Auto remediate any noncompliant resources

Cancel   Previous   Next

This default option creates a web ACL in each associated account within the organization; however, it will not apply the web ACL to any resources at that point. Alternatively, you could choose **Auto remediate any noncompliance resources** to automatically apply the new policy to all associated AWS accounts in the organization.

9. Select **Next** to move on to step 3 - **Define policy scope**:

Define policy scope

Policy scope

Policy scope defines the accounts and resources where you want to apply the web ACL.

AWS accounts this policy applies to

- ⦿ Include all accounts under my AWS organization
- ◯ Include only the specified accounts and organizational units
- ◯ Exclude the specified accounts and organizational units, and include all others

Resource type

- ☑ CloudFront distribution

Resources

- ⦿ Include all resources that match the selected resource type
- ◯ Include only resources that have all the specified resource tags
- ◯ Exclude resources that have all the specified resource tags, and include all other resources

Cancel   Previous   Next

Here, you can select which accounts within the organization this firewall policy should be applied to, in addition to specifying which resources should be included/excluded. Use the appropriate options to configure the policy as you need. For this example, I have selected the defaults as shown.

10. Click **Next** to move onto step 4: **Configure policy tags**:

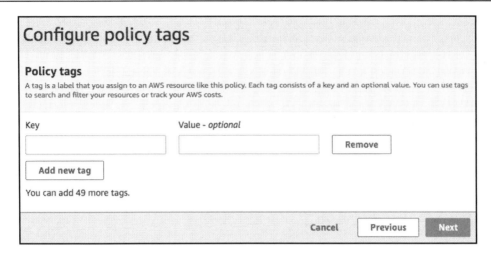

11. Add any tags that you require as needed and click **Next** to move onto step 5: **Review and create policy**. This will show you all of the configuration changes you made in the previous steps, 1 through 4.

> Beware: If you create the policy, it will cost you $100. If you do not want to create the policy, click **Cancel**.

12. If you do want to proceed, then you can select **Create policy**.

To summarize, AWS Firewall Manager uses AWS WAF rules that are grouped together within a rule group. These rule groups are then added to an AWS Firewall Manager policy, which in turn is associated with a different account within your AWS organization.

So far, we have covered application security using AWS WAF and Firewall Manager. Let's look at how we can also offer application protection via ELBs.

Managing the security configuration of your ELBs

ELBs are seen as a fundamental component of AWS architecture when implementing solutions to automatically scale and manage requests put upon your applications and services.

ELBs are essentially used to control, manage, and distribute incoming requests to a specified resource group, therefore load balancing these requests across a fleet of designated EC2 instances, containers, Lambda functions, or IP addresses. How you architect the placement of your targets within your resource groups is down to you, but by utilizing multiple **Availability Zones** (**AZs**) will certainly help to increase the level of resiliency of your solutions should a failure occur within a specific AZ. Best practice dictates that you should architect your solutions making full use of the AWS global infrastructure.

Before we delve deeper into the topic of ELBs, let's first understand the types.

Types of AWS ELBs

At the time of writing this book, there are three different variants of the AWS ELB that you can select and configure. Understanding the differences between them will help you select the correct ELB for your needs. They are as follows:

- **Application Load Balancer**: This is typically used to support the incoming traffic destined for your web applications when running the HTTP or HTTPS protocols. It offers a number of advanced features, such as TLS termination and advanced routing options, allowing you to route incoming requests to different ports on the same host.
- **Network Load Balancer**: If low latency and high performance are key to your application architectures, then you might want to select a Network Load Balancer, which can easily support millions of incoming requests per second.
- **Classic Load Balancer**: This was the original AWS ELB; however, this has now been superseded by the previous two ELBs, in particular the Application Load Balancer, and AWS recommends that you use the Application Load Balancer instead of the Classic ELB – *unless* your application resides within the older EC2 classic environment.

 For more information on load balancers, including their configuration and differences, please see my blog post at `https://cloudacademy.com/blog/elastic-load-balancers-ec2-auto-scaling-to-support-aws-workloads/`.

Managing encrypted requests

When configuring your ELBs, they can be defined as internal or internet-facing. Internal ELBs only have private internal IP addresses and can only serve requests that originate from within your own VPC. However, internet-facing ELBs are different. They have public DNS names that are resolved to publicly accessible IP addresses, in addition to their own internal IP address used within your VPC.

Therefore, as with many services that traverse the public internet, you may want to implement a level of encryption to increase the security of your solution and minimize threats against your infrastructure. When using ELBs, this encryption can be achieved for your requests through the use of server certificates.

If you select the HTTPS protocol as a listener during the configuration of your ELB, then additional configuration is required under step 2 of the configuration process to manage the encryption, including a server certificate and security policies. HTTPS is simply the encrypted version of the HTTP protocol and by using the HTTPS protocol, you are able to serve encrypted requests originating from external hosts to your load balancer:

A listener has to be configured for every ELB as it controls how incoming requests are routed to your targets based on the protocol used.

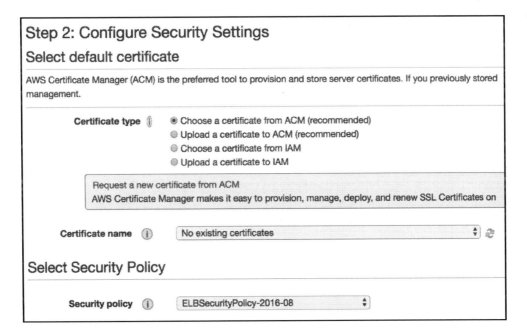

As you can see, you are required to select a certificate to be associated with your ELB when using a secure protocol, such as HTTPS. The certificate allows the ELB to terminate the incoming encrypted request from the external host, decrypting it as a part of this process before routing the same decrypted request to your ELB target group.

The certificates themselves are X.509 certificates provisioned by a **certificate authority (CA)**. A CA is simply an entity that provisions and issues digital certificates. You can use certificates generated by your own CA outside of AWS; however, your ELBs will easily integrate with the **AWS Certificate Manager (ACM)** service.

When configuring your certificate type, you will be asked to select one of four different options:

> ◉ Choose a certificate from ACM (recommended)
> ◎ Upload a certificate to ACM (recommended)
> ◎ Choose a certificate from IAM
> ◎ Upload a certificate to IAM

As highlighted in the screenshot, its recommended by AWS to use the ACM to generate and source your SSL/TLS public certificates. This is largely due to its integration with the ELB component.

The two options relating to IAM allow you to use any existing third-party certificate that you may already have. In fact, you would have to use the IAM option if you were utilizing encryption with your ELBs within a region that was not supported by ACM. To gain an up-to-date list of the supported regions used by ACM, see the following link: `https://docs.aws.amazon.com/general/latest/gr/rande.html#acm_region`.

ACM allows you to import your own third-party certificates, much like the IAM option, but it also allows you to create new ones generated by ACM itself.

Requesting a public certificate using ACM

Let's look at the process behind requesting a new SSL/TLS certificate using ACM so you can understand the steps involved:

1. From within the AWS Management Console, select the **Certificate Manager** service under the **Security, Identity, & Compliance** category:

Security, Identity, & Compliance

IAM

Resource Access Manager

Cognito

Secrets Manager

GuardDuty

Inspector

Amazon Macie 🗗

AWS Single Sign-On

Certificate Manager

Key Management Service

CloudHSM

Directory Service

WAF & Shield

Artifact

Security Hub

2. Select **Get started** under the **Provision certificates** option:

Provision certificates

Provide the name of your site, establish your identity, and let ACM do the rest. ACM manages renewal of SSL/TLS certificates issued by Amazon or by your own private Certificate Authority.

Get started

3. Select the **Request a public certificate** option:

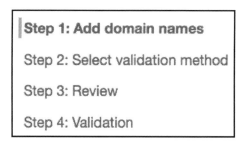

4. Finally, select the blue **Request a certificate** button.

You now have a four-step process to follow, starting with **Add domain names**:

Step 1: Add domain names

Step 2: Select validation method

Step 3: Review

Step 4: Validation

Let's go over them one by one:

1. Enter the domain name of the site that you want to secure with your SSL/TLS certificate and click the blue **Next** button:

2. You will then be asked to select a **validation method** (DNS or email):

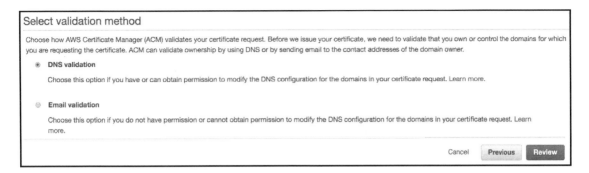

This validation is used to verify that you have control or ownership of the domain that you entered in the previous step. You have the options of **DNS validation** or **Email validation**. As shown, you can select the **DNS validation** option if you have permission to modify the DNS domain in your certificate request. If you do not have permission to do so, then you can use the alternate validation method of **Email validation**.

When using **DNS validation**, ACM will create additional CNAME records that need to be added to your DNS database. If you select **Email verification**, then ACM will send up to eight emails – three to contacts in the WHOIS database and up to five addresses for the domain specified. These emails request the approval of the certificate for the domain in question.

3. Let's presume DNS was selected, and click on the blue **Review** button. Review the options you entered for the domain and validation options and select **Confirm**.

4. From the final **validation** screen, you can export your DNS configuration to a file. This will contain all the information that you need to add your DNS database. If you are using Route 53 as your DNS provider and you have permission to write to the zone, then you can select the blue **Create record in Route 53** button. Select the blue **Continue** button.

It can now take a number of hours for the DNS records to be updated, depending on your DNS provider. Until then, your certificate request will show as **Pending**. Once the changes have been made, the status will change to **issued** and your SSL certificate will be ready for use.

Once your public SSL certificate is issued within ACM, you can then select that certificate when configuring your secure listeners within your ELBs using the **Choose a certificate from ACM (recommended)** option:

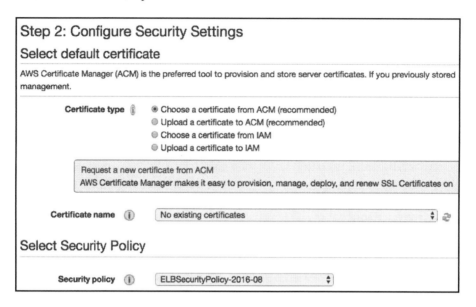

If you want to gain insight and understanding on how to use the IAM options for managing your certificates instead of ACM, see the following link: `https://docs.aws.amazon.com/IAM/latest/UserGuide/id_credentials_server-certs.html`.

In this section, we looked at how you can implement a level of encryption using your ELBs through the use of server certificates and how to request a certificate through ACM. Next, we'll go into depths on how you can secure your AWS API Gateway.

Securing your AWS API Gateway

API gateways are key components of many solutions that help to manage, control, secure, monitor, and deploy APIs, allowing communication with your backend applications and microservices running within your infrastructure. There are many variations of API gateways available on the market, but AWS has created its own, known as the **AWS API Gateway** service.

To see where API gateways fit within your architecture, let's take a look at a scenario.

Let's presume you are running a retail e-commerce website and customers from all over the globe can search your website, adding products to their shopping cart before ordering and paying for the items. The architecture supporting your website, to manage the multitude of requests and features on your website, would likely be orchestrated by tens or even hundreds of microservices, all operating independently, carrying out their own function.

For example, you'll likely have different services to manage search queries, present static content, manage authentication, enable encryption, personalize content, and so on. By having API Gateway acting as the first point of call to your application architecture, it can be used to provide a number of benefits, such as the routing of APIs to microservices, security features to manage authentication and access control, request caching, and being able to monitor all requests made, which can scale to hundreds of thousands of concurrent API calls.

 For detailed information on how to configure AWS API Gateway, please visit the AWS documentation found here: `https://aws.amazon.com/api-gateway/`.

In this chapter, we will focus on how we can use AWS API Gateway to enhance the security of the applications we deploy across our environment.

Controlling access to APIs

Using the same scenario as described previously, it's clear that we would have different levels of security that we would need to implement for our APIs.

To appeal to the maximum customer base, we would want anyone to freely access and browse our library of products on our website. Any APIs involved with presenting our content and search results would be considered **unauthenticated APIs** (public APIs), meaning that these could be used by anyone accessing our website landing page.

Now consider that someone has found a product that they would like to purchase, and they would like to add it to their own shopping cart within their own account and pay for the item. Here, we would see the need for **authenticated user APIs**, whereby the users would need to have undergone a level of authentication.

So, how is the access to these APIs controlled? Well, with AWS API Gateway, there are a number of different mechanisms that control who or what can call an API.

When it comes to controlling authentication and authorization, the following methods can be implemented.

IAM roles and policies

Using the IAM service, you are able to create policies to associate with a user, role, or group, which can dictate what permissions an identity has. This helps to manage who has access to manage, create, delete, and invoke APIs within API Gateway.

IAM tags

Following on from the preceding point, IAM tags can be used in conjunction with IAM policies when using condition statements within the policy. When using API Gateway, it's possible to associate tags with your resources. This allows you to reference these tags as a condition to help offer additional security controls, for example, defining which users can perform specific actions based on the resource tag. This offers an additional level of granularity to your IAM policies.

Resource policies

Whereas IAM policies are attached to a specific identity, resource-based policies are attached to resources. In this case, the resource is the API itself, allowing you to specify the principal that has been granted or denied access to invoke the associate API. Using resource policies, you can define how your API can be invoked, for example, from the following:

- Specific IP CIDR blocks/ranges/addresses
- Defined VPCs or VPC endpoints from any AWS account
- IAM users from a particular AWS account

VPC endpoint policies

These are another form of resource-based policy; however, this time the resource is a VPC endpoint, and through this policy, you can control access to any of your private APIs. VPC endpoints simply allow you to access AWS services using private IP addresses. Through their configuration, you can specify which APIs can be invoked by your internal traffic via any VPC endpoints you have configured. This can be used in conjunction with your API Gateway resource policies (mentioned previously) to offer an additional level of control.

Lambda authorizers

As the name implies, this method of security uses AWS Lambda functions to restrict who can invoke REST API methods. Lambda authorizers can either use bearer-based tokens to authenticate the request, including OAuth or **SAML (Security Assertion Markup Language)** or alternatively request parameters, such as HTML headers, paths, query string parameters, and stage variables.

When AWS API Gateway processes a request for API access, the identity of the request will be identified by the Lambda authorizer, which will generate a resulting IAM policy defining the access granted.

Amazon Cognito user pools

As discussed in `Chapter 5`, *Federated and Mobile Access*, Cognito user pools are scalable user directories that allow new and existing users to log in to mobile applications using the user pool, or they can alternatively federate their access via a social or enterprise IdP. Either way, a profile within the user pool is created for each and every user. These profiles contain no permissions of access to your AWS infrastructure; the purely allow the user to log in to your mobile app as a user to use the app.

With this in mind, you can configure your APIs to have a `COGNITO_USER_POOLS` authorizer. As a result, when this API is called, the user is authenticated via the Amazon Cognito user pool API gateway, whereby their token is validated before allowing access.

Summary

In this chapter, you might have realized that application security can be managed by a range of different AWS services, such as web ACLs, ELBs, and AWS API Gateway, depending on how your AWS architecture has been implemented. However, it is fundamental that you invest time and effort in ensuring you apply this level of security to prevent malicious activity against your applications. It is always best to implement security at every stage of your application development and deployment.

Using the services that AWS has designed and developed can help you to minimize the time and effort needed to implement your own methods that you might have used in the past. They have been tried and tested against some of the most common attack vectors, but having an understanding of these vectors will undoubtedly help you to not fall victim to such attacks. As a security practitioner, you should be aware of the OWASP top 10 and understand exactly what they are and the best methods to prevent them.

In the next chapter, we will be looking at DDoS attacks and how to prevent them using AWS Shield and the different options it provides through its advanced features.

Questions

As we conclude this chapter, here is a list of questions for you to test your knowledge regarding its material. You will find the answers in the *Assessments* section of the *Appendix*:

1. True or false: The main function of the AWS WAF service is to provide protection for your web applications from malicious attacks from a wide variety of attack patterns.
2. Which service allows you to manage WAF rules across a multi-account environment when using AWS Organizations?
3. Which AWS service must you enable as a prerequisite to use AWS Firewall Manager?
4. Which type of load balancer would you use if low latency and high performance are key to your application architectures?

Further reading

Whitepaper: *Using AWS WAF to Mitigate OWASP's Top 10 Web Application Vulnerabilities*:
`https://d0.awsstatic.com/whitepapers/Security/aws-waf-owasp.pdf`

DDoS Protection 9

Distributed Denial of Service (DDoS) attacks are very common, and if successful, they can have a hugely detrimental impact on an organization's service operation. Depending on the scale of the DDoS attack, it can render an entire website unavailable, and for e-commerce retail businesses, this could cost them significant losses in sales.

In this chapter, we will be looking at DDoS and how you can leverage AWS Shield to help protect your infrastructure from these malicious attacks. We will look at the differences between the two different tiers supported by Shield and how you can utilize the services of the AWS **DDoS Response Team (DRT)**.

This chapter will focus on the following:

- Understanding DDoS and its attack patterns
- Protecting your environment using AWS Shield

Technical requirements

There are no requirements for this chapter. However, within the chapter, if you would like to set up and configure AWS Shield Advanced (at a cost of $3,000 a month), then you need to ensure you have permission for this service. As an alternative, I will also cover the features of AWS Shield Standard, which comes as a free service.

For more information on how to grant access, please refer to `Chapter 4`, *Working with Access Policies*.

Understanding DDoS and its attack patterns

As mentioned previously, DDoS attacks are extremely common worldwide. To begin, the initiator of a DDoS attack will focus on a specific target, being a single host, network, or service to compromise, and this target will likely be a key component of an organization's infrastructure. During the attack, an attempt will be made to severely disrupt the performance of the target using a massive amount of inbound requests from a number of different distributed sources within the same time period.

This creates two problems, as follows:

- The additional traffic load is designed to flood the target and prevent authentic and legitimate inbound requests from reaching that target and being processed as real requests.
- The performance of the target is hindered, affecting the usability of the infrastructure and its associated resources. For example, should a DDoS attack be made against a web server running a website, anyone using the site would assume that the site was down and unavailable.

So far, we've just gotten a basic understanding of what a DDoS attack actually is. On a higher level, these attacks can be carried out using different patterns, which we will discuss next.

DDoS attack patterns

There are a number of different DDoS attacks that could be used to achieve the end goal of disruption. Let me explain a couple of these at a high level to help you understand the principles of DDoS attacks.

For the certification, you will not be tested on the different types of attacks and how they are initiated; this section was included as a foundation to the topic. More information on these topics is provided in the *Further reading* section at the end of the chapter.

SYN floods

This type of attack takes advantage of the three-way handshake that is used to establish a connection between two hosts, as can be seen in the following diagram:

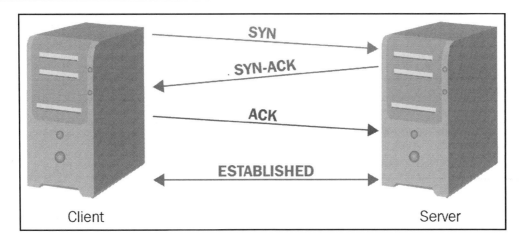

It is called a SYN flood because a huge amount of connections are made simultaneously to the attacked host, these being the SYN seen in the diagram. In the host's attempt to establish these incoming connections, the host responds with a SYN/ACK packet. Typically, to complete the handshake, the sender will then respond with a further ACK packet; however, the sender does not send this final response. As a result, this leaves a huge amount of open connections on the host, resulting in a large number of resources being utilized unnecessarily. This then leaves minimal resources available to then process legitimate requests.

HTTP floods

As expected from reading about the previous DDoS attack, the target is subjected to a substantial amount of HTTP requests, for example, GET or POST requests, which, in turn, consume valuable resources on the host. Much like a SYN flood, this results in a lack of available resources to process and serve legitimate requests on the server, rendering the performance of the host unusable.

Ping of death (PoD)

As suggested by the name, this isn't something that's going to help your environment! A PoD attack is initiated by a malicious user sending a number of oversized IP packets to a host through a series of pings. The maximum size of an IP packet is 65,535 bytes. However, due to the fragmenting of the packets sent, when they are reassembled into a single packet on the host, they are larger than the allowed size. This manipulation causes the host to suffer from memory overflow detrimental to its performance.

So far, DDoS has been explained and the general principles behind the attacks, but just bare knowledge about these attacks is of no use if we cannot do anything to stop them, right? Moving forward, let's focus on an AWS service that has been specifically designed to help protect your environment from DDoS threats, this being AWS Shield.

Protecting your environment using AWS Shield

In the previous chapter, we discussed the **Web Application Firewall (WAF)** service and Firewall Manager. AWS Shield is closely related to these applications. AWS Shield is a managed AWS service that helps to mitigate DDoS attacks on the applications running within your environment.

This section will take you through the two tiers of AWS Shield, explaining the differences between them, allowing you to understand which tier would be best for your own environment. You will also see how to activate AWS Shield Advanced tier.

The two tiers of AWS Shield

Your environment and how much protection you require, and at which level, will determine the AWS Shield tier that you implement within it. Currently, there are two tiers available:

- **AWS Shield Standard**: The first tier is freely available to anyone with an AWS account.
- **AWS Shield Advanced**: The second tier is a premium tier that comes with a range of additional features and protection. However, this comes at an additional cost.

By visiting `https://aws.amazon.com/shield/getting-started/`, you can see the full list of differences between the two tiers.

AWS Shield Standard

If you already have an AWS account, then this standard tier is available to you at no additional cost. It can be used to protect your environment from some of the more common DDoS attacks operating at the network and transport layer of your infrastructure when using Amazon CloudFront or Route 53. When utilizing AWS WAF, it can also be used to help mitigate some common application layer attacks.

AWS Shield Standard operates in real time in an always-on model. It automatically detects specific traffic signatures that could indicate an imminent attack against your infrastructure.

AWS Shield Advanced

AWS Shield Advanced offers a wider scope of advantages, features, and DDoS protection compared to AWS Shield Standard. One of the biggest additional features that it supports is application traffic monitoring and support for large-scale DDoS attacks. With this in mind, AWS Shield Advanced is recommended for organizations where these kinds of attacks could be significant for business productivity.

It also has advanced feature sets when it comes to visibility and reporting against layer 3, layer 4, and layer 7 attacks (network, transport, and application). Plus, it comes with access to a 24/7 specialized DDoS response team at AWS, known as DRT.

One last point I want to make about AWS Shield Advanced is that it comes with cost protection. This could be very advantageous in the event of a significant attack. During an attack, services such as Amazon Route 53, Amazon CloudFront, Elastic Load Balancing, and EC2 may escalate to cope with the flood of traffic. The cost protection with Shield Advanced would mitigate you having to pay for these additional spiked costs.

With all of these great features and protection also comes a cost. AWS Shield Advanced currently stands at $3,000 a month, plus data transfer fees.

Activating AWS Shield Advanced

In this section, I want to provide a quick overview of how to activate AWS Shield Advanced:

1. From the AWS Management Console, select **WAF & Shield** under the **Security, Identity, & Compliance** category:

2. Click the blue **Go to AWS Shield** button:

3. You will now be presented with a splash screen showing the core differences between Shield Standard and Shield Advanced. To activate Shield Advanced, you must select the blue **Activate AWS Shield Advanced** button:

AWS Shield

As an AWS customer, you automatically have basic DDoS protection with the AWS Shield Standard plan, at no additional cost beyond what you already pay for AWS WAF and your other AWS services. For an additional cost, you can get advanced DDoS protection by activating the AWS Shield Advanced plan. The following table shows a comparison of the two plans.

Features	AWS Shield Standard	AWS Shield Advanced
Active monitoring		
Network flow monitoring	✔	✔
Automated application (layer 7) traffic monitoring	-	✔
DDoS mitigations		
Helps protect from common DDoS attacks, such as SYN floods and UDP reflection attacks	✔	✔
Access to additional DDoS mitigation capacity	-	✔
Visibility and reporting		
Layer 3/4 attack notification and attack forensic reports	-	✔
Layer 3/4/7 attack historical report	-	✔
DDoS response team support		
Incident management during high severity events	-	✔
Custom mitigations during attacks	-	✔
Post-attack analysis	-	✔
Cost protection		
Reimburse related Route 53, CloudFront, and ELB DDoS charges	-	✔
Status	Activated	Not activated
Price	No additional cost for all AWS customers	**$3,000/month** plus additional data transfer fees AWS WAF included at no additional cost Learn more

> **Activate AWS Shield Advanced**

 However, do be aware, there is a $3,000 cost per month when you activate it.

4. You will now be asked to agree to a number of terms and conditions before the service is activated. Once activated, you are subscribed to the service, and to unsubscribe, you must contact AWS Support.

If you have multiple accounts that you own, then it's recommended that you use AWS Firewall Manager to activate and configure Shield Advanced on these accounts. By doing so, you will only pay a single monthly bill of $3,000 for all your accounts, providing they are in the same consolidated billing configuration. For more information on how to set up and configure this, please see the following URL: `https://docs.aws.amazon.com/waf/latest/developerguide/getting-started-fms-shield.html`

Configuring AWS Shield Advanced

Once you have activated AWS Shield Advanced, you will then need to configure it to protect your resources. In this section, I will review the steps involved.

Selecting your resources to protect

Once you have activated AWS Shield, you must then determine which resources and services you would like to protect using the ARNs of the resources. If you are looking to protect an EC2 instance, then you should be aware that you must first associate an **elastic IP address** (**EIP**) with the instance. AWS Shield can then be associated with the EIP and will protect whatever resource that particular EIP is associated with.

Adding rate-based rules

Once you have selected which resources you are looking to protect, you can then add rate-based rules to help identify potential DDoS attacks from spiking traffic. If you remember from the previous chapter, a rate-based rule counts the number of requests received from a particular IP address over a time period of 5 minutes:

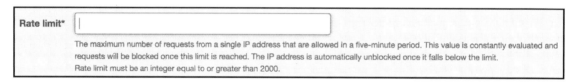

By selecting a rate-based rule, you can define the maximum number of requests from a single IP within a 5-minute time frame (this must be over 2,000, otherwise this setting falls within the boundaries of a standard rule). Once this limit is reached, all further requests are then blocked until the requests drop back below the defined threshold.

Adding support from the AWS DDoS Response Team (DRT)

Once your rate-based rules are configured, you have the option of adding support from the AWS **DDoS Response Team** (**DRT**). This is a specialized team at AWS who can help you to review, analyze, and monitor suspected malicious activity within your account and offer help and solutions on how to resolve a potential attack.

To help the DRT team with your investigations, they will need access to your AWS WAF rules web ACLs within your affected account. This obviously requires your authorization for them to access this information should you need their assistance. Should you require access to the DRT team, then you need to pre-authorize their access at this stage. If you *do not* want the DRT team to have access to your resources, then you must select **Do not grant the DRT access to my account** option.

If access to DRT is required, it will be governed by an IAM role that will have the `AWSShieldDRTAccessPolicy` managed policy attached, which trusts the service principal of `drt.shield.amazonaws.com` to use the role.

As with all monitoring systems, it is always recommended that CloudWatch alarms are configured and set up in addition to SNS for the notification of potential DDoS attacks. AWS Shield Advanced configures CloudWatch metrics and SNS to notify you of potential DDoS attacks.

Additional services and features

As an additional effort and level of protection against DDoS attacks, following on from AWS WAF and AWS Shield, it is also recommended, where feasible when serving web traffic, to use AWS-managed edge services such as AWS CloudFront and Amazon Route 53. AWS Shield integration with these edge services allows the architecture and AWS services to detect and mitigate potential DDoS attacks down to a sub-second level, significantly decreasing the chances of compromise.

Both Amazon CloudFront (with AWS WAF) and Route 53 offer the following protections:

- Layer 3, layer 4, and layer 7 attack mitigation (for example, UDP reflection, SYN floods, and application layer attacks).
- Being managed services, they are able to scale to absorb the additional traffic generated from application-layer attacks and so reduce the impact on your infrastructure.
- They are able to provide geo-location and the dispersion of additional traffic from larger DDoS attacks.

Amazon CloudFront (with AWS WAF) also offers protection from layer 6 attacks.

It is likely that you are already using elastic load balancers and autoscaling within your environment. However, if you are not, then these can also help to reduce the impact of a large-scale attack on your resources, which might be operating at the application or network level. By using application or network load balancers (ALBs or NLBs), they are able to quickly scale to meet the demands of additional loads that would be experienced during an attack, which would prevent your infrastructure from being overloaded as it would had it not got an ELB protecting it. When combined with autoscaling, your resources can be scaled to absorb the impact of the connections being initiated. These features will help to maintain the availability of your service during an attack.

Summary

In this chapter, we first learned about DDoS attacks and their attack patterns, where we saw just how serious these attacks can be and the damage that they can cause. In order to mitigate these attacks, we then learned about AWS Shield and the different tier levels it provides to support varied features against DDoS protection. We then followed this up with a quick demonstration of how you can activate and configure AWS Shield Advanced and use it to your advantage to mitigate DDoS attacks.

Remember that DDoS attacks are a very real concern for many organizations and are widespread globally. They can have a significant impact on your environment, and ultimately on your business' reputation. With the help of the information in this chapter, you will now be able to defend yourself by detecting these attacks by using AWS Shield.

In the next chapter, we'll be looking at incident response and how to prepare for incidents, and the necessary response actions to help isolate an issue.

Questions

As we conclude this chapter, here is a list of questions for you to test your knowledge regarding its material. You will find the answers in the *Assessments* section of the *Appendix*:

1. Which type of DDoS attack takes advantage of the three-way handshake that is used to establish a connection between two hosts?
2. How many tiers are there to choose from when working with AWS Shield?
3. True or false: AWS Shield Advanced is a premium tier that comes with a range of additional features and protection.

4. True or false: The DDoS Response Team (DRT) is a specialized team at AWS who can help you to review, analyze, and monitor suspected malicious activity within your account and offer help and solutions on how to resolve a potential attack.

5. True or false: By selecting a rate-based rule, you can define the maximum number of requests from a single IP within a 30-minute time frame.

Further reading

For additional information relating to AWS DDoS protection, I recommend reading the following AWS White Paper: https://d1.awsstatic.com/whitepapers/Security/DDoS_White_Paper.pdf?did=wp_cardtrk=wp_card

What is a DDoS attack?: https://aws.amazon.com/shield/ddos-attack-protection/

10
Incident Response

Inevitably, at some point, your organization will experience some form of security breach (incident) within a layer of their infrastructure. This could be the result of a simple misconfiguration within a deployment, thus creating a vulnerability, or from a malicious attacker external to your organization trying to obtain confidential data and compromise your systems. Either way, how you respond to a security incident as soon as it has been identified is critical to ensuring that the blast radius of the attack is minimized effectively and rapidly, thereby reducing the effect it has on the rest of your infrastructure.

Unfortunately, it is not possible to stop all security incidents from arising. As technology changes, new vulnerabilities, threats, and risks are introduced. Combine that with human error and incidents will undoubtedly occur. Because of these factors, there is a need to implement an **incident response** (**IR**) policy and various surrounding processes.

In this chapter, you'll learn how to prepare for such incidents and the necessary response actions you can use to isolate the issue. As a result, we will cover the following topics:

- Where to start when implementing effective IR
- Making use of AWS features
- Responding to an incident

Technical requirements

This chapter is largely theory and provides some best practices and recommendations in the event of a security incident occurring. As a result, there are no technical requirements in order for for you to be able to follow this chapter.

Where to start when implementing effective IR

To understand how to respond to a security incident within an organization, the business must first provide training for its staff and educate them on their corporate practices, procedures, and processes that are in place to safeguard the infrastructure. Security incidents can come in all shapes and sizes, from small and unlikely threats to immediate and imminent attacks whereby sensitive customer data could be stolen and extracted from your systems. With this in mind, training is an ongoing pursuit and, as such, you should employ and adopt runbooks that provide clear instructions and actions that you can carry out for particular security incidents that may occur and perhaps could be foreseen.

Over time, these security incident runbooks will be modified and adapted as new processes, techniques, and technologies are applied within your organization. Staff should be familiar with the security tools and features offered by AWS to help them prepare and manage the security incident. Again, this all begins with sufficient and adequate training.

You should also ensure that your security and support teams, as well as anyone who will be involved in responding to an incident, has the correct permissions. You might need to review your access controls, including federated access, access to assume roles cross-account roles, and general IAM permissions. You might want to create a number of roles with more privileged access that can only be assumed by specific users for use during incident response.

If you are not familiar with the **AWS Cloud Adoption Framework (CAF)**, which is a framework that has been designed by AWS to help you transition and migrate solutions into the AWS cloud based on best practices and recommendations, then I suggest that you review its contents. The following resource focuses on the security aspects of this framework: https://d0.awsstatic.com/whitepapers/AWS_CAF_Security_Perspective.pdf

As stated in the preceding link, this framework addresses four primary control areas:

- **Directive controls**: Establish the governance, risk, and compliance models the environment will operate within
- **Preventive controls**: Protect your workloads and mitigate threats and vulnerabilities
- **Detective controls**: Provide full visibility and transparency over the operation of your deployments in AWS
- **Responsive controls**: Drive the remediation of potential deviations from your security baselines

By following the recommendations highlighted by AWS CAF, you can start from a strong foundation when it comes to performing effective IR across your infrastructure and AWS accounts.

In addition to AWS CAF, I highly recommend that you review and read *AWS Security Incident Response Guide*, which can be found here: `https://d1.awsstatic.com/ whitepapers/aws_security_incident_response.pdf`. It was published in June 2020.

On top of this, being familiar with the AWS shared responsibility model should be mandatory for all security engineers involved with IR. It can't be highlighted enough that you need to understand where the boundary lies in terms of what you, as the customer, are responsible for, and what AWS is responsible for from a security perspective. You may remember from `Chapter 2`, *AWS Shared Responsibility Model*, that AWS has three different shared responsibility models – Infrastructure, Container, and Abstract – all of which have varying levels of responsibility between cloud customers and AWS. So, depending on your chosen service within AWS and which model it falls within, your responsibility for managing the security around that service will vary.

Now that we have a basic understanding of where to start, we can start looking at the different AWS services that will help us build an effective incident response strategy.

Making use of AWS features

AWS offers a wide scope of features and capabilities when it comes to assisting and helping you manage incident response, from investigative measures to proactive monitoring. In this section, we will quickly look at these features of AWS, some of which we've already learned about, or will learn about in the upcoming chapters in detail. Here, we will look at them from the IR perspective.

Logging

AWS has numerous services that offer logging capabilities that capture meaningful and vital information when it comes to analyzing the source of a threat and how to prevent it. Where possible, when using your chosen services, you should enable logging. This is often overlooked, which can be a huge regret for organizations should the worst happen. With active logging, you will have a much higher chance of being able to rectify an incident quickly and efficiently, or even prevent it from occurring by spotting patterns and trends.

Logging offers you the opportunity to baseline your infrastructure of what's *normal* and what can be considered *abnormal* operations. This helps identify and isolate anomalies easily, especially when combined with third-party logging and analysis tools.

Again, having logs running continuously and automatically by the supported AWS services allows you to view the state of your environment prior, during, and after an incident. This helps you gather intelligence and insight into where in your infrastructure the incident occurred and how to prevent it from happening again in the future.

Some examples of services that offer logging in AWS include Amazon CloudWatch logs, AWS CloudTrail logs, Amazon S3 Access logs, VPC Flow logs, AWS Config logs, and CloudFront logs. There are many more examples of logging within AWS and this will grow as AWS itself evolves. The main point is that logging is a great method of helping you resolve a security incident as and when it occurs, and these logs should be readily and easily accessible in the event you are responding to an incident as part of your IR policy.

 We'll cover logging as a whole in more detail in `Chapter 12`, *Implementing Logging Mechanisms,* where we will dive into each of these areas and services in great depth.

Threat detection and management

It is no surprise that AWS has a wide range of security services designed to help, protect, and guard your infrastructure. Within that scope, they also offer threat detection as another tool you can utilize to help you in your effort of minimizing security incidents.

AWS GuardDuty is a regional-based managed service powered by machine learning, specifically designed to be an intelligent threat detection service. It is used to monitor logs from other AWS services and features, including VPC Flow logs, DNS logs, and AWS CloudTrail event logs. AWS GuardDuty looks at these logs to detect unexpected and unusual behavior and cross-reference these analytics with a number of threat detection and security feeds that can help us identify potentially malicious activity and anomalies.

As I already stated, the service itself is powered by machine learning and, by its very nature, this allows the service to continually learn the patterns within your infrastructure and its operational behavior, which will, of course, evolve over time. Having a "big brother" approach allows GuardDuty to spot unusual patterns and potential threats, ranging from unexpected API calls and references that are not normally initiated to unexpected communications between resources. All of this could be the first sign of a compromised environment, and having insight into this through early detection is invaluable in reducing the impact of an incident.

From a security management point of view, we have AWS Security Hub, which integrates with other AWS services, such as Amazon GuardDuty, in addition to Amazon Inspector and Amazon Macie, plus a wide variety of AWS partner products and toolsets.

This scope of integration allows **AWS Security Hub** to act as a single pane of glass view across your infrastructure, thus bringing all your security statistical data into a single place and presented in a series of tables and graphs. If you are managing multiple AWS accounts, then Security Hub can operate across all of them using a master-slave relationship. The service itself operates as an always-on service, meaning it is continuously running and processing data in the background, which allows the service to automatically identify any discrepancies against best practices. The analysis of the data that's received by the different integrated services is checked against industry standards, such as the **Center for Internet Security (CIS)** benchmarks, thus enabling the service to spot and identify potential vulnerabilities and weak spots across multiple accounts and against specific resources. Early detection of weaknesses and non-compliance is valuable in ensuring that you safeguard your data.

One of the features of Security Hub is its insights. An insight is essentially a grouping of findings that meet a specific criteria base set from specific filters and statements. By using insights, you can easily highlight specific information that requires attention. AWS has created a number of managed insights, all of which can be found here: `https://docs.aws.amazon.com/securityhub/latest/userguide/securityhub-managed-insights.html`

The following are some examples of these managed insights:

- AWS users with the most suspicious activity
- S3 buckets with public write or read permissions
- EC2 instances that have missing security patches for important vulnerabilities
- EC2 instances with general unusual behavior
- EC2 instances that are open to the internet
- EC2 instances associated with adversary reconnaissance
- AWS resources associated with malware

In addition to these managed insights, you can also configure your own insights so that they meet criteria that might be specific to your own business security concerns.

 For more information related to Amazon GuardDuty and AWS Security Hub, please refer to `Chapter 14`, *Automating Security Detection and Remediation*.

Responding to an incident

Now that you have some background information regarding useful services, features, and how to ensure that you have a good foundation for your infrastructure by following the Cloud Adoption Framework and other best practices, let's look at some of the actions that you could take when an incident occurs.

Forensic AWS account

Having a separate AWS account for forensic investigations is ideal for helping you diagnose and isolate the affected resource. By utilizing a separate account, you can architect the environment in a more secure manner that's appropriate to its forensic use. You could even use AWS organizations to provision these accounts quickly and easily in addition to using a preconfigured, approved, tried, and tested CloudFormation template to build out the required resources and configuration. This allows you to build the account and environment using a known configuration without having to rely on a manual process that can be susceptible to errors and undesirable in the early stages of a forensic investigation. While performing your investigations, you should ensure that your steps and actions are auditable through the use of logging mechanisms provided by managed AWS services, in addition to services such as AWS CloudTrail.

Another benefit of moving the affected resource to a separate account is that it minimizes the chances of further compromise and effects on other resources when in its original source account.

Collating log information

Earlier in this chapter, I mentioned the significance of logs and the part they play in incident response. During an incident, it's critical that you are able to access your logs and that you know the process and methods for extracting and searching for data within them. You must be able to look at, for example, an S3 access log or AWS CloudTrail log and understand the syntax, parameters, and fields that are presented in order to process the information being shown. You may have third-party tools to do this analysis for you, but if you don't have access to those systems for any reason, you need to be able to decipher the logs manually.

If you have multiple AWS accounts, determine which ones can be shared with other accounts. To help with log sharing, you should configure cross-account data sharing with the use of CloudWatch and Amazon Kinesis. Cross-account data sharing allows you to share log data between multiple accounts that can then read it from a centralized Amazon Kinesis stream, thus allowing you to read, analyze, and process the data from the stream using security analytic systems.

 For more information on Amazon S3 access logs, AWS CloudTrail logs, and Amazon CloudWatch, please refer to Chapter 12, *Implementing Logging Mechanisms*, and Chapter 13, *Auditing and Governance*.

Resource isolation

Let's assume you have an EC2 instance that is initiating unexpected API behavior. This has been identified as an anomaly and is considered to be an abnormal operation. As a result, this instance is showing signs of being a potentially compromised resource. Until you have identified the cause, you must isolate the resource to minimize the effect, impact, and potential damage that could occur to other resources within your AWS account. This action should be undertaken immediately. By isolating the instance, you are preventing any further connectivity to and from the instance, which will also minimize the chances of data being removed from it.

To isolate an instance, the quickest and best way to do so would be to change its associated security group with one that would prevent any access to or from the instance. As an additional precaution, you should also remove any roles associated with the instance.

To perform a forensic investigation of the affected instance, you will want to move the EC2 instance to your forensic account (discussed previously). However, it is not possible to move the same instance to a different AWS account. Instead, you will need to perform the following high-level steps:

1. First, you must create an AMI from the affected EC2 instance.
2. Then, you need to share the newly created AMI image with your forensic account by modifying the AMI permissions.
3. From within your forensic account, you need to locate the AMI from within the EC2 console or AWS CLI.
4. Finally, you must create a new instance from the shared AMI.

For detailed instructions on how to carry out each of these steps, please visit the following AWS documentation: `https://aws.amazon.com/premiumsupport/knowledge-center/account-transfer-ec2-instance/`

Copying data

Again, following on from the previous example of a compromised EC2 instance, let's also assume that the instance was backed by EBS storage. You may just want to isolate and analyze the storage of this instance from within your forensic account, and this can be achieved through the use of EBS snapshots. These snapshots are essential incremental backups of your EBS volumes.

Creating a snapshot of your EBS volumes is a simple process:

1. From within your AWS Management Console, select the **EC2** service from the **Compute** category.

2. Select **Volumes** from under the **ELASTIC BLOCK STORE** menu heading on the left:

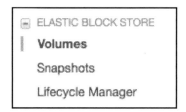

3. Select your volume from the list of volumes displayed:

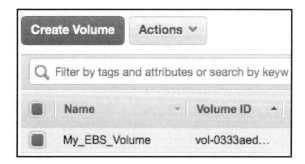

4. Select the **Actions** menu and select **Create Snapshot**:

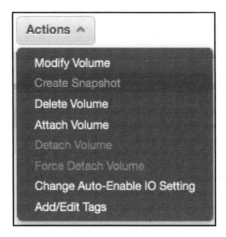

5. Add a description and any tags that are required:

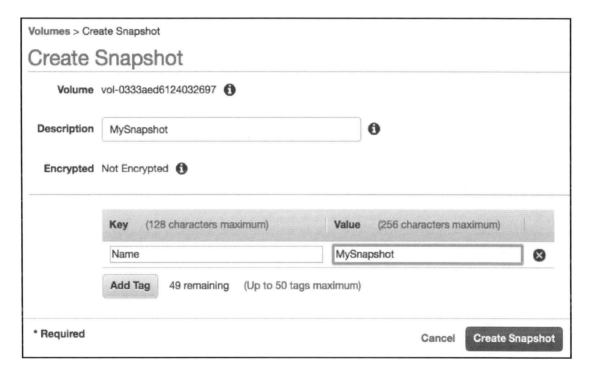

6. Select **Create Snapshot**. At this point, you will get a message stating that the requested snapshot has succeeded:

7. Click on **Close**.

8. You can now ensure that your snapshot has been created by selecting **Snapshots** from under the **ELASTIC BLOCK STORE** menu on the left:

9. From here, you will see your newly created snapshot:

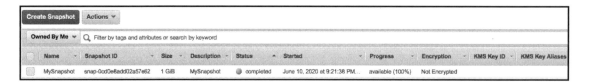

As you can see, it's a very simple process to create an EBS snapshot of your volumes.

Similarly, for AMI images, you must modify the permissions of your EBS snapshots so that you can share them from within another account. For more information on how to do this, please visit the following link: `https://docs.aws.amazon.com/AWSEC2/latest/UserGuide/ebs-modifying-snapshot-permissions.html`

Once the snapshot has been shared with the forensic account, incident response engineers will be able to recreate the EBS volume from the snapshot.

Forensic instances

Another option you can implement within your forensic account is forensic instances. These are instances that are specifically built to help you with your investigations and are loaded with forensic analysis tools and features. For example, if you had a compromised EBS volume, you could take a snapshot, copy the snapshot to your forensic account, build a new EBS volume from it, and attach it to your forensic instance, ready for investigation.

You can create a forensic instance in a few simple steps:

1. Select an AMI to be used for your forensic instance.
2. Launch an EC2 instance from this AMI. Be sure to use an EC2 instance that has a sufficient amount of processing power so that it can be used within your investigations.
3. Install all the latest security patches.
4. Remove all unnecessary software and applications from your operating system and implement audit and monitoring controls.
5. Harden your operating system as per best practices.
6. Install any software that you will be using to help you perform your analysis during your forensic investigations.
7. Once your packages have been installed, stop your instance and take an AMI image of that instance.
8. This process should be completed regularly and a new AMI should be built each time to ensure that the latest security fixes are in place.

In this section, we looked at the importance of implementing a forensic AWS account to isolate resources and help diagnose issues and incidents. We also looked at why we need to isolate the resource from the production network; that is, to minimize the blast radius of other resources being compromised. We then looked at the techniques we can use to obtain the data from the affected resource, before analyzing it with a forensic resource.

 For more information on launching your forensic instance, please review the AWS White Paper entitled *AWS Security Incident Response Guide*:
https://d1.awsstatic.com/whitepapers/aws_security_incident_response.pdf

A common approach to an infrastructure security incident

Before we come to the end of this chapter, I just want to quickly highlight a common approach to how you might respond to an infrastructure-related security incident involving an EC2 instance:

1. **Capture**: You should try and capture any metadata from the instance before you proceed and make any further changes related to your environment.
2. **Protect**: To prevent the EC2 instance from being accidentally terminated, enable termination protection while you continue to investigate.
3. **Isolate**: You should then isolate the instance by modifying the security group or updating the NACL to deny all traffic destined for the IP address of the instance.
4. **Detach**: Remove the affected instance from any autoscaling groups.
5. **Deregister**: If the instance is associated with any ELBs, you must remove them from any ELBs.
6. **Snapshot**: Take a copy of any EBS volumes via a snapshot so that you can investigate further without affecting the original volumes.
7. **Tag**: Using tags, you should highlight the instance that has been prepared for forensic investigation.

You will not be expected to know the commands to carry out the preceding steps via the AWS CLI, but should you wish to learn how to do this, please review the steps provided in the *AWS Security Incident Response Guide* White Paper: `https://d1.awsstatic.com/whitepapers/aws_security_incident_response.pdf`.

Summary

In this chapter, we looked at some of the recommendations regarding how to prepare for when a security incident occurs and some of the methods, services, and techniques that can be used to identify, isolate, and minimize the blast radius of damage across your environment.

Should you ever be contacted by AWS regarding a security incident, you must follow their instructions immediately and implement your own level of incident response in coordination with AWS's requirements.

The key to a successful incident response plan is planning and preparation. If you have read through this chapter well enough and have performed this element sufficiently, then you now stand a far higher chance of gaining control of the incident quicker and more effectively. Preparation is, in fact, the first element of the incident response life cycle within NIST Special Publication 800-61. Due to this, you must prepare for incidents and ensure you have your logging, auditing, monitoring, and detection services and features configured. You also need to have a way of isolating and removing affected resources from your production environment. You must also have the ability to investigate, analyze, and perform recovery for your affected systems.

In the next chapter, you'll learn how to secure connectivity to your AWS environment from your corporate data center using AWS **virtual private networks (VPNs)** and AWS Direct Connect.

Questions

As we conclude, here is a list of questions for you to test your knowledge regarding this chapter's material. You will find the answers in the *Assessments* section of the *Appendix*:

1. Which framework has been designed by AWS to help you transition and migrate solutions into AWS Cloud that's based on best practices and recommendations?
2. Which AWS service is a regional-based managed service that's powered by machine learning, specifically designed to be an intelligent threat detection service?
3. Which AWS service acts as a single-pane-of-glass view across your infrastructure, thus bringing all of your security statistical data into a single place and presented in a series of tables and graphs?
4. True or False: Having a separate AWS account to be used for forensic investigations is essential to helping you diagnose and isolate any affected resource.

Further reading

- *AWS Security Incident Response Guide*: `https://d1.awsstatic.com/whitepapers/aws_security_incident_response.pdf`
- *SANS Institute Information Security: Reading Room Digital Forensic Analysis of Amazon Linux EC2 Instances*: `https://www.sans.org/reading-room/whitepapers/cloud/digital-forensic-analysis-amazon-linux-ec2-instances-38235`
- **National Institute of Standards and Technology (NIST)** *Computer Security Incident Handling Guide Recommendations*: `https://nvlpubs.nist.gov/nistpubs/SpecialPublications/NIST.SP.800-61r2.pdf`

11
Securing Connections to Your AWS Environment

So far, we have looked at a number of security techniques to help you secure your AWS environment and the data within it. However, many organizations will be connecting to the AWS cloud from their own on-premises environment from within their own data center. As a result, you need to understand the different methods of secure connectivity between your own corporate site and that of the AWS cloud, allowing you to effectively extend your corporate network in a secure manner.

This chapter will look at some of the connectivity options and the security behind them to ensure you can maintain and implement a secure connection from your corporate environment to your AWS environment. We will be looking at the configuration of security options, such as routing and security groups, and the permissions behind connectivity options, such as an AWS **Virtual Private Network (VPN)** and AWS Direct Connect.

We will cover the following topics in this chapter:

- Understanding your connection
- Using an AWS VPN
- Using AWS Direct Connect

Technical requirements

To follow along with this chapter, you do not need any software or hardware. However, to get the most out of the information presented, you should have an understanding of the following:

- AWS route tables and basic routing principles (covered in `Chapter 7`, *Configuring Infrastructure Security*)
- Security groups (covered in `Chapter 7`, *Configuring Infrastructure Security*)
- IAM policies and policy syntax (covered in `Chapter 4`, *Working with Access Policies*)

Understanding your connection

If you are an organization building solutions on AWS, then you can easily access your resources and services via the internet, as many of you would have already experienced from using the AWS Management Console. From here, you can configure, deploy, and architect your infrastructure using the multitude of services that AWS offers. From a logical perspective, using the internet to connect to your AWS environment from your on-premises environment would look as follows:

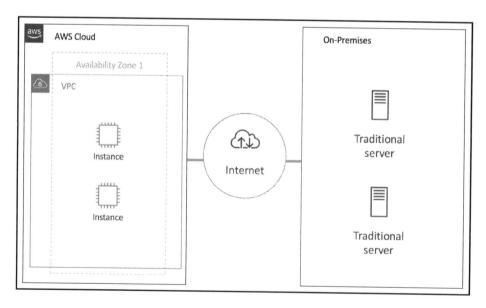

However, you might want to establish a more secure connection to these resources and connect to them as if they were an extension of your own internal network. To do this effectively and securely, you would need to enforce a private connection between your on-premises environment and AWS. This can be achieved via a couple of different connectivity options:

- By using a VPN connection
- By using a Direct Connect connection

In the following sections of this chapter, we will discuss both of these options in great detail. Let's begin with the VPN option first and the various configurations available to you.

This chapter will not explain how to configure and implement each of these connectivity options, but rather, the focus will be on the security aspects related to these solutions. For detailed implementation guides for these services, please see the relevant AWS documentation:

- **For VPNs:** `https://docs.aws.amazon.com/vpc/latest/userguide/vpn-connections.html`
- **For Direct Connect:** `https://docs.aws.amazon.com/directconnect/latest/UserGuide/dc-ug.pdf`

Using an AWS VPN

With an AWS-managed VPN site-to-site connection, a private connection is established between the on-premises site and **AWS Virtual Private Cloud** (**VPC**). This connection is established across the internet using two AWS components:

- A **Virtual Private Gateway** (**VPN gateway**)
- A customer gateway

As you can see in the following diagram, the VPN gateway is located on the AWS side of your architecture, and the customer gateway is associated with the remote customer location (on-premises):

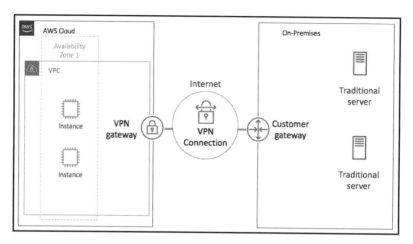

As this is a managed service, the VPN gateway component, which resides within AWS, is implemented and designed with redundancy in mind and actually consists of two endpoints, each of which is located in different data centers for resiliency (note: this is not depicted in the preceding logical diagram).

In addition to this, the VPN connection itself consists of two IPsec tunnels. But what is an IPsec tunnel?

IPsec, or **Internet Protocol Security**, is a secure network protocol suite allowing a cryptographic method of communication between two endpoints, such as between two gateways (creating a network-to-network connection), much like we have in the preceding example with AWS VPNs, or simply between two hosts, creating a host-to-host connection. The IPsec protocol simply outlines the required framework for implementing security at the IP layer, which can include functions such as encryption/decryption, authentication, and key management.

When an end-to-end connection is established between two gateways using a VPN connection with IPsec, the connection is referred to as a tunnel. Within a tunnel, the IPsec protocol wraps the entire data packet being sent, ensuring it's encrypted, and attaches a new header to the packet before it is sent to the other end of the tunnel.

Once your VPN gateway and customer gateway are configured, you need to configure routing options and security groups to enable communication between the site-to-site connections of VPC and your on-premises corporate network.

Configuring VPN routing options

Once you have created your VPN gateway and customer gateway, you are then in a position where you can begin to add routing configuration to your subnets to allow you to route traffic across to your corporate site via the VPN site-to-site connection.

Let's take a look at an example:

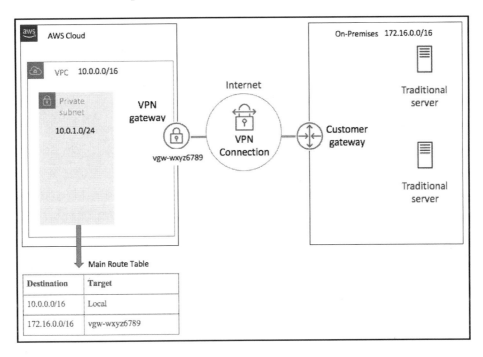

As you can see, AWS VPC has a `10.0.1.0/24` subnet within the VPC CIDR block of `10.0.0.0/16`. The main route table has a manually added static route pointing to the network address space within the corporate data center on the other side of the VPN connection. You will notice that this route has been added with the destination pointing to our VPN gateway (`vgw-wxyz6789`). As a result of this route, any traffic destined to this network will go via the VPN gateway.

A key point of understanding AWS routing in general is the principle of the *longest prefix match*. Understanding this can really help you troubleshoot routing issues. *Longest prefix match* determines how routes are prioritized in directing traffic to a target, especially when a route table has overlapping CIDR blocks—how will AWS determine where to send the traffic? Well, AWS will use the destination that has the most precise destination network listed, known as the *longest prefix match*.

For example, let's imagine you have the following route table:

Destination	Target
10.0.0.0/16	Local
172.16.0.0/16	pcx-1234abcd
172.16.1.0/24	vgw-wxyz6789

From the preceding table, we can understand the following:

- The first route is the local route of the VPC found in every route table.
- The second route points to a target relating to a VPC peering connection.
- The third route points to a VPN gateway, which then connects to a remote location.

If a packet was destined to a host on the 172.16.1.0 network, which target would it use? There are two routes that the route table could send the traffic to—the second and the third route. Both destinations fall into the network of a host on the 172.16.1.0 network. However, the third route has a longer prefix match in its destination field, and as a result, AWS routing would select this route as it's more precise.

Now, looking at the same route table, if a packet was destined for a host on the 172.16.2.0 network, there is now only one feasible route—the second one (the peering connection).

When using a VPN gateway, route propagation can be enabled. By enabling route propagation, all other routes to networks represented across your site-to-site VPN connection will be automatically be added within your route table, preventing you from having to manually add them. However, do be aware that should you encounter any overlapping CIDR blocks from propagated routes with static routes, then the static routes will always take precedence, regardless of the longest-prefix match principle between propagated and static routes.

If you don't use route propagation, then you will simply need to add in your static routes to your remote networks across the other side of the VPN connection.

Configuring your security groups

Once your routing has been configured and you have established a connection between your internal corporate network and AWS VPC, you will still need to configure and update your security groups to allow the required access inbound from your corporate network.

For example, if you intended to remotely connect to instances running in VPC from your corporate network using protocols such as RDP or SSH, then you need to open up these protocols within the security groups associated with your instances.

Using this VPC connection is one option of securing connectivity between your corporate infrastructure and AWS, which uses the internet as the underlying backbone of your connection. Now, let's take a look at AWS Direct Connection, which uses private infrastructure instead.

Using AWS Direct Connect

Similar to an AWS VPN connection, Direct Connect is another method of extending your own infrastructure and joining it to your AWS architecture as if it were a single network. However, with Direct Connect, you do not use a public network to initiate the connection. Instead, your connection runs across a private network via an AWS Direct Connect location.

These AWS Direct Connect locations are data centers where your own network and the network of AWS physically connect to each other via cross-connects using a standard fiber-optic cable between your router and an AWS Direct Connect router. These data centers are managed by AWS Direct Connect partners.

 For more information on these partners, please visit https://aws.amazon. com/directconnect/partners/.

Let's look at a diagram to help explain how this connection is established at a high level:

As you can see, there are three distinct locations involved to establish a link using AWS Direct Connect:

- Your corporate site where your own private network resides
- An AWS Direct Connect location (typically owned by an AWS partner)
- An AWS VPC within a specific AWS region

I have also highlighted two network segments. The network infrastructure highlighted by the dashed line on the right is managed by your organization and any of your associated network partners. You are responsible for implementing and managing the physical network infrastructure within this area. On the other hand, the physical network infrastructure highlighted by the dashed line on the left side is the responsibility of AWS.

With this segregation of physical network architecture, there are a number of networking prerequisites that need to be met prior to configuring and establishing a Direct Connect connection. From a network point of view, your network must meet at least one of the following requirements:

- Your organization works with one of the AWS Direct Connect partners, who is a member of the **AWS Partner Network (APN)**.
- Your network infrastructure has a co-location connection to an AWS Direct Connect location.

- Your organization works with an independent service provider allowing a connection to AWS Direct Connect.

Once you have established a physical network connection to an AWS Direct Connect location, you must also ensure that your network meets the following criteria:

- For authentication, your router must support both **Border Gateway Protocol (BGP)** and BGP MD5 (message-digest algorithm) authentication.
- Depending on the speeds required, your network infrastructure *must* use single-mode fiber. If you intend to use your Direct Connect connection as a 1 gigabit Ethernet connection, you have to use a 1000BASE-LX transceiver. For greater speeds of 10 gigabits over Ethernet, your transceiver must be a 10GBASE-LR.
- The port on your device must have manually configured speed and full-duplex mode enabled. However, auto-negotiation for the port must be disabled.
- You must ensure that you have 802.1Q VLAN encapsulation support across your network infrastructure, from your network source on-premises up to your customer/partner router at the AWS Direct Connect location.

An important element of Direct Connect is its ability to partition the connection into different virtual interfaces, so let's now take a look at these in more detail and see what they allow you to do.

Virtual interfaces

As mentioned, due to the requirement of enforcing 802.1Q VLAN encapsulation, you can partition the Direct Connect link into multiple connections, known as virtual interfaces. This allows you to gain access to other AWS services other than those within your VPC. For example, you could configure both a private and a public virtual interface. The private virtual interface will terminate within your VPC, establishing a private link between your corporate network and your VPC using private IP addresses. The public virtual interface, however, could be used to access all public AWS resources, such as objects stored in S3 with a public address space.

The following diagram shows how this would be represented:

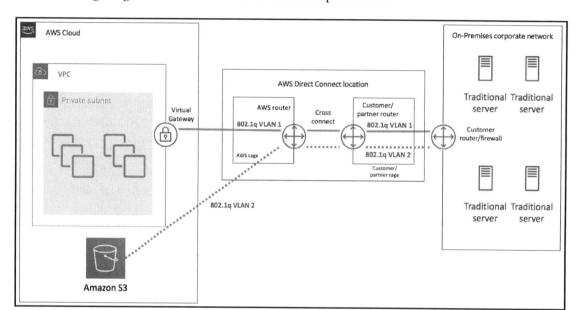

In this diagram, you can see that there are two virtual interfaces that are configured across the connection. Firstly, there is a private virtual interface, indicated by `802.1q VLAN 1`. Secondly, there is a public virtual interface that connects to publicly accessible AWS resources, such as configured S3 objects, indicated by `802.1q VLAN 2`.

Controlling Direct Connect access using policies

As with all AWS services, access can be controlled by a series of policies, and Direct Connect is no different. Configuring access policies allows you to instill granular access in relation to using and implementing Direct Connect.

When using identity-based policies, Direct Connect uses the prefix of `directconnect:` for any actions.

For a full list of Direct Connect actions, please visit `https://docs.aws.amazon.com/IAM/latest/UserGuide/list_awsdirectconnect.html`.

The following policy is an AWS-managed policy found within IAM titled
`AWSDirectConnectReadOnlyAccess`, and provides read-only access to AWS Direct
Connect via the AWS management console:

```
1  {
2    "Version": "2012-10-17",
3    "Statement": [
4      {
5        "Effect": "Allow",
6        "Action": [
7          "directconnect:Describe*",
8          "ec2:DescribeVpnGateways",
9          "ec2:DescribeTransitGateways"
10       ],
11       "Resource": "*"
12     }
13   ]
14 }
```

Following on from this, the following policy is another AWS-managed
policy, `AWSDirectConnectFullAccess`, and provides full access to AWS Direct Connect
via the AWS management console:

```
1  {
2    "Version": "2012-10-17",
3    "Statement": [
4      {
5        "Effect": "Allow",
6        "Action": [
7          "directconnect:*",
8          "ec2:DescribeVpnGateways",
9          "ec2:DescribeTransitGateways"
10       ],
11       "Resource": "*"
12     }
13   ]
14 }
```

You will notice, in these two example policies, that there are two `ec2:` actions referring to
VPN gateways and transit gateways. I have already explained what a VPN gateway is
earlier in this chapter. However, an AWS transit gateway is something slightly different.
Without digressing too much, let me quickly explain what it is.

A transit gateway enables the connectivity of multiple AWS VPCs and remote on-premise
networks together via a central transit hub. This transit gateway can accept connections
from VPCs, VPNs, and Direct Connect connections within a single region and route traffic
between all connected networks. Multi-region transit gateway connectivity will likely
become possible soon; however, at the time of writing this chapter, it is only feasible within
a single region.

OK, back to the policy management of Direct Connect. When it comes to identifying resources relating to the Direct Connect, there are four different **Amazon Resource Names (ARNs)**, which are as follows:

Resource Type	Amazon Resource Name
dxcon	arn:${Partition}:directconnect:${Region}:${Account}:dxcon/${ConnectionId}
dxlag	arn:${Partition}:directconnect:${Region}:${Account}:dxlag/${LagId}
dx-vif	arn:${Partition}:directconnect:${Region}:${Account}:dxvif/${VirtualInterfaceId}
dx-gateway	arn:${Partition}:directconnect::${Account}:dx-gateway/${DirectConnectGatewayId}

Using these resources types, you can create more granular policies relating to specific connection IDs, LAGIDs (**Link Aggregation Group IDs**: https://docs.aws.amazon.com/directconnect/latest/UserGuide/lags.html), virtual interfaces, and DC gateway IDs.

For example, if you wanted to reference a specific interface identified as dxcon-1234abcd in AWS account 6666777788889999, you would reference the ARN in your policy statement, as follows:

```
"Resource": "arn:aws:directconnect:us-
east-1:666677788889999:dxcon/dxcon-1234abcd
```

You can also use tagging to help manage permissions to your Direct Connect resources. As with most resources in AWS, you can associate tags; for example, you can add a tag to a virtual interface, perhaps to identify different environments. Once tags have been applied, you can then add conditions within your policy to govern what actions can be carried out based on the result of the condition.

As an example, the following policy will allow an identity to delete a virtual interface on the condition that the resource's environment tag matches the development value:

```
{
"Version": "2012-10-17",
"Statement": [
  {
    "Effect": "Allow",
    "Action": [
      "directconnect:DeleteVirtualInterface"
    ],
    "Resource": "arn:aws:directconnect:*:*:dxvif/*",
    "Condition": {
      "StringEquals": {
        "aws:ResourceTag/environment": [
          "development"
        ]
      }
    }
  }
```

```
        },
        {
          "Effect": "Allow",
          "Action": "directconnect:DescribeVirtualInterfaces",
          "Resource": "*"
        }
      ]
    }
  ...
```

For more information on access policies and JSON policy syntax, please refer back to Chapter 4, *Working with Access Policies*.

Summary

In this chapter, we looked at both VPN site-to-site connectivity and Direct Connect as a means of connectivity to your AWS infrastructure from your on-premises location via both public and private infrastructure. We saw that VPN connectivity uses the internet as an intermediary network to connect to your AWS infrastructure, whereas Direct Connect uses a private network that physically connects your corporate network to that of AWS within a specific region. Direct Connect generally provides a more consistent and reliable connection and offers enhanced throughput up to a speed of 10 gigabit Ethernet.

When using either option, consideration needs to be given to your routing configuration, security groups, and access policies. This chapter was designed to cover some of these points; however, for greater in-depth configuration of some of the routing protocols, such as BGP, please refer to the AWS documentation.

In the next chapter, I will be focusing on how AWS allows you to implement various logging capabilities across multiple different services, and so we will be looking at S3 server access logs, VPC flow logs and traffic mirroring, AWS CloudTrail logs, and the CloudWatch logging agent.

Questions

As we conclude, here is a list of questions for you to test your knowledge of this chapter's material. You will find the answers in the *Assessments* section of the *Appendix*:

1. When configuring a VPN connection, a VPN gateway is configured as well as what other type of gateway?
2. True or false: when an end-to-end connection is established between two gateways using a VPN connection with IPsec, the connection is referred to as a tube.
3. Does Direct Connect use a public or private network to establish a connection with AWS?
4. True or false: by enabling route propagation, all other routes to networks represented across your site-to-site VPN connection will be automatically added to your route table, preventing you from having to manually add them.

Section 4: Monitoring, Logging, and Auditing

4

In this section, we'll take a deep dive into the different methods of logging that are available when working with AWS. We'll cover the importance of logging and some of the different services and features that offer logging capabilities. You will learn how to implement S3 Server access logs, configure VPC Flow Logs and Traffic Mirroring, learn how AWS CloudTrail Logs are captured and what they capture, and how to configure the CloudWatch Logging Agent.

Following this, you will be exposed to the world of cloud auditing and governance. We'll look at why audits take place and what you can do within AWS to maintain compliance with different governance controls. We'll also look at a number of different services that will be invaluable when it comes to providing evidence during an audit and how to configure services to ensure your solutions maintain a set level of compliance.

By the end of this section, you will be able to confidently plan for and approach an audit to meet any compliance required.

This section comprises the following chapters:

- Chapter 12, *Implementing Logging Mechanisms*
- Chapter 13, *Auditing and Governance*

12
Implementing Logging Mechanisms

With so many services available to use within AWS, there is a vast amount of information being sent and received, both internally and externally, from your account. With so much traffic and data, it's essential that you are able to track and record what is happening with your resources to allow you to monitor your environment for potential weaknesses or signs of attack that indicate a security threat.

Having the ability to configure and enforce logging across your services helps significantly in identifying potential issues, not just from a security perspective but also from a performance and availability perspective too. In this chapter, I want to look at some of the different logging options available to you within AWS that you should be aware of.

We will be covering the following topics in this chapter:

- S3 server access logs
- Flow logs and traffic mirroring
- AWS CloudTrail logs
- The CloudWatch logging agent

Technical requirements

To follow the demonstrations in this chapter, you need elevated privileges for the services discussed. For information on granting permissions, please refer to Chapter 4, *Working with Access Policies*.

Implementing logging

For many organizations, implementing effective logging and monitoring at the start of a project can sometimes be an afterthought, what with the never-ending pressure to launch new applications, architecture, and solutions. However, treating it as an afterthought inevitably ends up being a regrettable approach due to the value that logging brings to your environment, especially during a security compromise or a degradation in service and performance.

Many AWS services generate logs that provide a vast amount of information that you otherwise wouldn't necessarily have access to that can be written to persistent storage. They contain details that enable you to optimize and identify potential issues, or highlight improvements, and so they become a valuable asset within your solutions. Logs are typically in text form, allowing you to easily process, analyze, and extract the data that you need and are looking for.

It can be very easy to implement logging solutions with vast amounts of data that holds valuable information; however, it's challenging to interpret that information and respond to it appropriately.

There are many benefits to logging, which fit many different business requirements. Log data can be very effective in resolving and identifying incidents across your environments, helping to reduce the blast radius of a problem quickly and sometimes automatically. Many organizations must also implement logging capabilities to fulfill audit and governance compliance controls, which are an important requirement that can't be overlooked. More on auditing and governance is covered in Chapter 13, *Auditing and Governance*.

With this basic understanding of logging and the advantages it provides, let's now look at some of the different AWS services and the logs they produce.

Amazon S3 logging

I want to look at the S3 service first, which is the most widely used storage service that AWS provides. S3 provides you with almost limitless amounts of object storage, which can be used for many different use cases. As a result, its logging features are worth taking a look at.

There are two types of logging that can be found within S3:

- S3 server access logs
- S3 object-level logging

We'll go over them one by one.

Enabling S3 server access logging

Server access logs contain details about when a particular bucket is accessed. This information can be used to ascertain the frequency at which a bucket is accessed and by whom it is accessed. Before I continue, an Amazon S3 bucket is a container in which you store the objects that you upload to Amazon S3. It can be considered similar to a folder that you would get in a normal filesystem.

The data gathered by these access logs contains useful information that can be used to help you identify the source of a security incident. Here are just a few of the log details that are captured:

- The identity of the requester accessing the bucket
- The name of the bucket being accessed
- A timestamp identifying when the action was carried out against the bucket
- The action that was carried out against the bucket
- The HTML response status
- Any error codes that are applicable

> For a full list of log fields, please see: `https://docs.aws.amazon.com/AmazonS3/latest/dev/LogFormat.html`.

It is very simple to enable this logging at the bucket level; the process simply involves using an additional bucket to direct logs to, known as a target bucket. Ideally, this target bucket should be dedicated to logging for ease of management. A key point to remember when configuring S3 server access logs is that the source and target buckets must be in the same region and be owned by the same AWS account.

Let's take a look at how to implement this configuration via the AWS Management Console:

1. Log in to your AWS account via the AWS Management Console.
2. Select the **S3 service**.
3. Under **Buckets**, select the source bucket that you want to create logs for.
4. Select the **Properties** tab:

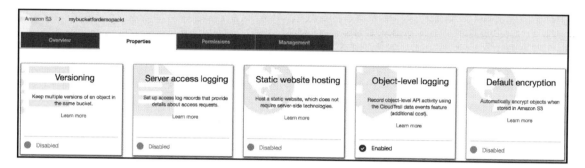

5. Select **Server access logging**. You will notice that it is currently disabled, which is the default option for any bucket that is created. If it was enabled, it would indicate so, much in the same way that the **Object-level logging** option is in the preceding screenshot:

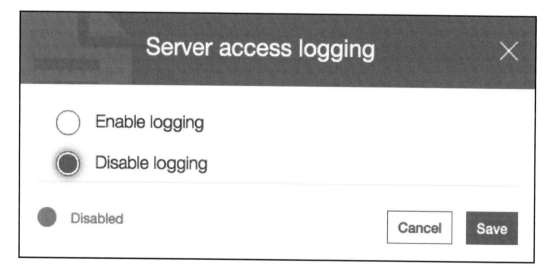

6. Select **Enable logging**:

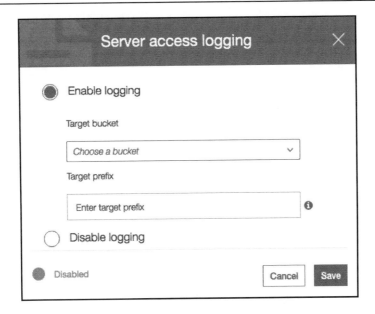

7. From the drop-down list, select the target bucket to be used. This target bucket will contain the logs gathered from the source bucket. If required, you can optionally set a **Target prefix** value; this will allow you to differentiate between your logs if you have multiple source buckets using the same target bucket. For example, you might want to add a target prefix of **audit/**, and then each log will have **audit/** as a prefix.

8. Once you have configured your target bucket and optionally a prefix, select **Save**. Server access logging is now enabled:

When a bucket is used as a target for S3 access logging from within the AWS Management Console, the **Access Control List (ACL)** permissions on the bucket are updated to allow the delivery of these log files by the log delivery group. This log delivery group is predefined by AWS and is used to deliver the logs to the target bucket from the source buckets.

The following screenshots show these permissions on the target bucket.

The first screenshot shows you that the **Log Delivery** group has write access to objects in the bucket and read access to read the bucket permissions. These permissions allow the log delivery group to send the log data to the target bucket:

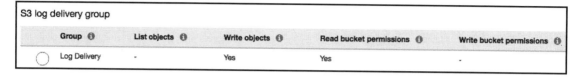

If you were to configure S3 access logging for use in the CLI, then you would need to manually add these ACL permissions to the target bucket for the logs to be delivered. For more information on how to configure this, please visit the following AWS documentation at: `https://docs.aws.amazon.com/AmazonS3/latest/dev/enable-logging-programming.html`.

The name of each S3 server access log file is constructed in the following format:

```
TargetPrefixYYYY-mm-DD-HH-MM-SS-UniqueString
```

`TargetPrefix` is the optional prefix that you can add as explained previously. `YYYY-mm-DD-HH-MM-SS` defines the year, month, day, hour, minute, and seconds, in UTC time, of the time at which the log was created. `UniqueString` provides no real value or meaning; it is simply used to prevent the file from being overwritten by another file with the same name.

The following screenshot shows some examples of S3 server access logs with a target bucket:

```
☐  📄  2019-11-21-14-19-47-88F556B746A4C313

☐  📄  2019-11-21-14-21-11-FDC9E6EF452F48C3

☐  📄  2019-11-21-14-21-49-B5E1DCFA2AE7F0B6

☐  📄  2019-11-21-14-22-19-02718399B49513DB

☐  📄  2019-11-21-14-24-29-2B39B042E9AE57FA
```

In addition to logging at the bucket level of Amazon S3, we also have logging at the object level, so let's now take a look at that.

S3 object-level logging

S3 object-level logging integrates with AWS CloudTrail data events. AWS CloudTrail is a service that records and tracks all AWS API requests that are made. These can be programmatic requests made using an SDK or the AWS CLI, from within the AWS Management Console, or from other AWS services.

When S3 object-level logging is enabled, you must associate it with a CloudTrail trail. This trail will then record both write and read API activity (depending on its configuration) for objects within the configured bucket. Although we are discussing Amazon S3 here, S3 object-level logging relies heavily on CloudTrail, and so I shall discuss CloudTrail data events later in this chapter when I dive deeper into AWS CloudTrail and its logging capabilities.

Now that we have looked at an example of how logging can be achieved for S3, I now want to look at how logging can be used at the network level, using VPC Flow logs.

Implementing Flow Logs

Within your AWS account, it's likely that you have a number of different subnets, both private and public, allowing external connectivity. You may even have multiple VPCs connected via VPC peering connections or via AWS Transit Gateway. Either way, you will have a lot of network traffic traversing your AWS infrastructure from multiple different sources, both internally and externally, across thousands of interfaces. Using Flow Logs gives you the ability to capture this IP traffic across the network interfaces that are attached to your resources, which could number in the tens of thousands in a corporate environment!

 For a recap of subnets and VPC infrastructure, please review the details found in `Chapter 7`, *Configuring Infrastructure Security*.

Flow Logs can be configured for the following resources:

- Your VPC
- A subnet within your VPC
- A network interface from your EC2 instances, or interfaces created by Elastic Load Balancing, Amazon RDS, Amazon ElastiCache, Amazon Redshift, Amazon WorkSpaces, NAT gateways, and Transit Gateway

As Flow Logs can capture information at these levels, it's a great way to help you identify security threats, such as network traffic that is reaching a resource or subnet that it shouldn't be. This might be down to overly permissive security groups or network ACLs, or other controls. Either way, it identifies weaknesses, allowing you to build a greater defense and remediate any potential vulnerabilities in your resources.

The logs themselves can either be sent and stored within Amazon S3 or sent to Amazon CloudWatch Logs. The logs need to be stored in a persistent data store to allow you to review them when required. Amazon S3 is a great way to store your logs, which can then be accessed by many different services for further analysis. Amazon CloudWatch can also be used as a central store for all of your logs that can be queried and sorted based upon different filters and visualized in dashboards.

Let's try implementing our own flow log. This will help us better understand the advantages that it brings us.

Configuring a VPC flow log for a particular VPC subnet

Creating a flow log is simple and can be done from the AWS Management Console. We'll create this and then decide whether to store it in Amazon S3 or CloudWatch, as well as understanding its format. So, let's begin:

1. From within the VPC dashboard of the AWS Management Console, select **Subnets**:

Virtual Private Cloud

Your VPCs

Subnets

Route Tables

Internet Gateways

Egress Only Internet Gateways

2. Select the subnet that you would like a flow log created for. At the bottom of the screen in the information pane, select the **Flow Logs** tab:

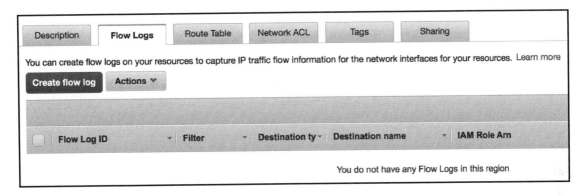

3. Select the blue **Create flow log** button (seen in the preceding screenshot):

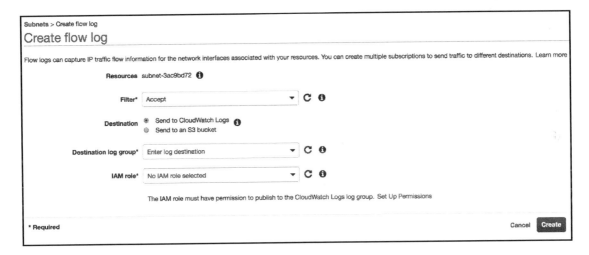

4. From here, you can configure the traffic that you want your flow log to capture. Using the **Filter** drop-down list, you can select either **Accept**, **Reject**, or **All**. This determines which traffic is to be recorded within the log.

5. Under the **Destination** option, you can choose to have the flow log data sent to either Amazon S3 or CloudWatch Logs. If you were to select CloudWatch Logs, you would then need to provide **Destination log group** and **IAM role** information to be used to deliver those logs. If you select S3 as the destination, your options change to the following:

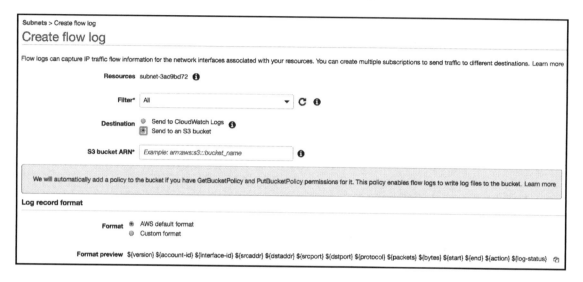

6. For this demonstration, I will select S3 as the destination, which means I need to add the **Amazon Resource Name (ARN)** of the destination bucket.

7. **Log record format** allows you to accept the default log file format:

```
${version} ${account-id} ${interface-id} ${srcaddr} ${dstaddr}
${srcport} ${dstport} ${protocol} ${packets} ${bytes} ${start}
${end} ${action} ${log-status}
```

Alternatively, you can create your own customized log file format, selecting a set of predefined options by using the **Custom Format** option. This will then present you with a drop-down list containing all available fields, which you can then select in any order. For this demonstration, I will select the default log file format.

We will discuss this file format in the upcoming subsection, so don't worry!

8. When you are happy with your options, select the blue **Create** button. You will then be taken back to the dashboard, where you can see your newly created flow log, which is given a flow log ID:

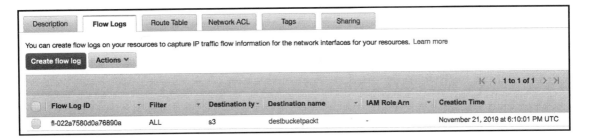

Once you have created your flow log, the only action you can then perform against it is deletion of the flow log.

If your flow log creation fails, then it is likely a permissions issue. When flow logs are created, permissions are added to the bucket policy of the selected S3 bucket, which allows the delivery of logs. These permissions are automatically applied as the user who is creating the flow log is also the owner of the bucket. If the user is not the owner of the bucket, then the following policy needs to be added manually, replacing the bold italics with your own details:

```
{
  "Version": "2012-10-17",
  "Statement": [
    {
      "Sid": "AWSLogDeliveryWrite",
      "Effect": "Allow",
      "Principal": {"Service": "delivery.logs.amazonaws.com"},
      "Action": "s3:PutObject",
      "Resource":
"arn:aws:s3:::bucket_name/optional_folder/AWSLogs/account_id/*",
      "Condition": {"StringEquals": {"s3:x-amz-acl": "bucket-owner-full
control"}}
    },
    {
      "Sid": "AWSLogDeliveryAclCheck",
      "Effect": "Allow",
      "Principal": {"Service": "delivery.logs.amazonaws.com"},
      "Action": "s3:GetBucketAcl",
      "Resource": "arn:aws:s3:::bucket_name"
    }
  ]
}
```

In this section, we looked at how to create a VPC flow log for a subnet, and we then directed that log data to an S3 bucket. In the next section, I want to explain how the log files themselves are defined.

Understanding the log file format

I briefly highlighted the log file format during the demonstration, but I just want to quickly highlight what each of those parameters is defined as. So, to clarify, the default log file format is as follows:

```
${version} ${account-id} ${interface-id} ${srcaddr} ${dstaddr} ${srcport}
${dstport} ${protocol} ${packets} ${bytes} ${start} ${end} ${action} ${log-
status}
```

These parameters define the following:

- version: The version of the flow log itself
- account-id: Your AWS account ID
- interface-id: The interface ID that the log stream data applies to
- srcaddr: The IP source address
- dstaddr: The IP destination address
- srcport: The source port being used for the traffic
- dstport: The destination port being used for the traffic
- protocol: The protocol number being used for the traffic
- packets: The total number of packets sent during the capture
- bytes: The total number of bytes sent during the capture
- start: The timestamp of when the capture window started
- end: The timestamp of when the capture window finished
- action: Whether the traffic was accepted or rejected by security groups and **Network Access Control Lists (NACLs)**
- log-status: The status of the logging, shown as one of three different codes:
  - OK: Data is being received.
  - NoData: There was no traffic to capture during the capture window.
  - SkipData: Some data within the log was captured due to an error.

To see a number of examples of log files taken from different interfaces, please visit: `https://docs.aws.amazon.com/vpc/latest/userguide/flow-logs-records-examples.html`.

In this section, we looked at the different parameters of VPC Flow logs to get an understanding of the data that they capture. But along with all the advantages they come with, do they also have limitations? Read on to find out.

Understanding log file limitations

Before you go ahead and think about creating flow logs across your infrastructure, do be aware that there are a number of limitations to using them. Some of the key points to be aware of are available at: `https://docs.aws.amazon.com/vpc/latest/userguide/flow-logs.html#flow-logs-limitations`.

That concludes this section covering VPC Flow logs and how they can be used at the network level to capture network data that's crucial in helping you to identify potential security attacks and threats. Attacks come from layers, and having the ability to create logs at each of these layers puts you in a good position to identify a threat quickly and eliminate it.

In the next section, I want to look at another network layer logging capability, but one that offers very different data to that of VPC Flow logs.

VPC Traffic Mirroring

VPC Traffic Mirroring, as the name implies, allows you to duplicate network traffic from elastic network interfaces attached to instances, so that the duplicated traffic can then be sent to third-party tools and services for traffic analysis and inspection.

When configured, the duplicated traffic is sent to a *target*; this could be a network load balancer, using UDP as a listener, which sits in front of a fleet of appliances dedicated to network analysis. Alternatively, you could simply use another EC2 instance as a target, pointing it to the **Elastic Network Interface (ENI)** of the instance. If required, these targets could also be in a different VPC for additional management.

Traffic Mirroring is a great addition to Flow Logs, as it provides a deeper investigative insight into network traffic. This helps you dissect packets more effectively, leading to a quicker root-cause analysis for both performance issues and security incidents. Reverse-engineering how a security threat progressed through your network allows you to better defend against it in future.

Each packet contains a lot of data and your own network team or security team might only be interested in certain elements. Using mirror filters, you can specify which element of a packet you need to capture. For example, you might only want to capture traffic running a certain port or protocol, or from a specific CIDR block.

More information on VPC Traffic Mirroring can be found at: `https://docs.aws.amazon.com/vpc/latest/mirroring/what-is-traffic-mirroring.html`.

Using AWS CloudTrail logs

As I mentioned previously when discussing S3 object-level logging, AWS CloudTrail is a service that records and tracks all AWS API requests made. These can be programmatic requests made using an SDK or the AWS CLI, from within the AWS Management Console, or from other AWS services. This makes it a fantastic service to comply with the specific governance and compliance requirements that you may have. Having a continuous log of all API activity within your account allows you to create a full audit history of operational activity, showing who or what has made specific changes to your specific resources and at what time.

To understand how CloudTrail logging works and the information that it captures, let me explain a few components of the service first:

- **Trails**: These are the fundamental building blocks of CloudTrail itself. They contain the configurable options that you want to monitor and track. For example, you can create a trail that monitors a single region, or multiple regions.
- **Events**: Each time an API call is made, AWS CloudTrail intercepts and captures that API request and stores it as an *event*. These events record key data relating to the API request, which is then stored within a log file. A new event is created for each and every API request made.
- **Log Files**: Log files are created approximately every 5 minutes and are delivered to and stored within a target S3 bucket as defined within the associated trail.

- **CloudWatch Logs**: In addition to storing your log files on S3, CloudTrail can also push your logs out to CloudWatch Logs for analysis and monitoring.
- **API Activity Filters**: These provide a search and filter functionality when looking at your API activity history from within the AWS Management Console.

If you are new to CloudTrail, let me show you how to create a new trail, which will also show how and where you can configure the options of the log files.

Creating a new trail

We will create a new trail using the AWS Management Console in this example. Follow these steps:

1. Log in to your AWS Management Console.
2. Select **CloudTrail** from the list of services.
3. Select **Trails** from the menu on the left:

4. Select the blue **Create trail** button. You will now be presented with a screen to configure your trail. Here, you will need to enter details relating to the name of the trail, whether you want the trail to apply to all regions, whether you want the trail applied to a specific region, and whether you want the trail to be applied to your AWS organization:

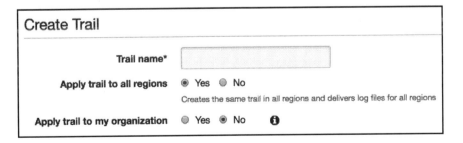

If your account is a part of an AWS organization and you are creating a new trail on the master account of that organization, then you can apply the same trail across all member accounts of that organization by selecting **Yes** for **Apply trail to my organization**. By doing so, users in the member account will be able to see the trail; however, they will not be able to modify it in any way or delete it. Also, by default, the users within the member accounts will not have access to the CloudTrail logs to ensure that access remains under the control of the master account.

One more point to mention is that by configuring this within the AWS Management Console, all trusted account permissions will automatically be applied to allow the service principal of `cloudtrail.amazonaws.com` to use the role `AWSServiceRoleForCloudTrail`.

5. You will then need to enter details for the management events. Management events are records of actions that are performed on or within resources in your AWS account. Your options are to record all read/write actions, just read actions, just write actions, or none. You can also choose whether you would like to use the trail to log **Key Management Service (KMS)** events as well:

Management events

Management events are records of actions that are performed on or within resources in your AWS account. These are also known as control plane operations. Learn more

      Read/Write events   ◉ All ◉ Read-only ◉ Write-only ◉ None **ⓘ**

      Log AWS KMS events   ◉ Yes ◉ No **ⓘ**

---

6. Next, you can opt in to logging insight events. Insight events are records that capture an unusual call volume of write management APIs in your AWS account. Do be aware that additional charges could apply for this feature:

Insights events

Insights events are records that capture an unusual call volume of **write management APIs** in your AWS account. Additional charges apply. Learn more

      Log Insights events   ◉ Yes ◉ No

---

7. Following insight events, you can then configure data events (plane operations), which can either be related to S3 or Lambda. Data events are records of resource operations performed on or within a resource. So, if you choose the S3 option displayed in the following screenshot, you can record all read calls, all write calls, or both read and write calls for S3 object-level API calls against specific buckets. Alternatively, you can record data events for all buckets within your account:

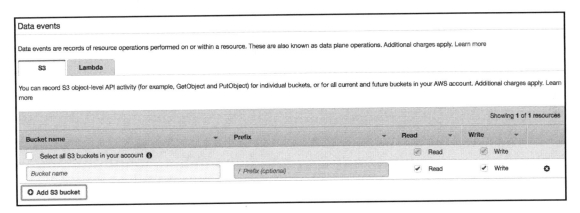

If you select the **Lambda** tab, you are presented with the following options, where you can record any Lambda Invoke API operations for the specific functions listed in the table. Again, much like S3 options, you can configure this to log all current and future Lambda functions:

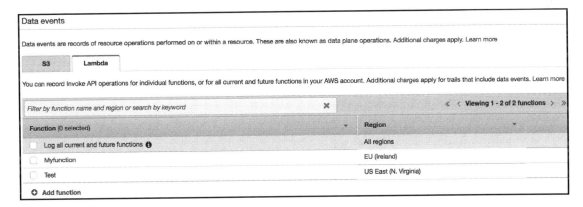

8. Next, you need to configure the storage location for the log files generated by the trail. You can either create a new S3 bucket or select an existing bucket. Under the advanced options, you can add additional details, such as a file prefix that should be used by the trail when storing log files within your selected bucket. Adding a prefix can help you quickly and easily distinguish between different log files:

Storage location

Create a new S3 bucket	⦿ Yes ◯ No
S3 bucket*	[_____] ⓘ
▾ **Advanced**	
Log file prefix	[_____] ⓘ
	Location: /AWSLogs/730739171055/CloudTrail/eu-west-1
Encrypt log files with SSE-KMS	◯ Yes ⦿ No ⓘ
Enable log file validation	⦿ Yes ◯ No ⓘ
Send SNS notification for every log file delivery	◯ Yes ⦿ No ⓘ

If your trail data is considered sensitive or confidential, then you can add a layer of encryption by choosing to encrypt the log files with **Server-Side Encryption using the Key Management Service (SSE-KMS)**. If this option is selected, you will be prompted to create a new **Customer-Managed Key (CMK)** or select an existing one. I will be covering KMS in detail in `Chapter 16`, *Managing Key Infrastructure*.

As an additional layer of security for your log files, you can enable log file validation. This essentially performs a check against your log file to see whether it has been tampered with after the log file has been delivered to your S3 bucket.

Finally, you can configure notifications for the delivery of every log file using **Simple Notification Service (SNS)**.

9. The final configurable element before creating your trail is configuring any tags to be used against the trail:

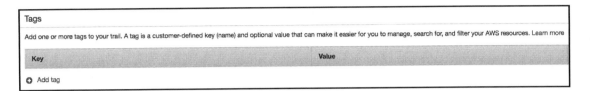

10. When you have finished your configuration, select the blue **Create** button to create your trail. You will then see your newly created trail on the dashboard.

Earlier, I mentioned that in addition to storing your log files on S3, CloudTrail can also push your logs out to CloudWatch Logs for analysis and monitoring; however, this configuration is not possible until the trail is created.

Configuring CloudWatch integration with your trail

Now that your trail is created, you have the option of integrating your trail with CloudWatch Logs. Let's run through the configuration process to do this:

1. Select your trail from within the CloudTrail dashboard.
2. Scroll down through the configuration of your trail until you get to the **CloudWatch Logs** section:

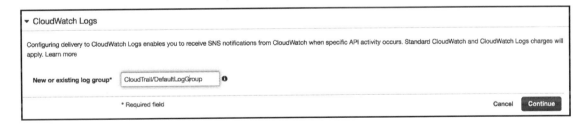

Here, either you can select an existing CloudWatch Logs group, if you have one configured, or alternatively you can have CloudTrail create a new one for you, which is what is shown in the preceding screenshot. Once you have selected your CloudWatch Logs group, select the blue **Continue** button.

3. To enable CloudTrail to deliver these logs to CloudWatch, permissions are required, and this is enabled in the form of a role that the CloudWatch service principal assumes to deliver the logs:

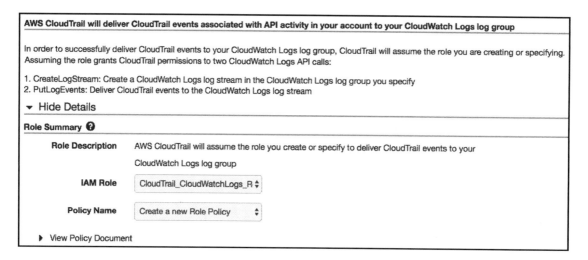

As you can see from the informational text in this image, access is required by CloudTrail to call the **CreateLogStream** and **PutLogEvents** APIs.

4. You must select the IAM role and the policy to enable this access. CloudTrail will create a default role for you, which is preselected, along with the ability for CloudTrail to create the policy as well (as shown in the preceding screenshot). The policy used is as follows:

```
{
  "Version": "2012-10-17",
  "Statement": [
    {
      "Sid": "AWSCloudTrailCreateLogStream20141101",
      "Effect": "Allow",
      "Action": [
        "logs:CreateLogStream"
      ],
      "Resource": [
        "arn:aws:logs:eu-west-1:730739171055:log-
```

```
group:CloudTrail/DefaultLogGroup:log-
stream:730739171055_CloudTrail_eu-west-1*"
      ]
    },
    {
      "Sid": "AWSCloudTrailPutLogEvents20141101",
      "Effect": "Allow",
      "Action": [
        "logs:PutLogEvents"
      ],
      "Resource": [
        "arn:aws:logs:eu-west-1:730739171055:log-
group:CloudTrail/DefaultLogGroup:log-
stream:730739171055_CloudTrail_eu-west-1*"
      ]
    }
  ]
}
```

5. When you have selected your options, select the blue **Allow** button for the configuration of permissions to take place. Your trail is now configured to send logs both to S3 and to CloudWatch Logs as well:

In this section, we covered how to create a new CloudTrail and then how to associate that trail with a CloudWatch Logs log group. Next, I want to dive deeper into AWS CloudTrail by looking at the contents of the log files generated by the trail.

Understanding CloudTrail Logs

In this section, I want to look at some snippets of the log files that are created by your trails so you can see some of the information that is captured.

As with many other policies within AWS, CloudTrail logs are written in **JavaScript Objection Notation (JSON)** format, and a new log entry (or event) is made each and every time an API is called.

These events, when written to a log file, may look similar to the snippets shown here:

```
"awsRegion": "eu-west-1",
"eventID": "6ce47c89-5908-452d-87cc-a7c251ac4ac0",
"eventName": "PutObject",
"eventSource": "s3.amazonaws.com",
"eventTime": "2019-11-27T23:54:21Z",
"eventType": "AwsApiCall",
"eventVersion": "1.05",
"readOnly": false,
"recipientAccountId": "730739171055",
"requestID": "95BAC3B3C83CCC5D",
"requestParameters": {
        "bucketName": "cloudtrailpackt",
        "Host": "cloudtrailpackt.s3.eu-
west-1.amazonaws.com",
        "key": "Packt/AWSLogs/730739171055/CloudTrail/eu-
west-1/2019/11/27/730739171055_CloudTrail_eu-
west-1_20191127T2321Z_oDOj4tmndoN0pCW3.json.gz",
        "x-amz-acl": "bucket-owner-full-control",
        "x-amz-server-side-encryption": "AES256"
"sharedEventID": "11d4461b-0604-46c4-b4c9-6a23b3e7f57c",
"sourceIPAddress": "cloudtrail.amazonaws.com",
"userAgent": "cloudtrail.amazonaws.com",
"userIdentity": {
        "invokedBy": "cloudtrail.amazonaws.com",
        "type": "AWSService"
```

Let me explain some of the parameters used within this single event taken from the event log stored on S3 and are useful when isolating issues from a security perspective:

- `eventName`: Highlights the name of the API being called (`"PutObject"`).
- `eventSource`: Determines the AWS service in which the API call was made. (`"s3.amazonaws.com"`)
- `eventTime`: This is the time that the API call was made (`"2019-11-27T23:54:21Z"`). This is in the format of yyyy-mm-dd T(IME) hh:mm:ss Z(UTC).
- `SourceIPAddress`: The source IP of the request used to make the API call. This displays the source IP address of the requester who made the API call. If this was the service in which the call was made, it will show the associated AWS service (`"cloudtrail.amazonaws.com"`).
- `userAgent`: Determines the agent method that initiated the request. This can be a number of different values. In our example event, I have `amazonaws.com`. It identifies that the request was made from within the AWS Management Console by a user.
- `Console.amazonaws.com`: Determines that the root user made the request.
- `userIdentity`: Contains additional information relating to the user agent.

So, what we can see from this log event is that AWS CloudTrail made a `PutObject` request to Amazon S3 to store its log file (this is shown under the `resources` parameter):

```
"arn:aws:s3:::cloudtrailpackt/Packt/AWSLogs/730739171055/CloudTrail/eu-
west-1/2019/11/27/730739171055_CloudTrail_eu-
west-1_20191127T2355Z_oFOj4tmndoH0pCW3.json.gz"
```

Having an understanding of what your CloudTrail logs contain can really help you grasp the value of having them. I suggest that you create a trail in your own account and review the contents of the logs to see how useful they can be. When working with more than one AWS account, it can be difficult to review all of your log files, so in the next section, I will explain how to consolidate your log files from multiple accounts into a single bucket.

Consolidating multiple logs from different accounts into a single bucket

In circumstances where you have multiple AWS accounts, you will want to implement a level of management and control. Thankfully, with AWS CloudTrail, you can consolidate logs from multiple accounts into a single S3 bucket, thereby reducing the amount of administrative effort needed to manage them:

 Before you begin, ensure that you have created a trail as shown in the previous demonstration in this chapter, with its target set as the required S3 bucket.

1. Log in to your AWS Management Console in the account that owns the S3 bucket.
2. Navigate to **S3** via the AWS Management Console dashboard and select the S3 bucket that you want to act as the central bucket for other AWS accounts. In this example, I have the **cloudtrailbucketstu** bucket:

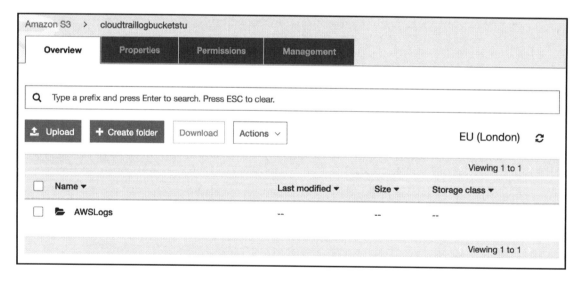

3. Select the **Permissions** tab:

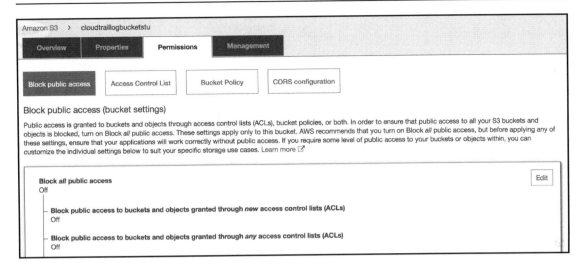

4. Now select **Bucket Policy**:

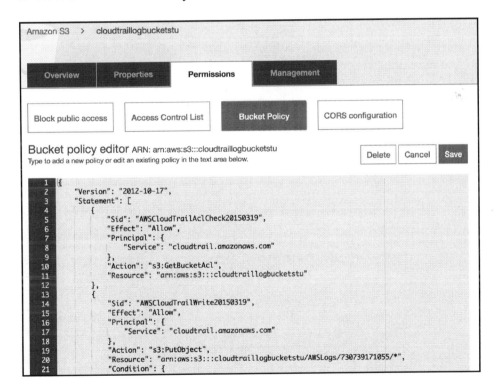

5. From here, you need to edit the policy to allow your other AWS accounts to access this bucket. You need to find the `Resource` section following the "`Action`": "`s3:PutObject`" section. In this example, it is listed as follows:

```
"Action": "s3:PutObject",
"Resource": "arn:aws:s3:::cloudtraillogbucketstu/AWSLogs/730739171055/*",
```

6. From here, you need to add another resource ARN, replacing the AWS account number with the account number of your other account. Ensure that you add a new resource for each account you want to add. It will then look something like the following:

```
"Resource": [
    "arn:aws:s3:::cloudtraillogbucketstu/AWSLogs/730739171055/*",
    "arn:aws:s3:::cloudtraillogbucketstu/AWSLogs/356903128354/*"
],
```

7. Here you can see that I have added another resource ARN. Select **Save**.
8. Log in to the AWS Management Console of the account that you just added the ARN for and navigate to AWS CloudTrail.
9. Create a new trail, following the steps from earlier in this chapter, until you get to **Storage location**:

10. Select **No** when asked whether you want to create a new S3 bucket; instead, add the name of the bucket from the primary account.
11. Continue to configure your trail as required and select **Create**. Your logs for this trail will now be delivered to the bucket specified from the primary account.

If I now log back in to my primary account and navigate to the S3 bucket, I will be able to see that a new folder has been created, identifying the account that I just added and showing that all logs are now being delivered to this bucket for each account:

The consolidation of logs into a single bucket can really help to ease the management burden when working with multiple accounts. When using CloudTrail at scale, this can help your teams manage logs more effectively in a single location, allowing you to enforce the correct level of access security on a single bucket, instead of having to do so for multiple buckets in different accounts.

Making your logs available to Amazon Athena

With so much valuable data within your CloudTrail logs, finding effective ways to query the data for specific entries can be made easier when using Amazon Athena.

Amazon Athena is a serverless service that allows you to easily analyze data being stored within Amazon S3, such as your CloudTrail logs, using an interactive query service that uses standard SQL. As a result, it is a very effective service to help you scan huge datasets. The configuration of Amazon Athena is outside of the scope of this book; however, more information on this service can be found at: https://aws.amazon.com/athena/.

Making your logs available to Athena to enable enhanced querying is a simple process:

1. From within the AWS Management Console, select **AWS CloudTrail**.
2. Select the **Event history** option from the left menu:

3. Select **Run advanced queries in Amazon Athena**:

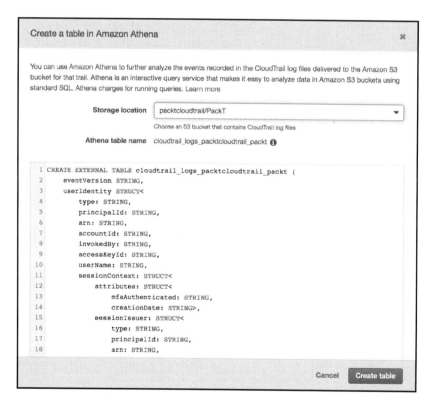

Can't find what you're looking for? Run advanced queries in Amazon Athena

4. From the **Storage Location** drop-down list, select the S3 bucket that contains your CloudTrail logs:

Create a table in Amazon Athena   ✕

You can use Amazon Athena to further analyze the events recorded in the CloudTrail log files delivered to the Amazon S3 bucket for that trail. Athena is an interactive query service that makes it easy to analyze data in Amazon S3 buckets using standard SQL. Athena charges for running queries. Learn more

Storage location   packtcloudtrail/PackT

Choose an S3 bucket that contains CloudTrail log files

Athena table name   cloudtrail_logs_packtcloudtrail_packt ⓘ

```
 1  CREATE EXTERNAL TABLE cloudtrail_logs_packtcloudtrail_packt (
 2      eventVersion STRING,
 3      userIdentity STRUCT<
 4          type: STRING,
 5          principalId: STRING,
 6          arn: STRING,
 7          accountId: STRING,
 8          invokedBy: STRING,
 9          accessKeyId: STRING,
10          userName: STRING,
11          sessionContext: STRUCT<
12              attributes: STRUCT<
13                  mfaAuthenticated: STRING,
14                  creationDate: STRING>,
15              sessionIssuer: STRUCT<
16                  type: STRING,
17                  principalId: STRING,
18                  arn: STRING,
```

Cancel   Create table

5. Select **Create table**. The table is then automatically created in Amazon Athena.

Using Amazon Athena, you can then create queries using SQL to search for specific content within your CloudTrail logs, enabling you to track and trace specific data that you want to be filtered within your results.

Using the CloudWatch logging agent

As you are probably aware, Amazon CloudWatch is the main monitoring service used in AWS and collects data and metrics from all the supported AWS services. This allows you to gain a better understanding of the performance of your environment. In addition to the built-in CloudWatch metrics, CloudWatch also allows you to collect valuable logging information from many different AWS services, such as EC2 instances, Route53, and CloudTrail.

Using CloudWatch logs as a central repository enables you to view real-time logging information from your services, which can be filtered and queried to search for specific events or error codes that you want to be made aware of, allowing you to respond accordingly.

In this section of the chapter, I want to explain how you can use the CloudWatch logging agent on your EC2 instances to enable you to send log data generated from your EC2 instances or any applications that may be running on your instance. This log data is in addition to the default CloudWatch metric data that is collected by CloudWatch.

There are a number of different ways to configure your instances. In this example, I will explain how to perform the configuration using the **AWS Systems Manager** (**SSM**). This will essentially involve three different steps:

1. Create the new roles that will be required.
2. Download and configure the CloudWatch agent.
3. Install the CloudWatch agent.

 During configuration, a CloudWatch agent configuration file will be created and stored in the parameter store in SSM. This part of the process is only required once. Once this configuration file has been created, the same file can be used on all your EC2 instances.

Creating new roles

You will need to create two new roles: one of these roles will have the permission to read and collect log data and send it to CloudWatch Logs to be written, and the other role is used to communicate with SSM to create and store your agent configuration file, allowing you to use the same agent configuration on your fleet of EC2 instances.

Create the first role, which will be used by your instances to collect log data using the following configuration information. I explained how to create roles in Chapter 3, *Access Management*, so please refer back to that if you need assistance in role creation. I have avoided going into the details here:

1. Select the type of trusted entity, then select **AWS service**.
2. Choose the service that will use this role – select **EC2**.
3. In the policy list, select both **CloudWatchAgentServerPolicy** and **AmazonSSMManagedInstanceCore**.
4. In **Role name**, enter CloudWatchAgentServerRole or another meaningful name.

For the second role, which is used with the parameter store, use the following configuration:

1. Select the type of trusted entity and select **AWS service**.
2. Choose the service that will use this role – select **EC2**.
3. In the policy list, select both **CloudWatchAgentAdminPolicy** and **AmazonSSMManagedInstanceCore**.
4. For **Role name**, enter CloudWatchAgentAdminRole or another meaningful name.

Once your roles are created, you need to download the CloudWatch logging agent and configure it.

Downloading and configuring the agent

Before downloading and installing the CloudWatch agent, you need to ensure that your EC2 instance is running at least version 2.2.93.0 of the SSM agent. If you need to update the SSM agent, please follow the instructions at: `https://docs.aws.amazon.com/systems-manager/latest/userguide/sysman-install-ssm-agent.html`.

Another prerequisite is that your EC2 instances need to have outbound internet access to enable them to send data to CloudWatch Logs. The endpoints and port information used for both logging capture and SSM can be found at: `https://docs.aws.amazon.com/general/latest/gr/rande.html#cwl_region`.

Once you have met the prerequisites, you can download the agent using SSM as follows:

1. From within the AWS Management Console, navigate to the SSM console found under the **Management and Governance** category.
2. Under **Instances and nodes** on the left-hand side, select **Run Command**:

▼ Instances & Nodes

    Compliance

    Inventory

    Managed Instances

    Hybrid Activations

    Session Manager

    Run Command

    State Manager

    Patch Manager

    Distributor

3. In the **Command document** search field, enter `AWS-ConfigureAWSPackage` to search for that document:

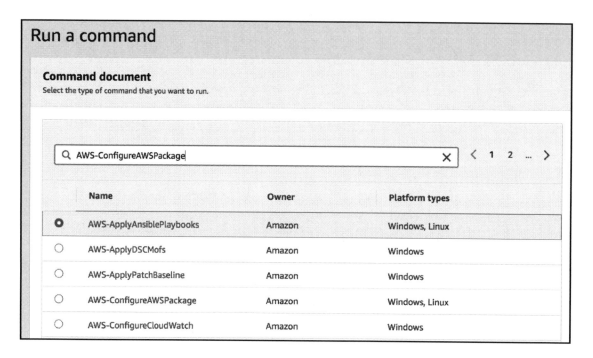

4. When the document is found, select it using the radio button:

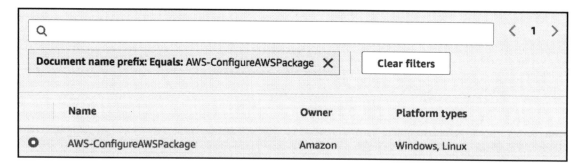

5. Under the **Command parameters** section, enter the details as shown here:

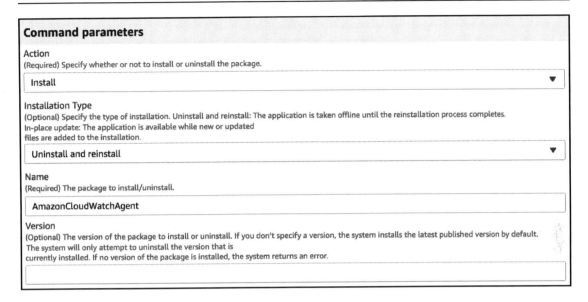

6. In the **Target** section, select your EC2 instance:

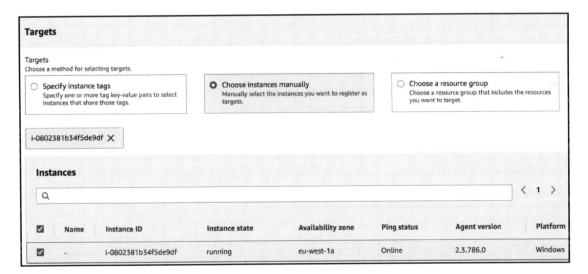

7. Under **Output options**, you can optionally add a destination for the output of the command either in S3 or a CloudWatch Logs log group:

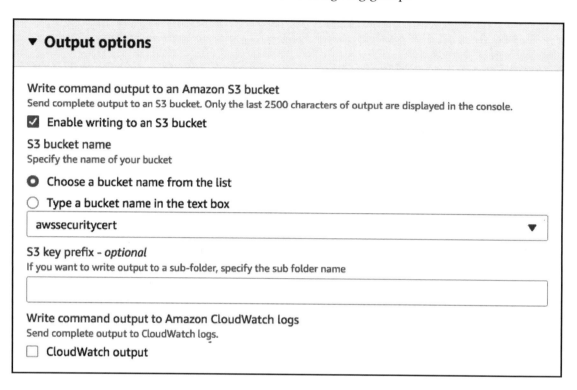

8. Select **Run**. You will then be shown the status of your command being issued:

Command status					
Overall status	Detailed status	# targets	# completed	# error	# delivery timed out
⏱ In Progress	⏱ In Progress	1	0	0	0

When the command has completed, you then have to create and modify the downloaded agent configuration file before it's installed on any of your other EC2 instances. This configuration file allows you to customize the agent via a series of questions. One of the easiest ways to create the configuration file for the agent is to use a wizard.

If you are running Linux, then enter the following command from your EC2 instance that you just issued the command on:

```
sudo /opt/aws/amazon-cloudwatch-agent/bin/amazon-cloudwatch-agent-config-wizard
```

If you are running Windows, then run the following:

```
cd "C:\Program Files\Amazon\AmazonCloudWatchAgent"
amazon-cloudwatch-agent-config-wizard.exe
```

You must then answer a series of questions, ensuring that you select **Yes** when prompted on whether to store the file in the SSM parameter store. This enables the configuration file to be copied to SSM, allowing it to be pushed out to your remaining EC2 fleet.

Installing the agent on your remaining EC2 instances

Finally, to install the configured CloudWatch agent for your remaining EC2 instances, you need to ensure that your EC2 instances meet some prerequisites.

Firstly, ensure that the EC2 instance is running the SSM agent version 2.2.93.0 or later. If you need to update a Linux-based instance, visit https://docs.aws.amazon.com/systems-manager/latest/userguide/sysman-install-ssm-agent.html; for Windows-based instances, visit https://docs.aws.amazon.com/systems-manager/latest/userguide/sysman-install-ssm-win.html.

Your instances must have outbound internet access to send CloudWatch logs to CloudWatch. For more information on understanding outbound internet access, please refer to Chapter 7, *Configuring Infrastructure Security*.

Once you have met the prerequisites, follow these steps to install the agent on your remaining E2C instances:

1. Attach the `CloudWatchAgentServerRole` role you created earlier to any instances that you want to install the CloudWatch agent onto.

2. From the SSM console, select **Run Command** and enter `AWS-ConfigureAWSPackage`:

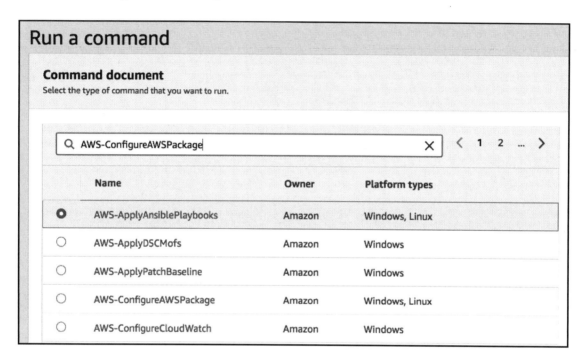

3. Under **Action**, select **Install**:

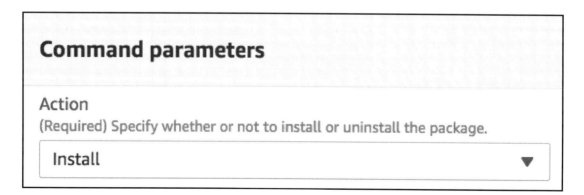

4. Under **Name**, enter the name of the package to install
   — `AmazonCloudWatchAgent`:

> **Name**
> (Required) The package to install/uninstall.
>
> **AmazonCloudWatchAgent**

5. In the **Targets** area, select the EC2 instance targets that you want to install the CloudWatch agent onto.
6. Select **Run**.

In this section, we focused on the CloudWatch logging agent and how it can be installed at scale, using the SSM service. By having the CloudWatch agent downloaded and installed on your EC2 instances, you now have the ability to capture more information on your EC2 instances to help you monitor their status and performance.

Summary

Within this chapter, we focused on Amazon S3, VPC Flow logs, AWS CloudTrail, and Amazon CloudWatch, all of which provided logging capabilities. I looked at how these were configured to capture log data to allow you to analyze them for suspicious activity.

An integral part of building a secure infrastructure is being able to collate and retrieve logs as and when required to help you identify the source of a threat even before it has happened. If you want to become an AWS security specialist, then take the time to investigate and understand which of the AWS services provide logs and how you can manage and monitor them to give you insight into your environment.

In the next chapter, I will be focusing on AWS auditing and governance and some of the services used to implement these measures, such as AWS Artifact, AWS CloudTrail, AWS Config, and Amazon Macie.

Questions

As we conclude, here is a list of questions for you to test your knowledge regarding this chapter's material. You will find the answers in the *Assessments* section of the *appendix*:

1. True or false: Amazon S3 server access logging is enabled by default.
2. Amazon S3 object-level logging closely integrates with which other AWS service?
3. Which logging feature allows you the ability to capture IP traffic across the network interfaces attached to your resources?
4. True or false: A VPC Flow Log can be configured for a subnet with a VPC.
5. Which AWS service can be used to easily query AWS CloudTrail logs, enabling you to search for specific data?

Further reading

- Security at Scale (AWS White Paper): `https://d1.awsstatic.com/whitepapers/compliance/AWS_Security_at_Scale_Logging_in_AWS_Whitepaper.pdf?did=wp_cardtrk=wp_card`

Auditing and Governance 13

Every organization is subjected to a level of governance and compliance, and this governance comes hand in hand with auditing. As an organization, you must be able to trace, track, and record different processes and operational steps to ensure that you as a company are following set guidelines, laws, and regulations. You have to able to prove at any given point that you as an organization are adhering to this level of governance, and this is referred to as auditing. Therefore, auditing provides a means and method of providing evidence to a third-party auditor that you meet specific criteria through implemented controls and processes. Failure to comply with governance controls, depending on the audit itself, can result in financial fines and/or criminal charges.

This chapter will look at some of the methods and AWS services that can play key parts in maintaining this governance and how a level of auditing can be achieved. As a result, we will be focusing on the following:

- What is an audit?
- Understanding AWS Artifact
- Securing AWS CloudTrail
- Understanding your AWS environment through AWS Config
- Maintaining compliance with Amazon Macie

Technical requirements

To follow the examples and demonstrations, you must have access to an AWS environment with elevated privileges to the following:

- AWS Artifact
- AWS CloudTrail
- Amazon S3
- AWS Config
- Amazon Macie

For more information on how to access these privileges, please refer to Chapter 4, *Working with Access Policies*.

What is an audit?

There are many different types of audits that a third-party external auditor can assess your organization on, for example, network security, data management, remediation management, and change management are just a few. The auditors may conduct the assessment by collecting evidence in a variety of ways, such as analyzing logs, physical inspection, reviewing procedures, and general inquiries. Before we begin this chapter, let's highlight some common audit compliance programs that you might see.

AWS complies with global compliance programs to meet the needs of its customers. A full breakdown of the compliance programs that they are subjected to and have certification for can be found at https://aws.amazon.com/compliance/programs/.

The following are the global compliance programs that AWS adheres to:

	ISO 9001	ISO 27001	ISO 27017	ISO 27018
CSA controls	Global Quality Standard	Security Management Controls	Cloud Specific Controls	Personal Data Protection
Report type	SOC 1: Audit Controls Report	SOC 2: Security, Availability, and Confidentiality Report	SOC 3: General Controls Report	

As you can see, many of these compliance programs focus on specific aspects of an organization's processes, such as ISO 27017, which looks at Cloud Specific Controls, and SOC 2, focusing on Security, Availability, and Confidentiality.

AWS also adheres to many other region-specific compliance programs, such as FedRAMP and HIPAA in the US, G-Cloud (UK) in the United Kingdom, and many more!

In each of these compliance programs, there is a set of audit controls that need to be met. For each control, evidence will need to be seen and collected to ensure that your organization meets the criteria of that control. Once the auditor is satisfied with the evidence, the audit control is classed as met. After each audit, a full report is carried out stating the controls that were passed and the ones that were failed, highlighting any certifications and accreditation achieved as a result of the audit.

Differences businesses, depending on the industry, need to follow different compliance controls, and just because AWS adheres to certain controls does not mean that you as a business running in AWS also meets those controls. You will be assessed on how you are running your infrastructure, processes, security, management, and more, to also ensure that you meet the controls required for your own audits conducted by external auditors.

With this basic understanding of what auditing is all about, let's now go one step further and look at some of the methods and AWS services that can play a key role in achieving this audit. Let's begin with AWS Artifacts.

Understanding AWS Artifact

Unlike other AWS services, AWS Artifact is not a service that you use to create a resource, such as an EC2 instance, a database, or a VPC. Instead, AWS Artifact is an on-demand portal to allow you to view and download AWS security and compliance **reports**, in addition to any online **agreements**. But what are these reports and agreements exactly?

- **Reports**: These are the reports that have been undertaken by external auditors of AWS, who have issued the relevant reports, certifications, accreditations, and other third-party attestations.
- **Agreements**: These allow customers to review and then accept any agreements that have been made with AWS that relate to your own individual account. If your account is a part of an AWS Organization, then all of the agreements for all accounts can be reviewed and accepted here in a central location, simplifying the management of AWS agreements.

You can access these reports and agreements from the AWS Management Console itself. Let's see how to do it.

Accessing reports and agreements

Accessing these reports is simple and you can do it from the Management Console. Follow these steps:

1. Log in to your AWS account and, from the AWS Management Console, click on the **Security, Identity and Compliance** category.
2. Now navigate to the **Artifact** dashboard. You are presented with two options, which help organize Artifact documents, these being **Reports** and **Agreements**:

Reports	AWS Artifact
Agreements	AWS Artifact features a comprehensive list of access-controlled documents relevant to compliance and security in the AWS cloud.

3. We'll look at **Reports** first, so click on it. Within the **Reports** section, you can find artifacts that relate to specific compliance and security requirements, such as SOC, PCI-DSS, IS27000 series, among many others. Here is a screenshot of the list of artifacts available:

ISO 27001:2013 Statement of Applicability (SoA)
Reporting period: Valid from 11/05/2019 to 11/05/2020

The AWS ISO 27001:2013 Statement of Applicability (SoA) indicates the ISO 27001 requirements applicable to AWS.

Get this artifact

ISO 27017:2015 Certification
Reporting period: Valid from 11/05/2019 to 11/07/2022

This certification, issued by an independent third-party auditor, validates that AWS complies with the ISO 27017 implementation guidance of cloud-specific information security controls that supplement the ISO 27002 guidance and the ISO 27001 standard.

Get this artifact

ISO 27017:2015 Statement of Applicability (SoA)
Reporting period: Valid from 11/05/2019 to 11/05/2020

The AWS ISO 27017:2015 Statement of Applicability (SoA) indicates the ISO 27017 requirements applicable to AWS.

Get this artifact

ISO 27018:2014 Certification
Reporting period: Valid from 11/05/2019 to 11/07/2022

This certification, issued by an independent third-party auditor, validates that AWS complies with the ISO 27018 implementation guidance of controls applicable to public cloud Personally Identifiable Information (PII) protection that supplement the ISO 27002 guidance and the ISO 27001 standard.

Get this artifact

ISO 27018:2014 Statement of Applicability (SoA)
Reporting period: Valid from 11/05/2019 to 11/05/2020

4. As you can see, for each artifact there is a blue button that allows you to **Get this artifact**. To view the artifact and download the document, you must select the blue button and then sign a **non-disclosure agreement** (**NDA**) with AWS relating to the information contained within the artifact. This NDA screen will look something like the following:

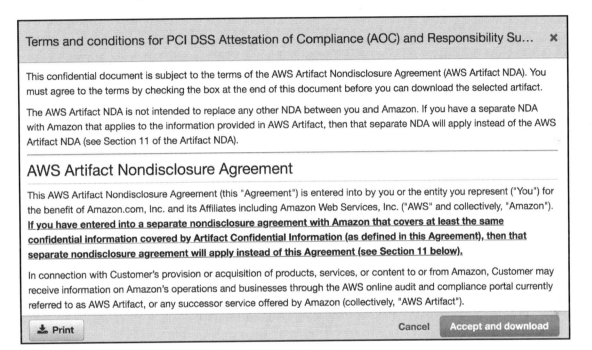

5. Once downloaded, these compliance artifacts can then be submitted to your own auditors to help achieve the level of governance and compliance that you need for your infrastructure.

6. Now let's move on to the **Agreements** dashboard. The **Agreements** section of AWS Artifact allows you to review, accept, and manage agreements for your account or organization such as the **Business Associate Addendum** (**BAA**) used for HIPAA compliance:

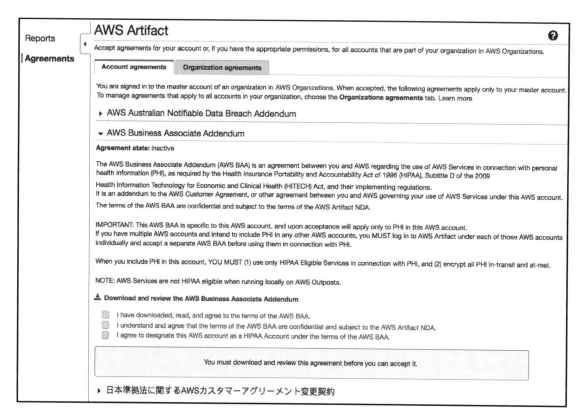

Account agreements shows any agreements that have been associated directly with your AWS account that you are currently viewing. If your account is the master account in an AWS Organization, then you will be able to view all of the account agreements for all member accounts using **Organization agreements**.

In this section, I explained how AWS Artifact can be used to help you provide reporting and agreement evidence from AWS to your auditors as and when required. This can be used in conjunction with your own evidence and reports gathered across your own infrastructure, which is what we will move on to next, starting with AWS CloudTrail.

Securing AWS using CloudTrail

In the previous chapter, I explained how you can create a new trail and configure logging mechanisms for AWS CloudTrail, in addition to diving into detail about the information captured, which provides great insight from an auditing perspective. However, here I just want to look at and highlight some of the best practices from a security perspective when configuring CloudTrail.

As we know, AWS CloudTrail is a great service to track and record all API activity on your accounts, which, as expected, can contain some very sensitive information that you would want to restrict access to. CloudTrail stores its logs in Amazon S3 by default, but as discussed previously, these can also be sent to CloudWatch Logs.

You may have heard over the past few years a lot of emphasis on Amazon S3 security controls, largely due to a string of data breaches where sensitive information had been exposed and was accessible to public users with malicious intent. However, much of this exposure was simply down to a lack of understanding from users of S3 about utilizing the available security controls that Amazon S3 offers, rather than a security design fault in the service itself. As a result, extra care should always be taken when storing sensitive information in any cloud storage. Thankfully, AWS has implemented further security enhancements, and in addition to an increase in user awareness of the service, it has helped prevent such accidents from happening since.

With this in mind, extra security controls on your CloudTrail data should be implemented. For example, you should always choose **Encrypt log files with SSE-KMS** in addition to selecting **Enable log file validation**. Let's see why these selections are important over the next two subsections.

The screenshots in the next section are taken from the configuration screen of an AWS CloudTrail trail. For more information on how to set up a trail, please see Chapter 12, *Implementing Logging Mechanisms*.

Encrypting log files with SSE-KMS

I will cover the full extent of the different S3 encryption options, in addition to how KMS works, in Chapter 16, *Managing Key Infrastructure.* However, at this stage, all we need to be concerned with is that it's possible to encrypt our CloudTrail logs files using either an existing or new KMS key. This is a very easy feature to enable as it's simply a checkbox and a KMS key selection:

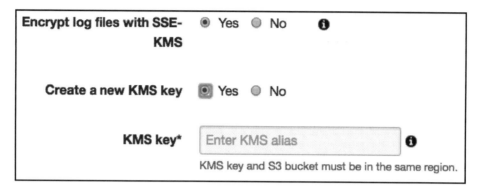

By doing so, all of your CloudTrail log data at rest will be encrypted unless you have access to the kms:decrypt action for the selected KMS key, in addition to access to the S3 bucket where your logs are stored. Adding this level of encryption ensures that only someone with access to decrypt the file can access the sensitive information that can be found within your log files. Due to the amount of information that can be contained in your CloudTrail log files, you will want to restrict access to them as much as possible, and this level of restriction might even be required to pass an audit control during an assessment.

Enabling log file validation

This checkbox is especially useful when you need to perform some forensic investigation into a security threat as it ensures that your log files have not been tampered with or modified at all from when they were written to your bucket in Amazon S3. To enforce this validation, CloudTrail uses algorithms such as SHA-256 for hashing and SHA-256 with RSA for digital signing:

Every time a new log file is delivered to S3 with validation enabled, CloudTrail will create a hash for it. In addition to this, and once an hour, CloudTrail will also create another file called a digest file that references each and every log file that was delivered within that hour, along with the associated hash. These digest files are signed using a private key of a public/private key pair used by CloudTrail for that region. Using the associated public key, you can then validate the digest files, which are stored in the same S3 bucket as your logs but in a different folder.

If you have read access to the bucket and you have *not* moved the files from their original bucket, then you can perform the validation by entering the following command using the AWS CLI:

```
aws cloudtrail validate-logs --trail-arn <trailARN> --start-time <start-time>
```

Additionally, you can add the following options to this command:

```
[--end-time <end-time>] [--s3-bucket <bucket-name>] [--s3-prefix <prefix>]
[--verbose]
```

These allow you to narrow your selection using specific parameters such as a set bucket name, prefixes, and time constraints.

 For a full listing of all the results and what they mean, please refer to the table within the AWS documentation at: https://docs.aws.amazon.com/awscloudtrail/latest/userguide/cloudtrail-log-file-validation-cli.html.

In addition to the aforementioned controls, you should also limit and control access to the S3 bucket in which the CloudTrail logs are stored. In addition to IAM permissions, limit access using bucket policies to only those who require access due to the sensitive information that can be found in the logs, which could, if accessed by a malicious user, provide a lot of information about your infrastructure, and potentially help to identify weak spots in your environment that could be used against you.

Auditing and governance do not simply require you to implement a level of logging, such as you can with AWS CloudTrail, but some audits will require you to demonstrate that you are restricting access to these logs as to ensure they do not become compromised and used as a method of gaining intelligence of intrusion. So, this section will be extremely helpful as you try and enforce additional control of your AWS CloudTrail logs.

Next, I want to move focus on to another service, AWS Config, which works in conjunction with AWS CloudTrail.

Understanding your AWS environment through AWS Config

With the number of services rising each year in AWS (currently at 168 services at the time of writing), it's easy to comprehend how difficult it can be to have an understanding of what resources you might be running within your environment. How can you keep up with what instances you have running and where, what are they running, and the resources still needed? You might be running infrastructure that's no longer required that got overlooked in among the thousands of virtual devices that are in production.

With the huge network of resources running within your account, do you have a clear understanding of which resource is connected to which? What ENI is connected to which instance? Which subnet is that instance running in? Which subnets are connected to which VPCs? Do you have a logical mapping of infrastructure that quickly and easily allows you to identify a blast radius should an incident occur, or visibility into resource dependencies should you change your configuration?

On top of that, do you know their current state of configuration? Are you certain they are running the latest patches, or is there a chance that some of your infrastructure is exposed and has been left vulnerable to potential security threats?

If someone makes a change to your infrastructure and environment, do you have an accurate record of that change, what changed, and when it changed?

Going back to compliance, how can you be assured that the resources that you are deploying and keeping meet compliance needs as dictated by both your internal and external controls and processes?

Answers to all of the above questions are generally required when performing audits, but gaining this information can be very cumbersome in traditional IT deployments, let alone cloud environments, which by their very nature are far more dynamic and are subject to a far higher rate of change. However, AWS is aware of these audit and compliance requirements and has an AWS service called AWS Config to help you address many of these questions in an automated, auditable, and compliant way.

For a comprehensive walk through of how to configure AWS Config, please see: `https://docs.aws.amazon.com/config/latest/developerguide/gs-console.html`. In this book, I want to focus more on the different components of AWS Config, and how they operate to help you understand how the service works and provides a level of auditing and governance checks. So, once you are set up, come back here to explore the various components of AWS Config.

To understand how AWS Config can help you achieve these results, let me explain some of the components of the service, which include the following:

- Configuration items
- Configuration streams
- Configuration history
- Configuration snapshots
- Configuration recorder
- Config rules
- Resource relationships
- Config role

Let's begin with our first component – **configuration items (CIs)**.

Configuration items

This is a fundamental element of AWS Config and is essentially a JSON file containing point-in-time snapshot information on the configuration data of attributes of a specific AWS resource within your environment that is supported by AWS Config (a full list of supported resources can be found at: `https://docs.aws.amazon.com/config/latest/developerguide/resource-config-reference.html`).

These attributes include its current configuration, any direct relationships the resource has with other resources, metadata, and events. A new CI is updated every time a change is made on that resource, for example, when a create, update, or delete API call is made against the resource.

To understand more about the construct of a CI, a table containing a list of components of a configuration item can be found within the AWS documentation at: `https://docs.aws.amazon.com/config/latest/developerguide/config-item-table.html`. Let's go over the components one by one:

- The **Metadata** section contains information and data about the configuration item itself.
- The **Attributes** section focuses on the data of the actual resource that the CI relates to.

- The **Relationship** section holds data related to any connected resource, for example, if the CI related to a subnet, the relationship could contain data related to the associated VPC the subnet was a part of.
- The **Current Configuration**, as the table explains, shows the same information that would be generated if you were to perform a `describe` or `list` API call made by the AWS CLI.

These CIs are effectively building blocks of AWS Config and are used by many other components of the service. Let's continue to see how these work together.

Configuration streams

When a change against a resource occurs in your environment, and as a result a new CI is created, then the CI is automatically added to a configuration stream, which is essentially an SNS topic. During the configuration of AWS Config, you can specify the SNS topic to be used for your stream:

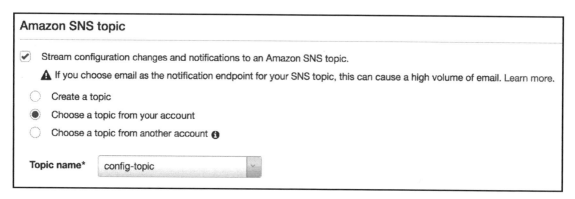

This enables you to monitor the stream and customize notifications for changes occurring to resources, helping you to identify potential issues or security incidents that are unexpected.

Configuration history

This is especially useful when it comes to audits and provides a complete history of all the changes made to a resource. By collating the CIs for a resource, AWS Config is able to assemble a history of modifications to that resource. The history of your resource can be accessed via the AWS CLI or via the AWS Management Console as a timeline of events. Also, as a part of the process, AWS Config will store a configuration history file of each resource type in an S3 bucket that is selected during the configuration of AWS Config.

Here, you can see the configuration history of an EC2 security group. It shows the date and time of any changes to the resource:

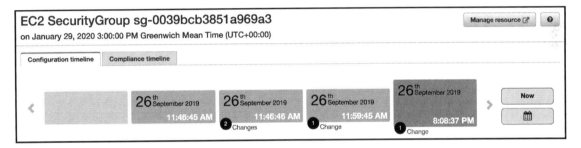

Using the AWS Management Console, you can select these changes and dive deeper to understand what element changed. Also, following a security incident or an outage, this history can be very useful to determine the timeline of events that led to the incident and can help you resolve it quickly and effectively.

Configuration snapshot

Again, using the building blocks of AWS Config, new CIs will be created allowing for a configuration snapshot to be constructed to get a point-in-time image of your AWS environment of all supported AWS resources with AWS Config in a particular region. This snapshot can be initiated by running the AWS CLI `deliver-config-snapshot` command and the results will be sent to your predefined Amazon S3 bucket.

Configuration recorder

You can think of the configuration recorder as the on and off switch for the AWS Config service. You must first enable the configuration recorder before the service can start creating your **configuration items (CIs)**. When you first configure AWS Config, the configuration recorder is automatically started, but once started, you can stop and re-enable it at a later date:

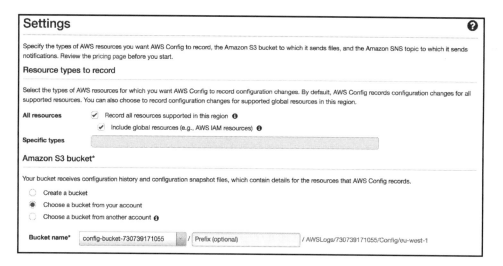

This shows the initial configuration screen and allows you to select the resource types that you want AWS Config to record. If you uncheck the **Record all resources supported in the region**, then you will be able to select from a drop-down list of **Specific types**, an example of which can be seen here:

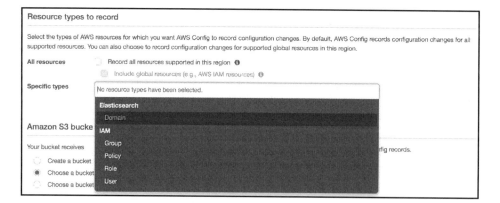

With your chosen resources selected and the destination S3 bucket selected to store your configuration history and snapshot files, the configuration recorder can begin resource changes.

AWS Config rules

From a compliance perspective, AWS Config rules are a great feature and should be implemented whenever you use AWS Config. Backed by AWS Lambda functions performing simple logic, Config rules automatically monitor your resources to ensure they are meeting specific compliance controls that you might need to introduce within your AWS environment. If a resource is found not to be compliant, you will be notified via SNS and the configuration stream, allowing you to take corrective action.

With Config rules, you can enforce a consistent deployment and configuration approach, ensuring all resource types are following set criteria, regardless of who or when the resource was deployed.

There are two types of Config rules available: those that can be *custom defined*, and those that are *predefined and managed by AWS*. These AWS rules are ready and available to use to save you having to create your own from scratch.

Let's take a look at how you can set up AWS Config rules to help with the compliance of your infrastructure.

Please note, you must have already set up and configured AWS Config (see the *Configuration recorder* section for more information).

1. Log in to the AWS Management Console and navigate to AWS Config under the **Management and Governance** category.
2. From the menu on the left-hand side, select **Rules**:

3. To add a new rule, select **Add Rule**:

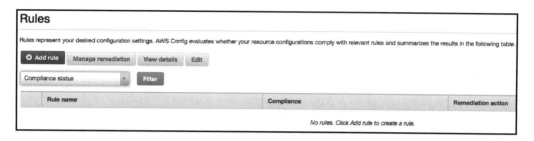

4. From here, you will be presented with a list of pre-configured AWS-managed rules. You can filter on these rules using the search box. As shown in the screenshot, I have searched for S3 and it has returned all compliance checks that relate to S3, of which there are 14. So it's likely that there is a compliance check that already exists that you are looking for, or at least a very similar one:

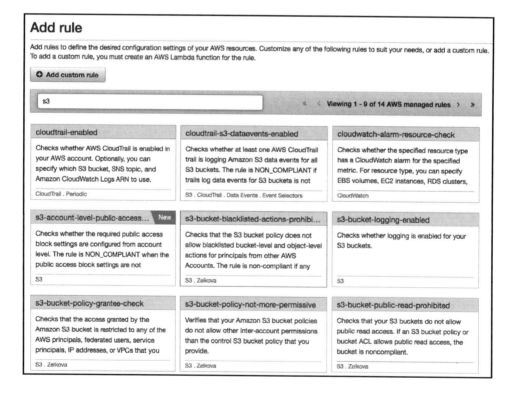

If there isn't a rule that matches your requirements, then you can select the **Add custom rule** button, which will allow you to select a Lambda function that will perform the logic of your compliance check. So, if you are familiar with AWS Lambda and are confident in the creation of a function, then you can create your own checks to fit your exact compliance needs.

5. For this demonstration, I am going to select the existing pre-configured AWS-managed Config rule **s3-bucket-server-side-encryption-enabled**. This will evaluate my S3 buckets to check which ones do not provide default server-side encryption:

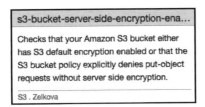

6. Once you have selected your Config rule, you are able to view its configuration and make additional configurational changes:

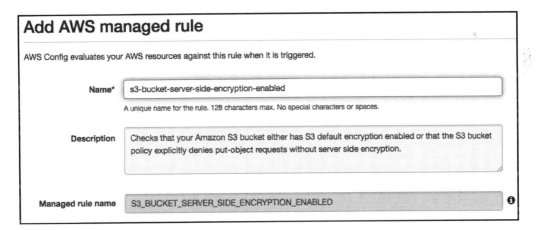

Firstly, you will be able to change the **Name** and **Description** to something more meaningful if desired. The **Managed rule name** section is protected and can't be changed. This is the actual Lambda function that is involved when the compliance check is run.

7. Next, you can configure the **Trigger** section:

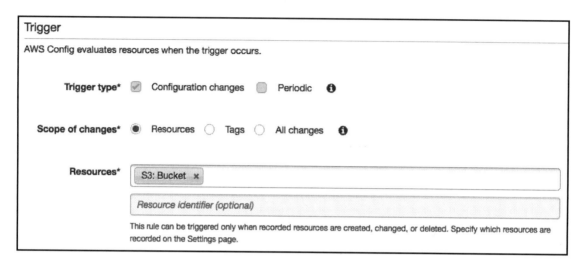

Here, you can make changes to affect how and when the compliance check is invoked. As this is a managed rule, the **Trigger type** is automatically set, however, if you were to create your own compliance check, you would be able to specify whether you wanted the check to trigger for every configuration change relating to the associated resources, or on a periodic basis regardless of any configuration changes in your environment.

Scope of changes allows you to specify the resources that you want the check to be associated with. As this is a check specifically to check the encryption status of S3 buckets, the scope of changes has been restricted to S3 buckets only.

8. Next, you have the ability to configure remediation options:

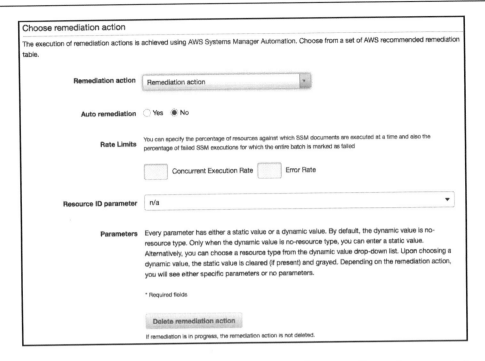

The **Remediation action** is a drop-down list of pre-configured automated remediation actions carried out by AWS Systems Manager Automation. An example use of this could be if you were checking to make sure EBS volumes were encrypted, and your compliance check found out that a volume wasn't, then you could select the following remediation action of **AWS-DetachEBSVolume**. This would prevent anyone from having access to the insecure EBS volume, allowing you to rectify the problem:

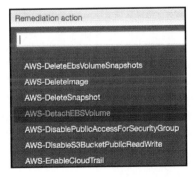

For this demonstration, I will leave the remediation action empty and will set the **Auto remediation** option as **No**, and all other options will be left as their default.

9. Once your configuration changes have been made, select the blue **Save** button. Your new rule will then begin its evaluation based on your configuration settings:

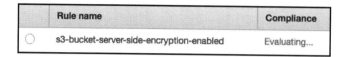

10. If any non-compliant resources are found, it displays its findings as shown. As you can see, this rule has found eight non-compliant S3 buckets:

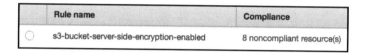

11. By selecting the **Rule**, we can dive deeper to find out exactly which resources do not provide the level of encryption required:

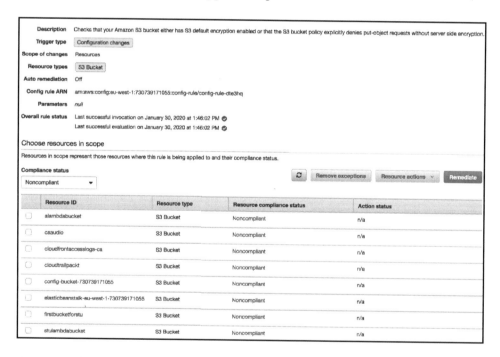

12. Using this information, we can easily uncover which buckets are affected and can choose to take any action that might be necessary.

Using AWS Config rules gives you the ability to very quickly and easily have a level of automated checks to help with your overall security posture and compliance. This also helps protect against any accidental human errors that have been made that might otherwise have gone unnoticed and could potentially have led to exposure or a vulnerability of some sort.

Resource relationships

The resource relationship component builds a logical mapping of your resources and their links to one another. Let's run through a quick example:

1. Select one of the resources from within AWS Config, for example, a particular subnet:

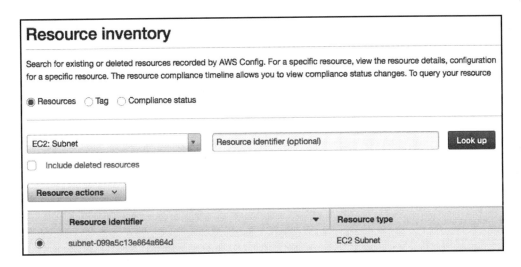

2. Now navigate through to the configuration timeline. From here, you can see the **Relationships** section:

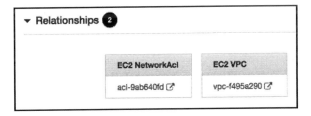

3. You can now clearly see which EC2 Network ACL and which VPC this subnet belongs to, and can quickly and easily select either of these resources to then navigate to the configuration timeline of that resource, for example, the EC2 VPC:

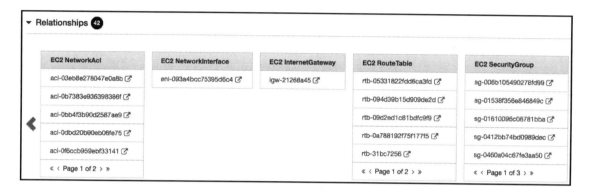

Here, we can see all the relationships that this VPC has, and so it becomes a very powerful tool to help you understand your logical mapping of resources very quickly and easily.

AWS Config role

During the configuration of AWS Config, you will be asked to specify a role:

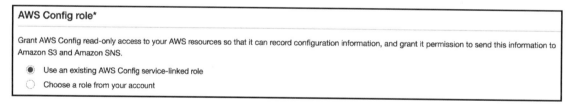

As stated in the screenshot, this is used to allow AWS Config to gain read-only access to your resources to record CI data. It will also be used to publish data to both your selected SNS topic for your configuration stream and your S3 bucket to store configuration history and snapshots. You can use an existing role within your AWS account, or allow AWS Config to select an existing service-linked role.

Now that we have seen the various components of AWS Config, let's briefly understand the Config process, which will help us understand how these components work together to provide the information necessary for the audit.

The AWS Config process

Before moving on to the next section in this chapter, let's just review the AWS Config process:

1. You must first configure elements of AWS Config, which in turn enables the **configuration recorder** to begin capturing and recording changes within your environment.

2. AWS Config will then actively identify and discover resources based upon your configuration.

3. For any changes, creations, and deletions of supported resources made within your environment where AWS Config is running, a **configuration item** will be created.

4. This change will be sent to the notification stream (**SNS topic**).

5. If you have any **Config rules** configured for managing compliance, AWS Config will evaluate any changes made to your environment and assess that change for any non-compliance. If a change of compliance state occured, a notification will be sent to the notification stream.

6. Should a **configuration snapshot** be initiated, a point-in-time snapshot of your environment will be captured and the output delivered to your predefined S3 bucket.

7. AWS Config will periodically update its **configuration history** for each resource type, which can be viewed via the AWS Config dashboard within the Management Console, in addition to reviewing the output stored in your designated S3 bucket.

As you have seen, AWS Config is a great service to help you manage your resources from an auditing perspective. It can provide you with a timeline of events, saving resource history, changes, and relationships. As an auditing tool, this is highly effective and can be used to provide a significant amount of auditing evidence during an audit being performed by a third party.

Now let's move on to another service that can be used to help you with your compliance program by protecting **personally identifiable information** (PII) – Amazon Macie, which tightly integrates with Amazon S3.

Maintaining compliance with Amazon Macie

Amazon Macie is a managed service, backed by machine learning, that provides an automatic way of detecting, protecting, and classifying data within your S3 buckets. By reviewing and continuously monitoring data object access patterns in S3 and associated CloudTrail log data, Amazon Macie can identify and spot any irregular or suspicious activity that sits outside of what Macie would consider familiar operations, potentially identifying a new security threat.

Some useful features of Amazon Macie include the following:

- The ability to use **natural language processing** (**NLP**) techniques to interpret data stored in S3, helping to classify it. To learn more about NLP, please visit `https://en.wikipedia.org/wiki/Natural_language_processing`.
- The ability to spot changes to specific security policies and ACLs that might affect who has access to your S3 bucket.
- The ability to categorize information, including sensitive security data such as **personally identifiable information** (**PII**), **protected health information** (**PHI**) data, access keys, and API keys.
- Customized configuration, allowing you to set and assign business values to certain types of data using a risk score. Depending on your business and what's considered critical, you can set your own values on what you consider a risk.

One of the key components of Amazon Macie is how it classifies data to help determine its level of sensitivity and criticality to your business. I now want to explain more about these classifications next.

 If you would like to enable Amazon Macie, please refer to: `https://docs.aws.amazon.com/macie/latest/userguide/macie-setting-up.html`.

Classifying data using Amazon Macie

Amazon Macie classifies data through a series of automatic content classification mechanisms. It performs its classification using the object-level API data events collated from CloudTrail logs.

There are currently five different levels of classification at the time of writing this book. Four of them can be seen from the Amazon Macie console from within the AWS Management Console, which can be enabled/disabled, and are shown as follows:

Classify data

Review and enable or disable the following settings that Macie uses to classify your monitored S3 objects. **Learn more**

Content type

Classify your S3 objects by content type, using an identifier embedded in the file header. Macie offers a set of managed content types. As Macie classifies your data, it automatically determines the content type of every S3 object. **Learn more**

File extension

Classify your S3 objects by file extension. Macie offers a set of managed file extensions. As Macie classifies your data, it automatically determines the file extension of every S3 object. **Learn more**

Theme

Classify your S3 objects by theme. Macie offers a set of managed themes. As Macie classifies your data, it automatically determines the theme(s) of every S3 object. **Learn more**

Regex

Classify your S3 objects by regex. Macie offers a set of managed regex. As Macie classifies your data, it automatically determines the regex of every S3 object. **Learn more**

First, we will go over the fifth type, which cannot be managed from the console.

Support vector machine-based classifier

The fifth type, **support vector machine-based classifier** is managed entirely by AWS with no modifications of any type and so is hidden from the console. This classifies each of your objects stored in S3 by analyzing the content within each object, in addition to its metadata, such as document length. Examples of these classifications include the following:

- Financial
- Application logs
- Web languages
- Generic encryption keys

For a full list and breakdown of the full list of classifications, please see the AWS documentation found: `https://docs.aws.amazon.com/macie/latest/userguide/macie-classify-objects-classifier.html`.

Content type

This classification looks at the classification of the actual file that is being stored, using an identifier that's embedded in the file header of the object. As an example, this classification could be identified as a *document* or *source code*. Each object stored is associated against a set of predefined content types, which would also indicate its risk factor.

A sample of these content types can be seen here, taken from the Management Console:

Content types

Name ▲	Description	Classification	Risk	Enabled	
application/cap	WireShark or Tcpdump Packet Capture	Binary	6	Yes	✎
application/epub+zip	application/epub	Document	1	Yes	✎
application/illustrator	Adobe Illustrator	Document	1	Yes	✎
application/java	Binary (Java)	Source Code	5	Yes	✎
application/java-archive	application/java-archive	Source code	6	Yes	✎
application/java-serialized-object	application/java-serialized-object	Source Code	5	Yes	✎
application/java-vm	application/java-vm	Source Code	5	Yes	✎
application/javascript	application/javascript	Document	1	Yes	✎
application/json	JSON	Plain Text	6	Yes	✎
application/msaccess	application/msaccess	Data Records	6	Yes	✎
application/msexcel	Microsoft Excel	Document	1	Yes	✎

As you can see, there are five different fields that are used in this classification method. The **Name** and **Description** fields define the file type that's associated with the object, such as a Microsoft Excel file, as seen in the last row of the excerpt of the preceding screenshot. The **Classification** is what Amazon Macie determines the file classification to be, such as binary, document, plain text, and so on. In the Microsoft Excel example, the classification is identified as **Document**.

When looking at the **Risk** column, it is rated from 1 to 10, with 10 carrying the highest risk. Again, our Excel document carries a low risk of just **1**. For each of the content types, you can choose to have these enabled or disabled, and it's worth pointing out that this is the only value that you can change for each classification type by clicking on the *pencil* symbol.

File extensions

Quite simply, instead of looking at the content type of the object, as in the previous classification, this determines a classification based upon the actual file extension of the object. A sample of these file extensions can be seen here:

File extensions

Name ▲	Description	Classification	Risk	Enabled	
7z	7-Zip compressed file	Archive and compressed	3	Yes	✎
abc	SolidWorks CAD	Design	5	Yes	✎
accdb	Microsoft Access database	Data records	6	Yes	✎
apk	Application installable on Android	Archive and compressed	1	Yes	✎
bat	Batch file	Source code	5	Yes	✎
bin	Compressed archive. Readable by Java. Extractable by 7-zip	Archive and compressed	3	Yes	✎
bz2	Bzip2 compressed archive	Archive and compressed	3	Yes	✎
bzip2	Bzip2 compressed archive	Archive and compressed	3	Yes	✎
c	C source code	Source code	5	Yes	✎

The first column, **Name**, shows the actual file extensions that are supported by Macie, for example, we can see that a **bat** file is a **Batch file** (as per the **Description** field). The **classification** is then determined for each file extension, for example, **Archive and compressed**, **Design**, **Data records**, **Source code**, **Keychain**, **Executable**, and **Email data**.

Risk, again, ranges from 1 to 10 (10 being the highest risk) and each classification can either be enabled or disabled.

Themes

Classification by themes is very different compared to both content type and file extension. With themes, a classification is made using a list of predefined keywords that exist within the actual content of the object being stored. Using themes, Amazon Macie can assign more than one theme if multiple themes are detected within the object:

Themes

Theme title ▲	Minimum keyword combinations	Risk	Enabled		
American Express Credit Card Keywords	1	1	Yes	🔍	✏️
Attorney Client Privileged	2	5	Yes	🔍	✏️
Audit Keywords	3	2	Yes	🔍	✏️
Banking Keywords	1	1	Yes	🔍	✏️
Big Data Frameworks	2	4	Yes	🔍	✏️
Cisco Analysis Keywords	1	2	Yes	🔍	✏️
Confidential Markings	2	5	Yes	🔍	✏️
Corporate Growth Keywords	3	5	Yes	🔍	✏️
Corporate Project Plan	3	3	Yes	🔍	✏️
Corporate Proposals	3	2	Yes	🔍	✏️
Credit Card Keywords	1	1	Yes	🔍	✏️
Encrypted Data Keywords	1	5	Yes	🔍	✏️
Financial Keywords	1	1	Yes	🔍	✏️
Hacker Keywords	2	1	Yes	🔍	✏️

Theme title identifies the type of keywords that are associated, for example, **Encrypted Data Keywords**. **Minimum keyword combinations** shows how many words must exist within the object from the associated theme title for it to be classified with the related **Risk**. So, for example, there must be two keyword combinations from within the **Big Data Frameworks** theme title for it to be associated with that theme and associated a **Risk** level of **4**. If you select **Theme Title**, you can view the keywords that are searched for that theme:

Edit theme details

Theme title

Big Data Frameworks

Description

Big Data Frameworks

Classification

Training set keywords

mapreduce,map reduce,HDFS,kafka,zookeeper,hadoop,tika,cassandra,mahout,hbase,lambda

Minimum keyword combinations

2

Risk

4

Enabled

Yes - this theme is active

As you can see, the training set keywords that exist for the **Big Data Frameworks** theme include **mapreduce**, **map reduce**, **HDFS**, **kafka**, and **zookeeper** to name a few.

Again, the **Risk** level ranges from 1 to 10 (10 being the highest risk) and each theme title can be enabled or disabled.

Regex

Regex classifies an object based upon regular expressions, again found within the content of the object itself. It looks for a string of specific data or data patterns before associating a risk level:

Regex

Name ▲	Classification	Min number of matches	Risk	Enabled		
Arista network configuration	Regex	1	7	Yes	🔍	✏️
BBVA Compass Routing Number - California	Regex	1	1	Yes	🔍	✏️
Bank of America Routing Numbers - California	Regex	10	1	Yes	🔍	✏️
Box Links	Regex	1	3	Yes	🔍	✏️
CVE Number	Regex	1	3	Yes	🔍	✏️
California Drivers License	Regex	10	1	Yes	🔍	✏️
Chase Routing Numbers - California	Regex	50	1	Yes	🔍	✏️
Cisco Router Config	Regex	3	9	Yes	🔍	✏️
Citibank Routing Numbers - California	Regex	1	1	Yes	🔍	✏️
DSA Private Key	Regex	1	8	Yes	🔍	✏️
Dropbox Links	Regex	1	3	Yes	🔍	✏️
EC Private Key	Regex	1	8	Yes	🔍	✏️
Encrypted DSA Private Key	Regex	1	3	Yes	🔍	✏️
Encrypted EC Private Key	Regex	1	3	Yes	🔍	✏️
Encrypted Private Key	Regex	1	3	Yes	🔍	✏️

These tables are probably familiar to you by now and follow the same pattern as the previous classifications. Again, **Risk** ranges from 1 to 10, and each Regex can be enabled or disabled, and Macie can associate more than one Regex with each object.

Much like the themes, you can select a specific Regex name to gain additional information. The following is taken from the **Cisco Router Config** regex:

Edit regex details

Name

Cisco Router Config

Description

Cisco Router Config

Classification

Regex

Regex

service\ timestamps\ [a-z]{3,5}\ datetime\ msec|boot-[a-z]{3,5}-marker|interface\ [A-Za-z0-9]{0,10}[E,e]thernet

Min number of matches

3

Risk

9

Enabled

Yes - this Regex is used in analytics

Through the five different types of object classification, Amazon Macie will collate and gather all risk scores from each to identify its overall risk factor. The result is defined by the highest risk found from any of the classification types. Let's work this out with the help of an example.

So let's assume you had a *document* that returned the following values from its object classification:

Object classification	Risk values
Support vector machine-based	2
Content type	1
File extension	1
Theme	2
Regex	5

The overall risk associated with this object would be identified as 5 as that is the highest value received.

In addition to this object classification, Amazon Macie will also scan and perform the automatic detection of any **personally identifiable information** (**PII**) data found within each of the objects, which is based on industry standards (NIST-80-122 / FIPS 199). These automatic detections can identify the following PII data and assign a PII impact of either high, moderate, or low:

- Full names
- Mailing addresses
- Email addresses
- Credit card numbers
- IP addresses (IPv4 and IPv6)
- Driver's license IDs (USA)
- National identification numbers (USA)
- Birth dates

The PII impact is categorized as follows:

High	>= 1 full name and credit card >= 50 names or emails and any combination of other PII
Moderate	>= 5 names or emails and any combination of other PII
Low	1 to 5 names or emails and any combination of PII Any quantity of the PII attributes above (without names or emails)

The following screenshot shows the output of the data classification of PII data:

S3 objects by PII priority

The following list shows your Macie-monitored S3 objects grouped by the PII priority. **Learn more**

Q   none   97.83% (4,652)

Q   low   2.16% (103)

S3 objects by PII types

The following list shows your Macie-monitored S3 objects grouped by the PII types. **Learn more**

Q   ipv4   93.33% (98)

Q   cc_number   4.76% (5)

Q   birth_date   0.95% (1)

Q   name   0.95% (1)

In this screenshot, we can see that Amazon Macie detected that 2.16% (103) of the objects contained a PII priority of **low**. Also, when grouping the classification by PII types, it detected that 93.33 % (98) of the objects contained IPv4 data.

In this section, we looked at how Amazon Macie classifies data by content type, file extensions, themes, and regex to help determine a risk factor of the data being stored. By identifying high-risk data, we can put in additional measures to ensure it is being protected through encryption, for example.

Amazon Macie data protection

Earlier, I mentioned that Amazon Macie can identify and spot any irregular or suspicious activity sitting outside of what Macie would consider normal boundaries of operations, potentially identifying a new security threat using AWS CloudTrail logs. Using historical data to review access patterns, Amazon Macie uses AI/ML to identify potential security weaknesses and threats from different users, applications, and service accounts.

As you can see, Amazon Macie offers two features to identify threats – **AWS CloudTrail events** and **AWS CloudTrail errors**:

Protect data

Review and enable or disable the following settings that Macie uses to protect your monitored data. **Learn more**

AWS CloudTrail events

Use this setting to classify CloudTrail data and management events that occur within your infrastructure. **Learn more**

AWS CloudTrail errors

Use this setting to classify errors that can occur as various CloudTrail data and management events take place within your infrastructure. **Learn more**

Basic alerts

Use this setting to review existing and create new basic alerts that Macie can generate to inform you about unexpected and potentially unauthorized and malicious activity within your infrastructure. **Learn more**

Let's go over these features one by one.

AWS CloudTrail events

Amazon Macie will review API calls gathered from CloudTrail logs stored on Amazon S3 and depending on the type of API and the impact it can have on your security posture, it will associate a risk score, again ranging from 1 to 10 (with 10 being the highest). If we look at a sample of these API calls, we can see what it looks for:

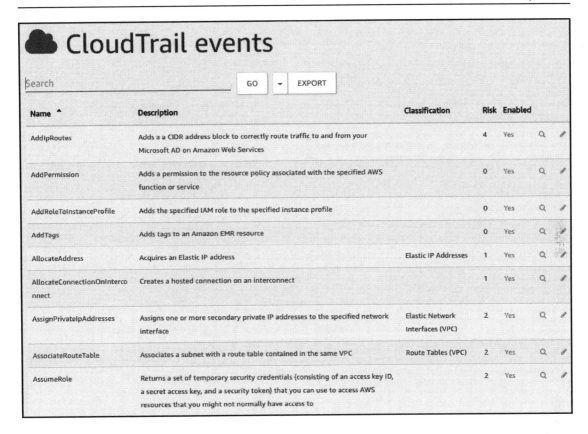

To make it easier to navigate, a search option is available to search for a specific API call. The table is self-explanatory and follows a similar approach to the object classifications we looked at previously.

By using the magnifying search option associated with each API call, you can query the CloudTrail data to understand where and how this API is being used. For example, here is a screenshot of the **AssumeRole** API, allowing you to dive deeper into all the details captured by CloudTrail:

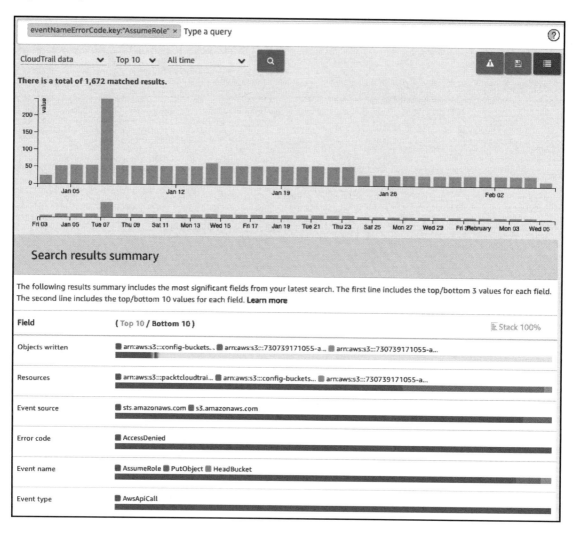

As you can see from the top section, this API was used multiple times and you can quickly see there was a peak on Tuesday 7th. If this was unexpected for a particular API, you could investigate the reason behind it further. At the bottom of the screenshot is a summary of the results that were used in conjunction with this API.

CloudTrail errors

This is an extremely useful feature as it captures any errors generated by an API call that CloudTrail has then captured, such as an **AccessDenied** response. This could be a sure sign that someone is trying to access something that they shouldn't be and could be the sign of a potential security attack or breach. There are many different errors that Amazon Macie looks for, which are assigned a risk value between 1 and 10 (10 being the highest risk). The following screenshot shows some of these errors:

Using the preceding example of **AccessDenied,** you can see this carries the highest risk factor or 10.

All of the results of the classification types and personally identifiable information and data risk values, along with any potential security problems found, are presented in a series of graphs and tables accessed via the Amazon Macie dashboard, which can be drilled down into to find further information. If you then couple this information with the ability to configure alerts for Amazon Macie's findings, it allows you to implement a series of strong compliance controls to meet stringent security controls that you need to adhere to.

Summary

In this chapter, we looked at some of the different services and features that we hadn't already covered thus far that can be used to help you meet your business audit requirements, certifications, and compliance controls. The services we looked at included AWS Artifact, AWS CloudTrail, AWS Config, and Amazon Macie.

Remaining compliant in the cloud can be a daunting task, but having an understanding of some of the logging capabilities and the services that can help you capture this information is vital. Being aware of the features of these tools will help you maintain a level of compliance and maintain full audit awareness.

In the next chapter, we are going to be looking at how you can utilize automation to quickly identify, record, and remediate security threats as and when they occur.

Questions

As we conclude this chapter, here is a list of questions for you to test your knowledge regarding its material. You will find the answers in the *Assessments* section of the *Appendix*:

1. Which AWS service is an on-demand portal to allow you to view and download AWS security and compliance **reports**, in addition to any online **agreements?**
2. Which security feature of AWS CloudTrail ensures that your log files have not been tampered with or modified after they have been written to your bucket in Amazon S3?
3. Which feature in AWS Config automatically monitors your resources to ensure they are meeting specific compliance controls?
4. Which service is backed by machine learning and provides an automatic way of detecting, protecting, and classifying data within your S3 buckets?
5. True or false: Amazon Macie classifies data through a series of automatic content classification mechanisms. It performs its classification using the object-level API data events collated from CloudTrail logs.

Section 5: Best Practices and Automation 5

In the first part of this section, we'll dive into the world of automation, learning how to use a variety of different AWS services to effectively detect, notify, and remediate security incidents that may arise within your environment. Then, we'll look at how to configure and use these services with each other to create a repeatable approach to resolving and responding to incidents without the need for manual intervention.

In the second part, we'll look at a variety of security best practices that should be adhered to at all times. These best practices are defined in such a way that they allow you to follow tried and tested processes and procedures that optimize your solutions, ensuring that security is built in at every layer of your architecture, thus minimizing the risk of security vulnerabilities and exposure.

This section comprises the following chapters:

- Chapter 14, *Automating Security Detection and Remediation*
- Chapter 15, *Discovering Security Best Practices*

14
Automating Security Detection and Remediation

So far, we have looked at many different types of security features and services, and the essential and secure controls and management they can bring to your solutions. However, when running your solutions at scale, you will want to ensure that you implement as much automation as possible when it comes to quickly identifying, recording, and remediating security threats as and when they occur. Automation provides an accurate and immediate response to an event that has taken place within your infrastructure, far quicker than a manual process involving a human could ever respond. Automated responses work on real-time data and are far more reliable than a manual process. As a result of this accuracy, reliability, and speed, using automation in a security context is always recommended.

This chapter will look at Amazon CloudWatch, Amazon GuardDuty, and AWS Security Hub, which are used to detect and automatically resolve and block potential security incidents.

The following topics will be covered in this chapter:

- Using CloudWatch events with Lambda and SNS
- Using Amazon GuardDuty
- Using AWS Security Hub

Technical requirements

To carry out the demonstrations in this chapter, you need to have access to an AWS account with permissions to administer Amazon CloudWatch, Amazon GuardDuty, and AWS Security Hub.

For details regarding permissions and access to these services, please refer to Chapter 4, *Working with Access Policies.*

Using CloudWatch events with AWS Lambda and SNS

In Chapter 13, *Auditing and Governance*, we looked at how AWS CloudTrail and AWS Config can be used to record and track changes to your infrastructure as soon as they happen, and how these events can be written to logs and processed by other services, such as Amazon CloudWatch. Using this data, you can configure controls to look for specific events for further investigation. These could be events that might signify a security breach or threat.

This is a simple method of implementing an automated level of remediation by monitoring and identifying events from different services to look for potential security breaches and implementing an automated response using AWS Lambda to rectify the problem. In addition to using CloudWatch log groups, we can use Amazon CloudWatch events.

For anyone who is unfamiliar with AWS Lambda, let me introduce the service quickly. AWS Lambda is a serverless compute service that automatically provisions compute power, allowing you to run code for your applications either on demand or in response to events without having to actually provision any compute instances yourself. Using this serverless technology removes a level of administrative responsibility of maintaining a compute instance; instead, that is all managed by AWS. This allows you to focus purely on the application logic and code.

Removing the need to provision and run an **Elastic Compute Cloud** (EC2) instance can provide significant cost savings, as when using AWS Lambda, it only charges you for compute power per hundred milliseconds of use, only when your code is running, in addition to the number of times your code runs.

CloudWatch events can be used to search for specific events within your infrastructure, which can trigger an automated response. We will learn how to do this using an example in the upcoming subsections.

For our example, let's assume that I have a **Virtual Private Cloud (VPC)** that contains no EC2 instances, and I want to ensure that this VPC never has *any* EC2 instances running on it as I want it to be purely used for other services and management. Any sign of an EC2 instance running could be a security breach. You could configure Amazon CloudWatch events to build an event pattern to detect when an EC2 instance is running and carry out an automated response in relation to that event. Let's see how to do this.

Detecting events with CloudWatch

Using Amazon CloudWatch, we will first create a rule that detects when an EC2 instance state changes to a `running` state. Follow these steps:

1. From the Amazon CloudWatch dashboard, select **Rules** under **Events** from the left menu:

2. Next, select **Create Rule**, and the following screen will be displayed:

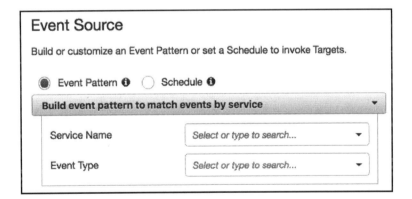

3. Using the drop-down list, select **EC2** for **Service Name**.

4. For **Event Type**, you can select **EC2 Instance State-change Notification**:

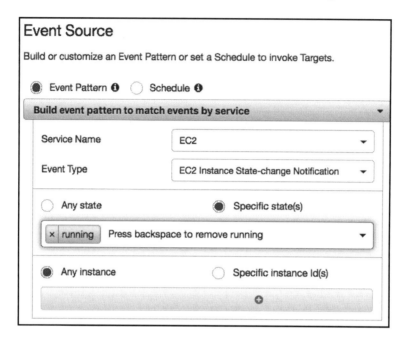

5. Select **running** under the **Specific state(s)** drop-down list.
6. Select **Any instance**.

   Your event pattern is now configured to record any events where an EC2 instance is listed as running, and this can be seen under **Event Pattern Preview**:

```
▾ Event Pattern Preview          Copy to clipboard   Edit
  {
    "source": [
      "aws.ec2"
    ],
    "detail-type": [
      "EC2 Instance State-change Notification"
    ],
    "detail": {
      "state": [
        "running"
      ]
    }
  }
```

Now that you have identified which event(s) you want to capture, you need to configure the response to those events.

Configuring a response to an event

The detection of an event is only the first part of the automated process. Next, we need to configure a response to define what action will be called upon when the event has been detected. A response can be called from a number of different AWS services, allowing you to utilize a variety of services to carry out a specific operation:

1. On the right-hand side of the console, you need to click on **Add target***:

2. Your targets are your event-response mechanisms, and the available targets include a number of different services, such as SNS topics, CloudWatch log groups, Kinesis streams, an SQS queue, an SSM `run` command, Lambda functions, code pipelines, and many more:

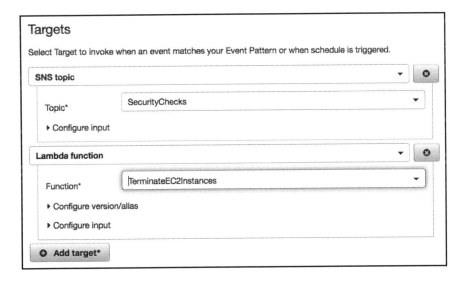

In this demonstration, I have selected two different targets, as you can see in the preceding screenshot:

- The first target I have selected is **SNS topic**, and I defined a topic that I want to be selected called **SecurityChecks**. This is a topic that I have created that a security team could be subscribed to so that they are notified when an EC2 instance is running.
- The second target is **Lambda function**, and I have selected an existing function called **TerminateEC2Instances**, which is designed to terminate the instance that is found running.

As you can see, in this scenario, if an EC2 instance was launched, the security team would be notified immediately by Amazon SNS for them to investigate how this EC2 instance was launched. In addition to this, the instance would also be terminated as quickly as it was found, running through the controls configured within the AWS Lambda function.

3. Once you have configured your targets, select **Next.** You will then be asked to give your CloudWatch event a name and a description:

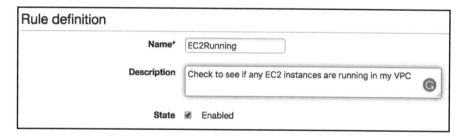

4. Ensure that the checkbox is ticked to enable the rule, and then select **Create Rule**.

Amazon CloudWatch is a great service that provides a range of monitoring and logging tools that are bundled into this area range of automation features. This method focused on how to automate a response to an event.

Configuring cross-account events using Amazon CloudWatch

If you have a multi-account environment, you can send events from one account to another account using the AWS CloudWatch **Event Bus** feature. This is a great way to consolidate the collation of events using a single account.

At a high level, the following steps need to be carried out.

1. On the receiver account, add permissions to the default event bus, allowing access from another account or from your AWS organization.
2. On the sender account, add a rule that points to the receiver account default event bus as the target of the rule.
3. Associate a role that has permissions to send events to the receiver's event bus.
4. Configure a rule in the receiver's account to match the events pattern of the rule generated in the sender account.

Let's take a look at how to configure this. For this demonstration, you need to have access to two AWS accounts within the same AWS organization. For more information on configuring AWS organizations, refer to `https://docs.aws.amazon.com/organizations/latest/userguide/orgs_tutorials_basic.html`.

One account will act as your receiver account and the other will act as the sender account.

From the receiver account, do the following:

1. Log in to the AWS Management Console and select **Amazon CloudWatch**.
2. Select **Event Buses** from the **Events** menu on the left:

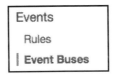

3. Select the blue **Add permission** button:

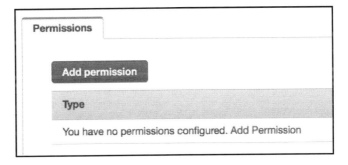

4. Select **Organization** under **Type** and select **My organization**, then click **Add**:

The receiver's event bus now has the ability to be accessed by accounts in the AWS organization.

Now, from the sender account do the following:

1. Carry out the same steps explained in the *Detecting events with CloudWatch* section at the start of this chapter, up until you configure a response to the event, where it should be defined as follows:

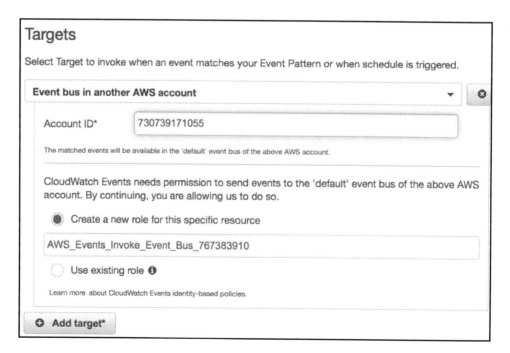

2. Enter the account number of the receiver account.

The sender account now has access via the role to send events as per the rule to the event bus of the receiver account.

From the receiver account, you now need to configure a new rule to match the event pattern of the rule you are receiving from the sender account, in addition to an added parameter:

1. Currently, the event pattern generated from the rule in the sender account looks as follows:

```
{
  "source": [
    "aws.ec2"
  ],
  "detail-type": [
    "EC2 Instance State-change Notification"
  ],
  "detail": {
    "state": [
      "running"
    ]
  }
}
```

2. You now need to create a new rule. Add the following parameter to the rule:

```
"account": [
    "356993128355"
],
```

Here, the account number is the account number of the sender's account. The event pattern should look as follows when added to the rule:

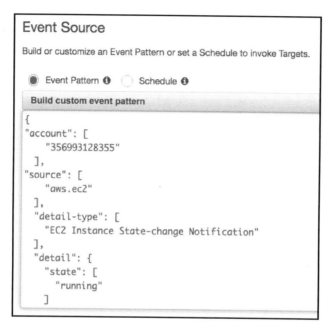

3. You can then configure the `Target` response for this rule as per the previous examples.

4. Adding the `account` parameter ensures that the rule configured in the receiver's account is not triggered when a matched event is received from a different account, especially if you are receiving events from more than one account.

In this section, we looked at how you can send all events from CloudWatch to a centralized AWS account, which can then respond with its own configured targets, such as a Lambda function or an SNS notification. This helps to implement a level of management and central control over how events are processed across a multi-account environment.

Next, I now want to discuss another AWS security service that we haven't touched on yet—Amazon GuardDuty, which can be used for both automation detection and the remediation of security incidents.

Using Amazon GuardDuty

For those of you who are unfamiliar with GuardDuty, it is a fully managed, intelligent threat-detection service, powered by machine learning, which continually provides insights into unusual and/or unexpected behavioral patterns that could be considered malicious within your account. Amazon GuardDuty can process and analyze millions of events that are captured through your AWS CloudTrail logs, DNS logs, and VPC flow logs from multiple accounts. These events are then referenced against numerous threat detection feeds, many of which contain known sources of malicious activity, including specific URLs and IP addresses.

Amazon GuardDuty is continually learning, based on the day-to-day activity of operations within your account, to understand and differentiate between normal behavior and what could be considered abnormal behavior, thereby indicating a threat within your infrastructure. This behavioral-based analysis allows GuardDuty to detect potential vulnerabilities and exploits, such as an API call that has been called unexpectedly or interactions and connectivity with unknown or unusual sources.

Being an *always-on* service, it provides a very effective method of identifying security issues automatically and without any performance impact, as the service runs entirely on the AWS infrastructure without the need of any local agents. Any findings by Amazon GuardDuty are presented to you in a list of priorities based on the findings.

With no initial upfront costs to enable GuardDuty, coupled with an ability to intelligently detect security threats without hindering the performance of your infrastructure, regardless of size, and providing centralized management by aggregating data from multiple AWS accounts, GuardDuty is a very effective tool in your effort to protect your AWS resources and any stored data.

Enabling Amazon GuardDuty

Amazon GuardDuty is a regional service, and so you must first select the region in which you want to enable the service. It is very easy and simple to enable:

1. From the AWS Management Console, select **Amazon GuardDuty | Get started**:

2. Select **Enable GuardDuty:**

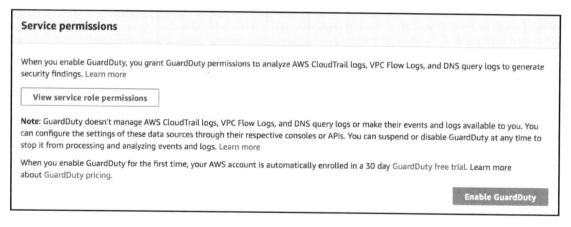

GuardDuty is now enabled. It will begin monitoring feeds from your DNS logs, CloudTrail logs, and VPC flow logs. Any findings that are found will be displayed within the dashboard—for example, the finding shown here:

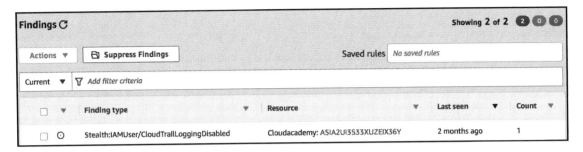

This shows that a finding highlighted unusual activity where a trail within AWS CloudTrail was stopped. By selecting the finding, we can gather additional information:

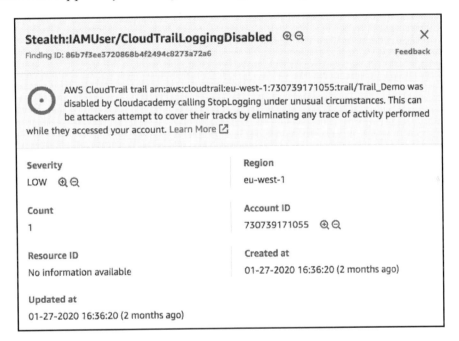

As you can see, it provides the reason behind the finding, plus the severity, and here, we can see that the severity is **LOW**. It also provides additional information, such as the account, the region, and timestamps.

> The severity for GuardDuty ranges from low to medium to high. More information on this can be found at `https://docs.aws.amazon.com/guardduty/latest/ug/guardduty_findings.html#guardduty_findings-severity`.

In addition to this high-level summary data, GuardDuty provides a whole host of other information that is very useful and important, as you can see here:

So, we now understand how to enable Amazon GuardDuty, and we have also seen how it detects unusual activity, which can be of great help. But finding a risk in not enough; it also needs to be remediated. So, let's learn how Amazon GuardDuty can be used to perform automatic remediation.

Performing automatic remediation

Amazon GuardDuty also has the ability to perform remediation on findings through automation, and again, this uses Amazon CloudWatch events to do so. From within Amazon CloudWatch, you can create a new rule, as in the previous demonstration, but instead of selecting **EC2** for **Service Name** as we did earlier, you could select **GuardDuty**, and select **GuardDuty Finding** for **Event Type**, as shown here:

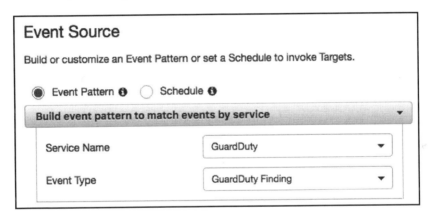

Again, you can configure your event target to then automatically implement a response, perhaps a Lambda function.

As you can see, using more than one service together can effectively help you actively monitor and detect security threats and vulnerabilities, as Amazon GuardDuty allows, and then implement mechanisms to automatically review and remediate a security issue—in this case, with a customized Lambda function.

Next, let's move on to another security service that helps us in automating our response to security incidents—AWS Security Hub.

I have mentioned AWS Lambda a couple of times in response to the automation of remediation, and so if you want to see a great example of how this can be implemented, please take a look at the following AWS blog post, which looks at how you can use AWS Lambda, Amazon CloudWatch events, and a DynamoDB table to alter security groups:

```
https://aws.amazon.com/blogs/compute/automating-security-group-
updates-with-aws-lambda/
```

Using AWS Security Hub

Another security service, AWS Security Hub, can also be used to help detect and remediate security incidents. It is designed to help you centralize many of your security findings, alerts, and compliance reports from numerous different AWS security services, including the following:

- AWS **Identity and Access Management (IAM)**
- Amazon Macie
- Amazon GuardDuty
- Amazon Inspector
- AWS Firewall Manager

In addition to these native AWS services, it can also be incorporated into any third-party partner solutions, such as Sumo Logic, Splunk, and many more, that you might already be using within your organization. A full list of these partners can be found at `https://aws.amazon.com/security-hub/partners/`.

By acting as a *security hub*, the service acts as a single-pane-of-glass approach to the security notifications used across your accounts. This allows the service to categorize and prioritize all events from multiple sources, allowing you to gain a deep understanding of any threats or vulnerabilities, in addition to being aware of what the highest priority from all of your feeds is. Let's see how.

Enabling AWS Security Hub

AWS Security Hub can be enabled from the AWS Management Console. Follow these steps:

1. When you first go to AWS Security Hub from the AWS Management Console, you will be presented with the following screen:

2. You first need to select the security standards that you would like to activate—either CIS AWS Foundations Benchmark (`https://www.cisecurity.org/benchmark/amazon_web_services/`) or PCI DSS. These standards allow Security Hub to run configuration and security checks continuously at an account-level based on the industry standards that you select.

    You can also see the AWS service integrations that AWS Security Hub operates on.

3. Once you have selected your security standards, select **Enable Security Hub.**

As you can see, you will then be presented with a series of interactive charts, graphs, and statistics displaying findings insights, and security standard compliance failures:

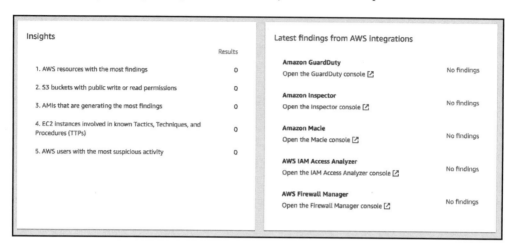

Let's go over these in the following subsections.

Insights

AWS Security Hub offers a number of predefined and managed insights, and these are used to highlight and identify any security-related weaknesses. The following screenshot shows an example of some of these:

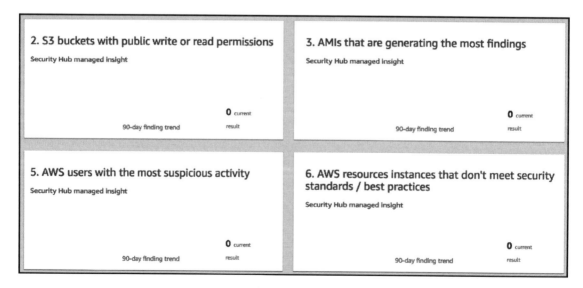

It is also possible to create your own insights using a serious of statements, identifiers, and filters to hone in on what you are trying to locate and isolate.

Findings

A finding is a security issue or a failed security check that has been detected by the integrated AWS service and third-party solutions. These interactions with other AWS services can be enabled or disabled:

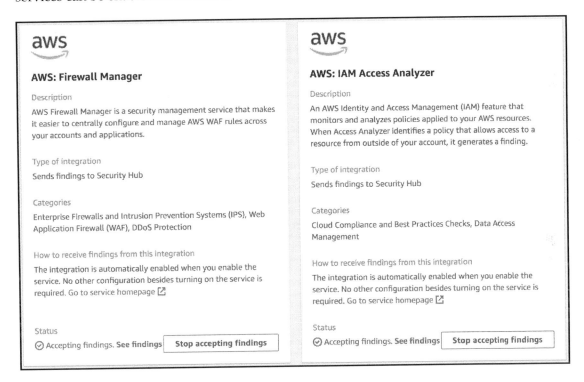

As you can see in the preceding screenshot, AWS Firewall Manager and AWS IAM Access Analyzer are third-party services that are sending their findings to Security Hub. These can be disabled by clicking on the **Stop accepting findings** button.

Security standards

As mentioned previously, these security checks assess your accounts continuously against the security standards enabled—for example, CIS AWS Foundations Benchmark. For each check, a severity is given, as well as remediation instructions should you experience a failure on these checks. The following screenshot shows an example of the checks that are undertaken, in addition to the defined severity of each check:

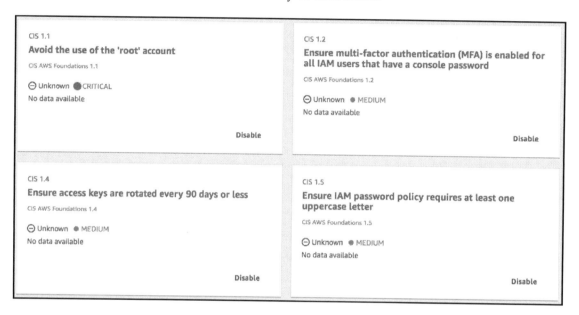

As you can see, if someone was actively using the **root** account, this would be considered a **CRITICAL** severity level, and would be highlighted as a security risk. Also, you have the option to disable the checks that you do not want to include, should you need or ever want to do so.

So far, we've seen how Security Hub can help us identify security incidents through insights, findings, and security standards. But you'd be right in thinking that mere identification is not enough and remediation is important.

Performing automatic remediation

Again, as with Amazon GuardDuty, AWS Security Hub also integrates with Amazon CloudWatch events to help you automate the remediation process of any findings found. This is configured from within the Amazon CloudWatch events dashboard by selecting **Security Hub** for **Service Name** and then the appropriate **Event Type** option:

Again, you can select from the available targets to carry out automatic remediation steps by your **Security Information and Event Management (SIEM)** tools.

It also integrates with **Amazon Detective**, which was a new service released at the AWS re:Invent conference in 2019. Amazon Detective helps to simplify the effort required to analyze and investigate the root cause of security incidents and suspicious activity through machine learning and log data received by multiple AWS services. More information on Amazon Detective can be found at `https://aws.amazon.com/detective/`.

Summary

In this chapter, we learned about the importance of automating responses to security incidents and looked at a few AWS services that help us achieve this automation—CloudWatch, GuardDuty, and Security Hub. As your environment scales and grows (and it will, especially when you begin to integrate multiple accounts, which Amazon GuardDuty and AWS Security Hub both support), it will become essential to implement a level of automatic detection and remediation to help you identify and resolve security incidents as and when they occur.

With the help of this chapter, you are now able to adopt a range of different AWS security services, such as Amazon GuardDuty, AWS Security, Amazon CloudWatch, AWS Lambda, and AWS CloudTrail, and use them as an asset to your security strategy. Not only can you now automatically put blocks in place as and when suspicious activity is automatically detected, but you can also notify your security teams, allowing them to investigate how it happened and apply the relevant measures to prevent it from happening again in the future.

In the next chapter, we will dive into a few security best practices that are tried and tested by many organizations to secure their cloud infrastructure. You will learn how to enable AWS Trusted Advisor and use the instrumentation to secure even-based remediation.

Questions

As we conclude, here is a list of questions for you to test your knowledge of this chapter's material. You will find the answers in the *Assessments* section of the *Appendix*.

1. True or false: CloudWatch events can be used to search for specific events within your infrastructure, which can trigger an automated response.
2. Amazon GuardDuty is able to process and analyze millions of events that are captured through your AWS CloudTrail logs, DNS logs, and which other logging mechanism?
3. Which AWS service acts as a single-pane-of-glass approach to your security notifications across your accounts?
4. True or false: AWS Security Hub integrates with AWS Trusted Advisor to help you automate the remediation process of any findings found.

15
Discovering Security Best Practices

For each of the AWS services that I have touched on so far, there are numerous best practices to follow and recommendations to adhere to when architecting your environments. These best practices are defined to allow you to follow tried and tested processes and procedures that optimize your solutions, ensuring that security is built in at every layer of your architecture and minimizing the risk of security vulnerabilities and exposures.

Within this chapter, I shall review some of the common security best practices that should be implemented where possible. I will also dive into AWS Trusted Advisor, which automatically highlights any deviation from a number of security best practices as defined by AWS. Finally, I shall take a closer look at penetration testing in AWS.

The following topics will be covered in this chapter:

- Common security best practices
- Using AWS Trusted Advisor
- Penetration testing in AWS

Technical requirements

To view and follow the demonstrations in this chapter, you must have access to AWS Trusted Advisor. For more information on managing permissions, please review `Chapter 4`, *Working with Access Policies*.

Common security best practices

There are so many AWS security best practices, and you should try and adopt as many as possible in an effort to enhance your security posture. I want to highlight and review a number of common best practices that are easy to implement and could play a huge role in protecting your solutions and data:

- **Enable Multi-Factor Authentication (MFA)**: In addition to a password that is required for users to authenticate to AWS, it is recommended to implement MFA to add a second layer of authentication. By using MFA, you are required to enter a randomly generated six-digit number once you have entered your password when using the AWS Management Console. This is a best practice for your AWS root account and any other user accounts that have elevated privileges. This was covered in `Chapter 3`, *Access Management*.

- **Enable AWS CloudTrail**: This service should be enabled within all regions that you operate your AWS solutions within. It is essential in helping you to monitor, log, and capture all API activity, which can then be used to identify any security threats within your environment. For details, visit `Chapter 13`, *Auditing and Governance*.

- **Remove your root accounts access keys**: You should not enable access keys for your root account that could enable programmatic access to your AWS account. These keys enable the user to authenticate to AWS resources programmatically using the AWS CLI, the SDK, or other development tools, and if these were compromised, a malicious user would have full access to and control over your AWS account. This was also covered in `Chapter 3`, *Access Management*.

- **Implement a strong password policy**: From within AWS IAM, you should ensure that you have created and implemented a strong password policy; the more complex the policy is, the stronger and harder to break your passwords will be:

Modify password policy

A password policy is a set of rules that define complexity requirements and mandatory rotation periods for your IAM users' passwords. Learn more

Select your account password policy requirements:

☑ Enforce minimum password length

    8   characters

☑ Require at least one uppercase letter from Latin alphabet (A-Z)

☑ Require at least one lowercase letter from Latin alphabet (a-z)

☑ Require at least one number

☑ Require at least one non-alphanumeric character (!@#$%^&*()_+-=[]{}|')

☑ Enable password expiration

Expire passwords in   30 day(s)

☑ Password expiration requires administrator reset

☑ Allow users to change their own password

☑ Prevent password reuse

    Remember 5   password(s)

- **Implement the Principle of Least Privilege (PoLP)**: Regardless of which policy you are using, one key point is to always implement security based on the PoLP. This essentially means that you should only ever grant permissions for an identity that the identity actually needs, and no more. For example, you should not allow full access to EC2 (`ec2:*`) for a user who only actually needs to use stop and terminate instances. Instead, you would assign the permissions of `ec2:stopinstances` and `ec2:terminateinstances`. By granting additional permissions, you increase risk and the level of potential damage should a breach of credentials occur. For more details, read `Chapter 4`, *Working within Access Policies*.

- **Encrypt, encrypt, encrypt**: Depending on the sensitivity of your data, you might need to implement a level of encryption to prevent it from being accessed as plaintext data. Whether your data is being sent in transit or stored at rest in AWS, you have a variety of ways to implement encryption to prevent it from being viewed should it fall into the wrong hands. I shall be covering more on encryption and using AWS **Key Management Service (KMS)** in Chapter 16, *Managing Key Infrastructure*.

- **Automation and Remediation**: As discussed in Chapter 14, *Automating Security Threat Detection and Remediation*, implementing a level of automation and remediation through a variety of managed services is crucial to being able to identify, classify, and remediate potential security vulnerabilities within your environment far quicker than you could manually. Services such as Amazon GuardDuty, AWS Lambda, AWS Security Hub, AWS CloudTrail, AWS Config, and Amazon Macie, to name but a few, are great for helping you to have an *eyes-on* approach to all activities undertaken within your environment.

Following these few simple best practices paves the way in providing a robust and secure environment that many of your deployed solutions will be tightly integrated with, giving you a great start in implementing a tight security posture. Failure to comply with these simple practices will provide easier access to your data and resources for those who aim to carry out malicious activity.

In order to help us adopt these best practices, AWS also provides us with a few services. Let's begin by looking at AWS Trusted Advisor.

Using AWS Trusted Advisor

The AWS Trusted Advisor service has been around for quite some time and continues to play an integral role in helping customers to optimize their AWS environment through recommended best practices. It acts, much as the name suggests, as an *advisor* to you and highlights and recommends enhancements against a number of predefined best practice checks across five different areas of your account:

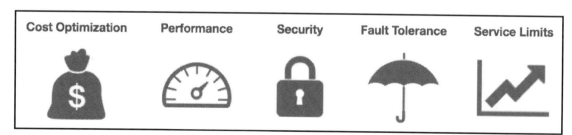

Cost Optimization   Performance   Security   Fault Tolerance   Service Limits

Within each of these areas, AWS Trusted Advisor has a list of predefined checks based on best practices that should be adhered to within your AWS account. Trusted Advisor would then highlight and identify any misalignment with these checks and suggest remediation steps to take action against the alert criteria. We will understand this better in the *Reviewing deviations using AWS Trusted Advisor* section, when we actually carry out a check in our environment. For now, just make sure you understand the basics.

The following points summarize and provide definitions of each of the five areas checked by Trusted Advisor:

- **Cost Optimization**: These checks help you to identify resources that are not being optimally used and see where you could save money by optimizing your infrastructure.
- **Performance**: Performance checks look at your resources to identify any resources that could make use of provisioned throughput and identifying resources that are over-utilized.
- **Security**: Here, the checks taken are used to identify weaknesses that could lead to vulnerabilities within your account.
- **Fault Tolerance**: The checks within this category are used to determine whether you have adequate resiliency and fault tolerance built into your environment – for example, through making use of multi-Availability Zone features and auto-scaling.
- **Service Limits**: This category checks whether any of your services have reached 80% or more against the allotted service limit. For example, you are only allowed five VPCs per region; once you reach four VPCs in a single region (80%), you will be notified.

For a full list of all the checks within each of these categories, please visit the following link, where you will be able to drill down into each of the checks to understand exactly what is being checked:

`https://aws.amazon.com/premiumsupport/technology/trusted-advisor/best-practice-checklist/`.

To the view the checks within Trusted Advisor for each of the categories, you can follow these steps:

1. From within the AWS Management Console, select **Trusted Advisor** from the **Management & Governance** menu on the service list page:

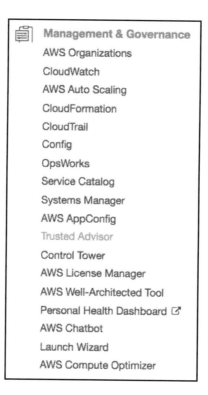

2. Select the category using the relevant icon from the dashboard:

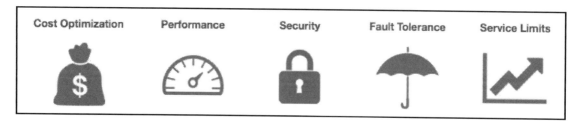

3. From here, you can then view the available checks within each category. As an example, the following screenshots show a check from each of the five categories:

- **Cost Optimization**: This check will review your EC2 instances to determine whether any of them have been running at 10% CPU utilization or less, or if the network I/O was 5 MB or less on 4 or more days over the previous 2 weeks:

Low Utilization Amazon EC2 Instances

Checks the Amazon Elastic Compute Cloud (Amazon EC2) instances that were running at any time during the last 14 days and alerts you if the daily CPU utilization was 10% or less and network I/O was 5 MB or less on 4 or more days. Running instances generate hourly usage charges. Although some scenarios can result in low utilization by design, you can often lower your costs by managing the number and size of your instances.

Estimated monthly savings are calculated by using the current usage rate for On-Demand Instances and the estimated number of days the instance might be underutilized. Actual savings will vary if you are using Reserved Instances or Spot Instances, or if the instance is not running for a full day. To get daily utilization data, download the report for this check.

Alert Criteria
Yellow: An instance had 10% or less daily average CPU utilization and 5 MB or less network I/O on at least 4 of the previous 14 days.

Recommended Action
Consider stopping or terminating instances that have low utilization, or scale the number of instances by using Auto Scaling. For more information, see Stop and Start Your Instance, Terminate Your Instance, and What is Auto Scaling?

- **Performance**: This check tries to identify any security groups that seem to have an excessive amount of rules, as too many rules can hinder a security group's performance:

Large Number of Rules in an EC2 Security Group

Checks each Amazon Elastic Compute Cloud (EC2) security group for an excessive number of rules. If a security group has a large number of rules, performance can be degraded. For more information, see Amazon EC2 Security Groups.

Alert Criteria
Yellow: An Amazon EC2-VPC security group has more than 50 rules.
Yellow: An Amazon EC2-Classic security group has more than 100 rules.

Recommended Action
Reduce the number of rules in a security group by deleting unnecessary or overlapping rules. For more information, see Deleting Rules from a Security Group.

- **Security**: This check looks for any unrestricted access to a resource that could be overly permissive, increasing the potential for a malicious user to gain access unnecessarily:

Security Groups - Unrestricted Access

Checks security groups for rules that allow unrestricted access to a resource. Unrestricted access increases opportunities for malicious activity (hacking, denial-of-service attacks, loss of data).

Alert Criteria
Red: A security group rule has a source IP address with a /0 suffix for ports other than 25, 80, or 443.

Recommended Action
Restrict access to only those IP addresses that require it. To restrict access to a specific IP address, set the suffix to /32 (for example, 192.0.2.10/32). Be sure to delete overly permissive rules after creating rules that are more restrictive.

- **Fault Tolerance**: This check will identify any RDS databases that have been deployed in a single Availability Zone in an effort to suggest that you use multi-Availability Zone deployments for high availability:

Amazon RDS Multi-AZ

Checks for DB instances that are deployed in a single Availability Zone. Multi-AZ deployments enhance database availability by synchronously replicating to a standby instance in a different Availability Zone. During planned database maintenance or the failure of a DB instance or Availability Zone, Amazon RDS automatically fails over to the standby so that database operations can resume quickly without administrative intervention. Because Multi-AZ deployments for the SQL Server engine use a different mechanism for synchronization, this check does not examine SQL Server instances.

Data for Amazon Relational Database Service (Amazon RDS) instances created in the Asia Pacific (Seoul) region (sa-east-1) is not available. We are working to fix this issue as soon as possible.

Alert Criteria

Yellow: A DB instance is deployed in a single Availability Zone.

Recommended Action

If your application requires high availability, modify your DB instance to enable Multi-AZ deployment. See High Availability (Multi-AZ).

- **Service Limits**: This check will determine whether more than 80% of your DyanmoDB-provisioned throughput limit has been reached for reads per account:

DynamoDB Read Capacity   Refreshed: 14 minutes ago

Checks for usage that is more than 80% of the DynamoDB Provisioned Throughput Limit for Reads per Account. Values are based on a snapshot, so your current usage might differ. Limit and usage data can take up to 24 hours to reflect any changes. In cases where limits have been recently increased, you may temporarily see utilization that exceeds the limit.

Alert Criteria

Yellow: 80% of limit reached.
Red: 100% of limit reached.
Blue: Trusted Advisor was unable to retrieve utilization or limits in one or more regions.

Recommended Action

If you anticipate exceeding a service limit, open a case in Support Center to request a limit increase.

At the time of writing this book, there are over 70 different checks that are performed against your resources and your account, and this list is continuously being updated and growing.

Understanding the availability of AWS Trusted Advisor

Now, you might be thinking that AWS Trusted Advisor is a great tool and you'll probably want to start using it right away if you don't already. However, the service is not freely available to everyone. The amount of AWS Trusted Advisor checks that you can use and access is dependent on your support plan with AWS – understanding this is important.

Each of the support plans offers different features, such as the following:

- Best practices
- Technical support
- Architecture support
- Proactive guidance
- Programmatic case management
- Account assistance
- Health status and notifications

 For a full list of AWS support plans and all of their features and what is included with each plan, please see: `https://console.aws.amazon.com/support/plans/home?#/`.

Access to Trusted Advisor falls under the best practices feature set, and as a result, the support plans for Trusted Advisor are set out as follows:

Feature comparison				Pricing example
Features	Basic Current plan	Developer	Business	Enterprise
Best practices	Access to 7 core Trusted Advisor checks	Access to 7 core Trusted Advisor checks	Access to all Trusted Advisor checks	Access to all Trusted Advisor checks

As you can see, there are four different support plans:

- Basic
- Developer
- Business
- Enterprise

For any AWS accounts that are on the Basic or Developer support plans, they will only have access to seven core Trusted Advisor checks.

For any accounts on the Business or Enterprise support plans, they will have access to all AWS Trusted Advisor checks across all five categories. There are also additional Trusted Advisor benefits that come with these two support plans, which include the following:

- **Notifications**: Allow you to create alerts and implement automation with the assistance of Amazon CloudWatch
- **Programmatic access**: Provides the ability to access and view any Trusted Advisor results via the appropriate AWS support APIs

The seven core checks that are accessible to everyone (through the Basic and Developer support plans) include six checks from the security category and the entirety of the service limit category (which is classed as one check but covers many different services). The checks are as follows:

The checks that are accessible for the security category include the following:

- S3 bucket permissions
- Security groups – specific ports unrestricted
- IAM use
- MFA of root account
- EBS public snapshots
- RDS public snapshots

The checks that are accessible for the service limits category include the following:

Service	Limits
Amazon DynamoDB (DynamoDB	Read capacity
	Write capacity
Amazon Elastic Block Store	Active volumes
	Active snapshots
	General Purpose (SSD) volume storage (GiB)
	Provisioned IOPS
	Provisioned IOPS (SSD) volume storage (GiB)
	Magnetic volume storage (GiB)
Amazon Elastic Compute Cloud	Elastic IP addresses (EIPs)
	Reserved Instances - purchase limit (monthly)
	On-Demand instances
Amazon Kinesis Streams	Shards
Amazon Relational Database Service	Clusters
	Cluster parameter groups
	Cluster roles
	DB instances
	DB parameter groups
	DB security groups
	DB snapshots per user
	Event subscriptions
	Max auths per security group
	Option groups
	Read replicas per master
	Reserved Instances
	Storage quota (GiB)
	Subnet groups
	Subnets per subnet group
Amazon Route 53	Hosted zones per account
	Max health checks per account
	Reusable delegation sets per account
	Traffic policies per account
	Traffic policy instances per account
Amazon Simple Email Service (Amazon SES)	Daily sending quota
Amazon Virtual Private Cloud	Elastic IP addresses (EIPs)
	Internet gateways
	VPCs
Auto Scaling	Auto Scaling groups
	Launch configurations
AWS CloudFormation	Stacks
Elastic Load Balancing (ELB)	Active load balancers
Identity and Access Management (IAM)	Groups
	Instance profiles
	Policies
	Roles
	Server certificates
	Users

If you are on the Basic support plan, then you can view these checks easily within the AWS Management Console by doing the following:

1. Selecting **Trusted Advisor** from the **Management and Governance** category on the service list page.
2. Selecting either the **Security** or **Service Limits** category and viewing the available services. From here, you can view each check in more detail.

Now that we have a basic understanding of what the service is and does, I want to show you what the interface and the findings look like when the set criteria have been breached.

Reviewing deviations using AWS Trusted Advisor

When you begin using AWS Trusted Advisor, over time you will see that the service begins to highlight potential issues within your account. In this section, I want to cover how to review the deviations that Trusted Advisor highlights and how to interpret the severity of the issues found.

From within the AWS Management Console, select **AWS Trusted Advisor** from the **Management & Governance** category list. This will then present you with the following dashboard:

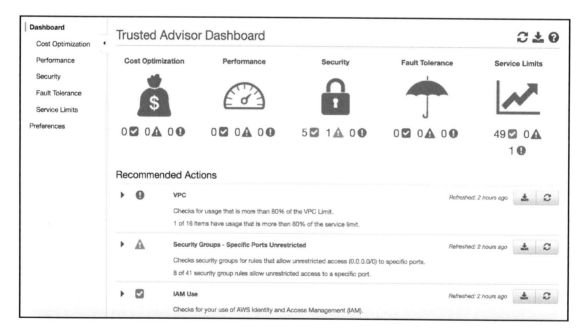

As you can see, you are presented with the five different categories that I explained earlier, each with a series of icons underneath that provide a high-level summary of the status of the checks within that category:

Let's understand what each of these icons signifies:

- The green square with a tick mark indicates the number of checks that successfully passed, where no action is required.
- The yellow triangle with an exclamation mark indicates the number of checks that require some level of investigation.
- The red circle with an exclamation mark indicates that immediate action and attention should be given.

My AWS account is only on the Basic support plan, and so I only have access to the free checks discussed earlier. Under the **Security** category, I can see that five of the six security checks passed successfully, but one element requires investigation, as signified by the yellow alert. Also, within the **Service Limits** category, I can see that I have a red alert for one of my checks. Let me take a look at both of these alerts.

Yellow alert

Firstly, we will try and understand the yellow triangle exclamation warning in my **Security** category. But how? There are two ways of doing so:

- You can select the alert from the **Recommended Actions** list, as shown in the previous screenshot.
- You can select the **Security** category icon showing the alert.

When selected, you can drill down into the check further to show the details captured. This shows my security alert:

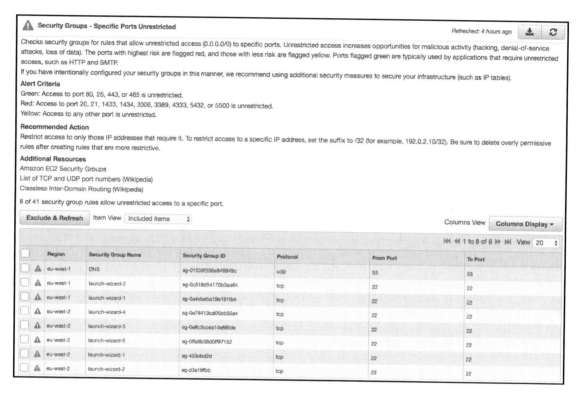

Let's take a closer look at the information presented on this page:

- Firstly, it identifies the check that this alert was issued against, this being **Security Groups - Specific Port Unrestricted**, which quite simply checks security groups for rules that allow unrestricted access (0.0.0.0/0) to specific ports.
- **Alert Criteria** defines the state at which this check is considered green, red, or yellow (its current state):
    - Green: Access to port 80, 25, 443, or 465 is unrestricted.
    - Red: Access to port 20, 21, 1433, 1434, 3306, 3389, 4333, 5432, or 5500 is unrestricted.
    - Yellow: Access to any other port is unrestricted.

- It also provides a suggestion for **Recommended Action**, and here it has indicated the following: **Restrict access to only those IP addresses that require it. To restrict access to a specific IP address, set the suffix to /32 (for example, 192.0.2.10/32). Be sure to delete overly permissive rules after creating rules that are more restrictive**.
- For additional clarification on the topics surrounding this issue, the check also supplies links to other resources, such as those shown here on Wikipedia and AWS's own documentation.
- Finally, at the bottom of the page, we can see a list of resources that were captured by this alert state, in which there are eight security groups.

So, my action to resolve this would be to restrict the source and destination addresses, instead of having the open access of 0.0.0.0/0 for these security groups.

If, for some reason, the configuration of one of these security groups was correct, despite this best practice, then I could exclude the resource from this check going forward to ensure that it didn't appear each and every time as an issue within Trusted Advisor. I could do this in two simple steps:

1. First, I would select the security group in question. In the example here, I have selected the **DNS** security group:

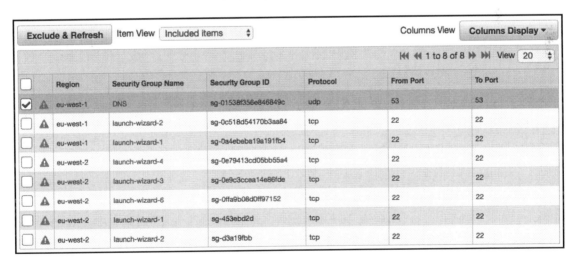

2. Then, select **Exclude & Refresh**, which you can see at the top of the table. AWS Trusted Advisor will then exclude that resource from its checks and refresh the entire listing:

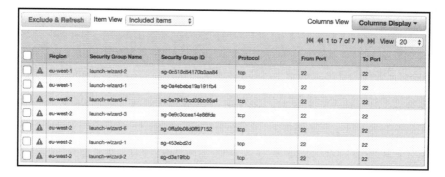

In this section, we reviewed a yellow alert, although it was not a critical find that needed immediate intervention. If left, then over time this could have become more of a security threat. So, essentially, yellow alerts still need rectifying, but it is not essential for you to act upon them immediately, whereas red alerts should require this level of response.

Red alert

Let me now take a look at the red alert from within the **Service Limits** category. To do so, select the alert from the main dashboard page:

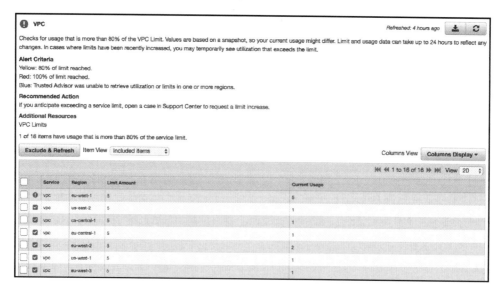

The service check limit seen here is for **VPC**. As explained previously, the service limit checks for usage that is more than 80% of the service limit; in this case, it's the VPC limit.

The alert criteria is either yellow (80% of the limit is reached), red (100% of the limit is reached), or blue (Trusted Advisor was unable to retrieve utilization or limits in one or more regions).

Based on this alert criteria, I can assume that I have five VPCs within a single region, and the recommended action to resolve this is to open a case in the Support Center to request a limit increase if I anticipate that I will require more than five VPCs in the affected region.

Looking at my list of VPCs, I can see that it is the **eu-west-1** region that does indeed have five VPCs within it:

		Service	Region	Limit Amount	Current Usage
	❗	vpc	eu-west-1	5	5
	☑	vpc	us-east-2	5	1
	☑	vpc	ca-central-1	5	1

As we have seen, AWS Trusted Advisor is a great tool for monitoring, getting advice, and getting recommendations about actions to take within your infrastructure based upon best practices that can help you to refine your architecture to the benefit of costs, performance, fault tolerance, service limitations, and most importantly, security! Having a service that is always analyzing your infrastructure and advising you to adhere to best practices, especially from a security perspective, makes this a very powerful service and helps you to maintain a stronger security posture.

Penetration testing in AWS

Firstly, what is a **penetration test**? A penetration test, or pentest, is essentially an authorized cyber attack on your own environment and infrastructure that is used to determine its weak points and vulnerabilities, in addition to its strengths, against defined security standards.

This is a good security practice to perform on your environments to understand the areas of improvement required at all layers of your architecture. It is better for an authorized attacker to find a weak spot, allowing you to fix and remediate the risk, than to have a malicious attacker who would exploit the flaw for their own gain.

However, within AWS, you must adhere to some strict policies and procedures when penetration testing. For example, you can't carry out penetration testing on whatever service you would like to; in fact, there are very few services that you can pentest without prior approval from AWS. These services are as follows:

- Amazon EC2 instances, NAT gateways, and elastic load balancers
- Amazon RDS
- Amazon CloudFront
- Amazon Aurora
- Amazon API Gateways
- AWS Lambda and Lambda Edge functions
- Amazon Lightsail resources
- Amazon Elastic Beanstalk environments

For the preceding "allowed" services, there are also some very strict rules regarding services that are not to be pentested under any circumstances – these are as follows:

- DNS zone walking via Amazon Route 53 hosted zones
- **Denial of Service** (**DoS**), **Distributed Denial of Service** (**DDoS**), simulated DoS, simulated DDoS
- Port flooding
- Protocol flooding
- Request flooding (login request flooding and API request flooding)

In addition to this, you are not allowed to carry out any kind of security assessment on AWS's own infrastructure or any of the services they offer.

Finally, the following terms and conditions should be adhered to at all times when it comes to pentesting:

- Pentesting will be restricted by service, network bandwidth, requests per minute, and instance type.
- Pentesting is subject to the terms of the AWS Customer Agreement (https://aws.amazon.com/agreement/) between you and AWS.
- You should abide by AWS's policy regarding the use of security assessment tools and services.

The preceding points and the full policy relating to the use of different assessment tools can be found at: `https://aws.amazon.com/security/penetration-testing/`.

Summary

In this chapter, we quickly went through some of the industry best practices that have been tried and tested, are easy to implement, and should be followed at all times. We then understood how AWS Trusted Advisor is a service that is based upon AWS best practices within your environment and covers not only security best practices but also those focused on cost optimization, performance, fault tolerance, and service limits. However, depending on your support plan, not all of the checks within Trusted Advisor may be available. Finally, we looked at the *dos* and *don't*s for the policies that must be followed, to ensure that you do not breach any security procedures set out by AWS when pentesting.

In the next chapter, we will be looking at AWS Key Management Service, known as KMS, and CloudHSM, which are two services used to manage encryption keys. Therefore, the next chapter will be very much focused on data protection using different encryption mechanisms.

Questions

As we conclude, here is a list of questions for you to test your knowledge regarding this chapter's material. You will find the answers in the *Assessments* section of the *Appendix*:

1. True or false: You should enable access keys for your root account that would enable programmatic access to your AWS account.
2. Which AWS service highlights and recommends enhancements against a number of predefined best practice checks across five different areas of your account?
3. Which check within AWS Trusted Advisor is used to determine whether you have adequate resiliency built into your environment, for example, through making use of multi-Availability Zone features and auto-scaling?
4. Which support plans only give access to seven core Trusted Advisor checks?
5. True or false: A penetration test, or pentest, is essentially an authorized cyber attack on your own environment and infrastructure in an effort to determine its weak points and vulnerabilities, in addition to its strengths, against defined security standards.

Section 6: Encryption and Data Security

6

The final section of this book covers encryption. We'll look at the different types of encryption used throughout AWS services and how to configure and implement encryption across a variety of different services. Then, we'll take a deep dive look at the **Key Management Service** (**KMS**). It's important that you understand this service and how it interacts with a number of different AWS services. We'll also look at another encryption service, AWS CloudHSM, how this differs from KMS, and when you should use one over the other.

Next, we'll look at data security, where we'll cover a range of different AWS services in order to learn how to configure and implement security features. These services include Amazon **Elastic Block Store** (**EBS**), Amazon **Elastic File Systems** (**EFS**), Amazon **Simple Storage Service** (**S3**), Amazon **Relational Database Service** (**RDS**), and Amazon DynamoDB.

Finally, to round off this section, we will provide two mock tests that will assess your understanding of the content in this book. Each mock test will contain 65 questions for you to answer.

By the end of this section, you will be able to implement data encryption features across a wide selection of AWS services to ensure your data remains protected at all times.

This section comprises the following chapters:

16
Managing Key Infrastructure

Understanding how to manage encryption keys and implement encryption is key to the Security– Specialty certification and, in particular, the AWS Key Management Service plays a big part. Data protection is always on people's minds when storing data within the cloud, and so understanding the different approaches to encryption and the different mechanisms available is an important topic to understand. Having a good understanding of how to encrypt data in AWS will allow you to confidently build secure solutions for you and your customers.

As a result, it's important that we cover KMS and that you are familiar with its workings and how it can be used by other AWS services to protect your data. Within this chapter, I will be covering the AWS **Key Management Service**, known as **KMS**, in addition to an overview of AWS CloudHSM, which is another service used to manage encryption keys.

The following topics will be covered in this chapter:

- A simple overview of encryption
- Exploring AWS **Key Management Service (KMS)**
- Exploring AWS CloudHSM

Technical requirements

To follow the exercises in this chapter, you must have access to the **Key Management Service (KMS)**, including the ability to create new CMKs. For more information on how to manage your permissions, please see Chapter 4, *Working with Access Policies*.

You must also have the AWS CLI installed on your client. If you do not already have it installed, please follow the steps at: https://docs.aws.amazon.com/cli/latest/userguide/cli-chap-install.html.

A simple overview of encryption

In today's world, data protection and data privacy is of the utmost importance not just to individuals, but also large organizations that are dealing with customer data on a huge scale. When data is not encrypted, that data is considered to be plaintext, meaning that anyone who has access to the data is freely able to view the data without any restrictions. If this data doesn't hold any sensitive data, then having data stored as plaintext is not an issue. However, if that data contains sensitive or confidential information within it, then the data should be encrypted.

This encryption should be applied both at rest and in transit. *Encryption-at-rest* means that the data is encrypted where the object is stored, for example, when data is being stored on an EBS volume or in an Amazon S3 bucket. On the other hand, *encryption-in-transit* ensures that an encryption mechanism is applied to data when it is being sent/received between two or more locations, for example, when data is being sent from an EC2 instance to an RDS database.

The encryption of data uses different mathematical algorithms and keys as a mechanism to alter plaintext data, making it unreadable. Once the encryption has taken place, the data is no longer considered to be plaintext; instead, it is referred to as ciphertext. The only way to decrypt the data again back to plaintext is to use the correct encryption key to revert the process. The encryption keys themselves are simply a string of characters, and the longer the string, the stronger the encryption is, and the harder it is to decrypt.

Symmetric encryption versus asymmetric encryption

At a high level, I want to explain the difference between symmetric and asymmetric encryption keys as this will help to understand how KMS works going forward, which uses both symmetric and asymmetric encryption.

Symmetric encryption uses a single key to encrypt and decrypt data. So if you were to encrypt a document using a symmetric key, in order to decrypt that same document, the user would have to have access to that very same key that performed the encryption to decrypt it. Examples of some common symmetric encryption algorithms include **Advanced Encryption Standard (AES)**, **Digital Encryption Standard (DES)**, and Triple DES:

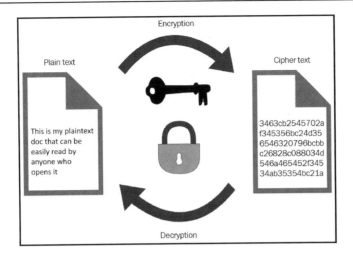

Asymmetric encryption keys differ from symmetric encryptionin that they use two keys to perform the encryption. The keys themselves are linked via a mathematical algorithm during their creation, where one of the keys can then be used to encrypt data (public key), and the second key (private key) is used in combination with the public key to decrypt the same data object. The keys themselves act as a public/private key pair. The public key can be given to anyone without restriction, whereas the private key must be kept private and NOT shared with anyone else. Anyone could encrypt data using your publicly shared public key; however, no one could decrypt that data unless they had the private key of that key pair. Some examples of asymmetric encryption include Diffie-Hellman, Digital Signature Algorithm, and RSA:

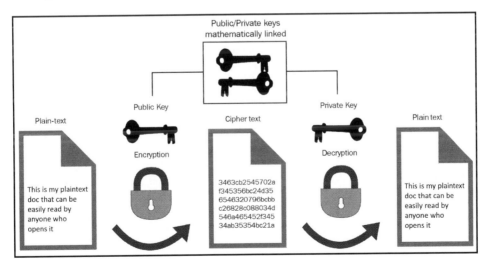

With this general understanding of symmetric and asymmetric encryption, we are now better equipped to understand how KMS works. So let's jump straight in.

Exploring AWS Key Management Service (KMS)

The AWS KMS service is essential if you want to encrypt your data at rest within your AWS environment. It is a managed service that allows you to create, store, rotate, and delete encryption keys to enable you to protect your sensitive data on AWS. It tightly integrates with a number of AWS services, such as RDS, S3, EBS, CloudTrail, and many more, offering a seamless and secure method of implementing encryption while utilizing a centralized key management repository.

KMS is a regional service, so you must be aware of this when architecting your encryption throughout your environment. You are unable to use a KMS key from one region in another region; for example, if you used a key in us-east-1, you would not be able to use that same key in eu-west-2.

As you can imagine, controlling access to KMS must be tightly monitored and, in fact, even AWS administrators are unable to access your keys within your KMS environment. Therefore, you need to be extremely careful when administering your KMS keys, since if you delete a key, AWS is unable to retrieve it back for you. You need to implement a robust set of access controls to your KMS service, ensuring that you implement the principle of least privilege to your key operators and administrators.

It's important to understand that KMS is not designed to perform encryption-in-transit. If you would like to implement in-transit encryption for your data instead of encryption-at-rest, you would need to adopt a different encryption mechanism, such as **Secure Sockets Layer (SSL)**.

As I mentioned previously, KMS integrates with CloudTrail, which means all API calls to keys are tracked and recorded, such as the following events:

- `CreateAlias`
- `CreateGrant`
- `CreateKey`
- `Decrypt`
- `DeleteAlias`

For a full list of events, please visit: `https://docs.aws.amazon.com/kms/latest/developerguide/logging-using-cloudtrail.html`.

Integration with CloudTrail allows you to audit when and where KMS keys and actions have been used.

Understanding the key components of AWS KMS

To truly understand how the AWS KMS service works, we need to dive into the different components of the service to see how they interact with each other. Over the next few pages, I will be discussing the following elements:

- Customer master keys
- Data encryption keys
- Key material
- Key policies
- Grants

Customer master keys

The **customer master key (CMK)** is the main building block of the KMS service as it contains the key material used for both encrypting and decrypting data.

KMS supports both symmetric and asymmetric CMKs. Any symmetric keys created and stored within KMS will be a 256-bit key that will, of course, be used for both encryption and decryption and will never leave the KMS service. The 'private' key of any asymmetric keys pairs that are created will be retained within the KMS service. Asymmetric keys were introduced into KMS in November 2019 and there are few differences between the two, including the following:

- Symmetric keys can be used to generate symmetric data keys in addition to asymmetric data key pairs.
- Importing your own key material is only supported for symmetric CMKs.
- Automatic key rotation is only supported for symmetric CMKs.
- When using a custom key store, you can only store symmetric CMKs.
- Asymmetric keys can either be used for encryption and decryption OR for signing and verification.

For a full comparison between both symmetric and asymmetric CMKs, please see the following resource at: https://docs.aws.amazon.com/kms/latest/developerguide/symm-asymm-compare.html.

It is possible to store your CMKs in a custom key store, instead of the KMS key store. These custom key stores can be created using an AWS CloudHSM cluster that you own and manage. Having your own CloudHSM allows you to have direct control over the **hardware security modules (HSMs)** that are responsible for generating key material. We will be discussing CloudHSM later in this chapter in great detail.

There are three different types of CMKs used by KMS that you need to be familiar with:

- AWS-owned
- AWS-managed
- Customer-managed

AWS-owned CMKs

These CMKs are owned and used by AWS services to encrypt your data. They do not reside within your KMS console or indeed within your account, nor do you have the ability to audit and track their usage. They are essentially abstracted from your AWS account. However, because they can be used by services used within your AWS account, those services do have the capabilities to use those keys to encrypt your data within your account.

They are managed and created by AWS, and so there is no management of these keys required. When it comes to the rotation of AWS-owned CMKs, it is down to the particular service that manages that particular key, and so the rotation period is varied from service to service.

Examples of AWS-owned CMKs include the following:

- The encryption used to encrypt all Amazon DynamoDB tables, which are encrypted by default with no option to disable this encryption
- Amazon S3 encryption using the S3 master key (SSE-S3)

AWS-managed CMKs

Much like AWS-owned CMKs, AWS-managed keys are managed by AWS. However, you are able to view the keys that are being used to encrypt your data from within the AWS Management Console, in addition to being able to audit and track their usage and view their key policies. However, because they are managed by AWS, you are not able to control their rotation frequency.

These keys are used by AWS services that integrate with KMS directly and are created by the service when you first add or configure encryption using that service within each region, since you will recall that KMS is a regional service. These keys can only be used by those services and cannot be integrated into your own cryptographic operations.

Here are examples of AWS-managed CMKs:

- The first time you select object encryption using Amazon S3's server-side encryption using KMS-managed keys (SSE-KMS), you can either select a customer-managed CMK, or there will be an AWS-managed CMK identified by **aws/s3** in the key selection list.
- When encrypting an EBS volume, this is again signified by **aws/ebs** as the key name.

Customer-managed CMKs

Finally, we have customer-managed keys, and these keys offer the greatest level of flexibility and control. Unlike AWS-owned and AWS-managed CMKs, with customer-managed keys, you have total control and governance over these keys. You are able to create, disable, or delete the key, configure the key policies associated with your key, configure grants, and also alter and adjust the key rotation periods and view full usage through the audit history of the key.

These keys can be used by other AWS services that integrate with KMS, and can be used instead of the AWS-managed keys if desired. Due to the additional flexibility offered by customer-managed keys, there is an additional charge for using your customer CMKs, whereas the other CMKs discussed can be used free of charge.

Let's try and create a customer-managed CMK. It is a simple process, so let's take a look step by step:

1. From within the AWS Management Console, make sure you are in the region that you would like to have the CMK. Remember that KMS is a regional service.
2. Select the **Key Management Service** under the **Security, Identity & Compliance** category.

3. Select **Customer managed keys** from the menu on the left:

> AWS managed keys
>
> Customer managed keys
>
> Custom key stores

4. Select the orange **Create Key** button. You will arrive at the following screenshot:

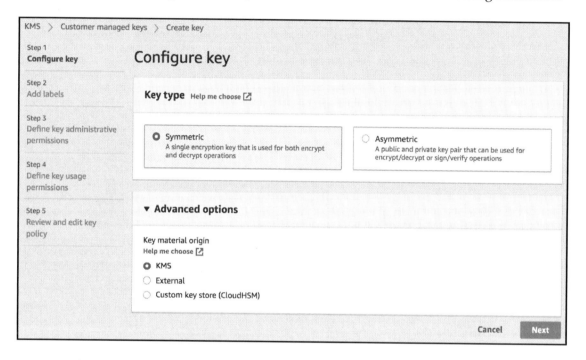

As you can see, there are now five steps to complete before your CMK is created. *Step 1* is **Configure key**.

5. Select either the **Symmetric** or **Asymmetric** key option depending on your use case. For this demonstration, I will create a symmetric key. **Advanced options** allow you to determine the origin of the key material. I will go into more depth on key material later in this chapter. For this demonstration, I will select **KMS** and click **Next** to move on to *step 2*, as seen in the following screenshot:

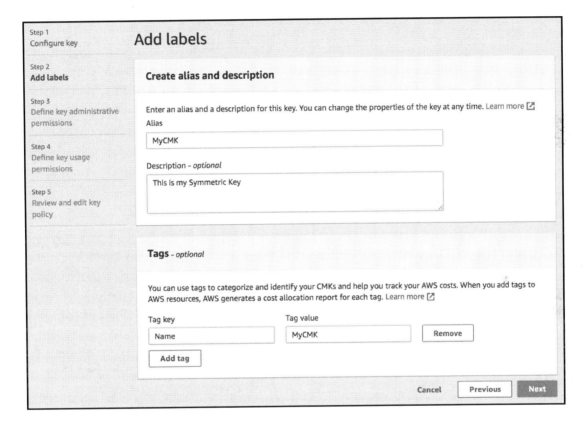

6. Enter an alias and an optional description, and if you would like to tag your CMK, then you can add your key-value tagging pairs, too. When you have added your details, select the **Next** button to move on to *step 3*, as seen in the following screenshot:

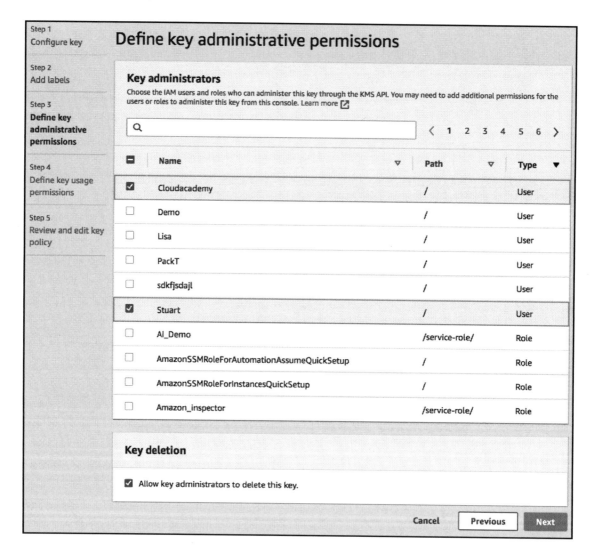

7. At this stage, you must select which IAM roles or users should be a key administrator. Key administrators can only administer the CMK and not use it to perform any encryption function that may be needed within the CMK. You can also decide whether you want the key administrators to have access to delete the key via a checkbox. Click **Next** to move on to *step 4*, as seen in the following screenshot:

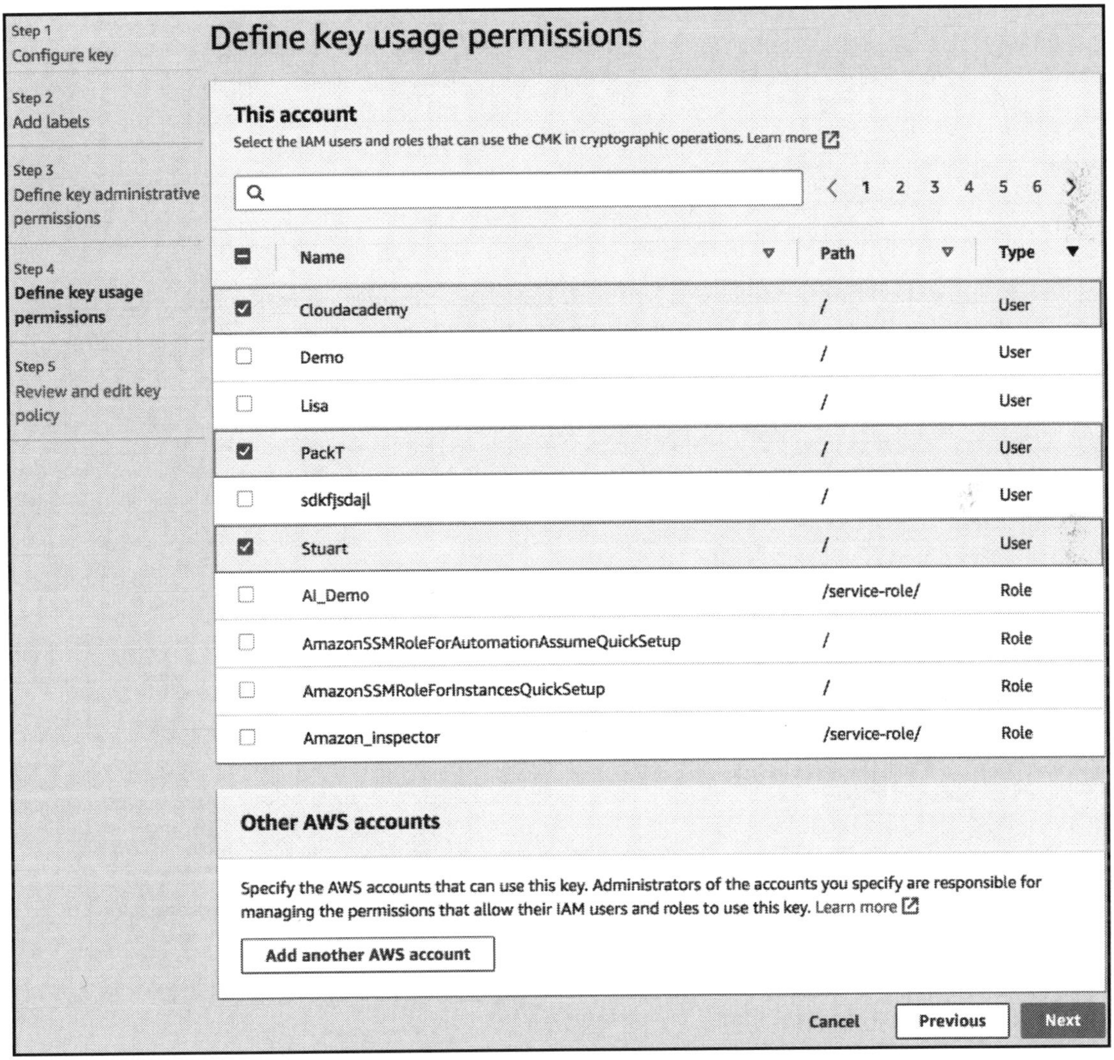

Step 1 Configure key	**Define key usage permissions**				
Step 2 Add labels	**This account**				
	Select the IAM users and roles that can use the CMK in cryptographic operations. Learn more				
Step 3 Define key administrative permissions	🔍	‹ 1 2 3 4 5 6 ›			
Step 4 **Define key usage permissions**	☐ Name ▽		Path ▽		Type ▼
	☑ Cloudacademy		/		User
Step 5 Review and edit key policy	☐ Demo		/		User
	☐ Lisa		/		User
	☑ PackT		/		User
	☐ sdkfjsdajl		/		User
	☑ Stuart		/		User
	☐ AI_Demo		/service-role/		Role
	☐ AmazonSSMRoleForAutomationAssumeQuickSetup		/		Role
	☐ AmazonSSMRoleForInstancesQuickSetup		/		Role
	☐ Amazon_inspector		/service-role/		Role
	Other AWS accounts				
	Specify the AWS accounts that can use this key. Administrators of the accounts you specify are responsible for managing the permissions that allow their IAM users and roles to use this key. Learn more				
	Add another AWS account				
			Cancel	Previous	Next

8. Here, you can now select which IAM users or roles you would like to be able to use the CMK in order to perform cryptographic operations. Additionally, you can also specify another AWS account that you would like to be able to use this key:

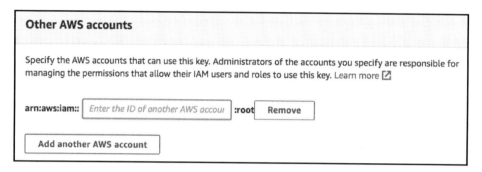

9. Once you have made your configuration and permissions choices, select **Next** to move on to *step 5*, as seen in the following screenshot:

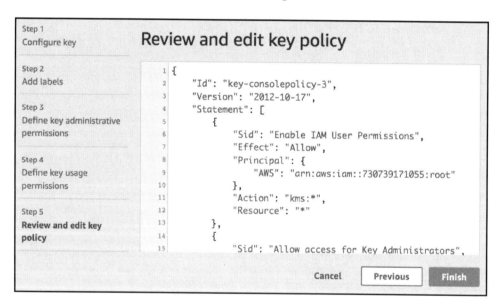

10. This final step allows you to review the key policy that has been generated based on the parameters that you selected during the previous screens. To finish creating the CMK, select **Finish**. Your customer-managed key will now show in the dashboard:

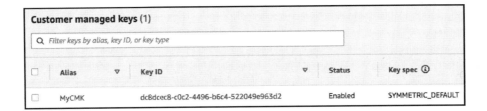

In this section, we looked at how to create a customer-managed CMK, which provides you with many more configurable options relating to the key when compared to AWS-owned and AWS-managed CMKs, including editing the key permissions and key policy defining who can use the key.

Data encryption keys (DEKs)

Now we have an understanding of CMKs, I want to talk about data keys. Data keys are created by CMKs. However, they do not reside inside the KMS service like CMKs do; instead, these are used outside of KMS to perform encryption against your data.

When a request to generate a data key is received by KMS, the associated CMK in the request will create the two **data encryption keys (DEKs)**; one will be a *plaintext* key, and also another *identical* key, but this will be encrypted:

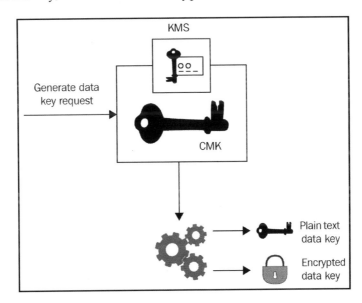

The process of using one key to encrypt another key like this is known as *envelope encryption*.

During the encryption process, the plaintext data key will be used to perform the encryption of your data using an encryption algorithm. Once the encryption has taken place, this plaintext data key will then be deleted and the encrypted data key will be stored and associated with the encrypted data.

At this point, your data is now encrypted, and the only way to access this data is to request for the encrypted data key to be decrypted by the CMK. However, that could only be requested by an entity who had the `kms:decrypt` permission associated with the CMK. I will discuss permissions further later in this chapter when I come to key policies.

To demonstrate an example of DEKs being used within AWS services, let me take a look at how both the encryption and decryption processes work for Amazon S3 **server-side encryption with KMS managed keys**, known as **SSE-KMS**.

Encryption

The following diagram shows a graphical representation of how the encryption process works when using SSE-KMS in Amazon S3:

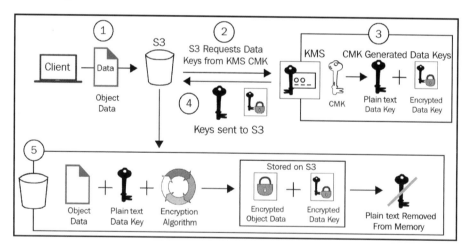

Let's go over the steps in the preceding diagram and see how encryption takes place:

1. Firstly, the client identifies the object(s) that are to be uploaded to S3, indicating SSE-KMS as the encryption mechanism, selecting either an AWS-managed or customer-managed CMK.

2. Amazon S3 will respond by initiating a request to generate DEKs from KMS to allow S3 to encrypt the data submitted by the client.

3. Using the CMK selected during *step 1*, KMS will then generate two data keys, a plaintext data key, and an encrypted version of that same data key.

4. KMS will send both of these data keys back to S3 to allow S3 to begin the encryption process using the plaintext data key.

5. At this stage, S3 then encrypts the object data with the plaintext version of the data key and stores the resulting encrypted object alongside the encrypted version of the data key. The plaintext data key will then be deleted and removed from memory.

Now that we have seen how the encryption process works, let's move on to the decryption process.

Decryption

This diagram shows a graphical representation of how the decryption process works when using SSE-KMS in Amazon S3:

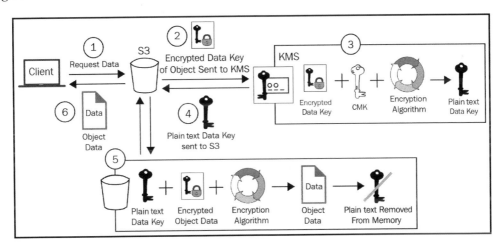

Let's go over the steps in the preceding diagram and see how decryption takes place:

1. A request is received by S3 to access an encrypted object via a client.

2. S3 is aware that the object is encrypted and sends the encrypted data key associated with the object requested to KMS.

3. KMS takes the encrypted data key and uses the original CMK to decrypt the data key to generate a plaintext version of the data key.

4. KMS sends the plaintext data key back to S3.
5. Using the plaintext data key, the encrypted object data can then be decrypted, returning a plaintext version of the object data, and the plaintext data key is deleted from memory.
6. The plaintext object is then sent back to the requesting client.

As you can see, the encryption process follows a logical process of obtaining the keys from KMS from outside of Amazon S3 before performing any encryption operations. The CMKs used in this process can either be AWS-managed or customer-managed.

KMS key material

Key material is essentially the data that is used to encrypt and decrypt data and is stored within your CMK. Hence, in the example I just covered with SSE-KMS, the CMK key material was used to encrypt a version of the data key as well as decrypt an encrypted version of the data key.

When you create your CMK, KMS automatically creates new key material for that CMK. However, when you are creating your own customer-managed CMKs, you can choose to create your CMK without any key material, allowing you to import your own into the key yourself. This method of key material assignment is known as **Bring Your Own Key (BYOK)**.

However, it is important to note that imported key material does not support automatic key rotation, but it is possible to manually rotate your keys with imported material.

Importing your own key material

In an early demonstration when we created a new customer-managed CMK, there was an option at *step 1* of configuring your key to select the key material origin under the advanced options. In the demonstration, I selected **KMS**, in order to use the key material generated by KMS:

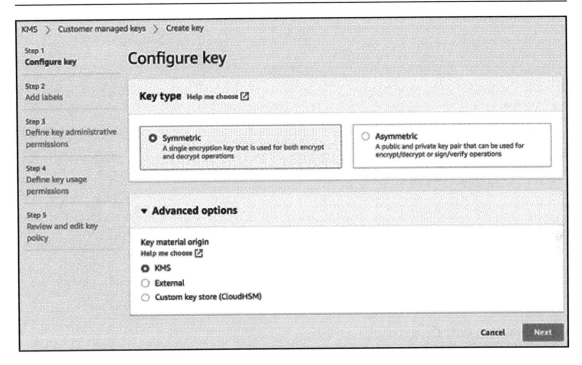

However, to import your own key material into a new customer-managed CMK, you can select **External** for the **Key material origin** option:

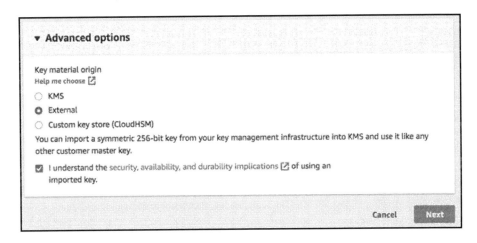

When doing so, you must also select the checkbox to confirm that you understand the security, availability, and durability implications of using an imported key.

After repeating the same steps from the earlier demonstration, you will then be asked to download the public key and import a token for your CMK. This is required in order to perform two functions.

- Firstly, the public key is used to encrypt your own key material before uploading it to KMS.
- Next, KMS will then decrypt it using the private key associated with that same public key.

The import token consists of metadata to ensure that the key material uploaded was uploaded and imported correctly.

There are a couple of additional points to bear in mind when performing this import. Firstly, the key material must be in a binary format when encrypting it with the public key. Also, when importing the key back into your CMK, you can choose to add an expiry date of the key material, at which point it will be deleted, thereby rendering the CMK unusable.

If the key material is deleted automatically through this expiration date, or manually at any time, the CMK can no longer be used for encryption. The only way to reinstate that same CMK is to import the same key material again, whereas if you were to delete the CMK, it is not possible to reinstate that same CMK.

Key policies

I now want to look at permissions associated with the CMK. Earlier, when I was explaining how to create a customer-managed CMK, we had options to review and modify key administrators and key users, which had an effect on the resulting CMK key policy.

The main function of the key policy is to determine who can both use the key to perform cryptographic operations, such as `encrypt`, `decrypt`, and `GenerateDataKey`, and many more, in addition to who can administer the CMK to perform functions such as deleting/revoking the CMK and importing key material into the CMK.

The policy itself is considered a resource-based policy as it is tied to the CMK itself and, as a result, it's not possible to use a CMK for any encryption unless it has a configured key policy attached.

Much like IAM policies, key policies are JSON-based and appear much like other IAM access policies from a syntax and structure point of view, so if you are familiar with IAM policies, then key policies will be easier to understand.

The key policies themselves also allow you to configure access and use of the CMKs in a variety of ways. As such, you can configure access to the CMK as follows:

- **Via key policies**: All access is governed by the key policy alone.
- **Via key policies and IAM**: Access is governed by the key policy in addition to IAM identity-based policies, allowing you to manage access via groups and other IAM features.
- **Via key policies and grants**: Access is governed by the key policy with the added ability to delegate access to others to use the CMK.

The key point to remember here is that, without a key policy, you are unable to control access to your CMKs. Let me now run through each of these options to explain how they operate.

Using only key policies to control access

When I created the key policy earlier in this chapter during one of the demonstrations, I was given the option to select any IAM users or roles that could act as administrators of the CMK. I selected the users **Cloudacademy** and **Stuart**, as seen here:

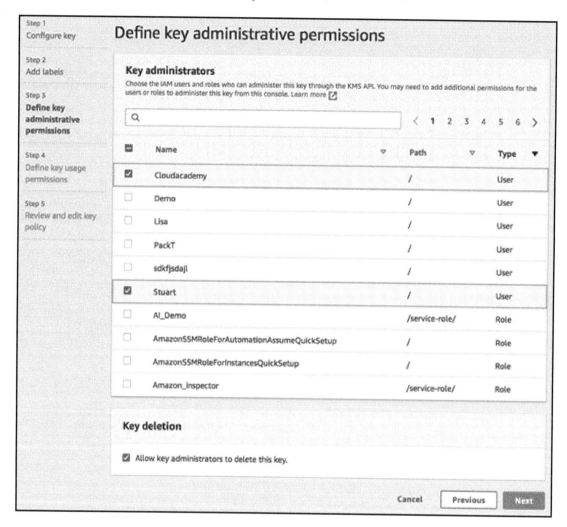

This resulted in an entry in the key policy as follows:

```
{
        "Sid": "Allow access for Key Administrators",
        "Effect": "Allow",
        "Principal": {
```

```
            "AWS": [
                "arn:aws:iam::730739171055:user/Cloudacademy",
                "arn:aws:iam::730739171055:user/Stuart"
            ]
        },
        "Action": [
            "kms:Create*",
            "kms:Describe*",
            "kms:Enable*",
            "kms:List*",
            "kms:Put*",
            "kms:Update*",
            "kms:Revoke*",
            "kms:Disable*",
            "kms:Get*",
            "kms:Delete*",
            "kms:TagResource",
            "kms:UntagResource",
            "kms:ScheduleKeyDeletion",
            "kms:CancelKeyDeletion"
        ],
        "Resource": "*"
    },
```

As you can see, the **Statement Identifier** (Sid) clearly identifies this section as Allow access for Key Administrators and lists both of the users that I selected using their respective ARNs. We can also see the entire range of actions that these users are allowed to perform as administrators. One point to note is that although key administrators are not able to use the CMK, they do have access to update the key policy to add themselves as a user!

Now, if we look at the user permissions set out for the users who can actually perform cryptographic operations using the CMK, which I configured as shown in the demonstration earlier in this chapter for three users, **Cloudacademy**, **PackT**, and **Stuart**, we have the following:

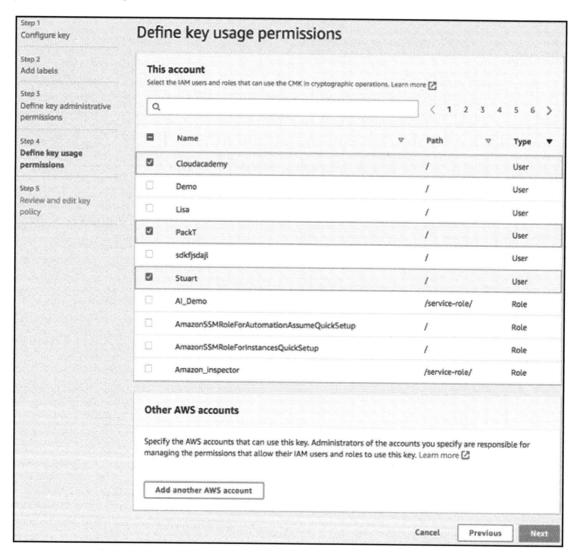

Again, this is reflected in the key policy of the CMK, as shown here:

```
{
            "Sid": "Allow use of the key",
            "Effect": "Allow",
            "Principal": {
                "AWS": [
                    "arn:aws:iam::730739171055:user/Cloudacademy",
                    "arn:aws:iam::730739171055:user/Stuart",
                    "arn:aws:iam::730739171055:user/PackT"
                ]
            },
            "Action": [
                "kms:Encrypt",
                "kms:Decrypt",
                "kms:ReEncrypt*",
                "kms:GenerateDataKey*",
                "kms:DescribeKey"
            ],
            "Resource": "*"
        },
```

As you can see, the permissions set for the users allow them to perform the encryption/decryption actions of data using the CMK, in addition to being able to generate data keys.

Using key policies in addition to IAM

Every time a new CMK is created, the root of the account in which the CMK is created will always have full access to the CMK within the key policy. This ensures that you will always be able to have admin access to the CMK because the root account can't be deleted, whereas other user can be.

In addition to this, granting the root account with full access also provides another very useful function. It enables you to use IAM policies to grant access to the CMK for both the key administrator and users.

When a policy is created, you will see a section at the beginning of the policy that looks like this:

```
{
            "Sid": "Enable IAM User Permissions",
            "Effect": "Allow",
            "Principal": {
                "AWS": "arn:aws:iam::730739171055:root"
            },
```

```
            "Action": "kms:*",
            "Resource": "*"
        },
```

You can see that the `Sid` is labeled as `Enable IAM User Permissions`.

Without this section within the key policy, it would not be possible to use IAM permissions to grant access for other IAM roles or users to your CMK.

Using IAM, you can then set specific permissions as you would for other resources across AWS. These permissions can be set for both key administrators and key users. For example, I could use the following identity-based policy within IAM to allow them to use the CMK for cryptographic operations:

```
{
    "Version": "2012-10-17",
    "Statement": [
        {
            "Sid": "Stmt1586431030713",
            "Action": [
                "kms:Decrypt",
                "kms:DescribeKey",
                "kms:Encrypt",
                "kms:GenerateDataKey"
            ],
            "Effect": "Allow",
            "Resource": "arn:aws:kms:eu-west-1:730739171055:key/dc8dcec8-
c0c2-4496-b6c4-522049e963d2"
        }
    ]
}
```

This policy, when attached to a user, group, or role, would provide `Decrypt`, `DescribeKey`, `Encrypt`, and `GenerateDataKey` permissions to the resource `arn:aws:kms:eu-west-1:730739171055:key/dc8dcec8-c0c2-4496-b6c4-522049e963d2`, which is the ARN of my CMK.

Using key policies with grants

The last method of allowing access to your CMKs is via grants. Grants effectively allow you to programmatically delegate your permissions to another principal, but at a more granular level than key policies can.

It is not possible to create grants from within the AWS Management Console; they are programmatically created, and so you can use the AWS CLI instead.

A grant consists of two parties, the user who creates the grant, and the grantee who then uses that grant to perform cryptographic operations. However, the permissions given to the grantee can only be equal to, or more restrictive than, those associated with the user who issued and created the grant.

For a user to be able to create and revoke grants, they must have the following permissions, either within the key policy, or given via an IAM identity-based policy, providing IAM permissions are allowed:

- "kms:CreateGrant"
- "kms:ListGrants"
- "kms:RevokeGrant"

To facilitate understanding, let's try and create a grant ourselves.

In this demonstration, we have two users, Stuart and Alice. Stuart has permission to create grants in addition to being able to use the CMK for cryptographic operations, as we saw in the earlier key policies. Alice, however, does not have any access to use the CMK via the key policy or via IAM permissions.

For this demonstration, I will be carrying out all operations on my own laptop, so I want to create two AWS CLI profiles to be able to test access, one for Stuart and one for Alice. To do this, you will need to have the access key and secret access keys of your two users from within IAM:

1. Open your terminal on your laptop and, from the command prompt, enter the following command:

   ```
   aws configure --profile Stuart
   ```

   Replace Stuart with your own profile name.

2. Add your access key and secret access keys for your user.
3. Specify your default region (I have selected the region in which the CMK resides):

```
Stuarts-MBP-2:~ stuartscott$ aws configure --profile Stuart
AWS Access Key ID [None]: AKIA2UI3S33X3HCHX2F6
AWS Secret Access Key [None]: 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
Default region name [None]: eu-west-1
Default output format [None]:
Stuarts-MBP-2:~ stuartscott$
```

4. Repeat the same process for your second user, in this case, Alice, with – `aws configure --profile Alice`:

```
Stuarts-MBP-2:~ stuartscott$ aws configure --profile Alice
AWS Access Key ID [****************ZK37]: AKIA2UI3S33XZUHHRYE4
AWS Secret Access Key [****************xN0/]: 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
Default region name [eu-west-1]: eu-west-1
Default output format [clear]:
```

Now I have two profiles set up on my AWS CLI: `Stuart` and `Alice`, each with their own credentials.

5. Now, to confirm that `Alice` is not able to encrypt anything using our CMK, I can enter the following command using the AWS CLI:

   `aws kms encrypt --plaintext "Certification" --key-id alias/MyCMK --profile Alice`

6. This command will attempt to take the word `Certification` in `plaintext` and encrypt it using the name of my CMK, `MyCMK`, using the credentials of `Alice`:

```
Stuarts-MBP-2:~ stuartscott$ aws kms encrypt --plaintext "Certification" --key-id alias/MyCMK --profile Alice

An error occurred (AccessDeniedException) when calling the Encrypt operation: User: arn:aws:iam::730739171055:
user/Alice is not authorized to perform: kms:Encrypt on resource: arn:aws:kms:eu-west-1:730739171055:key/dc8dc
ec8-c0c2-4496-b6c4-522049e963d2
```

As we can see, I received an error of `AccessDeniedException`. The user `Alice` is not authorized to perform the encryption. So this confirms that at this stage, `Alice` is not able to perform encryption using the CMK.

7. Now if I perform the same procedure using the profile of `Stuart`, we can see the result here:

```
Stuarts-MBP-2:~ stuartscott$ aws kms encrypt --plaintext "Certification" --key-id alias/MyCMK --profile Stuart
{
    "EncryptionAlgorithm": "SYMMETRIC_DEFAULT",
    "KeyId": "arn:aws:kms:eu-west-1:730739171055:key/dc8dcec8-c0c2-4496-b6c4-522049e963d2",
    "CiphertextBlob": "AQICAHgykeN0jK4KwKoMCf9kmqmAu9RUF518dozkj5kL7HxjlwGkoDH/Ig7rXvlpqyj6rEZuAAAAazBpBgkqhki
G9w0BBwagXDBaAgEAMFUGCSqGSIb3DQEHATAeBglghkgBZQMEAS4wEQQMNMbKl3LQTIDgtDUnAgEQgCiT4HUs6C6kzJBN0462Wf64ESxySJL9Z
b93goVaLuh1nvP3c9qN1JBZ"
}
```

Now, because Stuart has permission to perform encryption, we can see that `plaintext "Certification"` has now been encrypted using `key-id`.

8. Next, I want to use the `Stuart` profile to create a grant and delegate access to allow `Alice` to perform encryption. To do so, I can enter the following command at the AWS CLI:

```
aws kms create-grant --key-id arn:aws:kms:eu-
west-1:730739171055:key/dc8dcec8-c0c2-4496-b6c4-522049e963d2 --
grantee-principal arn:aws:iam::730739171055:user/Alice --operations
"Encrypt" "Decrypt" --profile Stuart
```

This command creates a grant using the ARN of the CMK, followed by the ARN of the grantee principal, this being Alice, followed by the permissions I want Alice to inherit from Stuart, and in this example, I have selected `Encrypt` and `Decrypt`.

9. The resulting action generates two items, `GrantToken` and `GrantID`. Now, this `GrantToken` or `GrantID` is used to perform the encryption and decryption operations by Alice. We can test this access immediately using `GrantToken`, straight from the AWS CLI. When a grant is created, there may be a delay in being able to use the permissions and this is due to eventual consistency having to take place, but `GrantToken` allows immediate access.

So, in order to test Alice's access, we can enter the following command:

```
aws kms encrypt --plaintext "Certification" --key-id
arn:aws:kms:eu-west-1:730739171055:key/dc8dcec8-c0c2-4496-
b6c4-522049e963d2 --grant-tokens
AQpAMWIyNTQ4MjBiNzk1YjNjNTM3Y2U3YmRjOTZjOTk1Yjc0YTIxZTU4NGMxOWFkMjY
zMmUxMDJlY2U1NWM2OTUzNiKKAgEBAgB4GyVIILeVs8U3znvclsmVt0oh5YTBmtJjLh
Auz1XG1TYAAADhMIHeBgkqhkiG9w0BBwaggdAwgc0CAQAwgccGCSqGSIb3DQEHATAeB
glghkgBZQMEAS4wEQQM34N2MA3fY_EM9Zi1AgEQgIGZYYAviHWyHWfpJ42CfVJYO8xU
WDGgLnk_-TGy1uPar1Jv2ygz0Rgk-NYTV-
faKNjgnP5ZO5yLNYy2gWwx4SZwZMfiX_KXxLoHt67qpin1AfOqMBkFiJNZLbcnQXwEo
7MquaW1MrzInRwCRh5Ru9GUGTgFh-1DGe7k5K7PbG-
b_oEzz3wBgf0oKe6gX0_gOMmkhluLbs9wfF6KKiBKZwCIA66UdutUGglVeHL45dJ5eb
OAtRKJA1_xCwxKyA --profile Alice
```

This command will attempt to take the word `Certification` in `plaintext` and encrypt it using my CMK with the grant token that was generated by the grant using the credentials of Alice:

```
Stuarts-MBP-2:~ stuartscott$ aws kms encrypt --plaintext "Certification" --key-id arn:aws:kms:eu-west-1:730739
171055:key/dc8dcec8-c0c2-4496-b6c4-522049e963d2 --grant-tokens AQpAMWIyNTQ4MjBiNzk1YjNjNTM3Y2U3YmRjOTZjOTk1Yjc
0YTIxZTU4NGMxOWFkMjYzMmUxMDJlY2U1NWM2OTUzNiKKAgEBAgB4GyVIILeVs8U3znvclsmVt0oh5YTBmtJjLhAuzlXGlTYAAADhMIHeBgkqh
kiG9w0BBwaggdAwgc0CAQAwgccGCSqGSIb3DQEHATAeBglghkgBZQMEAS4wEQQM34N2MA3fY_EM9Zi1AgEQgIGZYYAviHWyHWfpJ42CfVJYOBx
UWDGgLnk_-TGy1uPar1Jv2ygz0Rgk-NYTV-faKNjgnP5ZO5yLNYy2gWwx4SZwZMfiX_KXxLoHt67qpin1AfOqMBkFiJNZLbcnQXwEo7MquaWlM
rzInRwCRh5Ru9GUGTgFh-1DGe7k5K7PbG-b_oEzz3wBgf0oKe6gX0_gOMmkhluLbs9wfF6KKiBKZwCIA66UdutUGglVeHL45dJ5eb0AtRKJA1_
xCwxKyA --profile Alice
{
    "EncryptionAlgorithm": "SYMMETRIC_DEFAULT",
    "KeyId": "arn:aws:kms:eu-west-1:730739171055:key/dc8dcec8-c0c2-4496-b6c4-522049e963d2",
    "CiphertextBlob": "AQICAHgykeN0jK4KwKoMCf9kmqmAu9RUF518dozkj5kL7HxjlwFx53Q2vrj9PebN/c5JbogHAAAAazBpBgkqhki
G9w0BBwagXDBaAgEAMFUGCSqGSIb3DQEHATAeBglghkgBZQMEAS4wEQQMayomRgb/+ty7hGxhAgEQgChtNrWlmRYzv8B79GAzxe8k21xR/4U5a
oKihqmcRUe+bph6YN4Pa3gz"
}
```

And here we can see that Alice can now perform encryption using the CMK.

10. When eventual consistency is achieved using the the `GrantID` of the grant, which may require a few minutes, then you can simply issue the very first command we tried at the beginning of this demonstration to test Alice's access, as shown here:

```
aws kms encrypt --plaintext "Certification" --key-id alias/MyCMK --
profile Alice
```

AWS KMS is a service tightly integrated with many other services, and for good reason. It's a great way to implement data protection controls using cryptographic keys based on a service that is validated under FIPS 140-2 (**Federal Information Processing Standard Publication 140-2**).

Using KMS, you can adopt a very customer-controlled approach by creating all of your own keys to have full ownership of how the CMKs are used, or you can lean on the AWS-managed CMKs to help you implement levels of encryption quickly, securely, and effectively.

AWS KMS is featured heavily within Domain 5, so it's important you understand the key principles and understand how it works. I therefore recommend getting some hands-on experience with creating some CMKs and understanding how they work and familiarizing yourself with consoles and concepts.

Next, we will move on to another managed service that is used for data encryption – AWS CloudHSM.

Exploring AWS CloudHSM

AWS CloudHSM is another managed service that is used for data encryption. Being fully managed, many aspects of implementing and maintaining the HSM are abstracted, such as the provisioning of hardware, patching, and backups, plus it also has the great advantage of automatically scaling on demand.

HSM stands for **Hardware Security Module**, which is specialized security hardware and validated to FIPS 140-2 Level 3. These HSMs can be used to generate and create your own encryption keys.

Using AWS CloudHSM is required when you require additional control and administrative power over your encryption compared with KMS. Although KMS is supported by its own FIPS-enabled HSM, you have no control over those HSMs behind the service, whereas with CloudHSM, you have control over those modules. You should also be aware that AWS is not able to access your keys or any cryptographic material within your HSMs.

With certain compliance and regulatory requirements, you will be required to use an HSM to generate your keys, or an HSM might be required to be used as a cryptographic key store. In addition to simply generating keys and storing them, an HSM also allows you to carry out the following tasks:

- The use of different encryption algorithms to cater for both symmetric keys and asymmetric keys
- Management of both symmetric and asymmetric cryptographic keys, including both importing and exporting keys
- Signing and verifying signatures
- The ability to use a cryptographic hash function to compute **hash-based message authentication codes (HMACs)**

I mentioned previously that AWS CloudHSM can integrate with AWS KMS, and this comes in the form of using AWS CloudHSM as a custom key store.

A custom key store allows you to store CMKs outside of KMS, and instead store them within a CloudHSM cluster that you have created. You might want to use CloudHSM as a custom key store in KMS if you have a requirement where your key material can't be stored within a shared environment. Additionally, you might need to ensure that your key material is backed up in multiple AWS regions.

 There was a time in the history of AWS CloudHSM where there was a USD 5,000 upfront fee. However, this is no longer the case and there are no upfront costs associated with CloudHSM. Instead, you pay per hour to use the service, with costs varying from region to region.

CloudHSM clusters

When you deploy your CloudHSM, it is deployed as a cluster and, by default, this cluster size is 6 per account, per region. However, you can configure your cluster to have a single HSM all the way up to 28 HSMs. The more HSMs you have, the better the performance will be. To avoid complications with key synchronization, AWS CloudHSM manages that for you. If you add additional HSMs to your cluster after the original creation, AWS CloudHSM will take a backup of all of your users, policies, and, of course, your keys, and then deploy that backup onto the new HSM within your cluster.

For additional resiliency and high availability, you should place your HSMs within your cluster in different availability zones within your region. The cluster architecture of AWS CloudHSM can be summarized as shown here:

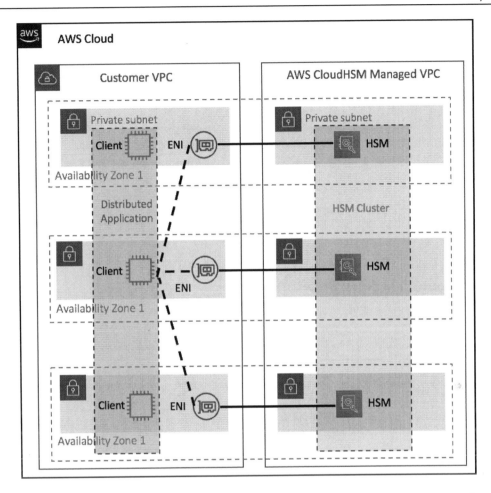

One important point to note is that when you configure your cluster and you specify your subnets/availability zones as locations, what in actual fact happens is an **Elastic Network Interface (ENI)** is deployed in your subnets, which then links to an HSM in a VPC owned and managed by AWS.

In this diagram, the VPC on the right is managed by AWS for CloudHSM, while the VPC on the left is a customer VPC.

When creating your clusters with more than one HSM, you will automatically have load balancing enabled, and when you deploy your HSMs between multiple availability zones, you inherently implement high availability for your cluster. If a particular availability zone was temporarily unavailable, you would still have access to the remaining HSMs in other availability zones.

To communicate with your HSMs, you need to use client software for AWS CloudHSM. This software can be installed on an EC2 instance. The clients used with the software must be able to communicate with the ENIs within your chosen subnets of your VPC.

Creating a CloudHSM cluster

To create a CloudHSM cluster is a very simple process. Let's take a look:

1. From within the AWS Management Console, select **CloudHSM** from the **Security, Identity and Compliance** section.
2. Select **Create cluster**:

3. From here you will need to complete the first page of configuration, which will look as follows:

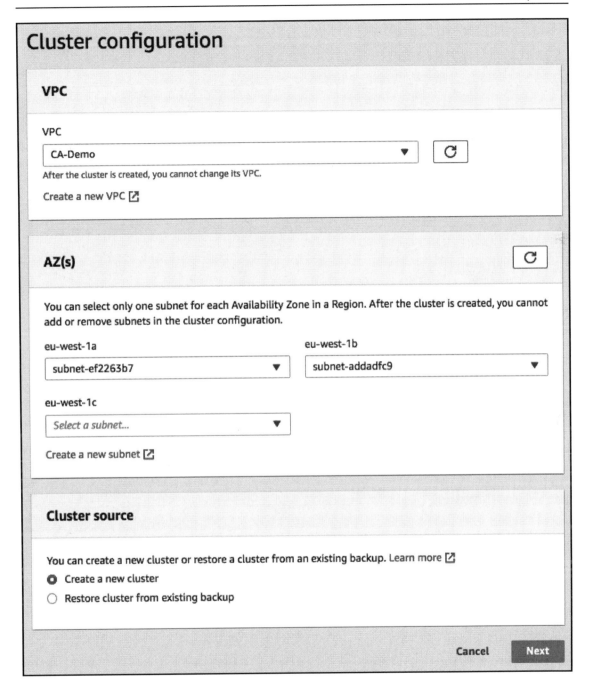

On this screen, make the following selections:

- Under **VPC**, select your VPC that you would like your CloudHSM cluster to be associated with.
- In the **AZ(s)** section, select which availability zones you would like your cluster to reside in.
- Finally, in **Cluster source**, you can either select to create a new cluster or restore from an existing backup. In this example, we are going to create a new CloudHSM cluster.

4. Click on **Next**:

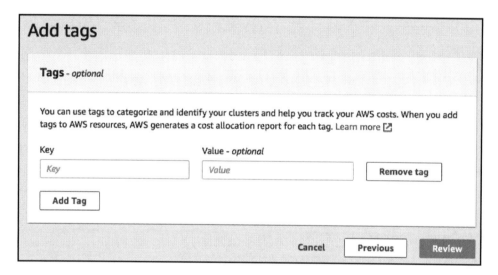

5. Here you can add any tags that you would like to be associated with your cluster. When you have added your tag information, select **Review**:

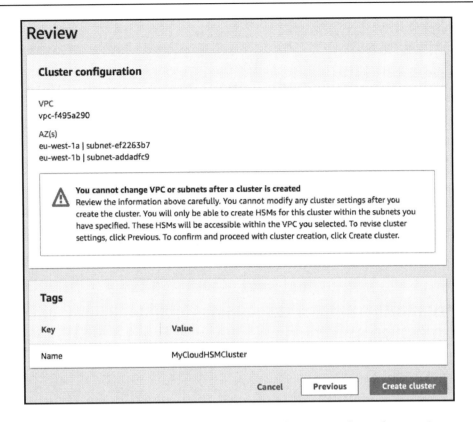

6. Here you will be asked to review your configuration from the previous steps. You will notice a warning that lets you know that once you have created your CloudHSM, you can't change the VPC or subnets that it is associated with, so ensure you are happy with your selection. Once you have confirmed your selections are correct, select **Create cluster** to create your cluster.

In this section, we looked at the simple steps involved in creating a new CloudHSM cluster within an existing VPC across multiple subnets.

AWS CloudHSM users

In the final part of this chapter, I want to explain some of the different user types that AWS CloudHSM uses and the differences between them. Different users have different permissions, and these user types are defined as follows:

- **Precrypto Office**
- **Crypto Office**

- **Crypto User**
- **Appliance User**

Precrypto Office

When you create your very first HSM within your cluster, the HSM will contain a **Precrypto Office (PRECO)** user that contains a default username and password. When your first HSM is set up, you will need to connect to it and log in to the HSM to activate it. Until you do so, your HSM will remain in an initialized state.

When connecting to the HSM, you will need to use the PRECO credentials and then change its own user password. Doing so will activate your HSM and your PRECO user will then become the Crypto Office user. The only permissions that PRECO has is to change its own password and perform read only operations on the HSM.

Crypto Office

The **Crypto Office (CO)** user has greater permissions than that of the PRECO user as it has the ability to perform some user management tasks, such as user creation, deletion, and password changes. It can also perform a number of administrative-level operations, including the following:

- Zeroise the data on the HSM, which allows the CO to delete keys, certificates, and data on the HSM.
- Identify the number of HSMs within the cluster.
- Obtain HSM metadata, including IP address, model, serial number, and firmware and device IDs.
- View synchronization statuses across HSMs in the cluster.

Crypto User

A **Crypto User (CU)** is able to perform cryptographic functions within AWS CloudHSM, including the following:

- Perform encryption and decryptio
- The ability to create, delete, wrap, unwrap, and modify attributes of key
- Sign and verif
- Generate digests and HMACs.

Also, much like the CO, CUs are also able to zeroise data and basic cluster information such as the IP address and serial number.

Appliance User

The **Appliance User (AU)** is a user that exists on all HSMs and is used to carry out the cloning and synchronization actions of your HSMs. The AWS CloudHSM service itself calls upon the AU to ensure that the synchronization of your HSMs within your cluster is maintained.

From a permission perspective, the AU carries the same permissions as the CO. However, it is unable to change passwords, or add/remove any other users.

To conclude, let's quickly compare the user permissions of all the user types we just covered:

Operations	Precrypto Office (PRECO)	Crypto Office (CO)	Crypto User (CU)	Appliance User (AU)
Obtain basic cluster information (number of HSMs in cluster, IP address, serial number, and so on	No	Yes	Yes	Yes
Zeroize HSMs (delete keys, certificates, and data on the HSM)	No	Yes	Yes	Yes
Change own password	Yes	Yes	Yes	Yes
Change any user's password	No	Yes	No	No
Add and remove users	No	Yes	No	No
Get synchronization status	No	Yes	Yes	Yes
Key management operations	No	No	Yes	No
Encrypt, decrypt, sign, verify, generate, and digest HMACs	No	No	Yes	No

This table provides an easy reference for the permissions associated with the different users across AWS CloudHSM.

In this section, we looked at CloudHSM and how it can be used to give you additional administrative control when compared to that of KMS by having added control over the hardware security modules of CloudHSM. Sometimes, from a governance perspective, you might need to use CloudHSM instead of KMS if you need that added level of control and ownership.

AWS Secrets Manager

Although AWS Secrets Manager is not solely focused on key infrastructure, it does offer the ability to maintain a level of security protection for any API keys, in addition to other secrets. You might be wondering what is actually considered a *secret*? Within Secrets Manager, a secret is something that you want to remain hidden and protected instead of being available with open access to anyone who can read it. This can include database credentials across Amazon Redshift clusters and Amazon RDS, instance passwords, plaintext, or, like I mentioned earlier, API keys.

AWS Secrets Manager holds, protects, and contains this sensitive information for you, allowing other services and applications to call for the secret via a simple API call. This negates the need for your application developers to hardcode any secret or credentials within your applications. Instead, when a secret value is required, an API call to AWS Secrets Manager is triggered that will then return the value. This method is far more secure than hardcoding secrets.

When working with secrets, such as passwords, it is important to rotate them across a given schedule to reduce the likelihood of them becoming compromised, much like we did with the password policy we discussed in Chapter 15, *Discovering Security Best Practices*. As a part of AWS Secrets Manager, it can automatically manage the rotation of secrets, meaning you don't have to manually do this yourself.

We have already discussed the KMS service within this chapter, and so it might be no surprise that AWS KMS is tightly integrated into AWS Secrets Manager to help encrypt your secrets' values that are being stored. It is important that any secrets are stored as encrypted. After all, they are of significant importance and must be protected as much as possible.

Due to the critical nature of the data being stored, it is important to be able to audit the secrets as to who, what, and when they are being accessed by. Thankfully, AWS CloudTrail is also integrated to maintain a log of when each secret is requested to ensure that a full audit trail of the secret can be maintained.

 More information on AWS CloudTrail can be found in Chapter 12, *Implementing Logging Mechanisms*, and Chapter 13, *Auditing and Governance*.

Obviously, managing access to the secrets held is of the utmost importance and needs to be managed accordingly. In addition to KMS encryption, you can use fine-grained policies, both identity-based and resource-based, to efficiently and securely manage who and what has access to each secret. By maintaining the principle of least privilege (discussed in Chapter 15, *Discovering Security Best Practices*), you can enforce a strict level of access control.

Identity-based policies are attached to users, groups, or roles and define what actions can be used against the specified secret, and these are managed within the IAM service. Resource-based policies are attached directly to the secrets themselves and define which principals can perform which actions against that secret. It is not possible to configure these from within the AWS Management Console, and so these need to be configured and attached to your secrets using the AWS CLI. For example, the following command would add a resource policy saved as resource.json to an existing secret named My_RDS_Secret:

```
aws secretsmanager put-resource-policy --secret-id My_RDS_Secret --
resource-policy file://resource.json
```

Now that we have an understanding of AWS Secrets Manager, let's take a look at how to create a secret within the service that can be called upon by other services:

 To follow this demonstration, you will need to have an RDS database running. For more information on how to set up an RDS database, please refer to the AWS documentation at: https://docs.aws.amazon.com/AmazonRDS/latest/UserGuide/USER_CreateDBInstance.html.

1. From within the AWS Management Console, select **Secrets Manager** from the **Security, Identity & Compliance** category:

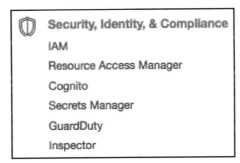

2. Click on **Store a new secret**:

3. You will now need to enter a number of configuration fields as shown:

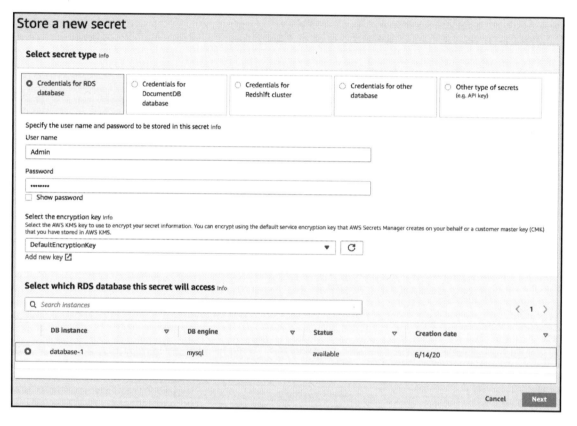

Here, you need to make the following selections:

- You can select the type of secret that you would like to store. In this demonstration, I have selected **Credentials for RDS database**. However, other options are available as well.

- If selecting **Credentials for RDS database**, you will need to enter the username and password that will be stored in your secret. The credentials of this username and password will grant you access to the RDS database selected.
- You will then need to select your encryption key. You can either select the **DefaultEncryptionKey** as shown, which will be set up by AWS Secrets Manager with KMS automatically, or you can select an existing CMK that you have already created.
- Finally, you must select the RDS database instance with which this secret will be associated.

4. When you have entered your details, click on **Next**, where the following screen will appear:

You must supply a name for your new secret, and optionally a description with optional tagging information.

5. Select **Next** when you have entered the relevant information where you can configure options for rotating your secret:

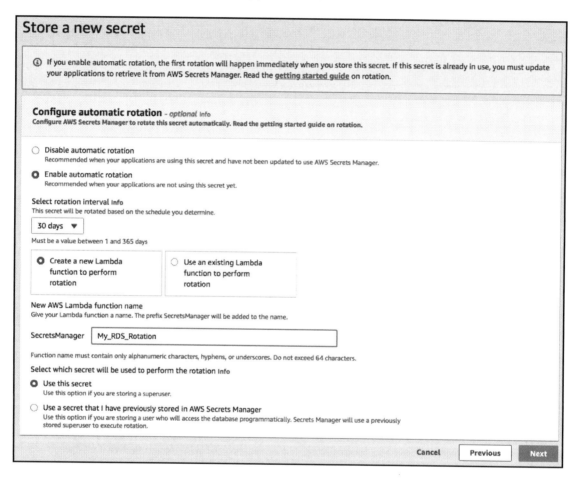

Here, the following selections can be made:

- You can either enable or disable automatic rotation. Enabling automatic rotation is the recommended option for the reasons previously mentioned.
- If you enable automatic rotation, you can select between 30, 60, and 90 day rotation periods.

- The rotation will be undertaken by a Lambda function. You can either select to have a new Lambda function created to perform the rotation, or select an existing one. If a new Lambda function is to be created, you must select a name for the function.
- Finally, you need to select which secret will be used to perform the rotation.

6. Select **Next** when you have configured the automation rotation settings where you will be presented with a **Review** screen to review the options selected during the creation:

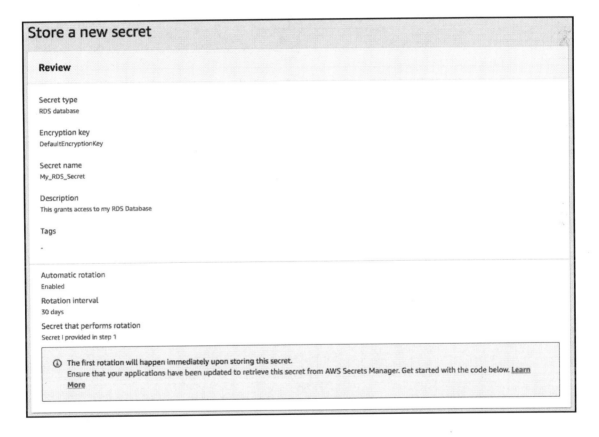

Store a new secret

Review

Secret type
RDS database

Encryption key
DefaultEncryptionKey

Secret name
My_RDS_Secret

Description
This grants access to my RDS Database

Tags
-

Automatic rotation
Enabled

Rotation interval
30 days

Secret that performs rotation
Secret I provided in step 1

ⓘ The first rotation will happen immediately upon storing this secret.
Ensure that your applications have been updated to retrieve this secret from AWS Secrets Manager. Get started with the code below. **Learn More**

7. When you are happy with the options selected, click on **Store a new secret**. Your secret will then be created and stored in the dashboard:

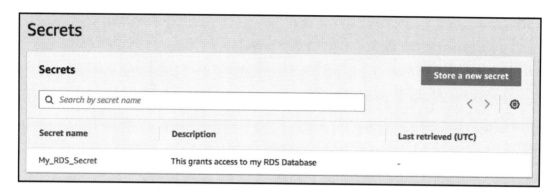

8. To view the value of the secret, you can select the secret. Select **Retrieve Secret Value.** This will then show you the secret:

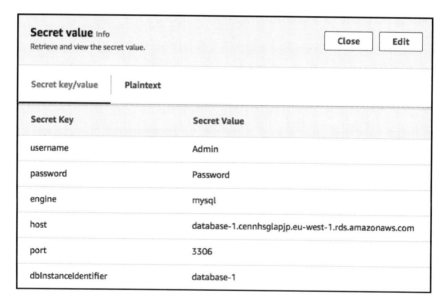

Alternatively, you could use the AWS CLI or AWS SDK to retrieve the value using the following commands, provided that access was granted to allow the retrieval of the secret value:

- API/SDK: `GetSecretValue`
- AWS CLI:`get-secret-value`

As you can see, AWS Secrets Manager is a great service that allows you to centrally manage and control access to your secrets that can be used by your applications and services without having to manage that layer yourself. Using a centrally encrypted and managed service offers many benefits and removes a lot of the administrative burden of managing it yourself, in addition to helping you to improve the security posture of your environment.

Summary

In this chapter, we covered the key services that are used to implement encryption within your AWS environment, specifically, the AWS Key Management Service, and AWS CloudHSM. We began with a quick overview of encryption and then understood AWS KMS and its components, including CMKs, DEKs, key material, key policies, and grants. In the section on CloudHSM, we understood how CloudHSM is deployed as a cluster and the cluster architecture, as well as the different types of users and permission levels.

Remember that KMS offers a managed service with the underlying HSMs containing your CMKs hidden and managed by AWS. AWS CloudHSM allows you to deploy your own HSMs within specific subnets of your AWS infrastructure, thereby allowing you to maintain the HSMs themselves with your own key infrastructure.

With the help of this chapter, you are now aware of the differences and similarities between both KMS and CloudHSM and have an understanding of when to use each of them. By applying this knowledge, you now have the key ingredients to design, architect, and implement solutions using each of these services, ensuring that your data is being protected with the appropriate level of cryptographic controls, and thereby safeguarding your data from being exposed and easily read.

In the next chapter, we will continue looking at encryption, but this time how it is implemented across a variety of different services covering both storage and database services.

Questions

As we conclude, here is a list of questions for you to test your knowledge regarding the material covered in this chapter. You will find the answers in the *Assessments* section of the *Appendix*:

    1. True or False: Asymmetric encryption uses a single key to encrypt and decrypt data.

2. Which component is the main building block of the KMS service as it contains the key material used for both encrypting and decrypting data?

3. There are three different types of CMKs used by KMS that you need to be familiar with; AWS-owned, customer-managed, and which other?

4. Which component of KMS is used to determine who can use the key to perform cryptographic operations, such as `encrypt`, `decrypt`, and `GenerateDataKey`, in addition to who can administer the CMK?

5. Which AWS service offers the ability to maintain a level of security protection for any API keys, in addition to other secrets?

Further reading

- White Paper – AWS Key Management Service Cryptographic Details: `https://d0.awsstatic.com/whitepapers/KMS-Cryptographic-Details.pdf`
- White Paper – AWS Key Management Service Best Practices: `https://d0.awsstatic.com/whitepapers/aws-kms-best-practices.pdf`
- White Paper – Security of AWS CloudHSM Backups: `https://d1.awsstatic.com/whitepapers/Security/security-of-aws-cloudhsm-backups.pdf`

17
Managing Data Security

In the previous chapter, we learned how AWS **Key Management Service (KMS)** and CloudHSM are used to generate encryption keys to encrypt data across different AWS services. In this chapter, I want to look at encryption again, but with a focus on how encryption is implemented across a variety of different services, covering both storage and database services, including Amazon **Elastic Block Store (EBS)**, Amazon **Elastic File System (EFS)**, Amazon **Simple Storage Service (S3)**, Amazon **Relational Database Service (RDS)**, and Amazon DynamoDB. Some of the encryption methods that we will discuss will integrate with KMS, and some of them will not.

When using these services, you will often be storing confidential and sensitive information, and so it's key to understand some of the methods for protecting the data that is being stored in these services. You will learn how to implement encryption across these services, looking at encryption at rest and in transit.

The following topics will be covered in this chapter:

- Amazon EBS
- Amazon EFS
- Amazon S3
- Amazon RDS
- Amazon DynamoDB

Technical requirements

To follow the demonstrations in this chapter, you should have permissions to perform encryption and decryption across the following services:

- Amazon EBS
- Amazon EFS
- Amazon S3

- Amazon RDS
- Amazon DynamoDB

For more information on how to manage permissions, please refer to `Chapter 4`, *Working with Access Policies*.

Amazon EBS encryption

I want to start with the EBS encryption service as it tightly integrates with the KMS service, which we already discussed in the previous chapter. EBS volumes provide persistent block-level storage to your EC2 instance, providing more flexibility for your instance storage capabilities. One advantage of using EBS volumes is the simplicity you can apply to encrypting sensitive data stored on these volumes.

When a volume is encrypted, it does not impact or affect the **Input/Output Operations per Second (IOPS)** of your volume and has a very minimal effect on latency. The encryption process is also transparent in its operation, and so, as a result, there are no specific actions required by your applications to access the data.

At the time of writing, EBS encryption is supported on the following instance types; however, I suggest you review the latest supported instances at `https://docs.aws.amazon.com/AWSEC2/latest/UserGuide/EBSEncryption.html#ebs-encryption-requirements`:

- **General-purpose**: A1, M3, M4, M5, M5a, M5ad, M5d, M5dn, M5n, T2, T3, and T3a
- **Compute-optimized**: C3, C4, C5, C5d, and C5n
- **Memory-optimized**: cr1.8xlarge, R3, R4, R5, R5a, R5ad, R5d, R5dn, R5n, u-6tb1.metal, u-9tb1.metal, u-12tb1.metal, u-18tb1.metal, u-24tb1.metal, X1, X1e, and z1d
- **Storage-optimized**: D2, h1.2xlarge, h1.4xlarge, I2, I3, and I3en
- **Accelerated computing**: F1, G2, G3, G4, Inf1, P2, and P3

When EBS encryption is enabled, both the root and data volumes can be encrypted and the encryption applies to all data residing on the volume, in addition to data moving between the EBS volume itself and the associated EC2 instance. Plus, when snapshots are created, the encryption settings will be applied to the snapshot as well. By performing EBS encryption on your EC2 instances, it's possible to encrypt the boot volume as well as your data volumes.

In order to understand how this encryption works in a better way, let's try to encrypt an EBS volume ourselves.

Encrypting an EBS volume

In this section, we are going to look at a variety of ways that we can implement EBS encryption in different scenarios, as follows:

- How to configure encryption as we create a new EBS volume
- How to create an encrypted EBS volume from an unencrypted snapshot
- How to re-encrypt an existing EBS volume using a new **Customer Master Key (CMK)**
- How to apply default encryption to a volume

As you begin using EBS volumes, you might need to implement encryption at different stages, so let's take a look at how to perform some of these processes.

Encrypting a new EBS volume

To encrypt a new EBS volume, follow these simple steps:

1. From the AWS Management Console, select **EC2** from the **Compute** category.
2. Select **Volumes** from the **ELASTIC BLOCK STORE** menu on the left:

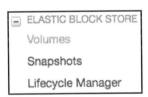

3. Select **Create Volume** to arrive at the following screen:

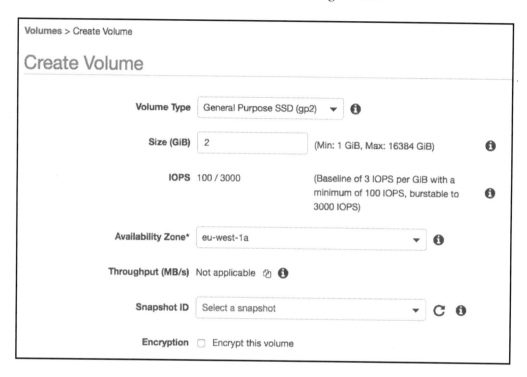

4. Select your desired **Volume Type**, **Size (GiB)**, and **Availability Zone** options. To apply encryption, select the tickbox beside **Encryption**, and this will provide you with additional options:

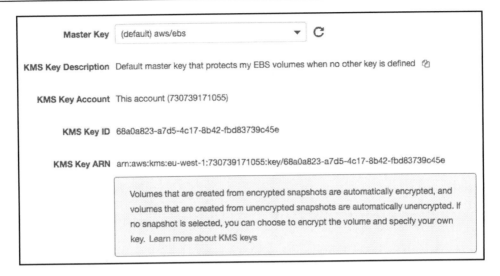

5. You first need to select your **Master Key** setting, which is effectively your CMK. If you have already created a customer-managed CMK within KMS, then you can select that key here. Alternatively, you can select the AWS-managed key instead. In the preceding example, I have chosen to select the AWS-managed key, which is automatically created by KMS for use with EBS only.

 Note that the data keys generated and encrypted by the CMK are stored alongside the encrypted data on your volumes. This data key is also then copied by any snapshots that are created to maintain encryption.

6. When you have selected your CMK to use for encryption via KMS, select **Create Volume**. The volume is then created and encrypted using the key selected:

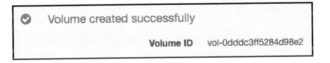

If a snapshot was then taken of this volume, that snapshot would also be automatically encrypted using the same CMK. Also, at this point, you can create a new volume from an existing snapshot by selecting a **Snapshot ID** option, as shown:

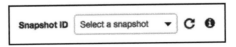

If you select a snapshot that is encrypted, then the new volume created from this snapshot will also be encrypted. Likewise, if the volume you select is unencrypted, then the volume will automatically be encrypted. However, you can choose to create an encrypted volume from an unencrypted snapshot. Let's see how to do this.

Encrypting a volume from an unencrypted snapshot

To create an encrypted volume from an unencrypted snapshot, follow these steps:

1. From within the AWS Management Console, select **EC2** from the **Compute** category.
2. Select **Snapshots** from the **ELASTIC BLOCK STORE** menu on the left:

3. Select your snapshot:

As you can see, this snapshot is not encrypted.

4. Select **Actions** | **Create Volume**:

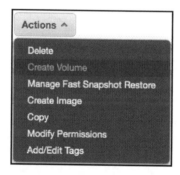

5. This will present the following familiar screen; however, notice how at the top, it highlights the snapshot ID that is used to create the volume. You can go ahead and select the **Encryption** checkbox, as in the previous demonstration, and select your required key to perform the encryption:

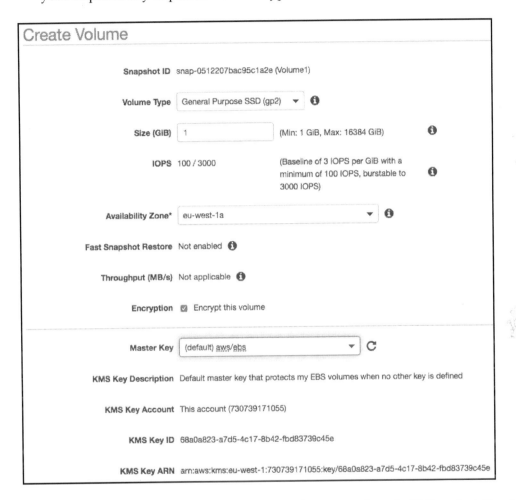

6. After you have selected your CMK to use for encryption via KMS, select **Create Volume**.

Your new volume will then be encrypted from an unencrypted snapshot. You might need to do this if your company adopts a new policy or standard that requires all EBS volumes to be encrypted. This allows you to implement that level of encryption while maintaining the data.

Re-encrypting a volume from an existing snapshot with a new CMK

You might want to re-encrypt an existing EBS volume with a new CMK if an existing CMK becomes compromised. This allows you to re-encrypt your volumes with a new CMK, thereby safeguarding your data:

1. From within the AWS Management Console, select **EC2** from the **Compute** category.
2. Select **Snapshots** from the **ELASTIC BLOCK STORE** menu on the left.
3. Select your snapshot that is encrypted:

	Name	Snapshot ID	Size	Description	Status	Started	Progress	Encryption	KMS Key ID	KMS Key Aliases
■	Volume2	snap-04b373d621b389506	2 GiB	EncryptedSna...	completed	April 17, 2020 at 12:35:36 P...	available (100%)	Encrypted	66a0a823-a7d...	aws/ebs

As you can see, this snapshot is encrypted using the AWS-managed **aws\ebs** key.

4. Select **Actions | Create Volume**:

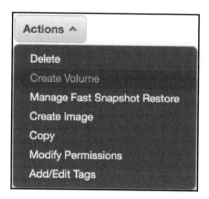

5. You will now have the option of selecting a different encryption key. In the example here, I have selected a customer-managed CMK, called **MyCMK**:

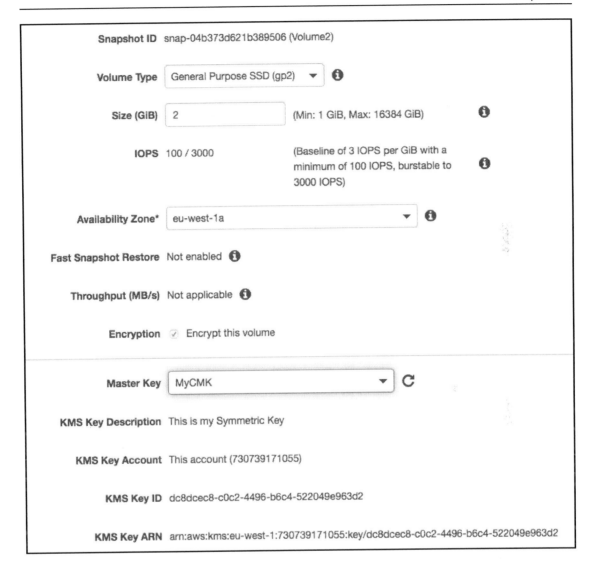

6. After you have selected your CMK to use for encryption via KMS, select **Create Volume**. Your new volume will then be encrypted using a different CMK:

Let's now look at how to apply default encryption to your EBS volumes.

Applying default encryption to a volume

You can configure your AWS account to apply a default regional encryption setting for your EBS volumes. This prevents you from having to manually select the option of an EBS volume being encrypted, which could be easily missed. Applying a default option ensures that any new EBS volumes created will be encrypted by default and so provides a greater level of protection.

This can be configured from within the AWS Management Console:

1. From the AWS Management Console, select **EC2** from the **Compute** category.
2. In the top right-hand corner of the console, under **Account Attributes**, select **Settings**:

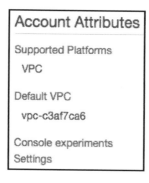

3. This will display the following screen:

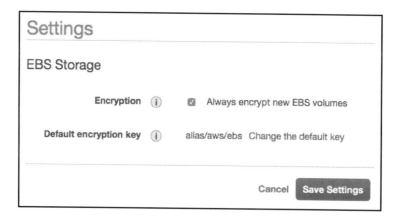

From here, you can select **Always encrypt new EBS volumes** so that encryption is done automatically. Additionally, you can select your default key; in this example, I have selected the AWS-managed **aws/ebs** key.

4. Once you have selected your key, select **Save Settings**.

From this point onward, all *new* EBS volumes will be encrypted by default using this key. Any existing volumes will not be affected. Activating this change will also automatically encrypt new volumes when they are created from unencumbered snapshots.

In this first section of the chapter, we covered the EBS encryption service offered by AWS. In the next section, let's turn our attention to a storage service known as Amazon EFS.

Amazon EFS

Amazon EFS is used for file-level storage, which has the capacity to support access for thousands of instances at once. Being a file-level storage system, it behaves much like most other filesystems and utilizes standard filesystem semantics; for example, it adheres to a file hierarchy structure with folders and subfolders and you can easily rename and lock files, and so on. It also provides low-latency access, making this a great service for many of your file storage needs, from home directories to big data analytics.

Being a storage service, there will, of course, be times when you will need to encrypt your data for additional protection, and EFS supports both in-transit and at-rest encryption.

Again, much like EBS, which we just discussed, EFS also uses the KMS service to encrypt its data. When encryption is enabled, all data, as well as metadata, is encrypted before it is written to a disk using the configured KMS CMK key.

Let's start by looking at how to enable encryption at rest when using EFS, before moving on to how EFS also supports encryption in transit.

Encryption at rest

You can enable encryption at rest using the AWS CLI, an SDK, or the AWS EFS API; alternatively, you can use the AWS Management Console. In this example, I am going to show you how to configure encryption for a new EFS filesystem using the AWS Management Console:

1. From the AWS Management Console, select **EFS** from the **Storage** category:

2. Select **File systems** from the menu on the left, and then select **Create file system**:

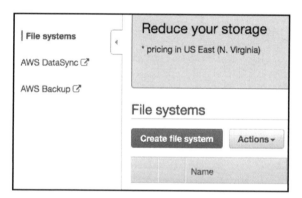

3. Select the VPC that you would like to create your EFS filesystems within, and select the subnets where you would like to create mount targets. Mount targets allow your resources to connect to your filesystem using a network interface called a mount target, which has an automatically assigned IP address. You should select all subnets that will need to connect to your EFS volume:

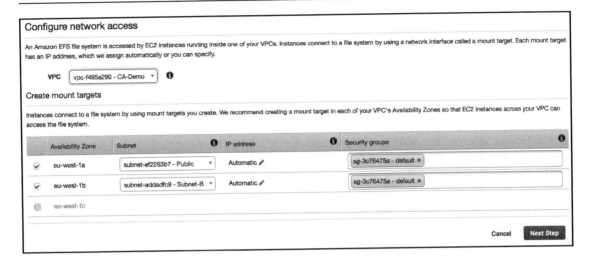

4. Select **Next Step**. Here, you have the option to add any tags that you need, in addition to configuring the life cycle management options and selecting throughput modes and your performance mode. Life cycle management allows you to select a specified number of days where inactive files can be moved to a different storage class to help you save on storage costs:

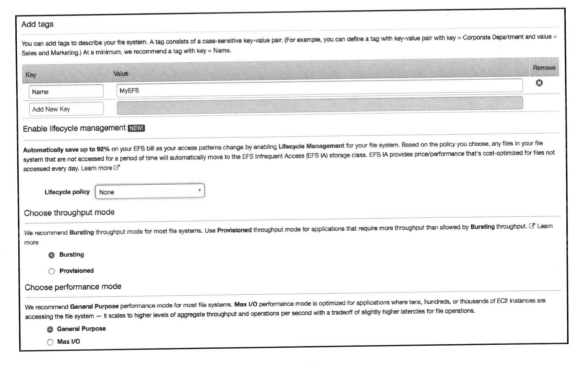

For more information on throughput modes and performance modes, refer to the AWS documentation at `https://docs.aws.amazon.com/efs/latest/ug/performance.html`.

5. After the performance mode section, there is an option to configure encryption:

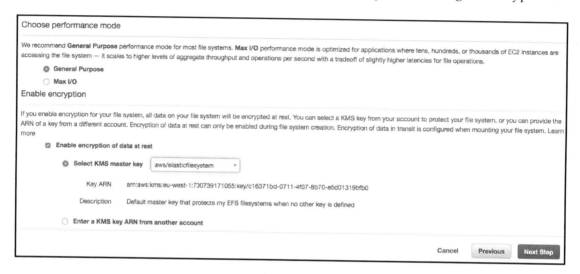

6. This is enabled via a checkbox, which then allows you to select a key, much like we did with EBS encryption. You can select either a customer-managed CMK or the default AWS-managed key, which I have done in this example: **aws/elasticfilesystems**. You can also select a KMS key from another account. When this option is selected, you must enter the ARN of that key:

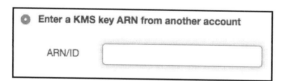

7. Select **Next Step**. This page allows you to set filesystem policies and configure access points:

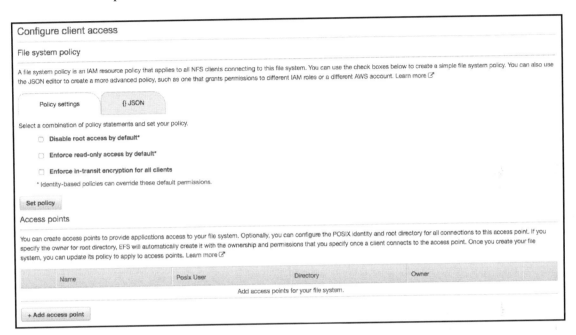

I don't want to divert your attention to discuss these points as it is beyond the scope of the exam, and so I want to keep the focus on encryption in this chapter. If you want to learn more about the filesystem policies for EFS, then please refer to `https://aws.amazon.com/blogs/aws/new-for-amazon-efs-iam-authorization-and-access-points/`.

8. Here, there is an **Enforce in-transit encryption for all clients** option. Now, I know we are configuring at-rest encryption here, but during the setup of your EFS filesystem, you might want to enable this. By doing so, it will only accept connections from clients that have initiated a connection using **Transport Layer Security (TLS)**, which is effectively in-transit encryption. If you select this option, and the client did not connect to EFS using in-transit encryption, then the connection will be dropped.

If you select this option, you can view the policy that is applied by selecting the {}JSON tab, which appears as follows:

```
1 ▾ {
2        "Version": "2012-10-17",
3        "Id": "efs-policy-wizard-3d6d4cc8-c1a5-4270-9321-b52a0fffd359",
4 ▾     "Statement": [
5 ▾         {
6                "Sid": "efs-statement-7b9c3ff6-a031-419b-9d9c-cf9a629d8665",
7                "Effect": "Deny",
8 ▾             "Principal": {
9                    "AWS": "*"
10               },
11               "Action": "*",
12 ▾             "Condition": {
13 ▾                 "Bool": {
14                        "aws:SecureTransport": "false"
15                    }
16               }
17           },
18 ▾         {
19               "Sid": "efs-statement-33acffc7-9d1c-486d-b3d4-9d5dadbadcbf",
20               "Effect": "Allow",
21 ▾             "Principal": {
22                    "AWS": "*"
23               },
24 ▾             "Action": [
25                    "elasticfilesystem:ClientMount",
26                    "elasticfilesystem:ClientWrite",
27                    "elasticfilesystem:ClientRootAccess"
28               ]
29           }
```

As you can see, between lines 6–17, the policy denies connections on the condition of secure transport *not* being used.

9. Select **Next Step** to be taken to the **Review** screen:

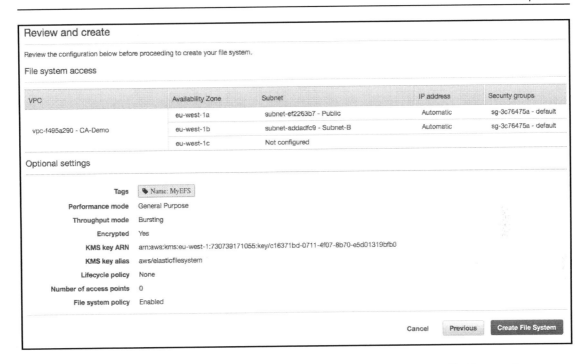

File system access

VPC	Availability Zone	Subnet	IP address	Security groups
	eu-west-1a	subnet-ef2263b7 - Public	Automatic	sg-3c76475a - default
vpc-f495a290 - CA-Demo	eu-west-1b	subnet-addadfc9 - Subnet-B	Automatic	sg-3c76475a - default
	eu-west-1c	Not configured		

Optional settings

Tags	🏷 Name: MyEFS
Performance mode	General Purpose
Throughput mode	Bursting
Encrypted	Yes
KMS key ARN	arn:aws:kms:eu-west-1:730739171055:key/c16371bd-0711-4f07-8b70-e5d01319bfb0
KMS key alias	aws/elasticfilesystem
Lifecycle policy	None
Number of access points	0
File system policy	Enabled

10. If you are happy with your configuration, select the **Create File System** button, and your EFS filesystem will be created:

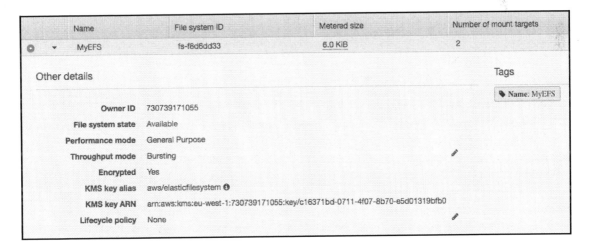

Name	File system ID	Metered size	Number of mount targets
MyEFS	fs-f6d6dd33	6.0 KiB	2

Other details

Owner ID	730739171055
File system state	Available
Performance mode	General Purpose
Throughput mode	Bursting
Encrypted	Yes
KMS key alias	aws/elasticfilesystem ⓘ
KMS key ARN	arn:aws:kms:eu-west-1:730739171055:key/c16371bd-0711-4f07-8b70-e5d01319bfb0
Lifecycle policy	None

Tags

🏷 Name: MyEFS

As you can see, when it's created, you will be shown the details screen, where you can see that your encryption is enabled for data at rest using the specified key from KMS.

With EFS being a shared storage service with many different use cases that can be used at a huge scale, it's very important to implement a level of encryption at rest if the data being stored is sensitive in any way to provide that added level of security, especially when this can be achieved with just a few clicks.

Encryption in transit

Before you can use your EFS filesystem, you need to mount an EFS target on your EC2 instance. This can be done by using the EFS mount helper, which is the easiest method. For more information on how to mount your EFS filesystem on an instance, please refer to the documentation at `https://docs.aws.amazon.com/efs/latest/ug/mounting-fs.html#mounting-fs-mount-helper`.

When mounting your EFS filesystem, you have the option of enabling encryption in transit using TLS as a mount option, which uses a client tunnel process. This listens on a local port where the EFS mount helper will redirect NFS traffic to.

Once you have completed the steps using the link to the AWS documentation, follow these steps to configure in-transit encryption:

1. Connect to your EC2 instance using SSH and log in with the appropriate credentials for your instance.
2. To complete the mount process of your EFS filesystem run the following command, replacing the text in bold and italics with your own filesystem identifier and directory:

```
sudo mount -t efs  -o tls fs-12345678:/ /mnt/efs
```

Now that we have covered EFS, let's now move on to explaining how encryption is carried out in Amazon S3.

Amazon S3

Amazon S3 provides an object-level storage solution, allowing you to save objects up to 5 terabytes in size. Being a storage solution, and one of the most commonly used storage services within AWS, S3 provides a variety of encryption mechanisms to suit different requirements and compliance concerns.

There are five different encryption options available to encrypt your S3 objects, as follows:

- Server-side encryption with S3-managed keys (SSE-S3)
- Server-side encryption with KMS-managed keys (SSE-KMS)
- Server-side encryption with customer-managed keys (SSE-C)
- Client-side encryption with KMS-managed keys (CSE-KMS)
- Client-side encryption with customer-managed keys (CSE-C)

The difference between server-side and client-side encryption is fairly simple. With server-side encryption, the encryption algorithm and process are run from the server-side—in this case, within Amazon S3. Client-side encryption means that the encryption process is executed on the client first, before the data is sent to S3 for storage.

Let's take a closer look at each of these methods to work out the exact process that takes place for both the encryption and decryption actions.

Server-side encryption with S3-managed keys (SSE-S3)

This diagram shows the three-step *encryption* process when using SSE-S3:

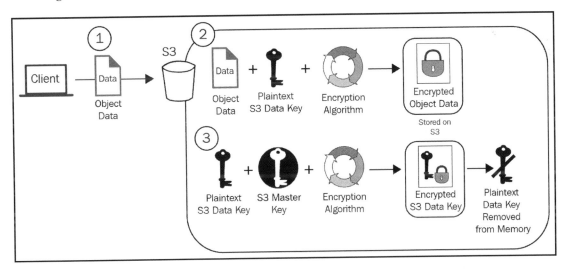

Let's understand the process:

1. The client selects their object(s) to upload to S3 and indicates the encryption mechanism of SSE-S3 during this process.
2. S3 then takes control of the object and encrypts it with a plaintext data key generated by S3. The result is an encrypted version of the object, which is then stored in your chosen S3 bucket.
3. The plaintext data key that is used to encrypt the object is then encrypted with an S3 master key, resulting in an encrypted version of the key. This now-encrypted key is also stored in S3 and is associated with the encrypted data object. Finally, the plaintext data key is removed from memory in S3.

This diagram shows the four-step *decryption* process when using SSE-S3:

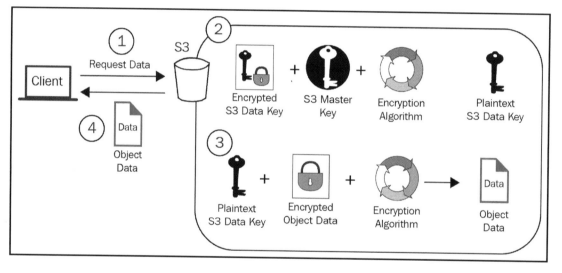

Let's understand the process:

1. A user requests access to the encrypted object via a client.
2. S3 is aware that the requested object is encrypted and so takes the associated encrypted data key of the object and uses the S3 master key to decrypt the data back into a plaintext data key.
3. This plaintext data key is then used to decrypt the encrypted data object to produce a plaintext version of the object.
4. Once the object is decrypted, S3 returns the data object to the client.

As you can see, the encryption process is completely transparent to the user and they are not required to interact with S3 in a different way; the same access method is used and all encryption processes are handled by S3, as long as the user that requested access has the required permissions to the data object in an encrypted form.

Server-side encryption with KMS-managed keys (SSE-KMS)

I covered this in the previous chapter, but for completeness, I will reiterate the process in this section, too.

This diagram shows the five-step *encryption* process when using SSE-KMS:

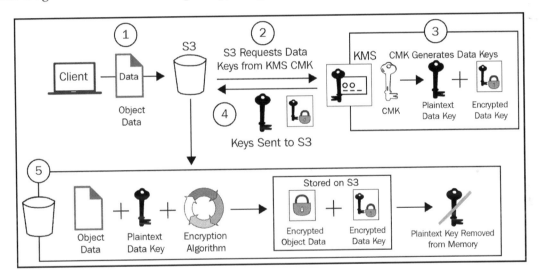

Let's understand the process:

1. Firstly, the client identifies the object(s) that are to be uploaded to S3, indicating SSE-KMS as the encryption mechanism, selecting either an AWS-managed or customer-managed CMK.
2. Amazon S3 will respond by initiating a request to generate **Data Encryption Keys (DEKs)** from KMS to allow S3 to encrypt the data submitted by the client.
3. Using the CMK selected in *step 1*, KMS will then generate two data keys: a plaintext data key and an encrypted version of that same data key.

4. KMS will send both of these data keys back to S3 to allow S3 to begin the encryption process using the plaintext data key.

5. At this stage, S3 then encrypts the object data with the plaintext version of the data key and stores the resulting encrypted object alongside the encrypted version of the data key. The plaintext data key will then be deleted and removed from memory.

This diagram shows the six-step *decryption* process when using SSE-KMS:

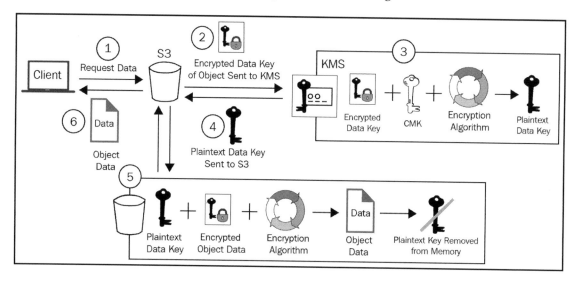

Let's understand the process:

1. A request is received by S3 to access an encrypted object via a client.

2. S3 is aware the object is encrypted and sends the encrypted data key associated with the requested object to KMS.

3. KMS takes the encrypted data key and uses the original CMK to decrypt the data key to generate a plaintext version of it.

4. KMS sends the plaintext data key back to S3.

5. Using the plaintext data key, the encrypted object data can then be decrypted, returning a plaintext version of the object data, and the plaintext data key is deleted from memory.

6. The plaintext object is then sent back to the requesting client.

Similarly to SSE-S3, this process is also transparent to the end client, but again, they can only access the object if the required permissions are in place.

Server-side encryption with customer-managed keys (SSE-C)

This diagram shows the two-step *encryption* process when using SSE-C:

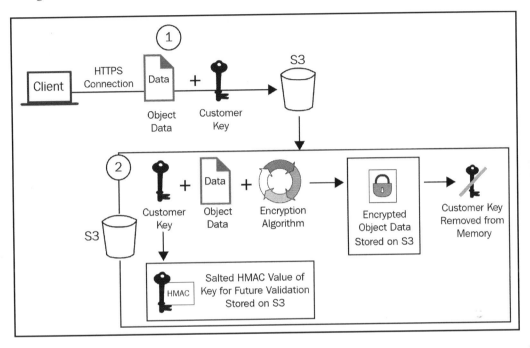

Let's understand the process:

1. The client uploads the object(s) to S3, along with the customer-provided key across an **Hypertext Transfer Protocol Secure (HTTPS)** connection. If SSE-C is being used and HTTPS is not used during the uploads, then it will fail and reject the communication. The channel needs to be encrypted as the key is being sent with the object.

2. S3 will then take the customer-provided key and the object and perform the encryption of the object. In addition to this, S3 will generate a salted HMAC value of the customer key to enable the validation of future access requests. This HMAC value and the encrypted object are then stored in S3 with an association to each other. Again, the plaintext customer-provided key is then removed from memory.

This diagram shows the four-step *decryption* process when using SSE-C:

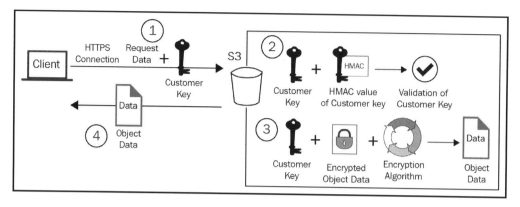

Let's understand the process:

1. A user requests access to the encrypted object on S3 via an HTTPS connection. With this same request, the customer key is also sent to S3.
2. S3 uses the stored HMAC value of the key to validate and confirm that the key sent is the correct key.
3. Upon successful validation, the customer key is then used to decrypt the object data.
4. The plaintext version of the object data is then sent back to the client.

As you might have noticed, here, the process was slightly different from SSE-S3 and SSE-KMS as the key is sourced from the client, rather than by S3. As a result, you need to include encryption with your request, using a number of different request headers in the AWS SDK:

- The `X-amz-server-side-encryption-customer-algorithm` header: Used to specify the encryption algorithm. The header value here must be `AES256`.
- The `X-amz-server-side-encryption-customer-key` header: This header is used to provide a 256-bit, Base64-encoded encryption key for S3 during both encryption and decryption operations of your objects.
- The `x-amz-server-side-encryption-customer-key-MD5` header: This header provides a Base64-encoded 128-bit MD5 digest of your encryption key. This is used by S3 as a form of integrity check to make sure the encryption key wasn't tampered with or experienced any errors during transmission.

Now that we have looked at the different encryption mechanisms using server-side encryption for Amazon S3, let's look at the client-side encryption options.

Client-side encryption with KMS-managed keys (CSE-KMS)

This diagram shows the six-step *encryption* process when using CSE-KMS:

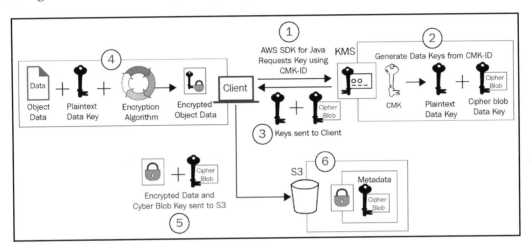

Let's understand the process:

1. The client will use an AWS SDK and, in this example, the Java client, to request data keys from KMS using a specified CMK.
2. Using the CMK selected in *step 1*, KMS will then generate two data keys: a plaintext data key and a cipher blob of the first key.
3. KMS will then send these keys back to the requesting client.
4. The client will perform the encryption against the object data with the plaintext version of the data key and then store the resulting encrypted object.
5. The client then uploads the encrypted object data and the cipher blob version of the key created by KMS to S3.
6. The final stage involves the cipher blob key being stored as metadata against the encrypted object, maintaining a linked association.

This diagram shows the six-step *decryption* process when using CSE-KMS:

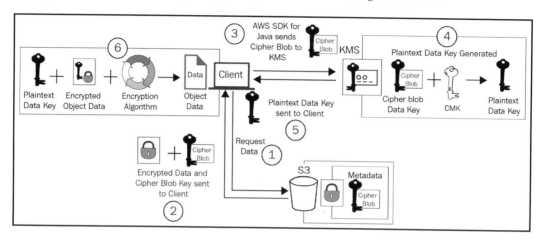

Let's understand the process:

1. A user requests access to the encrypted object in S3.
2. The encrypted object is retrieved from the S3 bucket and sent back to the client, along with the associated cipher blob key.
3. The Java client will then send the cipher blob back to KMS to generate a plaintext data key.
4. KMS uses the original CMK that was used during the encryption process, along with the cipher blob, to create and generate a plaintext version of the data key.
5. KMS then sends this plaintext data key back to the requesting Java client.
6. Once the Java client receives the plaintext key, it can then use it to decrypt the object that it has already received back from S3.

You will have noticed that all of the encryption operations were conducted on the client, using the AWS SDK. At no point did S3 perform *any* encryption operations. Even when the object was requested to be accessed again, S3 simply sent the encrypted data object back to the client to allow the client to perform the necessary steps.

Client-side encryption with KMS-managed keys (CSE-C)

This diagram shows the four-step *encryption* process when using CSE-C:

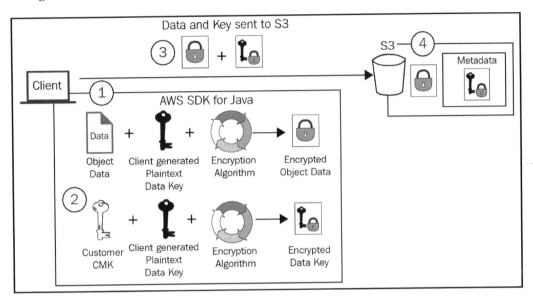

Let's understand the process:

1. The client will use an AWS SDK and, in this example, the Java client, which will create a randomly generated plaintext data key, which is then used to encrypt the object data.
2. A CMK created by the customer then encrypts this plaintext data key.
3. At this point, the encrypted data key and the encrypted object data is sent from the client to S3 for storage.
4. S3 then takes the encrypted data key and associates it with the encrypted object and stores both in S3.

This diagram shows the four-step *decryption* process when using CSE-C:

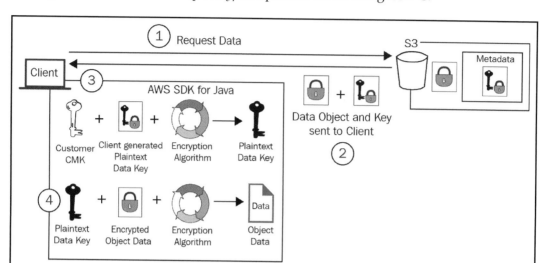

Let's understand the process:

1. A user requests access to the encrypted object in S3.
2. S3 responds by sending the requested object data, along with the associated encrypted data key, back to the client.
3. Using the AWS SDK, the customer CMK is then used with the encrypted data key to generate a plaintext version of that same data key.
4. The encrypted object can then be decrypted using the plaintext data key and its contents accessed.

As with CSE-KMS, you can see here that all encryption/decryption operations are handled by the client itself; the server (S3) has not been involved with this process, other than storing the encrypted data that is sent.

We have now covered five different mechanisms for encrypting data on Amazon S3. Having this choice allows you to implement the best level of protection for you based on your data needs, controls, and governance. Although each method is secure, they each also provide you with a different level of management and, depending on what data you are storing, you might be required to have added control.

That now covers the encryption options available in Amazon S3. So far in this chapter, we have only covered encryption in Amazon storage services. Next up, I want to move on from encryption in storage services to instead look at encryption options for database services—in particular, Amazon RDS.

Amazon RDS

Amazon RDS is a relational database service that is capable of running multiple different database engines, which include Amazon Aurora, PostgreSQL, MariaDV, MySQL, the SQL service, and Oracle Database. They can be run across a variety of different instance types, which can be optimized for performance and memory.

Again, much like the storage services, you will need to be careful when architecting your databases based on the data that is going to be stored on them, and so, of course, they also have encryption capabilities, which are very easy to implement.

Firstly, let's take a look at encryption at rest for an RDS database.

Encryption at rest

When at-rest encryption is configured, your database instance, tables, and any snapshots or automated backups taken of that database will be encrypted using AES-256 (**Advanced Encryption Standard**) encryption. You should also note that you can only encrypt an RDS database during its creation, so be sure to understand your encryption requirements before creating your database.

Configuring at-rest encryption is enabled by a simple checkbox from the AWS Management Console:

1. From the AWS Management Console, select **RDS** under the **Database** category:

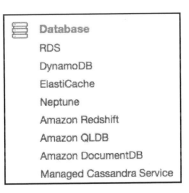

2. Select **Create Database**:

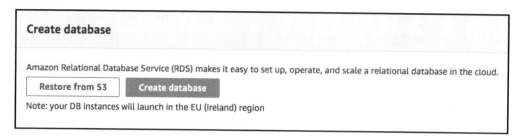

3. Scroll down to the **Additional configuration** section and expand the category by selecting it:

> ▶ **Additional configuration**
>
> Database options, encryption enabled, failover, backup enabled, backtrack disabled, Performance Insights enabled, Enhanced Monitoring enabled, maintenance, CloudWatch Logs, delete protection enabled

4. From here, you can scroll down to the **Encryption** section:

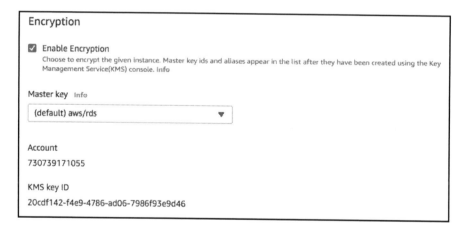

From here, you can either select a customer-managed key or, as in the preceding example, you can select the AWS-managed key for the service, **aws/rds**. You should be aware that once you have selected your key, you cannot change it to a different key, going forward, for that database instance.

5. Once you have configured the rest of your database options and created your database, your database instance and tables will be encrypted using the specified key.

If you're using SQL Server or Oracle as your database engine type, then you can also encrypt your database instance at rest using **Transparent Data Encryption** (TDE). However, if you do use TDE and the RDS encryption shown in the preceding screenshot together, you might see a performance impact, and you *must* use different encryption keys for each method.

> For more information on TDE configuration with SQL Server, go to `https://docs.aws.amazon.com/AmazonRDS/latest/UserGuide/Appendix.SQLServer.Options.TDE.html`.
>
> For more information on TDE with Oracle, go to `https://docs.aws.amazon.com/AmazonRDS/latest/UserGuide/Appendix.Oracle.Options.AdvSecurity.html`.

Encryption in transit

You will, of course, be connecting to your RDS database via an application of some kind, and when this data is being retrieved, you will want to ensure that the data remains encrypted. Amazon RDS utilizes **Secure Sockets Layer/Transport Layer Security (SSL/TLS)**. Which database engine you are using will depend on the configuration process of each one.

Refer to the following links if you want to understand how to configure and implement in-transit encryption for your database type:

- **Microsoft SQL Server database instance**: `https://docs.aws.amazon.com/AmazonRDS/latest/UserGuide/SQLServer.Concepts.General.SSL.Using.html`
- **Oracle Database instance**: `https://docs.aws.amazon.com/AmazonRDS/latest/UserGuide/CHAP_Oracle.html#Oracle.Concepts.SSL`
- **MySQL database instance**: `https://docs.aws.amazon.com/AmazonRDS/latest/UserGuide/CHAP_MySQL.html#MySQL.Concepts.SSLSupport`
- **MariaDB database instance**: `https://docs.aws.amazon.com/AmazonRDS/latest/UserGuide/CHAP_MariaDB.html#MariaDB.Concepts.SSLSupport`
- **PostgreSQL database instance**: `https://docs.aws.amazon.com/AmazonRDS/latest/UserGuide/CHAP_PostgreSQL.html#PostgreSQL.Concepts.General.SSL`

Databases often contain data that is sensitive in nature, and understanding how encryption can be used at rest by RDS is something you should be familiar with when going into the exam. You will often need to maintain an enhanced level of security when using databases, and encryption is a fundamental element of that.

Finally, I want to take a look at the encryption options for Amazon DynamoDB.

Amazon DynamoDB

Amazon DynamoDB is a fully managed key-value and document NoSQL database, designed for high performance (single-digit milliseconds) across multiple regions. Being fully managed, AWS is responsible for many of the maintenance tasks, such as architecting high availability, backups, and patching.

Much like Amazon RDS, DynamoDB also comes with encryption options for both at-rest and in-transit encryption.

Encryption at rest

By default, at-rest encryption using server-side encryption is enabled on all DynamoDB tables, and this option cannot be turned off or disabled. Again, this method of encryption uses the KMS service.

Unlike Amazon RDS, where you have to use the same KMS key for the duration of the database, with DynamoDB, you can swap your encryption key at any given time. For example, you could create your DynamoDB database with the AWS-managed key for DynamoDB, and then at a later date, if you created your own customer-managed CMK, you could select this new key as the key to be used for your encryption.

By default, your DyanmoDB primary key, local and secondary indexes, backups, global tables, and **DynamoDB Accelerator** (**DAX**) clusters are all encrypted, which helps to maintain a high level of compliance.

DynamoDB encryption options

When you create your DynamoDB database, you have three options to encrypt your database with. Let's take a look at these options in the console:

1. From the AWS Management Console, select **DynamoDB** from the **Database** category:

2. Select **Create table**:

3. You will then be presented with the following screen:

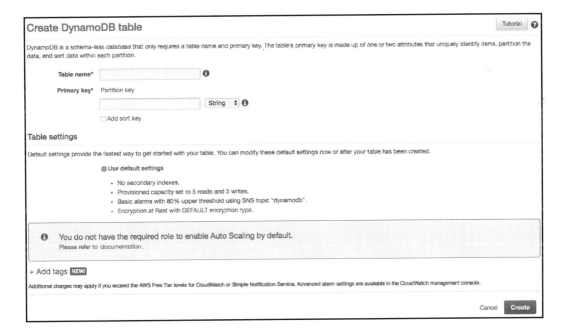

4. Uncheck the **Use default settings** checkbox under **Table settings**.
5. Scroll down to the **Encryption At Rest** section:

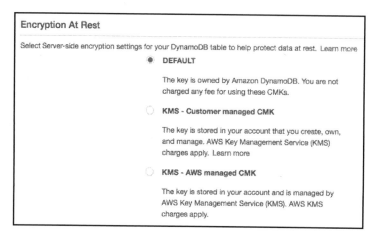

Here, you can see that there are three options:

- **DEFAULT**: This is a key that is owned by Amazon DynamoDB and provides the default encryption for your tables. It is free of charge and is stored outside of your AWS account
- **KMS - Customer managed CMK**: Select this option if you want to use your own customer-managed KMS key, which is stored in your own AWS account. Using your own CMK incurs a cost.
- **KMS - AWS managed CMK**: This final option allows you to use an AWS-managed key. Again, this also incurs a cost, and it is also stored in your AWS account.

The option you select largely depends on your data requirements, procedures, and what controls you are bound to from a compliance perspective. If you want the additional features that come with KMS, then you can select either of the KMS keys; but again, if you wanted further administrative control over the keys used in KMS, then you could select the customer-managed CMK option. However, if that level of administrative control is not required, then the AWS-managed CMK would suffice.

Encryption in transit

When your application needs to communicate with your DynamoDB table, it will do so using HTTPS, which is an encrypted HTTP connection. Also, all responses from DynamoDB will also use HTTPS. This ensures that communication between your application and your database remains protected and encrypted, at which point any data stored is also protected using server-side at-rest encryption.

You can also use the Amazon DyanmoDB encryption client to perform encryption of data locally before sending it to your DynamoDB database. For more information on the encryption client, please refer to the AWS documentation at `https://docs.aws.amazon.com/dynamodb-encryption-client/latest/devguide/what-is-ddb-encrypt.html`.

Summary

In this chapter, we covered the different mechanisms that different AWS storage and database services use to protect your data, such as EBS, EFS, S3, RDS, and DynamoDB. Most of them use KMS in some way via the CMK, which we discussed in the previous chapter. This integration of KMS makes it easy for other AWS services to implement their own server-side encryption options.

If you have your own AWS account, take a look at each of these services and the encryption option available to you to reiterate what we covered within this chapter. This will help you maintain a solid understanding of encryption across services, especially those that integrate with KMS.

In the next chapter, you will be able test the knowledge that you have gained throughout this book to check your understanding and readiness for the exam.

Questions

As we conclude, here is a list of questions for you to test your knowledge of this chapter's material. You will find the answers in the *Assessments* section of the *Appendix*:

1. What does IOPS stand for?
2. Which AWS service provides persistent block-level storage to your EC2 instance, providing more flexibility to your instance storage capabilities?
3. Which AWS service is used for file-level storage and has the capacity to support access to thousands of instances at once?

4. True or false: you can enable encryption at rest using the AWS CLI, an SDK, the AWS EFS API, or the AWS Management Console.

5. By default, at-rest encryption using server-side encryption is enabled on all DynamoDB tables. Which AWS service is integrated to perform this encryption?

18
Mock Tests

Mock exam 1

1. When IAM policies are being evaluated for their logic of access, which two of the following statements are incorrect?
    1. Explicit denies are always overruled by an explicit allow.
    2. The order in which the policies are evaluated does not matter regarding the end result.
    3. Explicit allows are always overruled by an explicit deny.
    4. Access to all resources is denied by default until access is granted.
    5. Access to all resources is allowed by default until access is denied.

2. Your security team has been tasked with implementing a solution to monitor your EC2 fleet of instances. Upon review, you decide to implement Amazon Inspector. What are the three prerequisites that you would need to implement before using Amazon Inspector? (Choose three answers)
    1. Deploy Amazon Inspector agents to your EC2 fleet.
    2. Create an IAM service-linked role that allows Amazon Inspector to access your EC2 feet.
    3. Create an Assessment Target group for your EC2 fleet.
    4. Deploy an Amazon Inspector log file to your EC2 fleet.
    5. Configure Amazon Inspector so that it runs at the root of your AWS account.
    6. Create an IAM group for your EC2 fleet.

3. After analyzing VPC flow logs, you notice that restricted network traffic is entering a private subnet. After reviewing your **Network Access Control Lists (NACLs)**, you verify that a custom NACL does exist that should be blocking this restricted traffic. What should you check to resolve the issue to ensure that the traffic is blocked at the subnet level?

    1. Check the inbound security group of the instances in the private subnet to ensure it is blocking the traffic.

    2. Check to see if the custom NACL has the restrictions associated with the private subnet.

    3. Check your VPC flow log configuration to see if it is configured to block the restricted traffic.

    4. Check the Main NACL associated with your VPC to see if it is conflicting with your custom NACL.

4. When using AWS Shield, which type of rule counts the number of requests received from a particular IP address over a time period of 5 minutes?

    1. Standard-based

    2. Flow-based

    3. Rate-based

    4. Integer-based

5. Following a breach on your network, an instance was compromised and you need to perform a forensic investigation of the affected instance. You decide to move the EC2 instance to your forensic account. Which steps would you take to carry out this process?

    1. Create an AMI from the affected EC2 instance and then share that AMI image with your forensic account. From within your forensic account, locate the AMI and create a new instance from the shared AMI.

    2. Create an AMI from the affected EC2 instance and then copy that AMI image to your forensic account. From within your forensic account, locate the AMI and create a new instance from the shared AMI.

    3. Create an EBS snapshot of the affected EC2 instance and then share that snapshot with your forensic account. From within your forensic account, launch a new instance and create a new volume using the snapshot and attach it to the instance.

    4. Create an EBS snapshot of the affected EC2 instance and then copy that snapshot to your forensic account. From within your forensic account, launch a new instance and create a new volume using the snapshot and attach it to the instance.

6. What is the Log Delivery Group account used for within Amazon S3?
   1. This is a customer-defined group that's used to deliver AWS CloudTrail logs to a bucket.
   2. This is a predefined group by AWS that's used to deliver S3 server access logs to a bucket.
   3. This is a predefined group by AWS that's used to deliver AWS CloudTrail logs to a bucket.
   4. This is a customer-defined group by AWS that's used to deliver S3 server access logs to a bucket.

7. After reviewing the following excerpt from a CloudTrail log, which statement is true?

```
"awsRegion": "eu-west-1",
"eventID": "6ce47c89-5908-452d-87cc-a7c251ac4ac0",
"eventName": "PutObject",
"eventSource": "s3.amazonaws.com",
"eventTime": "2019-11-27T23:54:21Z",
"eventType": "AwsApiCall",
"eventVersion": "1.05",
"readOnly": false,
"recipientAccountId": "730739171055",
"requestID": "95BAC3B3C83CCC5D",
"requestParameters": {
        "bucketName": "cloudtrailpackt",
        "Host": "cloudtrailpackt.s3.eu-
west-1.amazonaws.com",
        "key":
"Packt/AWSLogs/730739171055/CloudTrail/eu-
west-1/2019/11/27/730739171055_CloudTrail_eu-
west-1_20191127T2321Z_oDOj4tmndoN0pCW3.json.gz",
        "x-amz-acl": "bucket-owner-full-control",
        "x-amz-server-side-encryption": "AES256"
```

   1. A PutObject operation was performed in the cloudtrailpackt bucket without encryption.
   2. A PutObject operation was performed in the cloudtrailpackt bucket in the eu-west-2 region.
   3. A PutObject operation was performed in account 730739171055 using encryption.
   4. A PutObject operation was performed on 2019-11-27 in the packt bucket using encryption.

8. You have just joined a new startup organization as a security lead. Processes dictate that all your RDS databases must be deployed with Multi-AZ configured. For any new RDS deployments, you want to check whether high availability is enabled for your Amazon RDS DB instances. What should you configure to ensure that this process is being followed?
    1. Use AWS Config to set up the `rds-multi-az` compliance check.
    2. Use CloudWatch logs to detect RDS single AZ deployments.
    3. Use CloudTrail logs to search for RDS deployments with the `rds-multi-az=false` parameter.
    4. Use SNS so that you're emailed every time an RDS single AZ deployment is configured.

9. Which of the following is NOT considered a security best practice?
    1. Enable **Multi-Factor Authentication (MFA)**.
    2. Remove the root account access keys.
    3. Associate IAM users with a single resource-based policy.
    4. Enable AWS CloudTrail.

10. You are using the KMS service called `encrypt_me` to perform encryption within Amazon S3 using a customer created CMK in `eu-west-1`. A colleague explains that they are unable to see the CMK when they try to use it to encrypt data in a bucket named `encrypt_me_too` in `us-east-1`. What is the most likely cause of this?
    1. Your colleague does not have permission to encrypt with the CMK.
    2. CMKs are regional, so it will not appear in `us-east-1`.
    3. If a CMK has been used on one bucket, it can't be used on another.
    4. The CMK has become corrupt and it will need to be recreated within KMS.

11. A developer in your organization requires access to perform cryptographic functions using a customer-managed CMK. What do you need to update so that you can add permissions for the developer to allow them to use the CMK?
    1. KMS policy.
    2. CMK policy.
    3. Key policy.
    4. Encryption policy.

12. KMS Key Policies allow you to configure access and the use of the CMKs in a variety of ways. Due to this, you can configure access to the CMK in many different ways. Which of the following is NOT a method of allowing access?
    1. Via Key Policies – all access is governed by the Key policy alone.
    2. Via Key Policies and IAM – access is governed by the Key policy in addition to IAM identity-based policies, allowing you to manage access via groups and other IAM features.
    3. Via Key Policies and Grants – access is governed by the Key policy with the added ability to delegate access to others so they can use the CMK.
    4. Via Key Policies and IAM Roles – associating the Key policy with the role, thereby granting permissions to resources and identities that the role is associated with.

13. Which is NOT a valid method of S3 encryption?
    1. Server-Side Encryption with S3 Managed Keys (SSE-S3)
    2. Server-Side Encryption with CMK Managed Keys (SSE-CMK)
    3. Server-Side Encryption with KMS Managed Keys (SSE-KMS)
    4. Server-Side Encryption with Customer Managed Keys (SSE-C)
    5. Client-Side Encryption with KMS Managed Keys (CSE-KMS)
    6. Client-Side Encryption with Customer Managed Keys (CSE-C)

14. Your IAM administrator has created 20 IAM users within your organization's production AWS account. All users must be able to access AWS resources using the AWS Management Console, in addition to programmatic access via the AWS CLI. Which steps must be implemented to allow both methods of access? (Choose two.)
    1. Associate each user with a role that grants permissions that allows programmatic access.
    2. Create a user account with their own IAM credentials and password.
    3. Create an access key and secret access key for every user.
    4. Add the user to the power users group.
    5. Implement **Multi Factor Authentication (MFA)** for each user and configure their virtual MFA device.

15. You are configuring a number of different service roles to be associated with EC2 instances. During the creation of these roles, two components are established: the role itself and one other. Which component is also created, following the creation of a service role?
    1. An IAM group that the role is attached to
    2. An instance profile
    3. Temporary instance access keys
    4. A new instance associated with the new service role

16. Microsoft **Active Directory Federation Services (ADFS)** can be used as an **Identity Provider (IdP)** to enable federated access to the AWS Management Console. As part of the authentication process, which API is used to request temporary credentials to enable access?
    1. `AssumeRoleWithSAML`
    2. `AssumeIDP`
    3. `AssumeADFS`
    4. `AssumeRoleUsingADFS`
    5. `AssumeFederationRole`

17. When configuring your IdP from within IAM, which document do you need to provide that includes the issuer's name, expiration information, and keys that can be used to validate the SAML authentication response (assertions) that are received from the IdP?
    1. SAML response document
    2. Metadata document
    3. IDP federation document
    4. IDP document

18. Your CTO has asked you to find a simple and secure way to perform administrative tasks and configurational changes remotely against a selection of EC2 instances within your production environment. Which option should you choose?
    1. Use the `Run` command in AWS Systems Manager.
    2. Use built-in insights in AWS Systems Manager.
    3. Use State Manager in AWS Systems Manager.
    4. Use Session Manager in AWS Systems Manager.

19. Your organization is running a global retail e-commerce website in which customers from around the world search your website, adding products to their shopping cart before ordering and paying for the items. During a meeting to redesign the infrastructure, you have been instructed to define a solution where routing APIs to microservices can be managed, in addition to adding security features so that users can manage authentication and access control and monitor all requests that are made from concurrent API calls. Which service should you implement to manage these requirements?
    1. Amazon CloudFront
    2. AWS Lambda@Edge
    3. AWS API Gateway
    4. AWS API Manager
    5. AWS Shield

20. Your organization has been the victim of a massive DDoS attack. You have decided to use the AWS **DDoS Response Team (DRT)** for extra support to help you analyze and monitor malicious activity within your account. To help the DRT team with your investigations, they need access to your AWS WAF rules web ACLs. How can you provide this access?
    1. Using an IAM role with the `AWSShieldDRTAccessPolicy` managed policy attached, which trusts the service principal of `drt.shield.amazonaws.com` to use the role
    2. Using an IAM role with the `AWSShieldAccessPolicy` managed policy attached, which trusts the service principal of `shield.drt.amazonaws.com` to use the role
    3. Using an IAM role with the `ShieldDRTAccessPolicy` managed policy attached, which trusts the service principal of `drt.shied.amazonaws.com` to use the role
    4. Using an IAM role with the `AWSShielDRTAccess` managed policy attached, which trusts the service principal of `drt.amazonaws.com` to use the role

21. One of your instances within a private subnet of your production network may have been compromised. Since you work within the incident team, you have been asked to isolate the instance from other resources immediately, without affecting other production EC2 instances in the same subnet. Which approaches should be followed in this situation? (Choose two.)
    1. Delete the key pair associated with the EC2 instance.
    2. Remove any role associated with the EC2 instance.
    3. Update the route table of the subnet associated with the EC2 instance to remove the entry for the NAT gateway.
    4. Change the security group of the instance to a restricted security group, thereby preventing any access to or from the instance.
    5. Move the EC2 instance to the public subnet.

22. You have implemented a VPN connection between your data center and your AWS VPC. You then enabled route propagation to ensure that all the other routes to networks represented across your site-to site VPN connection are automatically added within your route table. However, you notice that you now have overlapping CIDR blocks between your propagated routes and existing static routes. Which statement is true?
    1. The routes will be automatically deleted from your route table as having overlapping CIDR blocks is not possible in a route table.
    2. Your static routes will take precedence over propagated routes.
    3. Your propagated routes will take precedence over your static routes.
    4. The longest prefix match will determine which route takes precedence.

23. Your CTO has explained that they are looking for a solution to be able to monitor network packets across your VPC. You suggest VPC flow logs, but the CTO wants to implement a solution whereby captured traffic is sent to a Network Load Balancer, using UDP as a listener, which sits in front of a fleet of appliances dedicated to network analysis. What solution would you suggest to the CTO?
    1. Use the AWS Transit Gateway to capture packets and use the NLB as a Target.
    2. Use Traffic Mirroring to capture packets and use the NLB as a Target.
    3. Use VPC Tunneling to capture packets and use the NLB as a Target.
    4. Use Traffic Capture to capture packets and use the NLB as a Target.
    5. Use VPC Transit to capture packets and use the NLB as a Target.

24. You have been tasked with defining a central repository that enables you to view real-time logging information from different AWS services that can be filtered and queried to search for specific events or error codes. Which of the following would you use?

    1. Amazon GuardDuty

    2. Amazon S3 Server Access logs

    3. Amazon Kinesis

    4. Amazon CloudWatch logs

    5. AWS Config logs

25. Which feature of AWS CloudTrail can be used for forensic investigation to confirm that your log files have not been tampered with?

    1. Select **Encrypt Log Files with SEE-KMS**.

    2. Select **Log File Validation**.

    3. Select **Encrypt Log Validation**.

    4. Select **Enable Log Tamper Detection**.

26. Which service is being described here? "_____ is a fully managed intelligent threat detection service, powered by machine learning, that continually provides insights into unusual and/or expected behavioral patterns that could be considered malicious within your account."

    1. AWS Config

    2. Amazon Inspector

    3. AWS Trusted Advisor

    4. Amazon GuardDuty

27. When it comes to data encryption, it is important to understand the difference between asymmetric and symmetric key encryption. Select the statements that are true. (Choose two.)

    1. Symmetric encryption uses a single key to encrypt and decrypt data.

    2. Asymmetric encryption uses a single key to encrypt and decrypt data.

    3. Symmetric encryption keys use two keys to perform the encryption.

    4. Asymmetric encryption keys use two keys to perform the encryption.

28. You need to encrypt data being stored across your EBS volumes in your VPC with minimal management, but you want to be able to audit and track their usage. Which type of AWS KMS key will you use?

    1. AWS owned

    2. AWS managed

    3. Customer managed

    4. Customer owned

29. You have been asked to ensure that your organization's data is encrypted when stored on S3. The requirements specify that encryption must happen before the object is uploaded using keys managed by AWS. Which S3 encryption option is best suited for this?
    1. SSE-KMS
    2. CSE-KMS
    3. SSE-S3
    4. CSE-C
    5. SSE-C

30. What is the disadvantage of importing your own key material into a customer-managed CMK?
    1. It does not support automatic key rotation.
    2. It does not support the creation of data encryption keys.
    3. The key material automatically expires after 12 months.
    4. You are unable to define additional key administrators.

31. When encrypting an EBS group, which kind of keys can be used? (Choose three.)
    1. AWS managed CMK key
    2. AWS owned CMK key
    3. AWS created CMK key
    4. Customer CMK key
    5. Customer DEK key

32. You have been tasked with granting permissions for your IT corporate workforce of 500+ users so that they can access the AWS Management Console to administer and deploy AWS resources. Your organization currently uses **Microsoft Active Directory (MSAD)** to authenticate users internally. None of your users currently have IAM user accounts and your manager has asked you to configure their AWS access with the least administrative effort. Which method would be best?
    1. Create 500 AWS users accounts and assign permissions to each account accordingly.
    2. Configure web identity federation with LDAP, allowing it to query MSAD as your authentication into your AWS account. This is used in configuration with AWS roles.
    3. Configure SAML 2.0 federation with LDAP, allowing it to query MSAD as your authentication into your AWS account. This is used in conjunction with AWS roles.
    4. Share access keys and secret access keys across your user base, allowing AWS Management Console access.

33. Take a look at the following IAM policy associated with a role. Which statement is true?

```
{
  "Version": "2012-10-17",
  "Statement": {
    "Effect": "Allow",
    "Principal": {"AWS": "arn:aws:iam::356903128354:user/Stuart"},
    "Action": "sts:AssumeRole",
    "Condition": {"Bool": {"aws:MultiFactorAuthPresent": "true"}}
  }
}
```

1. The user "Stuart" is denied access to assume the role.
2. Any users can assume the role if the user has used MFA to verify their credentials.
3. The role can be assumed for the user "Stuart" if the user uses MFA as an authentication method.
4. The principal is allowed to assume the role using existing permissions granted by MFA.

34. Which policies do NOT require a principal parameter within the context of the policy? (Choose two.)
    1. An Amazon S3 bucket policy.
    2. A key policy within KMS associated with a customer created CMK.
    3. An inline IAM policy.
    4. A **service control policy (SCP)**.
    5. A CloudHSM encryption policy.

35. You have just joined a new startup as a security engineer. One of your first tasks is to implement authentication for a new mobile application that is likely to scale to over a million users within the first few months. Which option is the best for handling scaling with minimal management?
    1. Implement Amazon Cognito with Enterprise Federation.
    2. Implement Amazon Cognito with SAML Federation.
    3. Implement Amazon Cognito with Social Federation.
    4. Implement Amazon Cognito with Mobile Federation.

36. Your engineering team has come to you to explain that they have lost the private key associated with one of their Linux instance-stored backed root volume EC2 instances, and they can no longer connect to and access the instance. Which statement is true in this circumstance?

    1. It is still possible to recover access as it has an instance-stored backed root volume
    2. When you lose your private key to an EC2 instance that has an instance-stored root volume, there is no way to reestablish connectivity to the instance
    3. Recreate a new key-pair for the instance using the `aws ec2 create-key-pair --key-name MyNewKeyPair` AWS CLI command
    4. Request a replacement private key from AWS using the associated public key

37. You are explaining the differences between security groups and Network Access Control Lists to a customer. What key points are important to understand when understanding how these two security controls differ from each other? (Choose three)

    1. Security groups are stateful by design and NACLs are not.
    2. NACLs are stateful by design and security groups are not.
    3. Security groups allow you to add a `Deny` action within the ruleset.
    4. NACLs allow you to add a `Deny` action within the ruleset.
    5. Security groups control access at the instance level.
    6. NACLs control access at the instance level.

38. Your new startup is deploying a highly-scalable multi-tiered application. Your VPC is using both public and private subnets, along with an application load balancer. Your CTO has defined the following requirements:

    - All the EC2 instances must only have a private IP address.
    - All EC2 instances must have internet access.

    What configuration is required to meet these requirements? (Choose two.)

    1. A NAT gateway should be deployed in the private subnet.
    2. A NAT gateway should be deployed in the public subnet.
    3. Add a rule to your main route table, directing all outbound traffic via the ALB.
    4. Launch the EC2 instances in the private subnet.
    5. Register EC2 instances with the NAT gateway.

39. You are experiencing an increase in the level of attacks across multiple different AWS accounts against your applications from the internet. This includes XSS and SQL injection attacks. As the security architect for your organization, you are responsible for implementing a solution to help reduce and minimize these threats. Which AWS services should you implement to help protect against these attacks? (Choose two.)

    1. AWS Shield
    2. AWS Firewall Manager
    3. AWS Web Application Firewall
    4. AWS Secrets Manager
    5. AWS Systems Manager

40. During the deployment of a new application, you are implementing a public-facing **Elastic Load Balancer (ELB)**. Due to the exposed risk, you need to implement encryption across your ELB, so you select HTTPS as the protocol listener. During this configuration, you will need to select a certificate from a **certificate authority (CA)**. Which CA is the recommended choice for creating the X.509 certificate?

    1. AWS Certificate Manager within AWS Systems Manager
    2. AWS Certificate Manager
    3. Select a certificate from IAM
    4. AWS Certificate Authority Manager
    5. Certificate Authority Manager within AWS Shield

41. Recently, you have noticed an increase in the number of DDoS attacks against your public web servers. You decide to implement AWS Shield Advanced to help protect your EC2 instances. Which configurational change do you need to implement before you can protect your instance using the advanced features?

    1. You must assign the EC2 instances within their own Public Shield subnet.
    2. Assign an EIP to the EC2 instance.
    3. Install the CloudFront Logging Agent on the EC2 instances.
    4. Install the SSM Agent on your EC2 instance.

42. Which layer of the OSI model do both Amazon CloudFront (with AWS WAF) and Route 53 offer attack mitigation against? (Choose three.)
    1. 2
    2. 3
    3. 4
    4. 5
    5. 6
    6. 7

43. Looking at the following route table, which target would be selected for a packet being sent to a host with the IP address of 172.16.1.34?

Destination	Target
10.0.0.0/16	Local
172.16.0.0/16	pcx-1234abcd
172.16.1.0/24	vgw-wxyz6789

- The first route is the local route of the VPC that's found in every route table.
- The second route points to a target related to a VPC peering connection.
- The third route points to a VPN Gateway that then connects to a remote location.

Your options are as follows:

1. 10.0.0.0/16
2. 172.16.0.0/16
3. 172.16.1.0/24
4. There is no feasible route

44. You have just joined a new network team. You are responsible for making configurational changes to your Direct Connect infrastructure that connects from your corporate data center to your AWS infrastructure. Take a look at the following policy detailing your access. Which statement is correct?

```
1 ▾ {
2       "Version": "2012-10-17",
3 ▾     "Statement": [
4 ▾       {
5           "Effect": "Allow",
6 ▾         "Action": [
7             "directconnect:Describe*",
8             "ec2:DescribeVpnGateways",
9             "ec2:DescribeTransitGateways"
10          ],
11          "Resource": "*"
12        }
13      ]
14  }
```

1. You have full access to make configurational changes as required to Direct Connect.
2. You have read-only access to Direct Connect.
3. You have full access to configure components related to Direct Connect Describe.
4. You have read-only access to Direct Connect, but you do have full access to VPN Gateways and Transit Gateway configurations.

45. An engineer has raised a concern regarding one of your buckets and wants to understand details about when a particular bucket has been accessed to help ascertain the frequency and by whom. Which method would be the MOST appropriate to get the data required?
    1. Analyze AWS CloudTrail log data.
    2. Analyze AWS Config log data.
    3. Analyze S3 Server access logs.
    4. Analyze VPC flow logs.

46. Amazon S3 object-level logging integrates with which other AWS service?
    1. Amazon CloudWatch
    2. Amazon Glacier
    3. Amazon EC2
    4. AWS Config
    5. AWS CloudTrail

47. You are currently monitoring the traffic flow between a number of different subnets using VPC flow logs. Currently, the configuration of the capture is capturing ALL packets. However, to refine the flow log details, you want to modify the configuration of the flow log so that it only captures rejected packets instead. Which of the following statements is true?

    1. You can't capture rejected packets in a VPC flow log.
    2. You can't change the configuration of an existing flow log once it's been created.
    3. The VPC flow log can be modified with these changes without any packets being dropped.
    4. The VPC flow log must be stopped before you can make configuration changes.

48. Your CTO is concerned about the sensitivity of the data being captured by AWS CloudTrail. As a result, you suggest encrypting the log files when they are sent to S3. Which encryption mechanism is available to you during the configuration of your Trail?

    1. SSE-S3
    2. SSE-KMS
    3. SSE-C
    4. CSE-KMS
    5. CSE-C

49. As part of your security procedures, you need to ensure that, when using the **Elastic File System (EFS)**, you enable encryption-in-transit using TLS as a mount option, which uses a client tunnel process. Assuming your filesystem is `fs-12345678` and your filesystem's identifier is `/mnt/efs`, which command would you enter to mount the EFS file stems with encryption enabled?

    1. `sudo mount -t efs  tls fs-12345678: -o / /mnt/efs`
    2. `sudo mount -t tls efs fs-12345678:/ /mnt/efs`
    3. `sudo mount -t efs  -o tls fs-12345678:/ /mnt/efs`
    4. `sudo mount -t ssl  tls fs-12345678:/ /mnt/efs`

50. You are configuring your AWS environment in preparation for downloading and installing the CloudWatch agent to offer additional monitoring. Which two tasks should you complete prior to installing the agent?
    1. Ensure that your EC2 instance is running the latest version of the SSM agent.
    2. Ensure that your EC2 instances have outbound internet access.
    3. Ensure that your EC2 instances all have the same tags.
    4. Ensure that any public EC2 instances are configured with an ENI.
    5. Ensure CloudWatch is configured for CloudWatch logging in your region.

51. You have been approached by your compliance team to define what data is encrypted on an EBS volume when EBS encryption has been enabled. Which of the following should you choose? (Choose three.)
    1. The root and data volume
    2. Just the data volume
    3. All data moving between the EBS volume and the associated EC2 instance
    4. All snapshots of the EBS volume
    5. Just the root volume
    6. The ephemeral volume associated with the EC2 instances

52. You are being audited by an external auditor against PCI-DSS, who is accessing your solutions that utilize AWS. You have been asked to provide evidence that certain controls are being met against infrastructure that is maintained by AWS. What is the best way to provide this evidence?
    1. Contact your AWS account management team, asking them to speak with the auditor.
    2. As a customer, you have no control over the AWS infrastructure or if it meets certain compliance programs.
    3. Use AWS Auditing to download the appropriate compliance reports.
    4. Use AWS Artifact to download the appropriate compliance records.

53. Which part of AWS CloudHSM can carry out the following functions?
    - Perform encryption and decryption.
    - Create, delete, wrap, unwrap, and modify attributes of keys.
    - Sign and verify.
    - Generate digests and HMACs.

Your options are as follows:

1. **Crypto Office (CO)**
2. **Crypto User (CU)**
3. **Precrypto Office (PRECO)**
4. **Appliance User (AU)**

54. You have a VPC without any EC2 instances, and for security reasons, this VPC must never have any EC2 instances running. If an EC2 instance is created, it would create a security breach. What could you implement to automatically detect if an EC2 instance is launched and then notify you of that resource?

    1. Use AWS CloudTrail to capture the launch of an EC2 instance, with Amazon SNS configure as a target for notification.
    2. Use CloudWatch Events to detect the launch of an EC2 instance, with Amazon SNS configured as a target for notification.
    3. Use AWS GuardDuty to detect the launch of an EC2 instance, with an AWS Lambda function configured as a target for notification.
    4. Use AWS Systems Manager to detect the launch of an EC2 instance, with Amazon SNS configured as a target for notification.

55. Which AWS CloudHSM user contains a default username and password when you first configure your CloudHSM?

    1. Crypto Office
    2. Crypto User
    3. Precrypto Office
    4. Appliance User

56. Amazon GuardDuty uses different logs to process and analyze millions of events that are then referenced against numerous threat detection feeds, many of which contain known sources of malicious activity, including specific URLs and IP addresses. Which of the following logs are NOT used by Amazon GuardDuty? (Choose two.)

    1. VPC flow logs
    2. S3 Server Access logs
    3. DNS logs
    4. CloudTrail logs
    5. CloudWatch Event logs

57. Which statement is true about a KMS key policy?
    1. It is an identity-based policy.
    2. It is a resource-based policy.
    3. You can only apply the resource using an IAM role.
    4. The same policy can be attached to multiple KMS keys in the same region.

58. You have just joined a company working within the security team that are utilizing third-party tools such as Sumo Logic and Splunk, in addition to a number of AWS security services, including AWS IAM and Firewall Manager. Your manager has asked you to review solutions in order to centralize findings from all toolsets and services. Which of the following solutions would you recommend?
    1. AWS Detector
    2. Amazon Macie
    3. Amazon GuardDuty
    4. Amazon Inspector
    5. AWS Security Hub

59. You have been asked to upload the company's own key material instead of using the key material generated by KMS. In preparation for doing this, you download the public key and import token. What format must your key material be in prior to it being uploaded?
    1. JSON
    2. Binary
    3. TAR
    4. TIFF

60. When configuring your access policies within IAM, what should you always consider as a security best practice?
    1. Always add an implicit "Deny" at the end of the policy statement.
    2. Implement the **principle of least privilege (PoLP)**.
    3. Only add a single statement within a policy.
    4. Implement identity-based policies instead of resource-based policies.

61. Which of the following is NOT considered an asymmetric key encryption mechanism?
    1. Diffie-Hellman
    2. **Advanced Encryption Standard (AES)**
    3. Digital Signature Algorithm
    4. RSA

62. AWS Trusted Advisor helps customers optimize their AWS environment through recommended best practices. Which of the following is NOT one of the five categories that it checks in your account?
    1. Cost Optimization
    2. Monitoring
    3. Performance
    4. Security
    5. Fault Tolerance
    6. Service Limits

63. Which of the following keys shows an AWS managed key when using Amazon S3 SSE-KMS?
    1. aws/s3
    2. aws/kms/s3
    3. s3/kms
    4. kms/s3

64. Which keys used in conjunction with KMS are used outside of the KMS platform to perform encryption against your data?
    1. Customer master key
    2. Data encryption key
    3. Data decryption key
    4. Customer data encryption key

65. Your organization is storing some sensitive data on Amazon S3. Using encryption, you have implemented a level of protection across this data. The encryption method you used was SSE-S3. Which type of key does this use?
    1. AWS owned
    2. AWS managed
    3. Customer managed
    4. Customer owned

Answers

1: 1,5	11: 3	21: 2,4	31: 1,2,4	41: 2	51: 1,3,4	61: 2
2: 1,2,3	12: 4	22: 2	32: 3	42: 2,3,6	52: 4	62: 2
3:	13: 2	23: 2	33: 3	43: 3	53: 2	63: 1
4: 3	14: 2,3	24: 4	34: 3,4	44: 2	54: 2	64: 2
5: 1	15: 2	25: 2	35: 3	45: 3	55: 3	65: 1
6: 2	16: 1	26: 4	36: 2	46: 5	56: 2,5	
7: 3	17: 2	27: 1,4	37: 1,4,5	47: 2	57: 2	
8: 1	18: 1	28: 2	38: 2,4	48: 2	58: 5	
9: 3	19: 3	29: 2	39: 2,3	49: 3	59: 2	
10: 2	20: 1	30: 1	40: 2	50: 1,2	60: 2	

Mock exam 2

1. New security policies state that specific IAM users require a higher level of authentication due to their enhanced level of permissions. Acting as the company's security administrator, what could you introduce to follow these new corporate guidelines?
    1. MFA
    2. TLS
    3. SSL
    4. SNS
    5. SQS

2. You have tried to configure your VPC with multiple subnets: a single public subnet and multiple private subnets. You have created an **Internet Gateway** (**IGW**) and are trying to update the route table associated with your subnet that you want to act as a public subnet as you wish this to point to the IGW as the target. However, you are unable to see the IGW. What is the most likely cause of this problem?
    1. You do not have permission to view IGWs.
    2. You have not associated the IGW with your region.
    3. You have not associated the IGW with your VPC.
    4. You have not associated the IGW with your subnet.

3. Your operations team is using AWS WAF to protect your CloudFront distributions. As part of configuring the web ACLs, the team is adding multiple condition statements to a single rule. Which three statements are true when combining statements within one rule?

    1. The conditions are ANDed together.
    2. All conditions must be met for the rule to be effective.
    3. If one condition is met the rule is effective.
    4. AWS WAF will not allow you to add multiple conditions to a single rule.
    5. Only one action can be applied to the rule.

4. You currently have a multi-account AWS environment that focuses heavily on web applications. As part of your security measures, you are looking to implement an advanced level of DDoS protection across all accounts. How would you implement a solution with cost optimization in mind that offers DDoS protection across all accounts?

    1. Activate AWS Shield Advanced on each AWS account.
    2. Activate AWS Shield Advanced on one account and set up VPC peering for all the other accounts.
    3. Configure consolidated billing for all the accounts and activate AWS Shield Advanced in each account.
    4. Configure AWS Security Hub to manage each account and activate AWS Shield Advanced within AWS Security Hub.

5. Your engineering team is trying to configure Amazon S3 server access logging. They want to use a source bucket named `MyBucket` within account A in `eu-west-2`, with a target bucket named `MyTarget` in account B in `eu-west-2`. However, they are not able to configure access logging. What is the most logical reason for this?

    1. The engineering team does not have cross-account access to the buckets.
    2. The source and target buckets need to be in the same account.
    3. The bucket permissions are restricting the engineering team's access.
    4. The source and target buckets need to be in different regions.

6. How can you enhance the security of your AWS CloudTrail logs? (Choose two.)

    1. Encrypt log files using CSE-KMS.
    2. Enable log file verification   .
    3. Encrypt log files using SSE-KMS.
    4. Enable log file validation.

7. As the IAM administrator, you have been asked to create a new role to allow an existing fleet of EC2 instances to access Amazon S3 directly with `PutObject` and `GetObject` permissions. Which of the following roles types would you create to do this?

    1. Another AWS account
    2. Web Identity
    3. SAML 2.0 Federation
    4. AWS Service
    5. Service Integration

8. You have been asked to assess your fleet of EC2 instances for security weaknesses while the instances are in operational use. Which of the following rule packages that can be used within Amazon Inspector would you recommend to run?

    1. **Center for Internet Security (CIS)** benchmarks
    2. **Common Vulnerabilities and Exposures (CVEs)**
    3. Security best practices
    4. Runtime behavior analysis
    5. Network reachability

9. Which of the following resources within your environment can be protected by the AWS Web Application Firewall service? (Choose three.)

    1. Amazon EC2
    2. Network Load Balancer
    3. Application Load Balancer
    4. API Gateway
    5. AWS NAT gateway
    6. Amazon CloudFront Distributions

10. You have configured some AWS VPC flow logs so that they capture network traffic across your infrastructure. Which of the following options are available as destinations that store the captured VPC flow logs? (Choose two.)

    1. Amazon S3 Bucket
    2. AWS Config
    3. Amazon Macie
    4. AWS Security Hub
    5. Kinesis Stream
    6. CloudWatch logs

11. Which AWS support plans provide the full capabilities of AWS Trusted within your AWS account? (Choose two.)
    1. Business
    2. Developer
    3. Basic
    4. Enterprise
    5. Corporate

12. Which of the following policies governs the maximum permissions that an identity-based policy can associate with any user or role, but does not apply permissions to users or roles themselves?
    1. Resource-based policies
    2. Organization Service Control Policies
    3. ACLs
    4. Permission boundaries

13. One of the subnets within your VPC is configured with the following NACL:

Rule #	Type	Protocol	Port Range	Source	Allow / Deny
100	ALL TCP	TCP (6)	0 - 65535	0.0.0.0/0	ALLOW
*	ALL Traffic	ALL	ALL	0.0.0.0/0	DENY

An instance in the subnet is configured with the following security group:

Type ⓘ	Protocol ⓘ	Port Range ⓘ	Source ⓘ
HTTP	TCP	80	0.0.0.0/0
RDP	TCP	3389	86.171.161.10/32

Which of the following connections would be allowed?

1. A host with an IP address of 86.171.161.10 trying to SSH to your EC2 instance
2. An engineer using the source IP address of 86.171.161.10 trying to RDP to the EC2 instance
3. If anyone, anywhere, was trying to use HTTP to get to the EC2 instance

Your options are as follows:

1. 1 and 2
2. 1, 2, and 3
3. 3
4. 2 and 3
5. 1 and 3

14. Which of the following services would fall under the abstract part of the Shared Responsibility Model? (Choose two.)
    1. Amazon **Simple Queue Service (SQS)**
    2. Amazon **Elastic Compute Cloud (EC2)**
    3. Amazon **Simple Storage Service (S3)**
    4. Amazon DynamoDB
    5. Amazon Relational Database Service

15. The following AWS Organizations SCP is in place for your account:

```
{
  "Version": "2012-10-17",
    "Statement": [
      {
        "Sid": "SCPPolicy",
        "Effect": "Deny",
        "Action": [
          "iam:AttachRolePolicy",
          "iam:DeleteRole",
          "iam:DeleteRolePermissionsBoundary",
          "iam:DeleteRolePolicy",
          "iam:DetachRolePolicy",
          "iam:PutRolePermissionsBoundary",
          "iam:PutRolePolicy",
          "iam:UpdateAssumeRolePolicy",
          "iam:UpdateRole",
          "iam:UpdateRoleDescription"
        ],
        "Resource": [
          "arn:aws:iam::*:role/IAM-Packt"
        ]
      }
    ]
}
```

Which statements are true? (Choose twoo)

1. All access is denied to delete all IAM roles.
2. All access is denied to update the `IAM-Packt` role.
3. All access is denied to assume the `IAM-Packt` role.
4. All access is denied to `DetachRolePolicy` for all roles.
5. All access is denied to `DeleteRolePermissionsBoundary` for the `IAM-Packt` role.

16. You currently have a number of resources based within your corporate data center and you also utilize some AWS resources within a VPC. Over the coming months, you are looking to incorporate more of your on-premise solutions with the cloud. From a security perspective, your CTO wants to implement a more reliable and secure method of connecting to your VPC. Which connectivity methods would you recommend in order to maintain a higher level of security? (Choose two)

1. Virtual Private Gateway
2. Virtual Private Network
3. Direct Connect
4. Connect Direct
5. Customer Private Gateway

17. Your company is looking to implement a link to AWS using AWS Direct Connect as the solutions architect. You explain that there are a number of prerequisites that need to be met from your own internal network. Which of the following is NOT a prerequisite for Direct Connect?

1. For authentication, your router must support both BGP and BGP MD5 authentication.
2. Your network infrastructure MUST use single-mode fiber.
3. The port on your device must have automatically configured speed and half-duplex mode enabled.
4. You must ensure that you have 802.1Q VLAN encapsulation support across your network infrastructure.

18. You have configured AWS Config rules to implement another level of compliance check. Your `s3-bucket-server-side-encryption-enabled` check has found five non-compliant resources. What action is taken by AWS Config?

    1. The default Amazon S3 encryption method is automatically applied to the non-compliant bucket.
    2. No further objects will be allowed to be saved in this bucket until the non-compliance associated with the bucket has been made compliant.
    3. No action will be taken; the non-compliance is for informational purposes.
    4. Objects in the non-compliant bucket will be moved to a different storage class.

19. You have been asked to present an AWS security introduction course to some of the business managers in your organization. As part of this process, you are going to explain the AWS Shared Responsibility Model. Currently, your organization works heavily with AWS **Elastic MapReduce (EMR)**, AWS **Relational Database Service (RDS)**, and AWS **Elastic Beanstalk (EB)**, so you will be focusing on the model that represents these services the most. Out of the different models, which of these services fit into them the best?

    1. Infrastructure
    2. Container
    3. Abstract
    4. Platform

20. Which statements are true regarding Amazon EC2 Key Pairs? (Choose three.)

    1. Key pairs use symmetric cryptography.
    2. Key pairs use public-key cryptography,
    3. The public key is maintained by the customer and must be downloaded,
    4. The public key encrypts the credentials.
    5. The private key decrypts credentials.

21. Which component of AWS Systems Manager can help you gain an overview of how the resources within your resource groups are operating and integrating with the following:

    - AWS Config
    - CloudTrail
    - Personal Health Dashboard
    - Trusted Advisor

Your options are as follows:

1. Resource Groups
2. Run Command
3. Built-in Insights
4. State Manager
5. Session Manager

22. When implementing a VPN connection between your corporate network and your AWS VPC, which components are essential to establishing a secure connection? (Choose two.)
    1. A VPN Gateway attached to your AWS architecture
    2. A Customer Gateway attached to your AWS architecture
    3. A Private Gateway attached to your AWS architecture
    4. A VPN Gateway attached to your corporate network
    5. A Customer Gateway attached to your corporate network
    6. A Private Gateway attached to your corporate network

23. AWS Trusted Advisor provides a "Service Limit" category. This category checks whether any of your services have reached a certain percentage or more against the allotted service limit. What is the percentage set at before an alert is triggered?
    1. 70%
    2. 75%
    3. 80%
    4. 85%

24. You are looking to implement AWS Firewall Manager within your organization as a way to manage your WebACL across multiple AWS accounts. As a prerequisite to using this service, you have enabled AWS Config. What two other prerequisites must be met before you can use AWS Firewall Manager?
    1. Enable CloudTrail logs.
    2. Add your AWS account to an AWS organization that has ALL features enabled.
    3. Add your AWS account to an AWS organization that has consolidated billing enabled ONLY.
    4. Select your primary account to act as the Firewall Manager Administrative account
    5. Enable AWS Shield across all AWS accounts.

25. What is the recommended running time for an AWS Amazon Inspector assessment?
    1. 1 hour
    2. 6 hours
    3. 12 hours
    4. 24 hours

26. You have just updated your KMS Key policy for one of your customer-managed CMKs. Within the Sid **Allow access for Key Administrators** section, you added the principal ARN of two of your engineers to maintain the same access as other key administrators. However, they complain, explaining that they are unable to use the CMK to perform cryptographic operations. What is the cause of this?
    1. The CMK is configured with `kms:encrypt -deny`.
    2. Key administrators are not able to use the CMK for cryptographic operations.
    3. The role associated with the engineers prevents the users from using KMS.
    4. You need to update the encryption policy for the CMK in the same region to provide access.

27. Which of the following are NOT actions that can be set within an AWS Web Application Firewall rule? (Choose two.)
    1. Reject
    2. Allow
    3. Deny
    4. Block
    5. Count

28. When using social federated access, any IdP that is **OpenID Connect (OIDC)** compatible can be used for authentication. Which of the following is not used for social federation?
    1. ADFS
    2. Facebook
    3. Amazon
    4. Google

29. Which of the following security policies are NOT written in JSON format?
    1. AWS IAM identity-based policies
    2. AWS KMS key policies
    3. AWS Organizational Service Control Policies
    4. AWS Amazon S3 ACLs

30. You have configured Amazon Inspector to run all the rules packages against your fleet of EC2 instances, which are running on both Linux-based and Windows operating systems. After examining the findings, you notice that there are no findings for Windows-based operating systems for the "Security Best Practices" rules package. What could be the explanation for this?
    1. The Security Best Practices rules package only discovers Linux-based operating systems.
    2. There were no issues found with the Windows-based EC2 instances.
    3. The Amazon Inspector agent on the Windows-based OS was not configured to detect this rules package.
    4. The role associated with Amazon Inspector did not permit this level of access.

31. You have configured a bastion host within the public subnet of your VPC. To connect to your Linux instances in your private subnet, you need to use the private key that is not currently stored on the bastion host. What method of connectivity can you use to gain access to the Linux instance?
    1. Copy the `*.pem` file from your localhost to your bastion host and then connect to your Linux instance.
    2. Use SSH forwarding.
    3. Connect to your bastion using SSL to encrypt the `*.pem` file, then connect to your Linux instance using the encrypted `*.pem` file.
    4. Use AWS Secrets Manager to maintain the `*.pem` files and call it using an API via the bastion host while it's connecting to your Linux instance.

32. You need to retrieve a secret stored in AWS Secrets Manager to gain access to an RDS database. You do not have access to the AWS Management Console, so you need to retrieve it programmatically. Which command should you use for this when using the AWS CLI?
    1. `get-secret-value-rds`
    2. `get-rds-secret-value`
    3. `get-rds-value`
    4. `get-secret-value`

33. Which of the following services and features of AWS do NOT offer DDoS protection or mitigation? (Choose one.)
    1. AWS CloudTrail
    2. Application Load Balancer
    3. Amazon CloudFront
    4. Amazon Route 53
    5. AWS WAF

34. To provide a single-pane-of-glass approach to the security notifications across your accounts, your organization has decided to implement AWS Security Hub. The first step of activating this service requires you to select a security standard. Which standards are available for you to select? (Choose two.)
    1. CIS AWS Foundations Benchmark
    2. PCI DSS
    3. ISO
    4. FedRamp
    5. SOC 2

35. To simplify authentication to specific AWS resources, you have decided to implement Web Identity Federation. Prior to configuration, what information do you need to obtain from the IdP first?
    1. Federated Sequence ID
    2. Federation Number
    3. Application ID/Audience
    4. Application Notice

36. Which AWS VPC secure networking component is being described here?

"A hardened EC2 instance with restrictive controls that acts as an ingress gateway between the internet and your private subnets without directly exchanging packets between the two environments."

    1. Bastion Host
    2. NAT gateway
    3. NAT Instance
    4. Internet Gateway

37. When trying to protect web applications, there are many different attacks that can be experienced, as explained within the OWASP top 10. Which type of attack is being described here?

"These are malicious scripts that are embedded in seemingly trusted web pages that the browser then executes. This can then allow a malicious attacker to gain access to any sensitive client-side data, such as cookie information."

    1. SQL injection attack

    2. String and regex matching

    3. **Cross-Site Scripting (XSS)**

    4. Broken access control

38. One of the key components of Amazon Macie is how it classifies data to help determine its level of sensitivity and criticality to your business through a series of automatic content classification mechanisms. It performs its classification using the object-level API data events it collated from CloudTrail logs. Currently, there are five levels of classification, but one of them is hidden from the console. Which one?

    1. Content type

    2. Support vector machine-based

    3. Theme

    4. File extension

    5. Regex

39. Using Amazon Macie, you need to classify your S3 data based on a list of predefined keywords that exist within the actual content of the object being stored. What would be the best content classification type to use to capture this information?

    1. Theme

    2. File Extension

    3. Regex

    4. Content type

40. When working with cross-account access, you must configure a Trusting account and a Trusted account. A user, "Stuart", in account A needs to gain access to an Amazon RDS database in account B. To configure access, cross-account access needs to be configured. Which steps need to take place? (Choose two.)
    1. From the Trusting account, create a cross-account access role.
    2. From the Trusted account, create a cross-account access role.
    3. Create a policy to assume the role in the Trusted account.
    4. Create a policy to assume the role in the Trusting account.

41. You are responsible for designing security solutions for protecting web applications using AWS Web Application Firewall. During a meeting with senior management, you are asked to highlight the core elements that construct the service. Which components would you highlight to the team? (Choose three.)
    1. Conditions
    2. Values
    3. Rules
    4. Web ACLs
    5. Thresholds

42. Which of the following traffic types are NOT captured by VPC flow logs?
    1. Ingress traffic to private subnets
    2. Egress traffic from public subnets
    3. Traffic to the reserved IP address for the default VPC router
    4. Traffic to the private IPv4 address of a NAT gateway

43. Which is NOT a method of installing the Amazon Inspector agent?
    1. A manual install via a script being run on the instance
    2. Using the `Run` command from within System Manager
    3. Installing the agent as a part of the initial assessment when defining your target
    4. Using an Amazon AMI that already has the agent installed
    5. Using the `Deploy` command from AWS Security Hub

44. Amazon GuardDuty has the ability to perform remediation of findings through automation. Which AWS service or feature does GuardDuty integrate with to allow this?
    1. AWS Security Hub
    2. AWS CloudWatch Events
    3. AWS CloudTrail
    4. AWS KMS

45. Your organization requires the use of MFA, but virtual MFA devices are not allowed. What other device options could you use? (Choose two.)
    1. U2F Security Keys
    2. Gemalto Token
    3. CMK keys
    4. SCP Token
    5. GuardDuty Security Keys

46. When AWS evaluates the permissions of an IAM user, a level of policy evaluation logic is applied to determine their resulting permission level. Which order are policies evaluated in?
    1. Resource-based, Identity-based, IAM Permission boundaries, and SCPs
    2. IAM Permission boundaries, Identity-based, Resource-based, and SCPs
    3. Identity-based, Resource-based, IAM Permission boundaries, and SCPs
    4. SCPs, Identity-based, Resource-based, and IAM Permission boundaries

47. Your systems engineers explain that they have deleted a key pair from the EC2 management console. However, they can still connect to EC2 instances that had this key pair associated with the instance. They are confused as to how this connectivity is still possible, even though the key pair was deleted. What explanation do you give them?
    1. When you delete a key pair from the EC2 Management Console, it will automatically reinstate it if AWS detects it is currently associated with existing EC2 instances to maintain connectivity.
    2. When you delete a key pair from the EC2 Management Console, it just deletes the copy of the public key that AWS holds; it does not delete the public keys that are attached to existing EC2 instances.
    3. When you delete a key pair from the EC2 Management Console, it removes the associated public key from the EC2 instance. It also allows open access until you create another key pair to associate with the instance.
    4. When you attempt to delete an active key pair from the EC2 Management Console, it is marked with a "hidden" tag, but NOT deleted. Only inactive key pairs are removed from the console.

48. As the lead security engineer, you have been asked to review how credentials associated with your RDS databases are managed and ensure there are no details hardcoded within your processes and applications. You need to implement a solution that offers greater protection that also enables the automatic rotation of credentials. Which services would you be using within your solution?
    1. AWS Security Hub with AWS KMS integration
    2. AWS Config with AWS Lambda and AWS KMS integration
    3. AWS Trusted Advisor with AWS KMS integration
    4. AWS Security Systems Manager with AWS Lambda integration
    5. AWS Secrets Manager with AWS KMS and AWS Lambda integration

49. S3 object-level logging integrates with which other AWS service component to record both read and write API activity?
    1. AWS CloudWatch Events
    2. AWS CloudTrail Data events
    3. AWS Config Rules
    4. AWS Trusted Advisor

50. As the AWS security lead, you are concerned that your IAM users have overly permissive permissions. Which element of IAM would you check to determine if permissions were not being used to allow you to implement the principle of least privilege?
    1. Permissions
    2. Policy Usage
    3. Policy Versions
    4. Access Advisor

51. You have been asked by your CTO to provide a list of all the EC2 instances within your production network that have missing patches. Which approach would be best to obtain this list?
    1. Use AWS Config to find a list of non-compliant patches across your EC2 fleet.
    2. Search AWS CloudTrail Patch logs to determine which patches are missing.
    3. Use Patch Manager within AWS Systems Manager.
    4. Use Query the Patch versions using Amazon CloudWatch metrics.

52. The security perspective of the AWS Cloud Adoption Framework covers four primary control areas: Directive controls, preventive controls, detective controls, and which other?
    1. Responsive controls
    2. Reactive controls
    3. Security controls
    4. Access controls

53. To maintain a high level of security across a VPN connection, it consists of two _____ tunnels, allowing a cryptographic method of communication between two endpoints. Select the missing word:
    1. SSL
    2. TLS
    3. IPsec
    4. AES256

54. A team of developers is currently assuming a role that has AmazonS3FullAccess permissions, in addition to varying levels of permissions to Amazon CloudWatch, Amazon SQS, AWS Lambda, and Amazon SNS. However, temporarily, you need to limit the developers in your AWS account to only read-only access to Amazon S3 while maintaining all other permissions. Which method would be best for this that also has the least administrative effort?
    1. Create a new role with the same access to Amazon CloudWatch, Amazon SQS, AWS Lambda, and Amazon SNS, in addition to `AmazonS3ReadOnlyAccess`.
    2. Set an in-line policy against the role with `AmazonS3ReadOnlyAccess`.
    3. Set a permission boundary against the role with `AmazonS3ReadOnlyAccess`.
    4. Set an AWS Organizations policy to `AmazonS3ReadOnlyAccess` and associate it with the AWS account containing the developers.

55. When working with the security components of VPCs, there are some key elements: Network Access Control Lists and security groups. Understanding the difference between them is key. Which of the following statements are true? (Choose three.)

    1. NACLs are stateless
    2. Security groups are stateless.
    3. There are no Deny rules for security groups.
    4. There are no Deny rules for NACLs.
    5. There is a Rule# field for NACLs.
    6. There is a Rule# field for security groups.

56. In a three-way handshake where a client-server is establishing a connection, which is the correct order for the operations to be carried out in?

    1. Syn, Syn-Ack, Ack
    2. Syn-Ack, Syn, Ack
    3. Ack, Syn, Syn, Ack
    4. Syn, Ack, Syn, Ack

57. Working at a mobile gaming company, you have just launched a new game with the hope that it will go viral. Using Amazon Cognito, you assigned permissions to users so that they can access the AWS resources that are used within the mobile app by using temporary credentials. This access can be granted to both federated users and anonymous guest users. Which component of Amazon Cognito enables you to assign permissions?

    1. User Pools
    2. Resource Pools
    3. Identity Pools
    4. IAM Pools

58. What action is being carried out against AWS Secrets Manager using this AWS CLI command?

```
aws secretsmanager put-resource-policy --secret-id My_RDS_Secret --
resource-policy file://resource.json
```

1. An identity-based policy is being applied to a group named `My_RDS_secret`.

2. A resource-based policy is being applied to a secret named `My_RDS_Secret`.

3. A resource-based policy named `My_RDS_secret` is being applied to a secret named `resource.json`.

4. An identity-based policy is being applied to a secret named `My_RDS_Secret` using the `resource.json` resource policy file.

59. From a threat detection and management perspective, which AWS service would you use to provide a single-pane-of-glass view across your infrastructure, thus bringing all of your security statistical data into a single place and presented in a series of tables and graphs?
    1. Amazon GuardDuty
    2. Amazon Detective
    3. Amazon Macie
    4. AWS Security Hub

60. You have just completed a large deployment of patches to your EC2 instances to ensure they all have the latest patches to minimize security vulnerabilities across your fleet. Your manager has asked you for compliance data to confirm your environment meets the patching criteria set out by the business. Which methods can be used to view compliance data? (Choose three.)
    1. AWS Systems Manager Artifact
    2. AWS Systems Manager Explore
    3. AWS Systems Manager Configuration Compliance
    4. AWS Systems Manager Managed Instances

61. You have been asked to implement an additional level of security within some of your IAM identity-based policies to restrict access based on the source IP address of 10.0.0.0/16 of the request. What optional parameter could you add to the policies to enforce this restriction?

```
1. "Criteria": {
            "IpAddress": {
                    "aws:SourceIp": "10.0.0.0/16"

2. "Condition": {
            "IpAddress": {
                    "aws:SourceIp": "10.0.0.0/16"

3. "State": {
            "IpAddress": {
                    "aws:SourceIp": "10.0.0.0/16"

4. "Context": {
            "IpAddress": {
                    "aws:SourceIp": "10.0.0.0/16"
```

62. To enhance the security of your APIs that are being used with the AWS API Gateway service, which method can't be used to control authentication and authorization?
    1. Resource-based policies
    2. VPC Endpoint Policies
    3. Lambda Authorizers
    4. AWS Config Rules

63. Which AWS Service can be used during SAML Federation connectivity to your AWS Management Console to gain temporary credentials and to create a console sign-in URL using the credentials generated by the service?
    1. AWS SQS
    2. AWS STS
    3. AWS SWS
    4. AWS SNS

64. To help you maintain a consistent and measurable condition of your EC2 instances, such as network settings, the installation of agents, and joining a Windows domain, you look to use AWS Systems Manager to help you manage operations. Which element of the service would you use to maintain these settings?

    1. State Manager
    2. Session Manager
    3. Resource Groups
    4. Patch Manager

65. You have to meet a requirement that states you must allow your private instances to access the internet. The solution must be highly available and involve minimal maintenance, and it must also have high bandwidth capabilities. A secure method of implementing this access would be to implement a NAT. Which NAT would you implement to meet these requirements?

    1. NAT Threshold
    2. NAT Instance
    3. NAT gateway
    4. NAT Transit

Answers

1: 1	11: 1,4	21: 3	31: 2	41: 1,3,4	51: 3	61: 2
2: 3	12: 4	22: 1,5	32: 4	42: 3	52: 1	62: 4
3: 1,2,5	13: 4	23: 4	33: 1	43: 4	53: 3	63: 2
4: 3	14: 1,3,4	24: 2,4	34: 1,2	44: 2	54: 3	64: 1
5: 2	15: 2,5	25: 4	35: 3	45: 1,2	55: 1,3,5	65: 3
6: 3,4	16: 2,4	26: 2	36: 1	46: 3	56: 1	
7: 4	17: 3	27: 1,3	37: 3	47: 2	57: 3	
8: 4	18: 3	28: 1	38: 2	48: 5	58: 2	
9: 3,4,6	19: 2	29: 4	39: 1	49: 2	59: 4	
10: 1,6	20: 2,4,5	30: 1	40: 1,3	50: 4	60: 2,3,4	

Assessments

Chapter 1

1. False
2. Five domains
3. 65 questions

Chapter 2

1. Infrastructure model
2. Abstract model
3. Infrastructure model
4. Container model
5. True

Chapter 3

1. Sevice roles
2. True
3. False
4. Multi-factor authentication

Chapter 4

1. JavaScript Object Notation
2. Resource-based policies
3. Principal
4. Trusted account
5. True

Chapter 5

1. False
2. Amazon Cognito
3. SAML federation and social federation
4. Identity provider
5. True

Chapter 6

1. False
2. True
3. AWS
4. AWS CloudTrail
5. AWS Systems Manager

Chapter 7

1. Virtual Private Cloud
2. **Internet Gateway (IGW)**
3. NAT gateway
4. True
5. False

Chapter 8

1. True
2. AWS Firewall Manager
3. AWS Config
4. Network load balancer

Chapter 9

1. SYN Flood
2. Two
3. True
4. True
5. False

Chapter 10

1. **Cloud Adoption Framework (CAF)**
2. Amazon GuardDuty
3. AWS Security Hub
4. True

Chapter 11

1. Customer gateway
2. False
3. Private
4. True

Chapter 12

1. False
2. AWS CloudTrail
3. VPC flow logs
4. True
5. Amazon Athena

Chapter 13

1. AWS Artifact
2. Logfile validation

3. AWS Config rules
4. Amazon Macie
5. True

Chapter 14

1. True
2. VPC flow logs
3. AWS Security Hub
4. False

Chapter 15

1. False
2. AWS Trusted Advisor
3. Fault tolerance
4. Basic and Developer
5. True

Chapter 16

1. False
2. **Customer Master Key (CMK)**
3. AWS-managed
4. Key policy
5. AWS Secrets Manager

Chapter 17

1. Input/output operations per second
2. Amazon **Elastic Block Store (EBS)**
3. Amazon **Elastic File Service (EFS)**
4. True
5. AWS **Key Management Service (KMS)**

Other Books You May Enjoy

If you enjoyed this book, you may be interested in these other books by Packt:

AWS Certified Advanced Networking - Speciality Exam Guide
Marko Sluga

ISBN: 978-1-78995-231-5

- Formulate solution plans and provide guidance on AWS architecture best practices
- Design and deploy scalable, highly available, and fault-tolerant systems on AWS
- Identify the tools required to replicate an on-premises network in AWS
- Analyze the access and egress of data to and from AWS
- Select the appropriate AWS service based on data, compute, database, or security requirements
- Estimate AWS costs and identify cost control mechanisms

AWS Certified SysOps Administrator - Associate Guide
Marko Sluga

ISBN: 978-1-78899-077-6

- Create and manage users, groups, and permissions using AWS IAM services
- Create a secure VPC with public and private subnets, Network Access Control, and security groups
- Get started with launching your first EC2 instance, and working with it
- Handle application traffic with ELB and monitor AWS resources with CloudWatch
- Work with S3, Glacier, and CloudFront
- Work across distributed application components using SWF
- Understand event-based processing with Lambda and messaging SQS and SNS in AWS
- Get familiar with AWS deployment concepts and tools including Elastic Beanstalk, CloudFormation and AWS OpsWorks

Leave a review - let other readers know what you think

Please share your thoughts on this book with others by leaving a review on the site that you bought it from. If you purchased the book from Amazon, please leave us an honest review on this book's Amazon page. This is vital so that other potential readers can see and use your unbiased opinion to make purchasing decisions, we can understand what our customers think about our products, and our authors can see your feedback on the title that they have worked with Packt to create. It will only take a few minutes of your time, but is valuable to other potential customers, our authors, and Packt. Thank you!

Index

Made in the USA
Columbia, SC
08 October 2020